THE EMERGENCE OF REGIONALISM IN MUMBAI

HISTORY OF THE SHIV SENA

SUDHA P. GOGATE

Popular Prakashan
www.popularprakashan.com

Published by Harsha Bhatkal
for Popular Prakashan Pvt. Ltd.
301, Mahalaxmi Chambers
22, Bhulabhai Desai Road
Mumbai 400026
www.popularprakashan.com

First Published 2014

(4378)
ISBN 978-81-7991-823-4

Design: Mahendra Ghanekar

Printed by
Repro India Ltd.
Mahape, Navi Mumbai 400 710

Foreword:
Regionalism in Mumbai

The emergence of Shiv Sena as a social movement was initially viewed by social scientists as specific instance of a world-wide trend - the organized resistance to immigrants followed by a demand for the better deal to the local ethnic groups. The arguments defending such unionising could be varied. The Shiv Sena was created, for instance, at an opportune time for uniting the Marathi speaking people to counter the "sinister" motive of the powers that be to separate Mumbai from the rest of Maharashtra at the time of linguistic reorganization of the Indian States. During the initial years, this organization thrived on frequent doses of patriotic emotionalism invoking the name of Shivaji, the founder of the Maratha Empire. During its formative years at least, championing of the cause of Marathi *manoos* was a deep-rooted conviction that most of the white-collar and even blue-collar jobs were denied to the local Marathi speaking populace. The Shiv Sena led violent agitations in the airline sector, railways, telephones and the banking sector to press for its demand for "80 percent reservation" of jobs in government and private sector for Marathis. These agitations which had reached its peak by mid-70s brought Marathi *manoos* in Mumbai together under the magic wand named the Shiv Sena. Even those who disliked, nay hated violence of any sort, were convinced in the heart of hearts of the raw deal the Marathi *manoos* was getting in the city.

Historically speaking, Thackeray himself would not have imagined then that his first public rally in 1966 would touch the emotional chord of a wide cross-section of Marathi *manoos* in Mumbai. Its instant success was so heady that Thackeray's language at public speeches grew more violent and his followers succumbed to translating his words into strong arm tactics and a life of violence. Having experienced that immigrants fear violent methods and threats create panic in them, Shiv sainiks got used to the diet of that sort. Arrogance, threats, strong arm tactics became their hallmark. Even so, it would not be a correct estimate of the Shiv Sena. It must be recorded that if Shiv Sena became a successful movement despite the demographic imbalance in, and the cultural character of, Mumbai with Marathi speakers losing their hold on Mumbai, it was because the Marathi speaking people were already harbouring ill-feelings of being slighted that the capital of their state did not culturally belong to them. Moreover, there were few Marathis in the best jobs, in the best schools and in the best residential areas. Shiv Sena appealed to Marathis in Mumbai on both the economic and cultural front. It goes to the credit of Shiv Sena that at present Mumbai's Marathi populace does not feel alien in "their own" city.

Dissolution of the Left-led Samyukta Maharashtra movement after the main demands were met and a separate state of Maharashtra with Bombay, now called Mumbai, as the state capital was created, vacuum was felt which had to be filled. No political party or organization was left to speak for the Marathi *manoos* in Mumbai. Shiv Sena footed the bill with the tacit understanding between leaders of both, the Shiv Seva and the ruling Congress Party.

Whether the formation of Linguistic States in India was the result or the cause of the emergence of regionalism is a moot point and much can be said on either side. In fact, the formation of the Linguistic States and its after effects has been a subject for an unending debate ever since. Rarely perhaps the emergence of regional spirit was more pronounced than in cosmopolitan Mumbai and Shiv Sena proudly represented that spirit. After half a century of the existence of the linguistic States, however, forces of regional spirit appear to be emerging in almost all the Indian States.

A social movement formed to safeguard interests of the local or regional people is not a sporadic instance. There are numerous examples all over the world. Industrialised and modern metropolises in the West too have encountered such situations in the past and are facing them even at present. It will be a cowardly denial to say that echoes of the strenuous and cold relationship of the local Americans towards Asian migrants are non-existent in the U.S. and other European countries. The difference lies only in the expression of the feeling whether pronounced and blatant or soft but blunt. In some areas the form of expression could be blatant while in other areas it could be in the form of mild resentment. Every society that undergoes transformation due to modernisation and industrialisation faces the strains of social mobilisation.

Therefore, there was nothing new or objectionable in Shiv Sena's formation. Whether Mumbai belongs to Marathis could be a debatable point. Demographic studies may prove otherwise. That Mumbai developed due to the contributions from non-Marathi communities, notably the Parsees and the Gujaratis, also cannot be denied. But it cannot also be denied that Mumbai had a distinct Marathi stamp on most socio-cultural and political activities for over a century and more. With that Marathi stamp losing its distinct identity, if the local Marathis felt uneasy about the loss of their hold on the city, it was understandable.

The decision taken at the highest level of the Shiv Sena leadership to catapult into a political party and join the forces of *'saffronisation'*, came as a jolt to many of its followers. Seldom does a social movement catapult into a political party worthy of notice. Shiv Sena supremo Bal Thackeray had pronounced from every available platform his distaste for real *politik*. That Shiv Sena should all of a sudden transform itself into a political party and join hands with a national party in the state of Maharashtra was not easy for the party followers to fathom, although for social scientists, it was a phenomenon worth studying. The followers were perhaps divided in their stand. At least the hardcore section felt that with joining the political bandwagon, Shiv Sena would have to dilute its original objectives. One substantial reason for this could be that a disgruntled and inward-looking Maharashtra that has historically sacrificed parochial interests at the altar of national concerns has of late begun to feel that the rest of the nation nurses some kind of misgiving and animosity towards it. In the lists of State Governors and Ambassadors appointed from time to time Marathi names appear few and far between. In the recognition by way of awarding national honours such as Padmashri, Padma Bhushan, the Marathi percentage is consistently falling. Over the last five decades many "outsiders" were 'foisted' on Maharashtra by the Central leadership of the Congress Party to be elected to Rajya Sabha and Lok Sabha from the Maharashtra State quota leaving the claims of Marathi leaders is a subject ever painful to the Marathi mind. National recognition, to them, is not commensurate with the contribution of the Marathi speaking people. This perception, firmly engrained in their minds was the fodder on which Shiv Sena exploited the situation. The Marathi leaders are used, misused and abused and their loyalty to Delhi is taken for granted, remained a refrain that the Marathis chanted over the years. That was the reason why this section of hardcore Shiv Sainiks had become the supporters of Bal Thackeray and admirers of the forceful language he employed. The other section of the Shiv Sena under Bal Thackeray blindly follows him. Their loyalty is unquestionable. Both these sections have one thing in common and that is their firm belief that Thackeray will always do what is good for Shiv Sena and the Marathi *manoos*. And they were right. Shiv Sena having declared itself as a political party not only remained a force to reckon with over the years but became a major regional political party in Maharashtra, with a threat to the national parties of providing a viable alternative.

Later the city centric Sena struck a responsive chord in rural Maharashtra with Sharad Pawar's joining the Congress in 1986. Pawar's co-option into the Congress left the traditionally anti-Congress backward castes with no choice but to support the Sena, which had been trying to make inroads under Chagan Bhujbal who was once a trusted lieutenant of Thackeray left his party to join the National Congress but soon distanced himself also from it to be in Pawar's Nationalist Congress Party. All these years Bhujbal is attempting to consolidate the OBC base in the State under his tutelage and has largely succeeded in fulfilling his ambition.

Shiv Sena has come a long way from its original incarnation of a social movement. For Bal Thackeray and his compadres the establishment and rise of Shiv Sena in Mumbai was a dream come true, may be at the connivance of the then ruling Congress party which wanted to build a formidable opposition to the unionism of the strong Communist lobby in Mumbai. With Communist influence in Mumbai contained, and power tasted Shiv Sena leaders were looking out for bigger role and it was not possible without entering into the political arena. The BJP offer with it newly found Hindutva plank, that is, the cause of upholding the cause of nationalist Hindu majority came in handy for Shiv Sena leaders.

But such a major change meant forsaking many of their earlier aims, policies and methods. The departure of Shiv Sena from its original position was masterminded by Bal Thackeray himself and he being shrewd enough he rode on both the chariot, though not simultaneously but off and on. Even if it meant that in its new avatar the party would have to bury many of the issues which were so dear to the Marathi-speaking population, he did not totally sidelined them, newer outfits like *Sthaniya Lokadhikar Samiti* and *Bharatiya Vidyarthi Sena* were allowed to tackle them. Having entered electoral politics Thackeray quickly learnt a lesson that attacking migrants in Mumbai is not good politics. South-Indians who were earlier easy targets went out of focus as Shiv Sena was obliged to shed at least some of radicalism when it first tasted victory in the 1985 Bombay Municipal Corporation elections. It was at this time Pramod Mahajan of the BJP came with an offer of alliance with Shiv Sena, for he knew that the BJP by itself had little chance of coming to power in Maharashtra. He did it knowing well that the Shiv Sena in Maharashtra had quickly spread its tentacles all over the State and that the BJP was the weaker force of the two. The alliance worked and came to power in 1995 defeating the mighty Congress under the leadership of Sharad Pawar. For the Shiv Sena-BJP alliance remained in power in Maharashtra between 1995 and 1999. That undoubtedly was the peak of Shiv Sena's glory. With a defeat in 1999 Assembly elections, the Shiv Sena-BJP alliance was out of power, a situation Bal Thackeray could never come to terms with and dreamt of coming to power again. Whatever the case, since then Shiv Sena has not looked back and has transformed itself into a major and vocal regional party in the State Assembly as also in Lok Sabha.

Much has been written on the changed posture of Shiv Sena and the role its supporters played in the State-level and National politics after it proclaimed itself as a regional political party. What the attitude of its promoters and leaders of the Shiv Sena was in the initial years when they claimed Mumbai for Marathi speaking people is all blocked only in the pages of its two mouthpieces, daily *Samana* and the weekly *Marmik* and also in contemporary newspapers over the last four and a half decades.

Now the Shiv Sena's aggressive posture against non-Marathis, particularly against "South Indians" is a thing of the past. With the new Hindutva line Sikhs are friends and South Indians are forgotten, even won over. Pakistanis continue to be the arch enemies and along with them Biharis who migrate to Mumbai in search of menial jobs are worth detestation and, since they "engage in crime", they deserve to be sent back to their original State. And so should be the Fate of Bangladeshis. "Close the gates for migrants to the city" has been a favourite war cry of Shiv Sena leaders. It comes in handy for them when other issues drop down.

This book, written two and a half decades ago, is a record of the reckoning of thought process of Shiv Sena leaders and a register of events of the first phase of Shiv Sena. It is a social scientist's enquiry into Shiv Sena's formation and modus operandi and as such it has its value for students and teachers alike. As it aims to analyze in depth the genesis of Shiv Sena as a social movement, it serves a purpose. The author's untimely demise two and a half decades ago unfortunately put a stop to further enquiry. Had she been alive, she would have also investigated in a competent way the causes and effects of the metamorphosis and the changed perspective of Shiv Sena.

Genesis of Shiv Sena as a social movement is the focus of the early part of the book where the author has relied on rigorous academic studies done by Mary Katzenstein (1979) and Dipankar Gupta (1982). Besides there are a number of interviews with aging socialist and communist leaders who are seen providing her incisive and critical insights into the early phase of the Shiv Sena. She would also have written about the second generation of the Thackerays on whom the mantle of leadership fell due to the aging and ailing "tiger of Mumbai". It is now left to the future social scientists to carry on the baton and continue to study this regional political party which initially started of as a social organization.

If at all an estimate of the impact of the Shiv Sena is to be attempted dispassionately, what will it be? Low though the ideological fount of the Shiv Sena may be, it must be admitted that it garnered a broad support base. From 1967 onwards, it relied instead on attacking Muslims and communists but nobody from within the ranks complained against this shift. Thackeray had already established his pre-eminence as a cultural hero of Marathi people in Mumbai and generated fear in the minds of non-Marathis. He was a tiger in Mumbai till the mid-1970s. In fact, in spite of the background conditions that favoured the rise of the Shiv Sena, it could still have been contained had not successive governments encouraged it. Y. B. Chavan whose creative leadership has been praised by almost all, had once said in public that Shiv Sena was valiantly upholding the proud tradition of Shivaji. Consequently, Bal Thackeray has always escaped the clutches of the law of the land in spite of the fact that he and his followers flagrantly broke it time and again. His fight for the Marathi cause is understandable, but how could he escape the charge that he de-intellectualised the Marathi community and insulated it from other communities? In the 19th century Marathis were preferred for employment, even by Parsee and Gujarati employers. They were known to be hard-working, god-fearing, honest, sincere, and they had respect for scholarship. Thackeray united them alright, but also made them insincere, dishonest, defiant and apathetic towards intellectual challenges. Like their leaders, Shiv Sainiks are dismissive of scholarship. Is the Congress Party any different? May not be.

But Shiv Sena, unlike the Congress, took the flag of the welfare of the Marathi *manoos.* There was a time when senior Thackeray ruled the Marathi mind. History is sure to record that he lost a golden opportunity. He taught his lieutenants to find quick fix solutions. A reason they caught the fancy of youngsters was that he told them not to read and increase their corpus of knowledge. He pooh-poohed all social, political and economic theories and told the youth that those were useless. He kept the vision of youngsters confined to the Marathi issue in which, no doubt, he pre-eminently succeeded. But in the ultimate analysis, the result has been stunted intellectual and cultural growth of the Marathi speaking people. A leader who could have achieved so much in reality achieved so little. Unfortunate for Maharashtra and the Marathi speaking people!

Mumbai — Aroon Tikekar

PREFACE

The present study is an attempt to explore the social matrix within which a regionalist movement emerged and took shape. The interest lies in locating the variables that contributed to and shaped the regionalist demands rather than in tracing the history and career of an association that led or carried out the movement.

Four chapters in the present work deal with variables linked with the discontent and emergence of the movement. Each of these chapters is divided into two sections. Section I consists of content-data from news-journals. Section II presents analysis and interpretation of the content-data.

I owe a debt of gratitude to my guide, Dr. Y. B. Damle, who encouraged me to pursue the present subject for a doctoral research thesis. His comments and criticism helped me all along to keep the work on the right track.

The Indian Council of Social Science Research, New Delhi, granted a doctoral fellowship for two years (1973-75) which enabled me to carry out this long-term project. The Women's University, where I work, was gracious in granting me leave of absence for the two-year period of fellowship. After I joined work, Dr. Neera Desai, Head of my Department, kindly spared me academic responsibilities beyond classroom teaching.

When I began the research I found few libraries had records of 'vernacular' newspapers and I had to approach the newspaper offices for the back issues of selected journals.

I am grateful to the management of these journals for giving me access to their issues. The library staff of the Journal Section of the Shasakeeya Vibhageeya Granthalaya (Vishrambaug Wada), Pune, the Mumbai Marathi Granth Sangrahalaya and the Central Library at the Town Hall, Mumbai, also helped me in ferreting out older issues unavailable elsewhere.

Smt. Khandwala, her colleagues at the SNDT Women's University Library, Shri A. C. Tikekar and members of the Library Staff of the University of Mumbai and Mr. Thorat of Council Hall Library often went out of their way to help me.

Several of my friends and colleagues contributed directly of indirectly to the completion of this work. I owe a particularly heavy debt to Smt. Sharayu Anantram and Shri Badrinarayan who gave unstinting help at all stages of the work. Both of them took time off to go through the manuscript and make useful suggestions.

Without the co-operation of all these persons and institutions I could not have done the work. The responsibility for any shortcomings in this work, however, is entirely mine.

August 1978 — Sudha Gogate

ACKNOWLEDGEMENTS

My sister Dr. Sudha Gogate (1932-87) completed her doctoral thesis in 1978 and in due course she received the Doctorate Degree from the Pune University. Almost immediately in 1980 she went to U.S. on an academic fellowship. Soon after returning, she assumed the responsibility of the Head of the Department of Sociology at the S.N.D.T. University, Mumbai. All this delayed the process of publishing her thesis in a book form. As she was thinking of spending some time on editing and preparing her thesis for publication, she fell ill and died rather suddenly in 1987. This further delayed the publication.

I am glad that this book is now being published. I sincerely thank Popular Prakashan for accepting the book for publication and doing everything necessary from editing to giving the book its final form. I am also thankful to Dr. Aroon Tikekar for writing the Foreword for this book.

Pune — Sharad Gogate

CONTENTS

Foreword
Regionalism in Mumbai: Aroon Tikekar iii

Preface xi

Acknowledgements xii

Introduction xv

I The Problem 1

II Methodology 19

III The Shiv Sena: Emergence and Growth 33

IV Problems of an Exploding Metropolis 96

V Economic Aspirations 147

VI The Maharashtrian Community 196

VII Self-View and the Protest Movement 313

VIII Conclusion 365

Appendix 385

Bibliography 414

INTRODUCTION

Modernisation and Change

With the end of colonial rule in Asia and Africa after the Second World War, many old societies with newly-acquired statehood faced problems of integration in the difficult process of nation-building. Self-rule promised the rich dividends of economic development, but it simultaneously led to rising expectations among individuals and communities. These expectations had been pushed into the background during the freedom struggle, when gaining independence was more important. For instance, the emergence of linguistic regionalist movements in India during the 1950s was an expression of the rising expectations of the large regional linguistic communities of a new nation.

These new nations in Asia and Africa had already begun their journey to modernisation - a long-drawn process of change - to which they were introduced by their contact with the colonial powers. Nation-building was a part of this wider process. It was unavoidable that they would stumble upon difficult problems during this process of continuous social change.

The social mobilisation, set in motion by the processes of industrialisation, urbanisation and by the large-scale migration of populations in their wake, and the continuous concentration of economic opportunities in a few urban metropolitan centres threw up a variety of problems – economic imbalances, violent eruptions, resistance, protest-movements and, occasionally, a critical breakdown of the social system in these modernising nations. India, too, was no exception. It had to face protest movements of the nativist and regionalist variety, for instance, led by the DMK, the Shiv Sena and the Telangana movement, to name a few.

The process of modernisation is always fraught with tension. It was not a very smooth transition even for the present-day developed nations, in spite of the fact that many of them were backed by the wealth and resources of their colonies. Public memory may be short-lived; studies and records by scholars, however, have a longer life. All along, American sociologists have observed and noted continuity and increase of inter-ethnic tensions and inter-group clashes in the train of expanding communications and widening of group contacts. (Odum, 1965, 398; Graham H.D. and Gurr T.R., 1969, 591) Resistance to change, protests, violent eruptions and occasional breakdowns were experienced by these developed nations. The available literature on the behavioural and historical studies of riots, rebellions and revolutions during the past 200 years in the Western world bears testimony to this.

However, it must be realised that the impact and the strains of the process would be felt differently by different societies. It is essential, therefore, to focus on the specific problems of different societies. A systematic study and understanding of India's problems would help in grappling with them more effectively.

Key to Abbreviations

- Mumbai Pradesh Congress Committee: BPCC
- Community Party of India: CPI
- Dravida Munnetra Kazagam: DMK
- Maharashtra Pradesh Congress Committee: MPCC
- Praja Socialist Party: PSP
- Sampoorna Maharashtra Samiti: SPMS
- Samyukta Maharashtra Samiti: SMS
- Samyukta Socialist Party: SSP
- Samyukta Maharashtra Parishad SMP
- Shetkari Kamgari Paksh (Peoples and Workers Party): PWP
- Shiv Sena: SS
- Maharashtra Ekikaran Samiti: MES
- Mumbai Citizens Committee MCC

Chapter - I

THE PROBLEM

In the mid-sixties, the city of Mumbai witnessed the sudden rise of a linguistic regionalist movement spearheaded by the Shiv Sena. It eventually gathered momentum and exploded into occasional violent riots around 1969-70. For many thinking persons, this was a totally unexpected and puzzling phenomenon – especially against the background of the recent formation of the new unilingual state of Maharashtra (1 May 1960). The spectacular growth of the Shiv Sena and its adoption of an aggressive stance towards outsiders were viewed with alarm, as a threat to the nation's unity. The Shiv Sena's demand for priority in jobs and housing for 'the sons of the soil' was looked upon as being contrary to the fundamental rights of the citizen conferred on him by the Indian Constitution.

The Shiv Sena, however, was not the only movement of its kind in India. There were anti-Bengali outbreaks in Assam in the early 60s and 70s. The Chaluvalligars of Karnataka nursed a hostile attitude to outsiders. The long-drawn violent riots of the Telangana movement* during 1969-70 against the 'Gair-Mulkis' from outside Telangana, are a case in point. All these movements seemed to have one characteristic in common, an attitude of hostility to outsiders, though the definition of an outsider changed from time to time. The Shiv Sena, perhaps because of its dramatic rise and its location in India's foremost metropolitan city, attracted the greatest attention from academic as well as non-academic quarters.

This study focuses attention chiefly upon the emergence of the Shiv Sena in Mumbai. Any regionalist movement is a complex, multi-dimensional phenomenon which needs a many-pronged and inter-disciplinary approach for understanding it.

Political scientists were the first among the social scientists to become interested in the study of the Shiv Sena. The Shiv Sena's agitational politics; its demand for priority to 'the sons of the soil'; its pronounced approval of limited dictatorship and stray references to the Nazi leader, Hitler as a hero; its huge rallies attended by thousands of people; and the protest marches of youthful Shiv Sainiks who often lapsed into acts of violence, were the dramatic aspects that brought the Sena into the limelight almost overnight. The Shiv Sena's quick initial success, its open hatred of communism, its anti-Muslim stance and its eventual growth into a political pressure group, drew the attention of politicians and political scientists alike. In an effort to understand this phenomenon, political scientists studied the Shiv Sena's organisational growth and the nature and characteristics of its leadership. Their interest lay in its Party-building processes; as a result, they focused their attention chiefly on its transformation from an earlier militant mass movement into a regional Party adjusting its aggressive stance in response to the political expediency and pressures of the Indian democratic system. (Ram Joshi, Nov. 1970) Some scholars were also interested in exploring the nature of the Shiv Sena's 'regional', 'revivalist', and 'anti-communist' politics. (Gangadharan, K.K. Dec. 1970; Fickett, L.P. Jr., 1971)

In their preoccupation with the style and issues of Shiv Sena politics, political scientists perhaps had little time and inclination to explore the social ecology of this movement, or to make an attempt to identify the socio-economic and other variables that might have been responsible for its rise. Beyond making references to certain variables such as 'latent but intense political discontent', 'worsening social-psychological situation', and the 'increasing economic competition', few political scientists concerned themselves with explaining the rise of this new phenomenon.

This, however, is not surprising. Most of the research conducted by social scientists on social movements has generally focused on the history and career of an association from the stages of collective unrest to the activities of formally organised groups – interest and pressure groups or political parties. In such studies, a movement gets identified wholly with the organisation, its goals and actions. However, a movement while often carried out by a group or an organisation is not wholly an associational phenomenon. By definition, a social movement (in whatever terms we define it, and quite a few definitions of social movements are available in sociological and social-psychological literature) is collective mobilisation and therefore essentially a phenomenon of change. The very word 'movement' suggests people on the move, people who are involved in the process of change rejecting existing arrangements, norms and/or values and seeking new arrangements or a fresh set of norms. A social movement thus arises out of its participants' dissatisfaction over the existing social arrangements, and some shared beliefs in the ways of changing those arrangements. One of the tasks in analysing a social movement is, therefore, to identify particular situations and/or the changes involved which generate discontent as also to specify their relation to the movement. (Gusfield, J.R., 1968)

Prerequisites of a Social Movement

A social movement has been defined as 'socially shared activities and beliefs directed towards the demand for change in some aspect of the social order'. (Gusfield, 1970; 2) Most definitions of social movements underline the factor of collective action for change. Collective mobilisation born of social unrest is considered a crucial ingredient of any type of social movement. Collective mobilisation includes harnessing the discontent of people and directing it to a goal of relevant change, through a group or an organisation. Such mass mobilisation takes place only if the popular discontent is a widespread phenomenon, sufficiently strong to stir people to seek a change or redressal of their grievances. Discontent over a common problem thus provides a social base and motivation for change. (Gusfield, J.R. 1968)

However, discontent alone is not enough. For an understanding of the goals and actions of a social movement, it is essential that we identify the sources of the popular discontent. Theoreticians trace the sources of the discontent to the strains in the established structured social relationships in the process of change and variously describe the fact, depending on the scholar's particular persuasion, as 'predispositions of the objective situation' (Hans Tooh, 1966, Ch 1); or as 'structural strains'. (Smelser N., 1962, Ch 1) These terms imply an impairment of established relationships or malfunctioning of the sub-systems due to changes in their context. A movement for restoration, renovation or overhauling of the relationship structure, thus appears to be a natural response. (Smelser, 1962, Gusfield, 1968)

Besides 'structural strains' and the patterns and forces that contribute to the movement ('structural conduciveness'), sociologists identify ideology or a belief system and leadership as other major ingredients or prerequisites of social movements. (Smelser, 1962; Hans Tooh, 1966; Gusfield, 1968) Broadly speaking, the ideology justifies and encourages collective action, supports and legitimises its goals and methods, while the leadership of the movement applies the ideology to the community's problems, interprets it to provide a myth of solution and a plan and programme for action. (Smelser, 1962; Tooh, 1966; Gusfield, 1968)

It is essential to briefly review certain popular notions, sometimes supported by academic theories, about the origin and growth of social movements. On the one hand, some of these ideas and theories overemphasise non-rational motivation of the leaders and participants of a movement. (Goodspeed, D.J., 1962; Kurt Riezler, Q.V. Gurr, 1970, 30) On the other hand, some others maintain that people are seduced into membership of social movements through the skill of the leaders and agitators who often are looking for their profits. (Eric Hoffer, 1966; Blumer, H. 1957, 147-48) To accept either of these positions is difficult.

One such popular theory about the Shiv Sena traces the roots of the movement to 'language-based chauvinism' and 'mass paranoia of Maharashtrians' kindled by the earlier Samyukta

Maharashtra Movement and exploited by the clever anti-outsider propaganda of the Sena leader, Bal Thackeray. (Gangadharan, K.K., 1970) This is a facile, pseudo-psychological explanation. There is little evidence to support a psychological theory that explains the rise of a mass movement by reference to the collective paranoia of a community. According to Ted Gurr, 'Aggression-prone victims of maladaptive socialisation processes are found in every society and among the actors in most outbreaks of political violence, but they are much more likely to be mobilised by strife than to constitute it in its entirety.' (Gurr, Ted, 1970, 31) Psychological explanations based on pathological traits and tendencies of leaders and followers of movements neglect the situational conditions out of which these movements arise. Mass following of the movements is a rational reaction of the people to economic and other social conditions which are felt to be intolerable. (Heberie R., 1968)

The other view, that social movements are contrived affairs or deliberate products of the leadership's clever manoeuvres, also neglects this fact. Unless the people are ready to listen to him, the agitator is likely to go unheeded, or may even be forced to withdraw. Even if we grant that appeals originate from people who are prone to look for profits, as Hans Tooh says, '... the vital fact remains that the needs appealed to are real needs. They existed before their exploitation. ... If needs did not precede appeals to some measure, attempts to appeal would be cries in the wilderness. ....The exploiter in this situation is not the originator of the problem, nor is he responsible for the eagerness with which his solutions are responded to. He is at best an individual who has sensed existing social deficit.' (Hans Tooh 1966, 87-88).

Many scholars engaged in the study of social movements reject these as simplistic explanations.

Theoretical Perspective

People's perception of themselves and their situation

It must be noted, however, that there is no simple unilinear relation between the hardships experienced by a group and the development of a movement towards change. In other words, there is no inevitable connection between structural strains and collective mobilisation. It is not the problem-situation in itself ('the predispositions of the objective situation' or 'structural strains', whichever way we describe the fact) that gives rise to people's uprisings. These are necessary but insufficient requisites. Human history is replete with situations wherein men have meekly permitted themselves to be subjected to inhuman inequalities and injustice with little resistance. Problem-situations originate discontent and liberate needs but they do not always produce social movements. (Gusfield, 1968, 446-447)

Only when 'the predispositions of the objective situation' concur with people's perception of an attainable change, are people motivated to bring about a change. Only when people can aspire and look for an improvement in their conditions, would they agitate for it. 'Research has shown that the absolute situation of a group is not instrumental in generating and focusing discontent as is the perception of what is just, expected and possible.' (Gusfield, 1968) And what they consider just, expected and possible depends on their past experience and present context.

If this is true, then it becomes a task of paramount importance for a student of social movements to explore the attitudes and expectations that motivate people to support or participate in collective action. As Weber maintains, human action is social and subjectively meaningful. 'To understand the conduct of others one must observe not only what they do but know what meaning they attach to their actions.' (Cohen, P.S. 1970, 81) It is the task of sociology to attempt 'interpretive understanding of social action in order thereby to arrive at causal explication of its course and effects.' (Weber, tr. Henderson and Parsons, 1947, 88)

A movement acquires meaning for a people because it addresses itself to their aspirations for change, to their expectations of improvement in their conditions, and offers a solution to their problems. Therefore, in the context of the present study, 'the definition of the situation' by the Maharashtrian community in their interactional setting of Mumbai and the self-view held by the community – the potential participants and supporters of the Shiv Sena movement – are factors of crucial significance in the birth and growth of this regionalist movement.

In other words, the origin of the people's discontent is in their sense of relative deprivation. The relative deprivation of the potential participants and supporters of the movement, the Maharashtrian community in this particular case, seems to be the major source and a causal factor responsible for the popular discontent. This factor, rather than economic competition or demographic concentration *per se*, seems to have mobilised the regionalist movement of the Shiv Sena.

Unemployment, job competition, overcrowding etc, are no doubt sources of strain for the urban system and for the people. It seems, however, that none of these objective factors by themselves triggered the collective action. These became a cause of intolerable discontent because of the community's perspective for self-appraisal. This factor in the situation is often overlooked when 'economic reasons' are put forward to explain the phenomenon.

A study of migrants to Mumbai, conducted by the Tata Institute of Social Sciences (Gore, M.S. 1970), had concluded that the lower-class Marathi citizen of Mumbai is comparatively less happy and less adjusted to the city than the lower-class North Indian or South Indian migrant. The study offers no verified explanation for this phenomenon but suggests the hypothesis of relative deprivation as a possible explanation. If the present study, based on content-analysis of newspapers and journals, bears out this hunch regarding the factor of relative deprivation, it would help to elucidate the puzzling findings of the said study and thus can make a small contribution to fill a gap in our understanding.

Relative Deprivation

Earlier than anyone else perhaps, Marx recognised and articulated the relative nature of human wants and their satisfaction. 'Our wants and their satisfaction have their origin in society; we therefore measure them in their relation to society and not in relation to the objects which satisfy them. Since their nature is social, wants are therefore relative.' (Marx q.v. Freedman, R., ed., 1971, 63) It follows that man's deprivation also is social in origin and therefore relative in nature.

Aberle defines relative deprivation as the negative discrepancy between the legitimate expectations and the actuality. (q.v. Ted Gurr, 1970, 25) In simple language, it means the perception of the gulf between expectations and the prospects of fulfiling these expectations. This is not the same as saying that people are deprived and angry because they do not get what they want. Relative deprivation is not a function of discrepancy between a 'want-get' ratio. As Ted Gurr puts it, 'People become most intensely discontented when they cannot get what they think they deserve, not just what they want in an ideal sense.' (Gurr, T.R. and Graham H.D., 1969, 596)

This connotation of the term 'relative deprivation' is slightly different from the one which has been in general currency in sociology. The term, as is well-known, was originally used by the authors of *The American Soldier*, in their socio-psychological study of the American army during the 1940s. (Samuel Stouffer, *et al*, 1949) The study does not offer any rigorous definition of the concept. The term is used to denote the feeling of an individual who finds himself lacking some status or conditions which he thinks he should have, his standards of what he should have being generally determined by reference to what some other person or group has. Later, the concept was used by W.G. Runciman in his study of attitudes to social inequality in 20th-century England, titled *Relative Deprivation and Social Justice* (1966).

In both the above-mentioned studies, the term *relative deprivation* underlines the aspect of subjective perception in deprivation. The concept implies that people may be subjectively deprived with reference to their expectations, even though an objective observer might not judge them to be in want; and, similarly, the existence of what the observer judges to be abject poverty, or 'absolute deprivation' is not necessarily thought to be unjust or irremediable by those who experience it. (Ted Gurr, 1970, 24)

In other words, relative deprivation depends on the frame of reference of the actor. As Runciman says, '...if people have no reason to expect or hope for more than they can achieve, they will be less discontented with what they have or even grateful simply to be able to hold onto it. But if, on the other hand, they have been led to see as a possible goal, the relative prosperity of some more fortunate community with which they can directly compare themselves, they will remain discontented with their lot until they have succeeded in catching up.'(Runciman, 1972, 10)

We must note however that the concept of relative deprivation excludes reference to fantasy wishes. It is deprivation felt with reference to expected goals or expectations which are distinct from aspirations that may include desires not feasible.

The concept of relative deprivation introduced by Stouffer S.A. *et al* (The *American Soldier*, 1949), was later formalised by R.K. Merton in his 'Social Theory and Social Structure' (1959, Chapters 8 and 9), and extended to a theory of reference group behaviour. Individuals see themselves as deprived (or privileged, hence 'relative gratification') by comparing their own situation with that of other groups and categories of persons. The extent to which they will see themselves as deprived will vary according to the category or group selected as the basis of comparison.

However, it may be recognised that value standards for self-appraisal can have sources other than reference groups. An individual's point of reference may be his own or his group's past condition or an abstract ideal, an active goal or an expected future state, etc., as well as a reference 'group'. This meaning of 'relative deprivation' goes a little beyond the conventional sociological usage of the term but may be considered as an extension of it. Relative deprivation, in this sense, is defined by Ted Gurr as 'actors' perception of discrepancy between their value expectations and their value capabilities. Value expectations are the goods and conditions of life to which people believe they are rightfully entitled. Value capabilities are the goods and conditions they think they are capable of getting and keeping.' (Ted Gurr, 1970, 24)

Values are the desired events, objects and conditions for which men strive. They are the goal-objects of human motivation, presumably derived from basic needs. Value satisfaction, therefore, means fulfilment of strivings or attainment of goals. Value expectations of a group are the average level of value satisfactions which the group believes it is justifiably entitled to. Value capability of a group is the average level of value satisfaction the group perceives itself as capable of attaining and maintaining in a situation. (Gurr, 1970, 24-29)

Relative Deprivation and Collective Discontent

Personal relative deprivation is distinct from deprivation shared by a collectivity or a class. The tension that develops from the perceived discrepancy between the 'ought' and the 'is' or the 'possible', when acute and shared by a large number of people, mobilises collective action. This happens when the expectations of socially-deprived people about the goods and conditions of life meet with frustration. An elaborate theory built by Ted Gurr about the causal relationship between relative deprivation and collective action covering violent civil strife, identifies three major patterns of social conditions that cause relative deprivation-induced collective discontent. These are patterns of Aspirational Deprivation, Decremental Deprivation and Progressive Deprivation.

Aspirational Deprivation

Aspirational Deprivation is a pattern of deprivation in which expectations increase and intensify while the perceived capabilities, i.e. conditions for their satisfaction, fail to keep pace with expectations. This is the familiar pattern of 'the revolution of rising expectations'. Those who experience aspirational relative deprivation become frustrated because they feel they have no means of attaining new or intensified expectations. It is the common experience of developing societies today that their exposure to new and better ways of life, through communication and developmental effort, increases people's expectations beyond the possibility of attainment, to the point of frustration. Also, the demonstration effect of other groups whose conditions are improving, leads to an experience of relative deprivation and people's expectation levels are often accelerated. Again, when social inflexibilities differentially restrict a group from attaining conditions enjoyed by other groups, the pattern is in operation.

Decremental Deprivation

The second, according to Gurr, the pattern of decremental deprivation, is a more common source of collective protest and violence. The pattern is seen when capabilities of a group are perceived to decline in the presence of relatively stable expectations. 'Men are likely to be more intensely angered when they lose what they have than when they lose hope of attaining what they do not yet have.' (Gurr, 1970, 50)

The pattern results when, for instance, people habitually used to normal political liberties, are deprived of them, or when people with fixed income face tax-rise or inflation. Gurr believes that the pattern is more commonly experienced by traditional segments of transitional societies; when, for example, middle-class groups are threatened with displacement by the upward mobility of groups below them on the socio-economic ladder.

Progressive Deprivation

The third pattern, known as progressive deprivation, was first introduced as the J-curve hypothesis by James C. Davies. He observed: 'Revolutions are most likely to occur when a prolonged period of objective economic and social development is followed by a short period of sharp reversal.' He maintained that the pattern precedes many a well-known revolution and rebellion. (Davies, J.C. 1962, 1969)

Progressive deprivation may be regarded as a special case of aspirational deprivation, in which a long-term, relatively steady improvement in people's material and social conditions, generates expectations about further continued improvement (i.e. expectations keep steadily rising) If, however, people's capabilities stabilise or decline after such a prolonged period of improvement, progressive relative deprivation is the result, according to Gurr; he holds that such a pattern is most common in societies undergoing simultaneous ideological and systemic change. Also, he cites as examples, the effects of economic depression in a growing economy, or the effects of the articulation of an ideology of modernisation in a society with structural inflexibilities, that obstruct improvement. (Ted Gurr, 1969, 597-603; 1970, 46-58)

Relative deprivation caused by these patterns of social conditions, may vary in magnitude, frequency and degree (or intensity). The magnitude is the extent of difference between the expected and the actual situations as experienced by a person. Frequency (also denoted as scope) of relative deprivation is the proportion of a group who feel it. The degree of relative deprivation is the intensity with which it is felt. It is the 'extent of the negative affect that is associated with perception of discrepancy'. In other words, it is the intensity of the anger or the discontent of the relatively deprived. (Runciman, 1972, p, 11; Ted Gurr, 1970, p, 29)

It then seems plausible to assume that the greater the intensity and scope of relative deprivation, the greater the magnitude of popular discontent.

Discontent and Collective Action

Underlying the relationship between discontent and collective action, especially violent behaviour, is the frustration-aggression mechanism in all probability a fundamental aspect of man's bio-psychic make-up. The assumption here is that men's frustration over some material and social conditions of their lives is a necessary precondition of collective action, group protest and acts of collective violence. The more widespread the frustration, the more intense and widespread would be the collective action. The discontent or frustration is a psychological variable and difficult to assess directly except by reference to its collective outcome. The assumption however, may be tested initially by evidence from psychology.

A large number of studies investigating the effects of frustration on aggression seem to support the essential validity of the frustration-aggression mechanism. When men feel thwarted in their attempt to get something they want, they are likely to become angry; when angry, the most satisfying inherent response for men seems to be to strike out at the source of frustration. According to the accumulated evidence, the frustration-aggression mechanism appears to be a built-in-disposition of man, subject, however, to influence by learning and the interplay of other internal and external stimuli. (Berkowitz, 1975, 222-225) Berkowitz defines frustration as 'thwarting', 'the blocking of ongoing goal-directed activity' or 'non-fulfilment of expectancy'. Frustration is thus different from an objective fact of deprivation, but comes very close to the connotation of relative deprivation which, in effect, is the perception of thwarting circumstances.(Berkowitz, 1975, 221-222; Gurr and Graham, 1969, 595-597)

This is not to say that all aggressive behaviour is spontaneous and instinctive. Aggression may be an emotional response to socially-induced frustration as well as a learned or rational response evoked by specific situations. Nature provides man with the capacity or disposition for aggressive behaviour when frustrated; it is the social circumstances that determine whether and how man exercises this capacity. Thus, the measure of men's anger at the perception of their deprivation is determined partly by the relative intensity or importance of their expectations, the degree of discrepancy itself, as well as by the number of alternatives that are yet open to them for the satisfaction of their expectations.

Collective Action and Social Variables

Besides the intensity and scope of deprivation-induced discontent, social variables also play a part in influencing collective action. Gurr, on the basis of data on collective strife from 114 nations (1961-65), states the following as major social factors that determine the course of collective action born of discontent:

1. The attitudes of the group and the society at large about the justifiability and utility of collective action, protest or agitation and of violence. These include the social norms, traditions and ideology that celebrate or support the collective struggle and the utilitarian beliefs in the success of collective action or violence.

2. The institutional support to collective action and the social-control mechanisms in operation in society are other relevant factors that encourage or delimit the recourse to collective action and its ability to shape the movement into existence and influence its later course. This means locating the social base of the movement, identifying the structural strains and the changes that give rise to the discontent – the mobilising energy of a movement. It also means exploring how the discontent gets related to the movement, how the generalised dissatisfaction becomes specific in terms of criticism of the existing order or situation and how the discontent gets focused into new demands and new definitions of rights and privileges.

Genesis Of The Shiv Sena

To obtain an insight into the genesis of the Shiv Sena movement and into the relative significance of various independent variables responsible for its rise, I consider it essential to ask the following questions:

1 How and why did the Shiv Sena arise in Mumbai?
2. How did it become a regionalist movement (and not a class movement)?
3. Why did it become an aggressive movement? How did the South Indian community become the target of its aggression?
4. Did the movement achieve its goals? What did it achieve for the community it claimed to represent?

To enable me to answer these questions, I had to search for answers to several ancillary queries.

1. Firstly, I considered it important to explore the roots of the discontent of the Maharashtrian community — the potential supporters and participants of the movement — at the time of the birth of the Shiv Sena. This would help obtain an insight into the motivation of the people who, in very large numbers, supported the Shiv Sena in its early days of 1966-69. I was particularly interested in understanding the reasons behind the popular support to the Shiv Sena.

i) For this I required data about the attitudes, expectations and perceived needs of the community. I expected other kinds of major frustrations besides the factor of unemployment, to contribute significantly to the discontent of the community. In the light of the points discussed earlier I was interested in exploring the nature of the sense of deprivation, if any, of the Maharashtrian community and its relation to the community's self image, at the time of the emergence of the Shiv Sena.

ii) What socio-historical factors supported and encouraged the self-image and the perspectives of the community? To answer this, I thought it would be useful to explore how far and in what way the Shiv Sena was related to the preceding Samyukta Maharashtra movement.

2. For understanding action, its subjective meaning needed to be linked to the objective situation.

i) I, therefore, wanted to know what objective factors in the situation, — socio-economic, political or cultural — contributed to the community's felt deprivations. For the purpose of structural analysis, what were the changes and strains in the established relationships that caused the discontent?

ii) How the subjective factors of the sense of deprivation and self-image and the objective factors of strains in the structure concurred, giving rise to the protest movement of the Shiv Sena; how the concurrence of subjective and objective factors stimulated or activated what Smelser calls generalised beliefs (Smelser, 1962, 16, 80-85); about the meaning of the situation, sources of strain and characteristics of these sources. How the Shiv Sena appeared on the scene to further elaborate and crystallise these beliefs into an 'ideology' and to provide solutions for the problem-situation.

iii) Why the movement took the form of a regionalist movement; how the general discontent of the community was transformed into the specific demands of 'priority for the sons of the soil' and of '80% of jobs for the local people', implying an indictment of the existing situation, and how and why the discontent was directed chiefly against South Indians.

3. i) What the nature of the leadership of the Shiv Sena was; what role it played in formulating the ideology, shaping the goals and programmes of the movement.
   ii) What the characteristic ways were in which the movement operated. Why the Shiv Sena movement became aggressive, unlike the earlier Samyukta Maharashtra Movement; what factors were responsible for the aggressive predictions of the Sena.
   iii) To what extent the goals of the movement were achieved.

Terminology

In the Indian context, the word 'regionalism' has been used in the recent past to represent regional patriotism or particularism often considered to be detrimental to national unity. During the 1950s, however, the term *regionalism* conveyed a different shade of meaning. Regionalism meant the principle of a region being the organisational basis for economic development. By the mid-1950s, it was generally accepted by the ruling elite that economic development had to proceed regionally. 'Region' in this context, however, did not denote a linguistic province but represented a wider geographical area covering two or three adjacent States or Provinces. Respecting this principle, the Zonal Council System was introduced into the constitutional structure of India (States Reorganisation Act-Part III), to promote economic development by bringing together into a larger unit, States having common problems and potentially competing claims on natural resources. This unifying feature of the zonal system or zonal division was meant also to counter the danger of 'provincial separation'. (Gazette of India–Extraordinary, 31.8.56, 756; Bondurant J.V., 1958)

In spite of the formation of zonal councils to counter 'provincial separation' the 1960s came to be described as one of 'the most dangerous decades'. (Selig Harisson, 1969) With the new demands for separate statehood for various linguistic regions, the older term 'linguistic provinces' — in use from British times — lapsed into disuse and instead the term 'linguistic regions' eventually came into fashion. As the demands for statehood for Maharashtra (1960), Nagaland (1963), Jharkhand and Punjabi Suba (1966) came to the fore, the term 'regionalism' gradually came to represent 'linguistic chauvinism'.

Region and Regionalism

Notwithstanding the variations in the points of view in the various social science disciplines, it is possible to draw a common denominator from the mutually reinforcing definitions of 'region'. A 'region' then would mean a unit of areal and cultural differentiation, distinguished by homogeneity of characteristics and an independent identity. (Vance, R.B., in Merril Jensen, 1965, 119-140) Homogeneity and identity of such a region are obviously multi-faceted and not derived from a single purpose such as of administration or economic organisation.

The term 'regionalism' which originates from 'region', thus underlines a concern for the region as a unit (of the larger gestalt), its homogeneity and identity.

The available literature on regionalism seems to suggest that the regionalist protest movements serve a function — that of focusing attention on the special needs and problems of particular regions and areas. This, in turn, sets into motion, the process of decentralisation of power and administration. If regionalism in the sense of regional decentralisation of power and administration fails to take shape, regionalism as a process of the asserting of regional identity perhaps begins to grow aggressive and eventually expresses itself as a protest movement.

If this analysis holds good the relationship between the two kinds of regionalisms is obvious. Whether this theory of relationship between the two regionalisms is applicable to the regionalist movement of the Shiv Sena, can be ascertained only upon concluding the present study.

Nativism

Nativism is yet another term that has been used in this context. Movements like the Telengana, the Shiv Sena and the Lachit Sena have often been described as *nativist movements.* Some scholars differentiate these 'nativist' movements from the earlier linguistic and ethnic movements like the Samyukta Maharashtra, the Andhra or that of the DMK. The argument is that even if both kinds of movements exploit ethnic and linguistic loyalties, the nativist movement distinguishes itself by its strong anti-migrant attitude. 'Nativism', it is claimed, is conceptually and empirically different from sub-national, ethnic or linguistic movements because of the greater degree of migrant-native conflict involved in it. (Katzenstein, Dec.1975) It is necessary therefore that we include this term in our review.

The meanings of the term *nativism* in sociology and social anthropology on the one hand, and in political science on the other, though related, vary considerably in their nuance or import. Their common denominator is the negative attitude or the attitude of resistance to 'the alien' or 'the migrant'.

Now, to apply the term 'native' or 'nativism' both at the national and sub-national/regional level (as in case of the Shiv Sena) is to render the term more ambiguous even if flexible. Such a use implies ignoring the subtle difference in the contexts and connotations of the term at the two different levels. A Bengali's negative attitude towards non-Bengali migrants is subtly distinct from the white American's resistance to Asian migrants. Though probably similar in their origin, the two attitudes seem to be differently conditioned.

Considering these ambiguities regarding the term nativism, I have preferred to use the term 'regionalism' to represent what may be called 'regional nativism'. Besides, it appears to me that the Shiv Sena movement is more than just an anti-migrant movement and includes elements of linguistic-ethnic-group movement.

CHAPTER II

METHODOLOGY

In the present research, my main problem was how to gauge the people's grievances, their sense of relative deprivation, if any, and how to obtain access to their views of themselves. A survey using the techniques of the questionnaire and the interview would indeed have yielded some information. However, I felt that such data might turn out to be too contrived, especially in respect of a self-view. Also by the time the present research was begun in 1972-73, much time had elapsed since the birth of the Shiv Sena, and therefore the usual techniques of the interview and the questionnaire, I felt, would not be of much use in obtaining information about people's attitudes during the pre-Shiv Sena days.

I decided, therefore, to use the technique of content analysis of Marathi journals, newspapers and, if necessary, other publications published during the period immediately before and after the emergence of the Shiv Sena movement. The hope was to obtain an insight into the regional community's attitudes and expectations, its relative deprivation, if any, and its appraisal of its position in Mumbai vis-à-vis the other communities.

Content Analysis in the Present Project

The selection of textual content for the present research was guided by the theoretical framework presented in the first chapter. As mentioned earlier, I was interested in exploring texts that would enable me to have an insight into the regional community's attitudes and expectations about their place or status in the metropolis of Mumbai and the nature of their hypothesised relative deprivation.

The Period of Coverage

I initially decided that the period of coverage for the purpose of the content-data of the present project should span a decade, from 1960 to 1970. The year 1960 was significant as the year the Maharashtra State was born; and 1970 was the year when a Shiv Sena member, for the first time, was elected to the State Legislature after contesting a key by-election — a clear landmark in the process of the transformation of the Sena from a movement to a pressure-group and political Party in regional politics. (This process of transformation, of course, had begun earlier when the Shiv Sena showed some signs of modification of its functional style to adapt itself to the demands of a democratic policy, and decided to contest civic elections to the Mumbai Municipal Corporation in March 1968).

However, when I actually began the work of collecting the content data, I found it very difficult to obtain older issues of the journals. Therefore, it was not possible to cover all the relevant issues of my chosen journals for the first two years, especially, the year 1960; also, some of the journals selected for the coverage, like the *Maharashtra Times*, for instance, had not yet come into existence.

Simultaneously I discovered that during these early years pertaining to the coverage, as also after 1969, there were relatively few entries on the relevant subjects i.e. the areas of relative deprivation or the self-view of the community (the exception being the entries articulating Maharashtrian aspirations around May 1960 — the time of the birth of Maharashtra State) Also, most of the entries of the later years, especially from 1969 onwards, are regarding the Shiv Sena, its programmes or politics rather than on the community's aspirations or deprivations. I, therefore, had to focus my attention chiefly on the period from 1962 to 1969 for the purpose of qualitative analysis. My record of content-data, however, is, for all practical purposes, complete for the period selected (1960-1970) barring a year or two each in respect of the *Loksatta* – 1960, 1961, the *Navshakti* – 1960, 1963, and *Maratha* – 1960, 1961, 1970. *The Maharashtra Times* came into existence only in 1962. For quantitative analysis I have included the entries of 1960-70.

To supplement the gap in data from the scheduled journals during the early years, I covered at a later stage, two newspapers from Pune, *Sakal* and *Kesari*, for 1960. This supplementary coverage brought into record, data on the aspirations of the community during 1960. This was also useful by way of a general check on the information and trends obtained in the coverage of the scheduled journals.

Choice of the Journals

Since the Shiv Sena movement has remained, even to this day, confined chiefly to the metropolis of Mumbai and the industrial areas in the vicinity, i.e. Mumbai city, its suburbs and a few satellite towns like Thane and Kalyan, I decided to include a few journals published from Mumbai for the content analysis.

The choice, for obvious reasons, was journals and newspapers in Marathi. Earlier, I had planned to cover the national press in English as well. The coverage of the English press was chiefly meant for comparative study, not necessarily meant to provide content vital to our present project. However, content analysis being a time-consuming and laborious technique, the handling of the large content-data obtained from the Marathi journals and newspapers left me with scant time to study the English press, and therefore the plan to cover it for comparative purposes was discarded.

The journals selected for coverage were all from Mumbai as mentioned earlier, and included five dailies and one weekly (the *Marmik*, the mouthpiece of the Shiv Sena). Our selection of the journals and newspapers for coverage of content data was based on the following criteria

1. Circulation: Wide circulation of a journal was one way of assuring that the attitudes and opinions mirrored in it were representative of a large majority of people.

2. Cross-section of views: These journals, which when taken together, projected a cross-section of political and economic views thereby covering or representing all sections of the Maharashtrian community.

Keeping these criteria in mind, I selected six journals

(i) *Loksatta* (Lks.) (ii) *Maharashtra Times* (Mht.) (iii) *Navshakti* (Nvs.) (iv) *Daily Maratha* (Mrt.) (v) *Navaka* (Nvk.) - all dailies, and (vi) *Marmik* (Mrm.) the only weekly.

1. Circulation

a. *Loksatta, Maharashtra Times* and *Navshakti* are three popular dailies with wide circulation all over Maharashtra and even outside the region. They belong to three different press-chains. *Loksatta* belongs to the Indian Express group, *Maharashtra Times* to the Times of India group and *Navshakti* belongs to the Free Press group.

b. To balance the coverage of these dailies belonging to the monopoly press-chains, three independent papers were selected: *Navakal*, the oldest (1923) of the selected dailies from Mumbai, established by a dedicated Congress worker during the freedom struggle; *Daily Maratha*, a very popular daily established by Acharya Atre, the leader of the Samyukta Maharashtra Movement; and lastly, the *Marmik* cartoon weekly, founded and edited by the Shiv Sena leader, Bal Thackeray.

2. Cross-section of Views

a. While the Marmik was the vehicle of the Shiv Sena's propaganda, Atre's Daily Maratha was a bitter opponent of the Shiv Sena and of the Marmik.

b. Navakal, an independent, pro-Congress daily and Navashakti of the Free Press group both supported the Shiv Sena to a considerable extent, especially during the early years of the movement (1966-1968).

c. Loksatta supported the Shiv Sena for a brief period during 1967-1968, especially at the time of the Barve-Menon contest in the fourth Lok Sabha elections, but later criticised it severely. Maharashtra Times largely followed a middle-of-the-road policy as far as the Shiv Sena was concerned.

I thus made efforts to obtain an unbiased and total picture of the situation through the coverage of the content-data from the journals by making a carefully balanced selection of newspapers for the study. In addition, I covered two more newspapers from Pune for the brief period of 1960, as mentioned earlier.

Being drawn from Marathi journals, the original data is obviously in Marathi. However, for the purpose of the present project, the data is presented in English. The English version is not a verbatim translation of the printed matter in Marathi but often a compact rendering. I have tried to keep to the spirit of the original, both in tone and meaning.

Criterion for Selection of the Content

The random sample method, normally used for selection of issues of journals and for collection of content-data, was not used for the present research because of the selective nature of data. I therefore, decided to go through as many issues as possible of the selected journals to obtain relevant data. Accordingly, I scanned almost all the available issues of the selected newspapers. Any content (falling under the three types Editorials, Reports and Articles, and Readers' Letters) that communicated information about the grievances, attitudes, opinions or the objective situation of the Marathi speaking people, about their self-image and about the Shiv Sena, came to be included in my data.

Classification of Content

1. Types and Units of content

What type or form of writing in newspapers and journals would yield me the information I was seeking and what type of writing should I include in my coverage? Initially, I thought of covering all genres of journalistic writing as far as they offered relevant content. However, on second thoughts, because it would make the data unwieldy, I excluded literary material like poems, short stories and visuals like cartoons, in spite of their considerable bearing on my subject. (*Marmik* has been significantly a cartoon weekly.)

i. Units of content

The collected content-types thus include news and news reports, write-ups and articles, interviews, editorials and readers' letters. Each report, interview, letter, editorial, in other words, each entry under the various content-types, was treated as one unit disregarding the length of the content or the number of paragraphs in it.

ii. Types of content

The collected data was then classified into three broad types or forms of content.

a. Readers' Letters had 660 letters voicing people's views and reactions.

b. Editorials covered 295 units.

c. News Reports and Articles had over 1500 units or entries including about 175 articles.

The three types of content-data together include over two thousand entries or units, spread over a decade (1960-70). Besides these, some entries from journals from Pune were used exclusively for qualitative analysis.—

a) **Readers' Letters**

These form the most valuable part of my data. These letters, like the proverbial tip of the iceberg, are indicators of a much greater volume of discontent seething below the surface. They give us a direct access into people's grievances and their self-image as a community, without the researchapter providing any stimulus to elicit the information wanted. (cf. Riley M.W., 1963, 243)

b) **Editorials**

Editorials are important because they represent the journals' authentic stand or outlook on issues of public concern. Here also, my care in the choice of journals enabled me in obtaining content-data that represented a cross-section of editorial opinion.

c) **News Reports* and Articles**

The data from news reports, regular columns and articles are treated together in spite of the distinction between these genres of writing. The articles, even those of independent writers, cannot be treated on the same level as readers' letters which

* To be referred to as 'reports' hereafter.

represent individual opinions and personal responses of people. Nor can they be included under editorials which represent the newspapers' authentic stand or attitude. The articles are either informative or critical, or both, and thus represent more of an objective assessment and therefore may be justifiably classified with news reports (i.e. reportage) which are accounts of factual events. Besides, the relatively small number of articles (less than two hundred) among the total entries under the heading of news reports (nearly one thousand five hundred), justifies, I thought, my inclusion of these with the reports.

The data from news reports, articles and editorials was used for supporting, complementing and verifying that obtained from readers' letters.

2. Categories and Themes

The units or the entries of each of the three types of content – editorials, reports and articles and the readers' letters – from each journal, were subjected to further classification into several categories representing different themes. (See Appendix I)

Here I may add that the categories of classification were not premeditated when I started collecting the data. I approached the journals with an open mind and collected whatever content-data I could, relating to the Maharashtrian community — its grievances, achievements, aspirations, self-views and other factual information about the community. On closer examination, subsequently, of the content-data I found that it lent itself to classification into the themes or categories used in the present project.

These themes included:

i) Various areas of deprivation ranging from those of employment opportunities to those of the status of the community and of the Marathi language, and even of the problem of unsettled disputes regarding the State's borders.

ii) Those related to the community's self-concept, its self-image and the image of other communities in the interactional setting of Mumbai.

iii) The theme of the Shiv Sena, positive and negative attitudes about the Sena, its programmes, leadership, etc.

Often, I came across an entry or a unit which dealt with more than one theme at a time. Classification of such entries was difficult, unless I had the aid of some guiding rule. I decided to put such an entry under two categories if both the themes communicated in the entry received more or less equal prominence in the content. An entry was put under three categories simultaneously — which happened only occasionally — if three themes received attention in the entry. However, care was taken not to extend the unit to four categories in any case.

Frequency of units under each category, for the three different content types of each of the selected journals, was counted year-wise. (Alongside, each unit was put on the affective scale under the proper index point. See below.) The count of frequency for each category served as a measure of the predominance of the category in the total communications and of its significance in mobilising popular discontent. The variations in the weight of categories according to time, type of content and a particular journal were noted while interpreting the data and drawing inferences.

3. Affective Scale*

After classifying the units of my content-data into various categories of themes (grievances, self-image and the Shiv Sena), they were further analysed and wherever relevant, as in case of the themes of grievances or deprivations, were also represented on a six-point affective scale of ascending order. The scale consists of the following six index-points

(i) Aspiration (ii) Grievance (iii) Frustration-Insecurity (iv) Protest (v) Demand, and (vi) Call for Action.

The successive six points of the scale are supposed to

* The affective scale was prepared after consultation and discussion with the following people active in social science and with experience in social research Dr. Y.B. Damle (Sociology), Dr. P.L. Bhandarkar (Sociology and Social Anthropology), Sharayu Anantram (Sociology), Kusum Damle (Psychology), Dr. A.W. Oak (Research in Education)

represent an increasing degree of intensity of a felt deprivation or of a grievance. The points on the ordinal scale are not claimed to be equidistant from each other. The selection of indices is a priori, based on the logic of psychological experience and is used to serve only as a broad or approximate indicator of the increasing intensity of people's relative deprivations.

In the process of my analysis, I came across many entries which exclusively communicated a 'protest' or censure of the conditions or of sources of strains. The frequency of 'protest' was much higher than that of 'demand' while 'demand' seemed to follow 'protest' with the progression of time. I feel I am justified in assigning to 'demand' a higher rank than to 'protest' on the affective scale, since 'demand' implies a more positive and articulate expression of the desire to alleviate frustration.

This leads us to another significant point regarding my scale. My ascending scale of six points consists of two aspects or dimensions — one of experience and the other of (overt) action. Aspiration, grievance and frustration refer to states experienced by individuals and groups, while protest, demand and call for action, even merely at the symbolic (vocal) level represent behaviour or action. 'Frustration' is the crucial meeting point — when experience transforms into the overt behaviour of protest. Failure of protest to obtain relief from frustration, leads to overt 'demand' and later to 'call for action' to relieve the frustration. The affective scale of six index points thus represents an ascending order of patterns of experience and of behaviour.

Distribution of Content Units on the Affective Scale

It is one thing to prepare a scale and quite another to carry out the distribution of given entries on the scale. It was relatively easy to classify the entries theme-wise, since each theme was clearly distinguishable from the other and problems of finer demarcation were involved therein. The only problem encountered in this context was when a particular entry spread over more than one theme. However, distributing the entries on the continuum of a scale representing states of experience and behaviour, and dividing them into distinct scale points was a rather difficult task. Besides, the communication in each entry differed in its style of expression, choice of words, method of presentation, etc., and specific words could not always serve as precise labels or symbols of specific states.

In spite of these difficulties, however, I found that the affective tone of an entry, taken as a whole, was unmistakably recognisable; certain phrases, idioms and words were found consistently repeated in the writings, expressing identical or similar ideas and feelings. It was not impossible, therefore, to distinguish the difference in the intensity of expression contained in the verbal statement. The choice of such words as 'injustice', 'unjust' or 'intolerable', and their repeated use in a piece of writing for instance, as distinct from the deployment of words and phrases like 'unfair', 'regrettable', 'painful', 'a matter of concern', etc., clearly conveyed a definite sense of protest, that was different from a sense of mere grievance. Calls 'to unite', 'to struggle', 'to come together to assert rights', could of course be easily identified. However, some careful examination of the content was necessary to distinguish a demand from aspiration, by the choice of the words conveying a sense of assertion, insistence and urgency. Again, frustration and insecurity could be detected relatively easily in contradistinction to grievance on the one hand and protest, or demand on the other, by the degree of intensity in expression. 'Frustration' and 'insecurity' were communicated in terms of despair and apprehension respectively at the 'loss of identity', 'loss of the language of the community', and in terms of the fear of 'the extinction of one's community (in the metropolis)', and in terms of 'others' conspiracy to oust one's community'.

If an entry included clear, articulate statements which could get distributed under more than one index-point, we noted such an entry under the respective index-points, but not exceeding three. Thus, if a piece of writing expressed in unmistakable terms grievances as well as demands for redressal for instance simultaneously, or frustration, protest and call for action, it was then entered under all the relevant index-points simultaneously, by a tick-mark against this entry, under each respective index-point-column. The frequency of tick-marks under each index-point of the scale was counted for every year of the decade and turned into value-points by multiplying the number of frequencies by the value-point for the respective index-point. This obtained a measure of total intensity expressed through the entries during a particular year. The affective intensity for various years could thus be compared.

It is true that every index-point on the present affective scale, theoretically speaking, covers the ground of the preceding index-point or rank. Thus the state of frustration covers the state of grievance, while grievance includes aspiration. The index of protest, on the scale, implies (according to the theoretical assumption of the scale), that the participants of a movement who voice a collective protest would not be moved to do so unless they had already covered the ground of 'frustration'. Similarly, positive demand for remedial action or for redress of a grievance implies a negative protest of the frustrating source or agent.

In this sense, a scale point or index which represents the degree of intensity on the affective scale is understood to cover or include the preceding scale-points representing lower degrees of intensity. However, while considering the affective value of an entry, I count its value-points solely by the index to which the entry is assigned; value points of preceding indices are not taken into account. I therefore feel that I am justified in assigning an entry to more than one scale-point (of the ascending scale), if and when the entry included articulate expressions of different degrees of intensity of grievance or deprivation.

Tables showing the distribution of units on the affective scale and in the categories representing various themes, and those correlating these distributions with the progression of time were prepared. These tables are presented in the relevant chapters. They are interpreted and discussed in their proper context.

Quantitative Analysis

Entries on the Affective Scale

If my analysis in the earlier chapter is correct and the people's severe discontent regarding their situation is responsible for the rise of the Shiv Sena movement, this fact ought to get reflected in the distribution of entries (units) on the affective scale. One would expect that during the early years of the chosen decade, 1960-1970, I would find a relatively small number of entries under the index of 'grievance', a relatively larger number of entries under 'aspirations' and almost no entries under the index points of 'protest' and 'demand'. With the progression of time it was expected that more and more entries would gather under 'frustration-insecurity' and under 'protest' and 'demand', till around the middle of the decade, i.e., around 1965-1966, entries would begin to appear under the index of 'call for action'.

Themes of Grievances

In the earlier chapter I had argued that the relative deprivation of the Maharashtrian community was the major factor responsible for the emergence of the Shiv Sena movement. I contended that the community's view of itself and its self-appraisal were the crucial variables, rather than merely the factors of job competition or of overcrowding which no doubt caused systemic strains.

If this analysis about the genesis of the Shiv Sena movement is incorrect and economic reasons are, or prove to be most crucial, I would expect the majority of the entries to collect under the theme of economic opportunities. If however, I came to find an equally large number of entries under the themes of (i) the social status of the community and/or (ii) the status of the Marathi language, I should then consider this to be a broad confirmation of my hypothesis. Also, if it is true that the people's perspective about their situation is a significant factor in transforming the economic and demographic or other strains, into the experience of stress and discontent, I expect this factor to reflect itself in terms of a good number of entries collecting under 'self-view'. Presumably, this point would also get reflected in the qualitative analysis of the entries under the related themes of 'self-view' and 'self and others'.

Qualitative Analysis

Besides carrying out the analysis based on the distribution

of entries under various themes and on the affective scale, the content-data was also subjected to a qualitative analysis, to obtain an insight into the community's view about itself and about 'others' in its social setting, and to understand the variety of the community's grievances which fermented the discontent that mobilised the movement.

The content data on the Shiv Sena too, was closely examined to understand the positive and negative attitudes to it and the nature of the popular support to it, to trace the evolution of its leadership, it s goals and objectives, the articulation of its programme, and the definition of its demand.

The job of analysing the content was carried out in the light of the hypothesis and the theoretical framework presented in the first chapter. Drawing upon content-data from six journals of differing complexions, I had the opportunity of comparing different sets of content-data, to avoid one-sided inferences based on isolated or biased records.

Besides, while content analysis has been the major technique of the present study, it is by no means the only source of data for drawing the inferences. I made efforts at all stages, to supplement and compare the content-data and its findings with other kinds of data available to a research scholar, from authentic sources such as government records, historical documents, research studies in Social Science and even occasional personal interviews. Also statistical data from the census and similar other reports were used for assessing my content-analysis findings and their interpretations before confirming them. This data is incorporated in the analysis and discussion carried out in separate sections of most chapters.

The Findings

It may be stated here briefly that my expectations based on my hypothesis seem to be broadly borne out by the findings of the content analysis and the supplementary data.

It appears that the widespread feelings of deprivation of the Marathi speaking community over a subordinate economic and social status, in relation to other communities of the metropolis, were crucial to the community's sense of severe frustration. Augmented simultaneously by raised expectations and increasing strains in the system under the changed circumstances after 1960, the popular frustrations got channelised into the violent protest movement of the Shiv Sena.

For a detailed presentation of the findings and their interpretations, one will have to wait until the concluding chapter of the thesis.

CHAPTER III

THE SHIV SENA: EMERGENCE AND GROWTH

Emergence

The Shiv Sena, named after Maharashtra's great and popular hero Shivaji, was born on 19 June, 1966; this was about six years after the establishment of the state of Maharashtra with Mumbai as its capital, on 1 May, 1960. Some two or three weeks before it was founded its advent was heralded in the pages of the *Marmik*, Bal Thackeray's Marathi cartoon weekly, which later became the mouthpiece of the Shiv Sena.

In the issue of the *Marmik* of 5 June 1966, a brief announcement appeared in a box regarding registration of the Sena's membership. The succeeding issue of 12 June 66 carried another announcement expounding the objectives and orientations of the Shiv Sena, under the heading 'Prolegomena to the Birth of Shiv Sena'.

The linguistic reorganisation of States has been carried out for furthering economic and industrial development of each of the linguistic regions and its linguistic communities. However, in the city of Mumbai, in Maharashtra, people of other provinces (*para-prantiya*, 'non-locals' or 'outsiders') have managed to establish themselves everywhere, in the name of 'cosmopolitanism'. As a result, the Marathi (speaking) people are being deprived of job opportunities and housing. Both the State Government and the Marathi people themselves have so far been rather generously accommodative and foolhardy not to have taken note of the situation. The Marathi people earned their claim to the city of Mumbai as the capital of their state only after a long-drawn struggle and the martyrdom of many. Was this all for living a life of the unprivileged and of the deprived in the city?'

Further, it complained:

'When many States of the Republic pursued the policy of priority to those speaking their own state language in jobs of all kinds, in State, Central Government, or private sector employment, why should not the Government of Maharashtra follow suit?'

Cynical of the Maharashtra Government's policy, the Prolegomena asserted:

We need a large organisation to force the State Government into some relevant action. The Marathi (speaking) people must gather together under the saffron banner and organise themselves into a powerful front for asserting Maharashtrian self-respect and their rights in the face of encroachment by people from other provinces.'

The Prolegomena also added:

'We have no hostility towards the people of other (linguistic) provinces, nor are they our enemies. But these people of other provinces give priority to the people of their own language groups and forestall others; why should we, the Marathi speaking people alone be obliged to accommodate outsiders? First comes the right of the Marathi (speaking) person for survival in his own state, and only then would follow the rights of the others. We demand 80% of all jobs — Government, semi-Government, and industrial for the Marathi people. We demand priority for the Marathi (speaking) people in the State Housing Board tenements. This is not a communal fight. This is an issue of the Marathi people's natural and just rights and we shall fight for these rights.'

This was the tone of the preliminary declaration accompanying the announcement regarding the registration to the Shiv Sena's membership.

The *Marmik* of 26 June 1966 gives us the news of the inauguration of the registration to the Sena membership in the presence of a statue of Shivaji, and at the hands of Prabodhankar Thackeray — Bal Thackeray's father, one of the erstwhile leaders of the non-Brahmin movement in Maharashtra. The *Marmik*, in this particular issue, claimed that, within an hour of starting, as many as two thousand young men's names were listed on the register. By the following day, the number shot up to ten thousand; it reached the mark of twenty thousand within a month, and within a period of three months i.e. by September it had shot up to thirty thousand. (*Marmik* 18.9.66)

Hirji Malik, in his article on the Sena, 'The Private Armies' (*The Illustrated Weekly of India* 15.3.70), estimated the Shiv Sena volunteers' strength to be somewhere between 80, 000 and 2 lakh in 1970. Even after making some allowance for exaggeration, the fact remains that at its advent, the Shiv Sena was received with unexpected enthusiasm. The speedy increase in *Marmik's* sales from 18,000 to 25,000 during 1966, furnishes another indication of the Shiv Sena's popularity in the first years of its existence.

What was in the *Marmik* and in the philosophy and programme of the Shiv Sena that appealed to the Marathi speaking people of Mumbai, especially those of the middle and the working classes and fired them with enthusiasm? What were the writings of Bal Thackeray and his colleagues in the journal, and what were the readers' responses?

The Background

Taking its inspiration from P.K. Atre's *Dainik Maratha* (The *Daily Maratha*), the *Marmik* assumed the role of the champion of the Maharashtrian cause, and around 1964-1965 it began to vehemently voice the grievances of the Marathi community. The *Marmik* was started on the 14 August 1960 as a cartoon weekly. It is little-known that its first issue carried a letter of gratitude from the editors, Bal Thackeray and his brother Shrikant, to Atre, the colourful journalist-leader of the Samyukta Maharashtra Movement. The *Daily Maratha* not only inspired, but also influenced the *Marmik* a great deal. The *Marmik* modelled itself in many ways after the *Daily Maratha*, though it lacked the satirical finesse of Atre's pen. The clever and well-drawn political and social cartoons appearing in the *Marmik*, however, were its own creation — a distinctive feature largely responsible for its popularity.

The *Marmik* served as an important communication link for the Shiv Sena's volunteer-members. Ram Joshi (1970) estimated the *Marmik's* circulation to be in the vicinity of 60,000 in the mid-sixties. The official sales figure was around 25, 000 and 37,000 in 1966 and 1969 respectively. (See Appendix A-I)

However, the actual readership may have easily exceeded one lakh. This readership, of course, was spread all over Maharashtra, though Mumbai no doubt provided the lion's share of patronage. Much of the political education of the Shiv Sena cadre — volunteers and office-bearers — took place through this weekly. The *Marmik* thus played a vital role in the formation of this movement and organisation. (See Ram Joshi, 1970)

From 1965, the *Marmik* published, for a period of about two years, in almost every weekly issue, lists of names of the officials and personnel in managerial cadres of a number of public and private industrial and business firms, as well as other institutions in Mumbai and in a few other places like Pune and Nashik in Maharashtra. It focused attention on the microscopic percentage of members of the Marathi community in these lists and on the large proportion of members of non-Marathi groups, especially of South Indian communities. The *Marmik's* allegation was that the high percentage of the non-Marathi and especially of the South Indian was due to deliberate manoeuvring, neither accidental nor coincidental.

The *Marmik's* Grievances

Migrants' influx to Mumbai

One of the preoccupations of the *Marmik's* columns and Bal Thackeray's speeches (and, in fact, even that of several leaders of the Samyukta Maharashtra Samiti and other parties) around 1965 and 1966 was the incessant and heavy influx into Mumbai of migrants from outside the State of Maharashtra, and apprehensions regarding its consequences for the Maharashtrian community. The apprehensions centred round the fear that the Maharashtrian community would be ousted from the city for all practical purposes, if such a trend continued indefinitely; and that some of the migrating communities which held economic power or possessed such values and skills that enabled them to earn this power, would ultimately monopolise the material rewards and economic opportunities which normally should and would have been available to the Marathi (speaking) community in their state capital.

For example, an article in the *Marmik* exhorted the Marathi community to wake up 'before they get driven out of their own capital'. (Mrm. 8.5.66)

The heading of another article was rhetorical: 'Who does Mumbai belong to? To the refugees and to the people of other States!' This article directed its resentment against the Sindhis who, in spite of having arrived as victims of the Partition 'soon captured the cloth markets of Mumbai' and became prosperous — owning buildings, houses and real estate in the city of Mumbai — while the majority of the Marathi people continued to live in *chawls*, small rented tenements.

Another community against whom resentment was expressed was the South Indian. 'Once one of them gets a footing in an office or industry, he invariably brings in his clan-members by using connections and influence' and 'when he makes headway, he promotes his clan-fellows too'. (Mrm.15.5.66)

Failures of the State Government

Housing

The editorial of *Marmik's* Maharashtra Day number ('Events that Make Maharashtrians Restive'), severely criticised the State Government for its failure to look after the very basic needs of food, shelter, clothing and jobs of the Marathi people — the native community of the State — 'in the name of cosmopolitanism and nationalism'. Maintaining that the State Housing Board was created to provide housing for the middle and working class people of Maharashtra, the editorial referred to the discussion in the Legislative Assembly of the State. Only about 35% of the Housing Board tenants were Marathi (speaking) persons and that the Minister's definition of 'Maharashtrian' which ingeniously included all those who were residents of Mumbai for a period of ten years, in effect excluded a number of Marathi speaking persons who were the natives of the State but who were left without the amenity of housing. (Mrm.1.5.66)

Another editorial commenting at a later date on the Housing Board's mismanagement and corruption alleged that many a

South Indian had obtained a tenement in Mumbai by presenting a false domicile certificate. (Mrm. 31.7.66)

Employment

The major complaint that the Maharashtra Day editorial had against the State Government was its failure to safeguard the Marathi community's interests regarding employment, in public, private, State and Central Government jobs. The editorial admitted: 'It is the shortcoming of the Maharashtrian community that it lacks entrepreneurship and business skills and nobody but itself can be held responsible for these lacunae.'

However, it still held the State Government responsible for making little effort to encourage these skills in the Marathi community. Further, it took the State Government to task for its failure in giving priority to Marathi people at least in jobs. The editorial pointed out that it could legitimately be demanded that lower-cadre jobs be given to the members of the local community of the State, especially when scarce resources like land, electricity and water were made available to industries by the State Government, and prognosticated: 'However, when all the higher posts are occupied by non-Marathi persons (persons from other provinces or States), it is difficult to expect that they would be concerned about giving greater scope to Marathi (speaking) workers or technicians.'

The same editorial then went on to point out the large proportion of South Indian officials and the microscopic quantity of Marathi officials and other types of employees at the MIG factory, Nashik, and further, drew attention to similar situations in Fertiliser Corporation of India, Trombay, Hindustan Antibiotics, Pimpri, and Indian Oil Corporation, Mumbai.

The editorial ended with a warning to the Maharashtra Government stating that if it failed to stall this kind of encroachment on employment in Maharashtra by non-Marathi communities the people will be forced to earn justice by setting the ministerial seats on fire. (Mrm.1.5.66)

Slums and Squatter Population

The editorial of 29.5.66 ('The Governing Elite of the Morrow') discussing the problems of metropolitan slums and hutments pleaded for urgent preventive measures considering the difficulties involved in the eradication of slums once they grew. The editorial was concerned about the deteriorating civic situation due to the heavy influx of people.

The editorial claimed that the Marathi (speaking) population of about 3 to 4 lakh among the 10 lakh slum-dwellers of metropolitan Mumbai, was already outdone by numbers coming from other States; it further bemoaned the concentration of anti-social activities like illicit brewing, bootlegging, etc., in slums and the existence of anti-social elements such as beggars, vagrants and criminals outlawed from other States, thanks to the prohibition policy of Maharashtra State.

The editorial criticised the indifference of the political parties in Mumbai to the problem of the influx of migrants and their vested interest in the slums as prospective vote banks. It held the industrialists, the businessmen and their top executives responsible for indirectly contributing to the problem of slums in Mumbai by the recruitment of persons from their own province and village, oblivious of the problem of housing them or of the unemployment existing among local workers.

The editorial was worried that as an upshot of all these events, the number of Marathi speakers in Mumbai was decreasing, to the detriment of the interests of the Marathi community, and cited the instance of the Home Minister of the State being heckled for making a speech in Marathi at a public meeting.

The editorial ended with a warning that if such a state of affairs continued, there would soon be a demand for separate Statehood for the city of Mumbai by the 'cosmopolitan' citizens of the metropolis, with the support of the Mumbai Pradesh Congress Committee.

The influx of out-of-State population into Mumbai and the apprehension of a probable demand the creation of a separate state for the metropolis are themes central to yet another editorial 'Salutations to Maharashtra'. (Mrm. 14.8.66)

Complaints against South Indians

Apart from the central theme of Mumbai's exploding population and the feeling of insecurity expressed over the status of the Marathi community in Mumbai, another theme which recurs is that of antagonism towards South Indians. The negative attitude towards them is ostensibly because of their alleged nepotism and clannishness. However, this expression of antipathy has more varied a background than merely that of the oft-repeated one of job competition.

i. The editorial of 14.8.66 alleged: 'In Tamil Nadu 70% to 80% jobs go to the Tamil people and the advertisements calling for jobs insist on domicile in Tamil Nadu and the knowledge of the Tamil language as qualifications required for employment. The norms of nationalism and cosmopolitanism, of the citizens' freedom of employment and of movement are apparently reserved for implementation only in the State of Maharashtra.' Merely, as a pointer to this, the editorial claimed, the *Marmik* reluctantly published a list of officials and other staff from various offices and establishments in Mumbai. (Mrm. 14.8.66)

ii. Another grouse expressed in the editorial 'The Farce of the Keralites' (20.2.66) was about how the South Indians refused to adapt to local food habits. The occasion for this reaction was the complaint of the Kerala representatives at the Jaipur Session of the Indian National Congress, that Keralites got only four kilos of rationed foodgrains per head simply because another portion of four kilos were grains other than rice. The editorial contended that in spite of rice being the staple food of coastal Maharashtra, the people there accepted available foodgrains considering the scarcity conditions in the country. (Mrm. 20.2.66)

A significant cause of resentment seemed to be the South Indians' resistance to the Marathi language, even after their migration to Mumbai.

iii. In reaction to a letter from a Keralite in Mumbai which appeared in the *Indian Express* (9.5.66), criticising the language of the State and claiming its implementation as an impediment to the non-Marathi person's employment opportunities, a

Marmik columnist comments that this attitude of resistance to the Marathi language itself is a stumbling block to migrants' integration. (Mrm. 22.5.66)

iv. The editorial of 5.6.66 entitled 'The Arab and the Camel' compared South Indians to the camel in Aesop's fable; this was occasioned by K.Kamaraj, the President of All India Congress Committee, telling a felicitation meeting in Mumbai that he would like to live in the city. Tamilians in Mumbai, the editorial observed, are often said to be identifying themselves with Maharashtra. But do they really? How many of them have learned Marathi even after settling in Mumbai for a living? How many of them associate themselves with Maharashtrian activities and organisations in the city? The editorial observes that most Tamilians in Mumbai avoid using languages other than Tamil or English. They have little understanding or sympathy towards Maharashtra, being indifferent to issues which vitally concern Maharashtrians e.g.Godavari waters. Yet they claim to have identified themselves with Maharashtra. Referring to anti-Brahmin, anti-Hindi and anti-North attitudes flourishing in Tamil Nadu and the DMK government's demand for an autonomous state, the editorial declares: 'We do not need the Tamil people (Madrasi) to teach us nationalism'. (Mrm.5.6.66)

The Shiv Sena and the Sampoorna Maharashtra Samiti — the Background

A few editorials and articles published in the *Marmik* around mid-1966 throw significant light on the Shiv Sena stand on the issues, parties and personalities which dominated the-then political scene in Mumbai. A sample of the content of these articles would also be useful as a pointer to the change that the Shiv Sena underwent during the critical period of the Barve-Menon contest in 1967.

The Samyukta Maharashtra Samiti (SMS), the organisation thrown up by the Samyukta Maharashtra Movement, was an alliance of the leftist opposition parties in Maharashtra, including the Communist Party of India. It was this coalition of leftist parties, which, for the most part, spearheaded the agitation for unilingual Maharashtra with Mumbai as its capital and, after its sustained efforts for five years (1956-60), achieved its goal on 1 May, 1960. However, soon after the formation of Maharashtra State, the SMS began to disintegrate, with the withdrawal of one of its member parties, the Praja Socialist Party. After a truncated existence for a couple of years, the SMS was dissolved in 1963. (Mrt. 4.8.63)

Although the SMS had achieved its major goal, the problems of the demarcation of Maharashtra's borders and of the inclusion of major Marathi speaking areas like Belgaum, Karwar, Goa and Nagar-Haveli remained undecided, to the dissatisfaction of the Marathi community. Some of the personalities and parties in the erstwhile coalition were therefore keen on the continuation of the alliance as a united political opposition to the Congress Party and wanted to reap the political benefits of the existing residue of people's discontent. Atre, the editor of the *Daily Maratha*, was one of the persons who took initiative and made considerable efforts at reviving the older SMS for mobilising mass support for the yet incomplete task of the integration of the border areas of Maharashtra. As a result of these efforts, was born the Sampoorna Maharashtra Samiti (SPMS), an alliance of parties led by the Communist Party of India and the Samajwadi Socialist Party. (Mrt. 12.4.66) It, however, never became as popular as its predecessor, the Samyukta Maharashtra Samiti.

Soon after the formation of the SPMS in mid-1966, the parties in this alliance decided to organise an agitation under its banner over the Belgaum-border issue (Mrt. 27.5.66; 30.5.66) In response to this move, the *Marmik* published an editorial (12.6.66) which welcomed the SPMS's decision of an agitation over Belgaum but expressed doubts over the Samiti's ability to deliver the goods.

The tone of the editorial 'The Sampoorna Maharashtra Samiti of Decimal Parties' (Mrm. 12.6.66), was surprisingly appreciative and generally welcomed the founding of a new alliance of opposition parties. This appears especially interesting in the light of later events — the emergence of the Shiv Sena and the Sampoorna Maharashtra Samiti as political opponents and their bitter campaign wars during the Barve-Menon parliamentary election.

> The *Marmik* editorial argued: 'For the defeat of the Congress, all the opposition parties of Maharashtra need to join hands on a common platform, to bring about a solution to the problem of the border areas of Karwar, Belgaum, etc., which has been shelved for long by the Congress government and the Congress high command.'
>
> Speaking of the SPMS, the editorial commented: 'The new Sampoorna Maharashtra Samiti would be able to bring some pressure on the Central Government for seeking a favourable solution to the vexing border issues only if it manages to win a large number of seats in the Maharashtra legislature.' The editorial further expressed hope that the able leadership of S.M. Joshi and S.A. Dange would carry out the tasks of the new coalition.
>
> The editorial however warned: 'The SPMS must win over the sympathy and support of the members of the Maharashtra Pradesh Congress Committee to ensure the Samiti's success in the elections in Maharashtra and to give a blow to the BPCC controlled by S.K. Patil.'

It is obvious that the Shiv Sena was well-disposed to the SPMS and expected it to mobilise the masses for solving Maharashtra's border problem shelved until then by the Congress government. This was on the eve of the founding of the Sena, the announcement of which was already made in the *Marmik*.

Some of the editorials written in the *Marmik* in mid-1966 also raised the issue of injustice to Maharashtra over the inclusion of the border areas of Belgaum and Karwar in Karnataka. These editorials, comparing notes with the Punjabi Suba agitation, repeated the complaint that the Central Government took notice of the people's grievances only when forced to by violent agitations. One of these editorials chastised the government for its ad-hoc policy and its appointment of a one-man Commission for the Belgaum-border issue, without laying down the directive principles for resolving border disputes between the States of the Indian Union.

Writing on the Belgaum border issue ('Do not Chide the Tiger of Sahyadri' – Mrm.15.5.66 and 'Maharashtra will have to Trample This Bait Underfoot' – Mrm. 3.7.66), the editorials blamed the Central Government for its apathy in laying down guiding principles for the demarcation of borders disputed by one or the other States, and the Government's ad-hoc decisions made purely under political pressure in the absence of a planned policy. The editorial contended that those who managed to make the greater noise, to create an atmosphere of violence and intimidation, were the ones to profit from the government's 'ad-hocism', whereas that particular community which expressed its discontent and demands through the means of elections and other parliamentary mechanisms (an obvious reference to the Belgaum and Karwar elections) suffered and are totally ignored.

The editorial further criticised the Central Government for continuously shelving the problem of properly defining Maharashtra's borders with its neighbouring States of Gujarat Maharashtra, Madhya Pradesh and Karnataka, even six years after the formation of the unilingual State of Maharashtra.

The editorial pointed out that only when the Congress suffered heavy losses in the 1957 elections, was Maharashtra's reasonable demand for a unilingual state conceded by the Government, although the All India Congress Committee had always accepted the principle of linguistic States.

The editorial thus held the Central and State Governments responsible for driving people to resort to agitational measures by their policy of turning a deaf ear to popular grievances.

The *Marmik* and S.K. Patil

Some editorials written in the mid-sixties reveal the *Marmik's* distrust and dislike for 'the shrewd and suave politician' S.K. Patil, styled as the one-time political boss of the Mumbai Pradesh Congress Committee. S.K. Patil held a high position in the All India Congress Committee and had occupied important cabinet portfolios until the Kamaraj plan led to the retirement of senior ministers. Patil was well-known for his ability to raise funds for the Party. The *Marmik's* hostility towards S.K. Patil was in line with that of the Maharashtrian community. During the Samyukta Maharashtra struggle, he was vehemently against the inclusion of Mumbai in Maharashtra State. Despite this, it is interesting that Patil was the first to obtain Bal Thackeray's help for a common cause — the election of S.G.Barve a Maharashtrian and the Congress candidate contesting against Krishna Menon.

The early *Marmik* editorials on Patil were very ironic and spare no sarcasm at his expense.

An editorial ('Why Shouldn't S. K. Patil Resign?') dated 26.6.66 written in the context of the-then railway accident near Matunga station in Mumbai, referred to this new addition to the mishap list of the railways, and in an ironic vein continued: 'Mr. Patil does not have to model his behaviour after that of Mr. Lal Bahadur Shastri, who, as Railway Minister resigned immediately after the Aliyalur accident.'

An editorial (Mrm. 4.9.66) which was highly critical of S.K. Patil came after the resignations of three ministers (Shantilal Shah, Homi Talyarkhan and Dr. Kailash) and seventeen other members of the State Ligislative Assembly — all from the BPCC — in August, 1966. The resignations were to protest against the Naik Government's alleged failure in handling the law-and-order situation at the time of the 'Mumbai Bandh' organised by the Sampoorna Maharashtra Samiti on two consecutive days — the 24th and 25th August.

In the *Marmik* of 4.9.66, an editorial entitled, 'What to do Mr. Patil's *Sadobas* (Stooges) Have to Say?' saw Patil's hand behind the drama of the resignation of the BPCC members in the ministry and the Legislative Assembly. The *Maratha*, in its editorials had also expressed similar views earlier. (Mrt. 28.8.66; 29.8.66)

The *Marmik* and the BPCC

The *Marmik* was highly critical of the BPCC in 1966 and earlier. Two series of articles, 'In the Capital of Maharashtra' and 'The Reawakening of Maharashtra', one by Prabodhankar Thackeray (Bal Thackeray's father), and the other under a pseudonym, but apparently by the same person, appeared in the July and August 1966 numbers of the *Marmik*.

Analysing the Maharashtrian situation in Mumbai in the mid-sixties, these articles held three major factors responsible for the shrinking status of Maharashtrians in Mumbai: (i) Mumbai's capitalist class (ii) the Mumbai Pradesh Congress Committee and (iii) the Government of Maharashtra.

i. It argued that the capitalist class of Mumbai that controlled its and Maharashtra's business and industry, was well-organised. With the commercial expansion of Mumbai after Independence, the importance of this capitalist class continued to grow, reducing the lot of the Marathi community to that of the passive bystander.

   This elite non-Marathi 'cosmopolitan' class upheld a definition of 'Maharashtrian' based on the criterion of domicile, ignoring the criterion of language though language was the very basis for the reorganisation of linguistic States.

ii. Regarding the BPCC, the articles observed:

   Through its economic resources, the capitalist class of Mumbai controls the BPCC. The BPCC thus represents the business entrepreneur class made up of non-Marathi communities, which have hardly any emotional ties with the region and people of Maharashtra; the BPCC's main concern is to safeguard the class interests of its representatives which clash with the class interests of the Marathi community. Consequently, the BPCC emerges as the staunchest opponent of Maharashtrian interests.

   The article further alleged that soon after the formation of Maharashtra State, the BPCC effectively suppressed the Maharashtrian voice by manoeuvring changes in the metropolitan constituencies for civic and parliamentary elections. The BPCC saw to it that Maharashtrian members did not get an important standing in the BPCC or in the Mumbai Municipal Corporation and its various committees, in the Assembly and Parliamentary seats from Mumbai, or on other civic bodies representing citizens' interests.

> The writer warned that the question of the Maharashtrian's status in Mumbai was not simply a matter of giving more jobs to Marathi persons. It involved a wider struggle for economic power. The Marathi community, which so far had laid itself open to exploitation, was now not willing to tolerate this subservience.

The final major factor responsible for the situation, according to the articles, was the weakness and inefficiency of the Maharashtra Government. The Maharashtra Government was reluctant to pursue a policy based on its own convictions. It was unable to rectify the situation because it was unwilling to hold its own against the economic power of the capitalist class, the political pressures and the authority of the Central Government.

iii. The writer further argued:

> In the keen economic competition of a growing city with a number of migrant communities, the State Government is unable to protect the Maharashtrian's rights and interests. In employment, and in State Government Housing, the migrant population is getting a larger share at the cost of the native community of the State. Political parties develop vested interests in the large migrant population (including hawkers, smugglers and slum dwellers) as they are prospective vote-banks. One can least expect these parties to voice the grievances of the Marathi community. The articles therefore appealed to the members of the Marathi community to set aside their feeling of dejection and inferiority and unite in a concerted effort to assert themselves without looking for help from political parties or from the State Government. (Mrm. 10.7.66; 17.7.66; 24.7.66; 31.7.66; 14.8.66; 21.8.66; 28.8.66; 4.9.66; 11.9.66; 18.9.66)

People's Response

Marmik's writing was received with enthusiasm and some Marathi journals and magazines even published interviews with Bal Thackeray. The *Daily Navakal*, then a pro-Congress independent newspaper from Mumbai, published an interview with the *Marmik's* editor, on 17.7.66, carrying the following introduction:

Maharashtra today, seems to have fallen on bad days, inspite of the arrival of Swaraj, and inspite of the formation of Maharashtra State. Waves of migrants are pouring unimpeded into the city of Mumbai. As a result, the Maharashtrian is facing keen competition for housing and for jobs. We find that the presence of non-Marathi persons in high executive posts invariably leads to recruitment of workers from States other than Maharashtra, ignoring the Marathi job seekers. Thackeray's Shiv Sena is meant for protecting the Maharashtrian's rights and fighting against this injustice; this is an essential part of the programme for the improvement of the Maharashtrian's status and economic condition.

Thackeray's concern was that the incessant flow of population into Mumbai had reduced Maharashtrians to a minority community at all levels of economic and civic life in the city and that, as a result, Maharashtrians were deprived of their rightful place and status in their State capital Mumbai. (Nvk. 17.7.66)

Who is a Maharashtrian?

In this interview, Thackeray spelled out, perhaps for the first time, the aims, objectives and the programmes of the Shiv Sena along with his definition of a Maharashtrian (which kept changing slightly, under the pressure of periodic political exigencies). According to Thackeray,

'A Maharashtrian is one who, along with his forefathers, has been living in Maharashtra' and 'not the one who comes to Maharashtra in mere pursuit of economic opportunities and keeps himself aloof from the native Marathi speaking community' as it were, 'in a South Indian colony'. (Nvk. 17.7.66)

The official publication of the Shiv Sena declared:

The Shiv Sena 'not only includes Marathi speaking Maharashtrians, but extends to all those of all castes, creeds and religions, who look upon Maharashtra as their homeland, who have been living here for generations together, carrying on trade or business contributing to the welfare and prosperity of Maharashtra and above all commingling their weals and woes with those of the sons of the soil'. (Kapilacharya, *Shiv Sena Speaks*, 1967, 7)

The extension of the 'Maharashtrian' from the 'Marathi speaking' to those 'who look upon Maharashtra as their homeland' referred chiefly to the Gujarati communities of Mumbai which had settled in the city ever since Mumbai became a trading centre for the British. (Kapilacharya, 7)

The latter definition appears to be liberal in including two categories firstly that of the Marathi speaking or the 'sons of the soil', and secondly, that of those who looked upon Maharashtra as their homeland. However the distinction between the two categories was apparently more verbal than substantive. It was not surprising therefore that the Shiv Sena treated the term 'Maharashtrian' interchangeably with 'the Marathi speaking' rather than with those *domiciled* in Mumbai. (Significance of this 'linguistic' approach is discussed in detail in Chapter VI)

Bal Thackeray further underlined the need of an organised protest against injustice to the Marathi community.

In the interview, Thackeray made the following demands of the State Government:

1. A policy of priority and reservation of 80 per cent of jobs in Maharashtra for the Marathi people.
2. Priority of reservation of 80 per cent of the allotments in the State Housing Board for members of the Marathi community.
3. Appointment of Maharashtrian officials at high levels on the State Housing Board, to protect Maharashtrian interests.
4. Re-organisation of the Employment Exchange in Maharashtra with the appointment of Maharashtrian officials to ensure implementation of the two demands mentioned earlier.
5. A policy of appointing Maharashtrian officials at high-level positions in the State Government service.

6. A policy and programme to encourage Maharashtrians to become self-employed in industries and business.
7. Immediate stoppage of allotment of State housing tenements by the system of drawing lots.
8. Priority to Marathi persons in the sale or lease of Municipal and public property.
9. Priority to Marathi hutment dwellers in housing schemes replacing slums.
10. Loans to Marathi persons' co-operative housing societies which lacked funds.
11. The urgent rehabilitation of the uprooted residents from the older localities of Mumbai.
12. A period of twenty years' domicile as a requisite for non-Marathi persons for eligibility in State Housing schemes.
13. A policy for the prevention of the proliferation of slums on public and private vacant land and prevention of pavement-dwelling.
14. The banishment of lepers, beggars and those found guilty of anti-social activities hailing from other States.
15. A policy of maintaining a check on Mumbai's population.
16. The use of regional language names and regional script for all railway stations in Maharashtra, as in Tamil Nadu and West Bengal.
17. Knowledge of Marathi, along with a stipulated period of domicile to be the requisite qualification for all those non-Marathi persons seeking eligibility to public services in Maharashtra.
18. Greater scope of programmes in the regional language (Marathi) on All India Radio, Mumbai, as in the case of other metropolitan cities.
19. Putting an end to all illicit, illegal and unlicensed industrial and commercial activities carried on (by non-Maharashtrians) in Mumbai.
20. The merger of the BPCC into the MPCC to end the unprecedented exception of a Pradesh Congress for a city.

These were some of the major demads of a total of 25 presented. Thackeray maintained that the demands were not parochial but necessary remedies to rectify the situation in Mumbai. All State Governments protected the interests of the native, regional community of their States and the Maharashtra Government would only be following suit if it implemented these demands.

Shiv Sena on the National Scene

In spite of the growing popularity of the *Marmik* and of Thackeray, the Shiv Sena had not yet been noticed by political parties or by the national press. But in November 1966, due to a certain untoward incident following a large Shiv Sena rally at Shivaji Park, it attracted the attention of public beyond the confines of the Maharashtrian community for the first time and coverage by the nationwide English press. The *Maharashtra Times* (31.10.66) reported a gathering of a lakh of people at the rally — a fact not mentioned by the English press. The *Maharashtra Times* compared these crowds to those at the Samyukta Maharashtra Samiti meetings.

It was this rally which brought about the speedy metamorphosis of Bal Thackeray from talented cartoonist to a popular leader of the middle and lower-middle strata of the Marathi community, and especially of Mumbai's Maharashtrian youth. As Thackeray spoke, people thronged to hear him and cheered him lustily. On the dais, along with Thackeray, sat Ramrao Adik, the chairman of the Maharashtra Hitavardhini, an independent association established earlier to protect and further Maharashtrian interests (it later became defunct).

In his speech at the rally, Thackeray appealed to the Marathi people 'to unite' and 'to assert their rights' and demanded for them 80 per cent of jobs and tenements in the State Housing. (Mht. 31.10.66) Though there was no direct instigation in his speech for violent action against any community, there were some incidents of stone-throwing at restaurants and the looting of some hawkers' stalls near Dadar railway station by mobs returning from the rally. (Mht. 11.11.66) Covering this news in prominent headlines: '12 Hurt as Mobs Storm Hotels/Hawkers Beaten Up' the English press (T. Ind. 1.11.66, Ind. Ex 1.11.66) brought the Shiv Sena on the national stage for the first time.

The incident invited considerable criticism in the regional and the English press. In spite of the wide criticism the Shiv Sena evoked on account of these attacks by mobs on non-Marathi establishments, the organisation continued to appeal to the Marathi community and especially to Maharashtrian youth. Newspaper comments and editorials in Marathi continued to be sympathetic to the Shiv Sena.

The *Navakal* devoted three editorials to the Shiv Sena and Marathi community's problems, during the particular fortnight following the rally. A *Navashakti* editorial bitterly commented:

'While the Maharashtra ministers give assurance that no injustice to Maharashtrians will be tolerated, non-Maharashtrian communities are illegally appropriating acres of land in Maharashtra (Mumbai).' The editorial of the *Navashakti* referred to the 'exaggerated reports about the rally' in the newspapers and dubbed them as a campaign to suppress the Maharashtrian voice raised at the rally against the 'Shrinkage of Maharashtrian life in Mumbai'. (Nvs. 5.11.66)

At the installation ceremony of the equestrian statue of Shivaji at the Shivaji Park grounds, the-then Central Minister Y. B. Chavan gave a new definition of the 'Maharashtrian' perhaps partly to accommodate non-Maharashtrian communities and partly to restrain the extremism of the Shiv Sena. 'Those who accept Maharashtra as the land of their life's mission or work *(karmabhoomi)* are Maharashtrians'. (Nvk. 8.11.66)

The *Navakal* editorial, accepting this definition, commented that those who come to live in Maharashtra to work out their life's mission would naturally be expected to identify themselves with Maharashtra and not hold themselves aloof from the mainstream of Maharashtrian life and culture. And those who did identify themselves with Maharashtra and Maharashtrians would have no difficulty in understanding the Maharashtrians' feelings of grief and belittlement at their low economic and consequent social status in their own capital city. (Nvk. 8.11.66)

Earlier, a *Navakal* editorial had observed: 'Irrespective of the exaggerated and prejudiced reports in the press about the Shiv Sena, it is as clear as daylight to all people concerned that

Maharashtrian sympathy and support turn to the Shiv Sena, because in truth Maharashtrians do feel restive and injured in this city. Because of this very reason they are gradually getting alienated from it. The Marathi person does feel that life in Mumbai is passing by him and excluding him. The cosmopolitanism of Mumbai throttles the growth of the economically poor Maharashtrian community'. (Nvk. 5.11.66)

In response to the State Minister's criticism of the Shiv Sena as not being the right means to resolve injustice to Maharashtrians, the editorial asserts that articulation of the demand for priority for the Maharashtrian is only an inevitable reaction to his rightful place being ignored and denied. This, the editorial comments, is not an expression of hate, but a matter of natural right. (Nvk. 6.11.66)

The nationwide publicity accorded to the incident in the English press, immediately brought about a spate of criticism and censure of the Shiv Sena from various quarters.

(Nvk. 3.11.66, Mrt. 4.11.66)

The Chief Minister Mr.V.P. Naik declared that an attack on non-Maharashtrian establishments was not the proper approach to resolve Maharashtrian grievances. At a public meeting, Home Minister D.S. Desai warned that the State Government had promised to maintain the cosmopolitan character of Mumbai, provided such 'cosmopolitanism' was not devoid of fair treatment to the Maharashtrian community. The Government on its part would tolerate no act of intimidation from any quarter since it was committed to protect all citizens irrespective of their language and region. (Nvk. 3.11.66, Nvs. 3.11.66)

The most stringent criticism came from the *Maratha.* It published readers' letters and also a letter from the hoteliers' association, condemning the violence following the Shiv Sena rally. Acharya Atre, the Chairman of the Sampoorna Maharashtra Samiti published a statement in the *Maratha* censuring the Shiv Sena under the banner 'A DMK kind of a Dravidistan (a parochial state) not wanted in Mumbai'. (Mrt. 2.11.66)

The *Maratha,* in its editorial, 'The Demon of Parochial Chauvinism', condemned the 'movement against non-

Maharashtrians and the violent attacks by mobs on these communities.' According to the *Maratha*, a movement started to safeguard Maharashtrian interests should appropriately confront the State's ruling powers and the capitalist class, rather than direct itself against non-Marathi citizens and Udipi restaurants of the city. The *Maratha* questioned why the Shiv Sena and its leaders had not joined the opposition parties. The editorial declared that the Shiv Sena, by its aggressive acts, was bringing Maharashtrians into disrepute and was providing a stick to non-Maharashtrians to beat the former with. The editorial commented 'By its anti non-Maharashtrian acts the Shiv Sena was only serving as an agent of those who still wished and conspired to sever Mumbai from Maharashtra and make it a centrally-administered city.' (Mrt. 3.11.66)

In spite of its criticism of the Shiv Sena, the editorial did express some opinions and attitudes parallel to those of Shiv Sena (Mrt. 3.11.66)

The editorial accepted that the Marathi community was shrinking fast in the capital city of Maharashtra after the formation of Maharashtra State for which the Marathi community had to struggle and agitate for long. It also conceded that Marathi persons were being set aside in all spheres of industry, business, trade and employment. It further accepted that Marathi persons, being economically under-privileged, found it extremely difficult to obtain housing in their own capital. However, the editorial held the ruling powers, the Congress Party and its ally, the capitalist class, responsible for this situation of Maharashtrians in Mumbai. The editorial maintained that the capitalist-dominated BPCC — a covert opponent of the MPCC — was the chief culprit in the plight of the Maharashtrians. According to the *Maratha*, 'the non-Marathi capitalists recruited non-Marathi personnel in industrial and commercial jobs to safeguard their class interests. They were apprehensive of a a well-organised trade union movement among the local Maharashtrian community'.

The other factor responsible for the Maharashtrian situation was, according to *Maratha*, the economic problem of imbalanced growth with concentration of all economic opportunities in

Mumbai alone, where a large number of migrants competed with Marathi people for these economic opportunities.

The *Maratha* maintained that the Marathi community had always received unfavourable and unjust treatment at the hands of the Congress, the ruling party in power in the country. Even though Maharashtra had become a separate state, the problem of its borders remained unsolved.

The editorial declared it was not solely the responsibility of Mumbai, the capital of Maharashtra, to look after an incessant flow of migrants from all over the country, to provide jobs and wages to all those who came here. Marathi persons must get jobs and housing on a priority basis in the city, commensurate with their status as native citizens of the state.

Because of these very reasons, the *Maratha* considered that the struggle for the Marathi community's rights had no room for hostility towards non-Maharashtrian communities. Such a struggle, according to the editorial, was to be directed against the State Government. The State Government, the editorial suggested, ought not to allow the non-Marathi community's rampant provincial nepotism, not only in the private sector companies, but also in the Central Government offices. (Mrt. 3.11.66)

Barve-Menon Contest and Shiv Sena

The Barve-Menon contest in the Parliamentary elections of 1967 turned out to be a crucial event in the development of the Shiv Sena movement. It provided a focal point for further crystallisation of the movement and articulation of its 'philosophy'. The contest (a) provided an opportunity for pitting the Shiv Sena against South Indians (b) the election campaigns encouraged its aggressive behaviour and thereby lent a background to its legitimisation, and (c) the contest also helped to consolidate the Shiv Sena's anti-communist stand, an aspect, which if in existence earlier, was expressed in undertones.

Krishna Menon, being a South Indian (at least by origin) and known for his leftist leanings, served as a focal point to motivate and direct the Shiv Sena's energies born of Maharashtrian frustration against South Indians. This event also achieved a more complete polarisation of the Sampoorna Maharashtra Samiti and the Shiv Sena, inspite of agreement between them on some points regarding the condition of Maharashtrians in Mumbai. These two parties and their leadership emerged during this election as the staunchest of opponents, even as foes, and the possibility of the SPMS slowly integrating Shiv Sena activists within its fold or drawing the Shiv Sena's support to fight for a common goal, totally withered away. Had Menon not contested this election from this constituency, matters might have developed differently. The crucial event of the Barve-Menon election forced the SPMS and the Shiv Sena to take opposing stands and provided the Shiv Sena with a chance for whipping up anti-South Indian, anti-communist propaganda in a situation where the distance between the communities was already growing.

The cordial relations that existed between Atre and Bal Thackeray during the Samyukta Maharashtra struggle mentioned earlier, had begun to deteriorate in the sixties. Thackeray, father and son, had severed ties with SMS leadership by 1963, and, since then, the Atre-Thackeray controversies on several minor personal issues were being debated in the pages of the *Marmik* and the *Maratha*. After the PSP left the SMS on the eve of the formation of Samyukta Maharashtra, the SPMS came under the influence of the CPI leadership. The *Maratha*, an independent paper owned by Atre which had served as the mouthpiece of the Samyukta Maharashtra Movement since its foundation in 1956, also slowly came under the influence of the CPI group. The two editors, Atre and Bal Thackeray fought bitter, wordy wars during the campaign for the Barve-Menon electoral contest.

The very evening the Barve-Menon election concluded, a hutment colony in Chembur, where a large number of South Indians lived, caught fire. The English press gave considerable publicity to the event suggesting that the Shiv Sena had a hand in this.

George Fernandes, on behalf of the Mumbai Citizens Committee, published an appeal to 'protect South Indians from intimidation and violence by an anti-social organisation called the Shiv Sena'. (Nvk. 2.3.67) The statement was signed by Atre, Dange, Rajni Patel, R.K.Karanjia, Comrade Kolhatkar and others. The allegation implicit in the statement, that South Indians were in danger in Mumbai and Maharashtra, was highly resented by the Marathi community of Mumbai and by the Marathi news media. A large majority of the Marathi community had sympathies for Barve and therefore to some extent even for the Shiv Sena which organised election campaigns to support Barve. The *Navakal* and the *Navashakti* published biting criticisms of the Citizens Committee statement and interpreted it as maligning the Marathi community in an effort to derogate the Shiv Sena. (Nvk. 3.3.67, 5.3.67; Nvs. 26.3.67, 5.3.67)

The article in the *Navashakti*, 'Cosmopolitan Goondaism', made a point that in cosmopolitan Mumbai, a large percentage of anti-social elements also hailed from outside the State, and mostly from the South, rather than from the native community of the State. If further maintained that South Indian anti-social elements were quite active in the northern suburbs of Mumbai during the election period and were responsible for causing considerable harassment to Barve's supporters. It was therefore wrong to malign an organisation or a community in the absence of sufficient and reliable evidence. (Nvs. 12.3.67)

Burning of hutments, in fact, was no new phenomenon at that time in Mumbai. A month before the elections there was a fire at the Dharavi slum which included a sizable population of Maharashtrians in addition to others. Even prior to 1967, there was a chain of fires in slums in the suburbs of Mumbai.

Culture of Intimidation

These incidents eventually led to a creation of a political culture of intimidation and violence during the election campaigns in Mumbai. The climate of the election campaign in which the Shiv Sena came to be labelled in the press as an extremist organisation of violent zealots, seems to have contributed considerably to the Shiv Sena's increasing reliance on an aggressive stance. However, there is no denying that the Shiv Sena had a role in creating a political climate of intimidation.

The Anti-communism of the Shiv Sena

The Barve-Menon contest crystallised the Shiv Sena's anti-communist stance. It provided Thackeray an opportunity to launch anti-communist propaganda and eventually to integrate this aspect into the 'philosophy' of the Shiv Sena. He thereby dragged a protest movement born out of popular discontent and grievances of a local nature, into a worldwide cold war between the rightist and the leftist camps. The anti-communist stance immediately brought the Shiv Sena onto the national horizon, transforming it from a protest movement into a prospective political party.

The Shiv Sena's transformation into an anti-communist organisation is not the object of my study and so it is of little direct concern. Anti-communism was not the objective of the Shiv Sena when it was established in 1966. In fact, it its early manifesto, the Shiv Sena had vouched to keep itself away from party politics.

The Shiv Sena's anti-communism was born out of Thackeray's reactions to the Communist Party's stand in the wake of the India-China conflict of 1962. It was particularly heightened during the propaganda wars of the Barve-Menon contest, since Menon was known for his leftist views and sympathies with the Communist bloc. The Shiv Sena's competition with the SPMS for leadership of the Marathi community kept this aspect alive and it eventually became an ingredient of the Shiv Sena's philosophy. However, the anti-leftist stand remains an appendix to the Shiv Sena's regionalist demands and is without a popular base.

Parallelism between the Shiv Sena and the SPMS

The parallelism between certain attitudes and viewpoints of the SPMS and of the Shiv Sena has already been pointed out. The SPMS had included in its 1967 election manifesto (Mrt. 11.2.67), the demand for 80 per cent of jobs for Maharashtrians and also the principle of priority in housing for the Marathi community. (Mrt. 20.2.67, Nvk. 3.3.67) The leaders of the SPMS had declared their support for Marathi as the language of the State Government administration and communication in

Mumbai and Maharashtra; whereby the Marathi speaking people would obtain a position of priority and importance due to them in State Government jobs and related employment.(Mrt. 26.1.67, Dange's interview; Mrt. Atre's editorial, 30.1.67)

In fact, the idea of founding the Shiv Sena came from the *Maratha's* editor, Atre, to be 'usurped and distorted' by Thackeray, as Atre later alleged. (Mrt. Ed. 18.2.67) On 27.1.64, Atre declared in the *Maratha's* eight-column banner: 'Acharya Atre to Found the Shiv Sena in Maharashtra.' His idea was to establish a voluntary force of disciplined Maharashtrian youth who would work for the good of Maharashtra, keeping itself free of political party affiliations and within the framework of democratic and nationalist principles.

The Barve-Menon contest contributed to the polarisation of the SPMS and the Shiv Sena and helped to crystallise further the Shiv Sena's anti-communist and anti-South Indian stands.

First in 1957 and later in 1962, Menon was elected to the Lok Sabha from the North Mumbai constituency as a Congress candidate. Menon was not a popular personality in Mumbai or in Maharashtra, inspite of his close contact with Nehru and his role in building India's foreign policy. In fact, in the 1957 and 1962 elections, that is, during the heyday of the Samyukta Maharashtra Movement, the Samyukta Maharashtra Samiti had opposed Menon, who then was a Congress candidate with Nehru's support. At that time, the *Maratha*, the mouthpiece of the SMS, the grand alliance of the opposition parties of Maharashtra, had opened a bitter election campaign against Menon. Atre's weekly, the *Navyug*, had then been critical of Menon's selection as a candidate in Mumbai setting aside the local Congress worker Indravadan Oza. (Navayug, 27.8.62) In fact, the *Maratha* and its evening counterpart, the *Sanj Maratha* bore the slogans: 'A Vote for Menon is an Insult to Maharashtra's Martyrs', and 'Menon from Mumbai is a Blemish upon Maharashtra'. (The *Sanj Maratha*, 17.8.62)

In spite of the SMS, Menon then got elected, partly due to Nehru's influence, due to his own reputation as an ambassador to the United Nations, and partly due to the support of the increasing South Indian population in the northern suburbs of Mumbai.

By 1967 however, the debacle of the war with China in 1962 had added to Menon's unpopularity in Maharashtra, excepting among the followers of the communist parties. Also, even after his resignation from Nehru's council of ministers, Menon continued to be in the capital and had little time to cultivate ties with the electorate. The question of a constituency for Menon remained undecided for long and was developing into a controversy. In December 1966, the press published the news that Menon was refused a Congress ticket from Mumbai. (Mrt. 3.12.66)

This time, it seems, in the absence of Nehru to back Menon's candidature, S.K. Patil was successful in withholding the Congress ticket from Menon for the North Mumbai constituency. The ex-chief minister of Kerala, R. Shankar, had reportedly offered Menon a seat from Kerala (Mrt. 5.12.66), but Menon showed little interest. He insisted on the North Mumbai constituency and ultimately proclaimed his decision to resign from the Congress and fight the election as an independent candidate from North Mumbai. (Mrt. 17.12.66)

At the time of the 1967 elections, Barve was denied a Congress ticket for Parliament from Pune by the MPCC. S.K. Patil, who had returned to Mumbai after being relieved of his position in the Central ministry in accordance with the Kamaraj plan, shrewdly offered Barve the Congress ticket from Mumbai. The intra-party hostilities between Patil (BPCC) and Chavan (MPCC) on the one hand, and between S.K. Patil and Menon on the other, are too well-known to need elaboration. S.K. Patil's strategy of offering a ticket to Barve from Mumbai when the MPCC had refused it to him in Pune seemed to be a diplomatic move, to kill two birds with one stone. No one interpreted S.K. Patil's selection of Barve for the North Mumbai seat as being parochial. He was known for his sympathies for capitalism, cosmopolitanism and a centrally-administered Mumbai, and his stand regarding Goa, Belgaum and Karwar was openly unfavourable to Maharashtra. By selecting Barve, however, he could checkmate both Chavan and Menon; though, later, the selection of Barve was interpreted in the light of subsequent developments as preference to a 'local' man. (A 'local' man was here meant not a Mumbai man obviously, but a Maharashtrian, a native of the State).

Barve, who had earned a name as an able administrator, naturally, was favoured by the majority of Marathi speaking voters. The Sampoorna Maharashtra Samiti earlier was thinking of putting up their own candidate from North Mumbai (prior to Menon declaring to contest independently) to oppose Barve, the Congress candidate; and Comrade Mirajkar (Marxist) was its possible, though controversial, choice. (Mrt. 16.1.67) However, when Menon declared his decision to contest the election as an independent, the SPMS did not put up its own candidate, but gave freedom to its followers to vote at their discretion, implying that they supported Menon. (Mrt. 21.12.66, 24.12.66 and 2.2.67)

Had Mirajkar contested the election on the SPMS ticket against Barve, chances of Barve's defeat might not have increased; but the contest would have escaped being coloured in terms of regional loyalties. The forces of intra-party politics in the Congress, and, in all likelihood, in the SPMS as well, seem to have conspired to pit Barve against Menon, giving scope for a full display of regional propaganda.

After Menon's decision to contest the election independently (Mrt. 17.12.66), E.M.S. Namboodiripad, the communist leader, suggested in a public speech in Mumbai, that Menon and the 'democratic' forces of the SPMS should cooperate. (Mrt. 30.12.66) Though there was no official arrangement agreement that the SPMS and Menon would support each other (the SPMS had some of its candidates standing for the State Assembly elections), it was the Samiti's decision to support Menon in the Parliamentary election. (Mrt. ed., 30.3.67)

Shiv Sena Support to Barve

In addition to his move of setting up Barve's candidature against Menon's in North Mumbai, S.K. Patil made clever use of the Shiv Sena for election campaigns in support of Barve. Perhaps the idea for the move was suggested by the Shiv Sena's own enthusiasm in supporting Barve or by the *Maratha's* tirade against the Shiv Sena that it was being used by Patil for the propaganda of the Congress.

S.K. Patil, in a press statement in February 1967, disowned connections with the Shiv Sena and confirmed his belief in the broader nationalist viewpoint. (Mrt. 2.2.67) On the other hand, the *Maratha* criticised Patil for the BPCC's clandestine backing of Shiv Sena goondaism and held Patil responsible for the transformation of the Shiv Sena into a diehard, aggressive organisation. (Mrt. ed., 17.2.67, 18.2.67) *The Daily Maratha* and the SPMS alleged that even the State Government encouraged the Shiv Sena by its soft-pedalling. (Mrt. 5.2.67)

On the day (1.1.67) Menon proclaimed his decision to contest the election as an independent at a public meeting at Shivaji Park (Mrt. 2.1.67) Thackeray addressed a Shiv Sena rally at Thane, attended by thousands of his followers.

Thackeray's speech at this meeting is an excellent example of a leader's effort at public persuasion and mobilisation of voters. He said:

'I am not a leader, nor do I wish to be one. There is no aura of greatness about me. I control no unions. And yet when I raise my voice to speak of Maharashtrian grievances, a large number of people gather, are stirred, and receive me with enthusiasm and cheers. If the great journalists of Maharashtra (an obvious reference to Atre) try to understand what is happening and why, they may not condemn the Shiv Sena as the 'Demon of Parochialism'.

We did work with the communists in the SMS. But we consider them traitors because in 1962, they were equivocal about the Chinese aggression, unwilling to categorically call it an aggression.

We do not want Menon because there is not a single thread by which he relates himself to us, the people of Maharashtra. He has done nothing for the people of Maharashtra, to solve their problems of a Samyukta Maharashtra or Goa or Belgaum-Karwar or any other.

Will the people of Kerala or Bengal elect a Y.B. Chavan or a V.P. Naik from their constituencies? The other day, at the Congress session at the Shanmukhananda Hall, Chief Minister Naik spoke with pride of the little Madras at Matunga in Mumbai. Would the people of the South and the North like to have a little Kolhapur in Bengal or a little Pune in Madras?

In Mumbai, we want rules and norms regarding employment, housing and economic opportunities similar to those that are implemented by other provinces for their own people. You cannot have nationalist and cosmopolitanist norms for one set of people and a different code for another. This we call injustice.

We would like to avoid conflict. But out tolerance cannot be stretched beyond a certain limit.

We have always criticised S.K. Patil as an agent of the capitalists and as one who mortagaged the nation to America for the PL-480. But remember, those who mortagage the country to Moscow or Peking are no better either!

We shall vote for all those who would be willing to voice our grievances and fight for them. We know that Barve has worked for Maharashtra and reinstated Pune on the Maharashtra map. We shall vote for him.' (Mrm. 15.1.67)

The press reports of Thackeray's speech do not mention his supporting Patil. However, Comrade Prabhakar Vaidya released a statement accusing Thackeray of lending support to Patil at the Thane rally. (Mrt. 5.1.67) The *Maratha* started a campaign against the Shiv Sena for its 'support to S.K. Patil'. In reply to this charge, Thackeray declared, rather belatedly, at a public meeting (15.1.67) that the Shiv Sena backed not Patil, but Manohar Kotwal, the dock workers' leader. (Mrm. 29.1.67) He criticised the *Maratha* for 'creating a mountain of support' for Menon, the 'outsider', whom the SMS had twice opposed earlier. (Mrm. 29.1.67)

The sparring between the *Maratha* and the *Marmik* contributed to the temper of the election campaigns of the candidates, giving an edge to the Shiv Sena's anti-South Indian stance and adding to it the dimension of anti-communism. The anti-communism of the Shiv Sena seems to be the result of the keen competition between it and the CPI-dominated SPMS to attract a common electorate in whose hands lay the fate of the two candidates -

Barve and Menon. The SPMS by including regional demands like the one of priority for Marathi speaking persons and reservation of 80 per cent of employment and housing, was exploiting the people's grievances against the government and the 'outsiders', as much as the Shiv Sena; but the Shiv Sena went a step further by identifying Menon as an 'outsider' and as a communist. (Communists, according to the Shiv Sena, had extra-national affiliations)

Shiv Sena propaganda had effectively mobilised Maharashtrian opinion in favour of Barve as seen from the election results of the Barve-Menon, and Menon-Tara Sapre* contests held in February and March 1967. On both occasions, Menon scored a slight edge over his opponent in the votes from North Mumbai; but this, however, was no match to that gained by his opponents in the Thane and Kalyan areas. These areas were predominantly Maharashtrian, unlike the northern suburbs with a mixed population including a high percentage of South Indian communities.

We have dealt with the issue of the Barve-Menon contest rather elaborately, chiefly to bring out the importance of this event in the shaping of the Shiv Sena as an organisation and a movement voicing the grievances and demands of a regional community in a 'cosmopolitan' city and especially, in the development of its militancy and anti-communism.

Shiv Sena's Politics of Protest

In its new role of the leader of the Maharashtrian community, the Shiv Sena began its agitational politics by taking out two protest morchas during 1967. The first was in January, which was in connection with the shifting of the Electronics Production Division of the Atomic Energy Centre from Mumbai to Hyderabad, an issue for which Atre's *Daily Maratha* had also been mobilising public opinion for a long time. (Mrt. 22.11.66, 30.12.66, 3.4.67 and 20.6.67) Both the *Maratha* and the *Marmik* were mobilising discontent over issues affecting the employment opportunities of the Marathi community, like the proposed

* In the by-election held after Barve's sudden death, Mrs. Tara Sapre, Barve's sister, was pitted against Menon who chose to re-contest.

shifting of the Vehicle Research and Development Establishment from Ahmednagar to Chennai and that of the large percentage of South Indian staff at the MIG factory at Ozar. (Mrt. 10.12.66, 12.1.67, 13.3.67, and 2.5.67)

The Shiv Sena tried to get an edge over the *Maratha* and the SPMS by taking out a protest march in connection with the shifting of the Electronics Production Division and copies of the *Maratha* were publicly burned by the mob, before it presented a memorandum to the Chief of the E.P.D., at the offices of the Atomic Energy Commission near the Gateway of India. (Mrm. 15.1.67)

The Shiv Sena organised another march on the 21 July, 1967, to the Council Hall (the State Legislative Assembly) to present a memorandum of its twenty-five demands to the Chief Minister V.P.Naik. There was efficient police bandobast to protect hawkers (a possible target of Sena attack) and shopkeepers en route; but no untoward incident was reported. In spite of the Sena's image as an organisation of aggressive youth, the 10, 000-strong crowd was largely peaceful as unanimously reported by newspapers. (Mrt. 21.7.67, 22.7.67; Nvk. 22.7.67, 23.7.67)

The march proved effective in drawing public attention to the Shiv Sena's demands, and in mobilising public opinion about these.

The memorandum also voiced apprehensions regarding (a) the recruitment of large number of South Indians to white-collar jobs and higher executive positions in establishments in Maharashtra. (b) Maharashtrians losing ground in their capital should the process of migration continue, and (c) migration of a large number of beggars, bootleggers, and squatters from the southern States.

The memorandum urged the State Government an early consideration of its grievances and demands. (Mrt. 21.7.67; 22.7.67)

The Shiv Sena Demands in the State Legislature

Following the march, the Shiv Sena's demands were taken up by several opposition members, especially by those of the PWP (the Shetkari Kamkari Pakshi i.e. the Peasants and Workers Party) to discuss the 'unfair treatment' to the Marathi community in the job market in Mumbai.

During the summer session of the State Assembly in March, 1967, Gulabrao Ganacharya (CPI) had assailed the State Government for its failure in safeguarding the interests of the Marathi community by not reserving a certain percentage of jobs for the local community of the State as was done in other linguistic States in the country. His complaint was two-fold (i) non-recruitment of Marathi persons in the industrial undertakings in and around Mumbai; and (ii) retrenchment of Marathi employees in certain industrial units in the Pune Municipal Corporation area. He suggested the formation of an all-Party committee to enquire into the situation and chalk out a proper policy to counter it. Similar complaints were made by several members of the opposition on the floor of the State Legislature (Nvk. 12.4.67) and the Maharashtra Legislative Assembly Debates, 1967. (Vol. 20-II, 5, 189-198)

Members of the opposition in the State Legislative Assembly criticised the Government for its failure to heed their warnings and to respond to similar demands made earlier by them on the floor of the house. The members also felt that the Government's indifference had been responsible for the outpouring of the people's discontent. During the discussion the Minister for Industries promised that the State Government would try its best to give priority to Marathi personnel in the State's new industries. Chief Minister Naik, in his reply, assured the members of the House of his Government's efforts to employ local people in the various departments of the State Government. He informed the House that he was holding personal meetings with industrialists to discuss the matter of priority to local men in industrial employment, as feasible within the constitutional framework. (Mrt. 3.8.67, 9.8.67, 10.8.67; Mrk. 3.8.68, 4.8.67, 10.8.67; Nvs. 10.8.67; Mht. 3.8.67; Mah.Leg. Assembly Debates, Vol. 21.-II, 29, 30, 35 and 39)

Shiv Sena – Militancy and Reactions

Notwithstanding its peaceful protest march, the Shiv Sena had come into disrepute because of the aggressive language used by its leaders and because of the scuffles that the Shiv Sainiks often allegedly got involved in. The Shiv Sena constantly invited censure from its opponents and even from its sympathisers, due to its arrogant and irresponsible language of 'solving issues on the streets'. (Mrt. 14.5.67, 17.5.67; Nvs. 12.5.67) During 1967, the Samyukta Socialist Party and the MPCC (whose senior members had occasionally associated themselves with the *Marmik's* anniversary functions) passed resolutions censuring the Shiv *Sena* and expressing grave concern over its violent activities. (Nvk. 15.5.67; Mrt. 15.5.67; Nvs. 15.5.67 and Nvk. 25.8.67) Another reaction to the emergence of the Shiv Sena was the rise of similar other senas, for instance, the Chaluvaligars in Karnataka and the Gopal Sena in Kerala. 'The Association for the Protection of all Communities', an organisation established at the initiative of some Kannada-speaking persons in the hotel and restaurant business, in Mumbai, condemned the 'anti-national' activities of the Shiv Sena. (Nvk. 11.8.67; T.Ind. 3.9.67) However, these organisations remained merely on paper in the absence of a mass base.

On 15 August, 1967, the Shiv Sena was allegedly involved in a serious melee at Koliwada, an old settlement of Mumbai's fisherfolk in Sion, a northern district of the city. The hutment colony at Sion-Koliwada, the place of the incident, housed a large number of South Indian migrants. The publicity the press gave to this incident invited immediate reactions from Southern leaders. Annadorai, the-then Chief Minister of Tamil Nadu, and Ramamurthy, the CPI (M) leader, announced their plans to dispatch two South Indian MPs to hold an enquiry into the alleged violence of the Shiv Sena against the South Indian residents of Koliwada. (Mrt. 21.8.67, 22.8.67)

Submitting their report to the Prime Minister, Krishnamurthi (DMK), and Umanath (CPI-M), the two MPs from the South, alleged that the Shiv Sena was creating an atmosphere of insecurity for the South Indian residents of Mumbai and demanded an enquiry into the Shiv Sena's affairs. (Mrt. 15.9.67)

In response to these allegations, Thackeray released a public statement: 'The Shiv Sena's struggle is not directed against any community as such, but it is meant to achieve fair treatment to the Marathi people and to assert their rights. Charges made without evidence by the Southern leaders, do not help to create a peaceful atmosphere.' (Mrm. 27.8.67)

The enquiry was regarded with great resentment not only by the Shiv Sena (Mrm. 27.8.67, 3.9.67), but by all sections of opinion in Maharashtra, except perhaps the communists. Though a number of editorials blamed Thackeray for his use of intimidatory language, most of them strongly disapproved of an independent enquiry and interpreted it as interference with the law and order situation of another state. Even the *Kesari*, whose editor was then the Secretary of the SPMS, criticised the enquiry. He laid the blame on the anti-Maharashtrian English press for giving undue publicity to minor incidents of tensions between communities and for building up stories of Shiv Sena intimidation. As an independent observation, the *Kesari* pointed out that a large number of anti-social elements existed among the South Indian hutment dwellers of Mumbai. (Ke. 1.9.67)

The *Marmik* published lists of residents of the Koliwada hutments, pointing out to its disproportionately small number of Marathi residents and claimed that the trouble started when Shiv Sena followers reported against some of the South Indian gang leaders of the locality. (Mrm. 27.8.67, 3.9.67) The publicity in the press and the importance given to the enquiry by the South Indian communist leaders, the *Marmik* alleged, were reactions born of their fear of losing ground in Mumbai to the Shiv Sena.

There is no denying, however, that Shiv Sena's image as a violence-prone organisation was born out of the aggressive language and the behaviour of the Shiv Sainiks and their leaders.

Shiv Sena Enters Civic Government

The Shiv Sena's success in 1967 in the elections for the Thane municipality was an important landmark. (Nvk. 16.8.67, Nvs. 20.8.67) This event ensured that the Shiv Sena would test its mettle in the Mumbai civic polls as well. It was the first step in the Shiv Sena's transformation from a movement and an organisation into a political pressure group and a party.

In October, 1967, at the Shiv Sena's large Dassera rally, with a crowd numbering two lakh, Thackeray declared that the Shiv Sena would contest the forthcoming Mumbai Municipal Corporation elections to be held in March 1968. (The English press reported a crowd of 25,000, while even the critics of the Sena from the Marathi press conceded that the gathering was nearly ten times larger.) (Sadhana 21.10.67, Mrm. 22.10.67) The news was flashed on the front pages of the English newspapers. (T.Ind. 28.12.67, Ind. Ex. 28.12.67)

Earlier, the CPI had challenged the Shiv Sena to hold a meeting in the working class area. This item appeared only in a few language newspapers. The Shiv Sena reportedly accepted the challenge and held meetings in the Parel-Lalbaug-Sewri area in December 1967, the meeting at Sewri on the night of the 27 December, being one in response to the challenge. (Mrm. 10.12.67, 7.1.68; Nvk. 2.1.68; Sakal, 4.1.68)

Shiv Sainiks returning from the meeting late at night were allegedly subjected to stone-throwing from Dalvi Building which housed the Girni Kamgar Union's office. The Shiv Sainiks it was alleged, retaliated by breaking into the Union Office and by burning its furniture, papers, records, files, etc. (Mrt. 7.1.68; Kesari, 8.1.68; Sakal, 9.1.68; and Mrm. 7.1.68)

All these incidents point to the long-drawn tussle between the Shiv Sena and the leftist parties, chiefly the Communist Party, for the leadership of the middle and the working class Maharashtrian community and to corner popular support.

The Shiv Sena's success in the civic elections to the Mumbai Municipal Corporation was the major event of 1968. Apart from the Shiv Sena the chief contestants were the Congress Party and the Sampoorna Maharashtra Samiti. During the election campaign, some of the leftist papers tried to build up the story of an arrangement reached between the Shiv Sena and the BPCC, and the Shiv Sena contesting the elections against the Congress was described as a 'trick to fool the people', the real objective being to 'defeat the SPMS'. (Link, 24.3.68) However, almost, simultaneously, A.K. Hafijka, the BPCC President complained of attacks on Congress workers by Shiv Sainiks and asked the

State Government to restrain the Sainiks in their activities. (Mrt. 15.3.68) The Shiv Sena had, in fact, an arrangement with the Praja Socialist Party in this civic poll. The increasingly tolerant attitude expressed by PSP leaders towards the Shiv Sena since September 1967, suggested the brewing of an alliance between the Shiv Sena and the PSP. (Mht. 7.9.67; Nvs. 12.9.67, 4.10.67; Sadhana, 21.10.67)

The SPMS and the Shiv Sena Civic Election Manifestoes

The SPMS declared in its election manifesto that its chief aim was to uproot the corrupt Congress, which had always worked against the interests of Maharashtra, from Mumbai. The SPMS promised a cleaner administration. Another SPMS promise was a housing programme for the poorer sections of society. Further, it is interesting to note that the SPMS also included in its programme, a rational policy 'to solve the problem of the daily influx of three hundred families into Mumbai and the expanding squatter population.' (Mrt. 9.3.68, 25.3.68)

On the other side, Thackeray also, under the obvious pressure of political expediency, evinced greater flexibility and a greater leniency in his definition of the Maharashtrian. He declared that the Shiv Sena considered all those as Maharashtrians, who, irrespective of their mother tongue, contributed their mite to build up Maharashtra and identified themselves with the life of its people. (Nvs. 20.2.67) Giving his new definition of Maharashtrian, at a public speech, he appealed to all migrants from other States to call themselves Maharashtrians instead of continuing to identify themselves as non-Maharashtrians. (Mht. 27.2.68) He restrained Shiv Sainiks who wanted to take out a protest demonstration against the South Indian film star, Sivaji Ganesan, who was in the city on a film-shooting schedule. Thackeray pointed out to the Sainiks that the actor, though a South Indian, had always treated with respect Maharashtra's great men like Shivaji and Bal Gandharva. (Mrm. 10.3.68; Lks. 2.3.68)

In a press interview, on behalf of the Shiv Sena candidates, Thackeray promised:

(i) a clean civic administration, (ii) efforts to solve the problems of hawkers' encroachment on pavements, (iii) efforts to solve the squatter problem, and (iv) fair distribution of water. (Mht. 83.68)

When an interviewer pointed out the newly-soft attitude of the Shiv Sena towards non-Marathi speaking persons, Thackeray retorted that there had been no change in his attitude and that he still believed that the stream of migrants to Mumbai must be stopped to save the metropolis; and that his definition of Maharashtrian did not include those who did not identify with their adopted region and pushed the interests of their own language-speaking brethren. It was to tell such people to identify with the people of Maharashtra, that he used the platform of the election campaign. (Lks. 9.3.68)

In the elections, the Congress contested 124 of the total of 140 seats and won 69. The Shiv Sena, which contested 97 seats, won 39; the PSP, contesting 32, won 14; the SPMS, which contested 129 seats in alliance with the Muslim League, won 9; the Jan Sangh won 6 out of the 70 seats contested; the Swatantra Party got one seat; two independent candidates were also selected. (Mrt. 17.2.68, 5.3.68; Link 24.3.68; Mrt. 27.3.68)

Analysing the defeat of the SPMS, the *Maratha* frankly admitted that neither the money invested in the election campaign nor the tactics of intimidation employed by the Shiv Sena, explained its thumping victory. It attributed the Shiv Sena's success to the Maharashtrian community's discontent with the BPCC, the lack of unity among its member parties, and its inability to focus on the Marathi community's problems and grievances regarding employment and housing. (Mrt. Ed. 28.3.68)

However, in June 1968, in the Pune Municipal Corporation elections, the Shiv Sena got only one of the seventy-two seats. (Mrt. 6.6.68, 16.6.68, 18.6.68, 19.6.68; E. and P. Wkly, July, 1968) This meant that the Shiv Sena's appeal was limited to the environs of metropolitan Mumbai. Beyond awakening Maharashrian sympathies towards the grievances of their metropolitan brethren, the Shiv Sena had failed to develop a programme that could actively engage and involve the non-urban Maharashtrian's interests. The base of the Shiv Sena, therefore, was built up of the urbanites of Mumbai and its immediate neighbourhood.

The Shiv Sena Organises Itself

By this time, the Shiv Sena had begun building itself into an organised structure – a requisite for entry into politics, for contesting elections or for functioning as a pressure group or a prospective political party. (For details or organisational structure, see Ram Joshi 1970) By the turn of the decade, the Shiv Sena had more than 120 units or branches spread over 140 districts of Mumbai's fifteen municipal wards. These units carried out day-to-day voluntary activities in their neighbourhoods, which involved the Shiv Sainiks in the welfare and entertainment programmes thereby filling a vacuum in the lives of urban Maharashtrian youth, especially the unemployed among them. The branch leaders met the top leadership in weekly meetings which functioned as a communication channel between the rank and file of the Sena and its leadership.

By the end of the sixties, the Shiv Sena had branched out into trade union activity (Bharatiya Kamgar Sena) and had also established its cine-branch (Chitrapat Shakha). It came to acquire influence in the Hindi cinema world, especially after the movement to 'ban' Hindi films produced in Madras.

Shiv Sena and Boycott of Hindi Films in the South

Then an event took place which created a storm in the film industry and perhaps contributed to the Shiv Sena's popularity among Mumbai's voters during the civic polls. At a public meeting on 26.2.68, Thackeray declared that Hindi films produced in Madras studios would not be allowed exhibition in Mumbai's cinema houses unless Madras cinema houses resumed screening of Hindi films. With the passing of the Official Languages Bill in the Parliament, in January 1968, the anti-Hindi stir in the south intensified and students under DMK influence had organised a boycott of Hindi films in Tamil Nadu. Thackeray's 'ban' on films produced in the South was generally seen by common people as a fitting response to the anti-Hindi stir. (Nvs. Ed. 4.5.68) AVM Studios, which had already initiated the advertising campaign for the release of their film (*Do Kaliyan*) on 1 March 1968 in Mumbai, were thrown into a quandary by this ban. Meiyappan, the AVM producer, met Thackeray for negotiations on 28 February, 1968. In his public statement he observed that Thackeray had no personal axe to grind against South Indians or South Indian films, but that he was unwilling to relent until the people in the South allowed screening of Hindi films in Tamil Nadu.

During further negotiations, Thackeray agreed to withdraw his 'ban' if the AVM producer promised to persuade the Government and the students in Tamil Nadu to permit re-exhibition of Hindi films in Madras. (Lks. 8.3.68, Mrt. 9.3.68, Mrm. 10.3.68)

However, before the issue was finally settled, all 70 cinema houses in Mumbai closed as a result of a dispute between film producers and film distributors and exhibitors. (Mrt. 20.3.68, 24.3.68)

The Shiv Sena Exploits Issue of Border Disputes

The border issue of Belgaum and Karwar provided the Shiv Sena with an opportunity to attract people from other regions in Maharashtra. The report of the one-man Mahajan Commission on the Maharashtra-Karnataka border dispute was published early in November 1967. (Mrt. 5.11.67) The general reaction in Maharashtra to the report was that it was prejudiced and a grave injustice to Maharashtra and the Maharashtrian people. The Sampoorna Maharashtra Samiti directed its followers to express their protest by burning copies of the report. (Mrt. 5.11.67) and there were several such bonfires in Mumbai, in the major cities of Maharashtra and in the border areas under dispute. (Mrt. 5.11.67, 14.11.67; Mrm. 19.11.67)

While the Mysore State Government and the Mysore Congress Committee accepted the Mahajan report *in toto* (Mrt. 10.11.67), the Maharashtra State Legislative Assembly rejected it on 30.11.67. (Mrt. 1.12.67) The SPMS, in its effort to mobilise the masses on the border issue, held an All-Party Conference (the Shiv Sena was excluded) at Kolhapur on the 2 and 3 December 1967. (Mrt. 2.12.67, 3.12.67, 4.12.67) The Kolhapur rally was perhaps the greatest achievement of the SPMS which in fact was created to fight for the border issue.

The SPMS had to suspend its agitation because a severe earthquake. The earthquake had its epicentre in Koyna in Maharashtra. The Congress also shifted the venue of its proposed AICC meet from Sangli. (Mrt. 11.12.67, 12.12.67) The rehabilitation of the Koyna victims followed by the Mumbai Municipal Corporation elections kept the political parties preoccupied until March 1968.

In May 1968, however, the agitation was revived, due to the efforts of the Maharashtra Ekikaran Samiti (the Maharashtra Integration Association), a body active in the disputed border areas of Belgaum and Karwar. Founded in 1946, the organisation had been independently carrying on an agitation for the inclusion of the Belgaum and Karwar districts in Maharashtra since 1955. Seven leaders of the MES went on a twenty-four hunger-strike outside the MPCC meeting venue in Mumbai, on the 21 and 22 May, 1968. (Mrt. 23.5.68) However, they were not supported by the SPMS in their efforts to bring pressure upon the State Congress leaders.

> Piqued by the SPMS's indifference, the *Daily Maratha*, in its editorial, 'Where has the Fire of the Samiti Gone?' criticised the Samiti for its lethargy and slackening of interest on the border issue, and for its failure to support the Ekikaran organisation. The editorial cautioned that the SPMS, which was born to fight for the border problem, would be doomed if it continued to be inactive and failed to co-operate and respond to the Ekikaran Samiti's call for help. The *Maratha* expressed regret that the member parties of the SPMS had neglected their common cause in order to pursue narrow Party interests. The *Maratha* however, declared, that it would keep its guns active to intensify efforts and mobilise the people for a just solution to the border problem. (Mrt. 23.5.68)

None of the member parties of the SPMS took much notice of the *Maratha's* caution. The CPI, the dominant member party of the SPMS, seemed reluctant to actively participate in the alliance. The Karnataka leaders meanwhile insisted upon the implementation of the recommendations of the Mahajan Commission. (Mrt. 28.5.68)

This provided the Shiv Sena a chance to step in and exploit the vacuum created by the SPMS lethargy, and try to extend its influence beyond Mumbai by allying with the MES.

During the visit of the Prime Minister Indira Gandhi to Mumbai in December 1967, Bal Thackeray had presented her with the Shiv Sena's memorandum on the Maharashtra-Karnataka border issue. In November 1968, Thackeray and other Shiv Sena leaders attended the 'Black Day' in Belgaum, an event held annually to commemorate the separation of Belgaum and Karwar from Mumbai State in 1956. At this meeting, Thackeray proclaimed that that was to be the last 'Black Day' meeting and promised the Shiv Sena's support to the MES in its struggle for the inclusion of Belgaum and Karwar districts in Maharashtra. (Statement by Sukhthankar, M.E. Samiti, May 1969; Mht. 14.11.68)

In December 1968, Thackeray declared that the Shiv Sena would launch an intensive agitation for bringing pressure upon the party in power to resolve the border problem. (Mht. 30.12.68) Earlier, he had met the Prime Minister, urging her to find an early solution to the problem. (Mht. 14.11.68) Later, at a mammoth meeting in Shivaji Park, on 2 February 1969, Thackeray announced that the Shiv Sena would continue with its agitation of stalling the entry of Central Ministers into the city of Mumbai (with the exception of the Prime Minister). At the Shivaji Park meeting, Thackeray also made mention of the co-operation assured by the PSP, the SSP, and the PWP (the Peasants and Workers Party) in the Shiv Sena agitation. Thackeray expressed the hope of extending the agitation beyond Mumbai into all parts of Maharashtra with their help. The leaders of the MES from Belgaum and Karwar districts and those of the PSP also made speeches at this meeting. (Mht. 3.2.69; Nvs. 3.2.69; T. Ind. 3.2.69)

The Shiv Sena Agitation and February Riots (1969)*

On 7 February 1969, Morarji Desai, the-then Deputy Prime Minister, visited Mumbai. Shiv Sena volunteers awaited Desai's

* For detailed news coverage, see Appendix A-III.

arrival at Mahim and Prabhadevi, the two points en route every visitors' entry to the city. At these points, Shiv Sena men were to present the Deputy Prime Minister with their memorandum; but could not do so. Reporting on the Prabhadevi incident, the *Maratha* observes

'As the car drove to Prabhadevi, it speeded up, past the protest-demonstrators and then there was heavy stone-throwing which broke a window-pane of the Police Commissioner's car. Two persons were injured by Morarji Desai's speeding car, and rioting broke out. The police resorted to lathi-charge. At Shivaji Park, Ranade Road (Dadar), and at the Citylight Cinema (Mahim), police chowkies and a garbage van were set on fire'. (Mrt. 8.2.69)

'As the riots spread to North Mumbai, the Police Commissioner clamped prohibitory orders on assemblies and processions on Saturday, the 8 February. Police resorted to lathi charge and tear gas to disperse mobs'. (Mrt. 9.2.69)

The main target of the rioters' ire seemed to be the milk booths, police chowkies, public buses under municipal control and post offices. An MPCC branch office in a lane at Dadar was also set on fire. Eventually, as the riots developed, even private shops and restaurants, too, came under attack. At Sewri, the Deputy Police Commissioner's car was attacked. Efforts were made, at some places, to burn railway ticket windows and railway bogies.

On 9 February 1969, the Police Commissioner clamped a curfew from 8 p.m. to 5 a.m., but with hardly any success. The *Maratha* reported the arrest of a thousand persons, including the Sena leaders, Thackeray, Manohar Joshi and Datta Salvi, in the early hours of 9 February. From 7 to 9 February, the police opened fire several times, in addition to the use of tear gas and lathi charge. (Mrt. 9.2.69, 10.2.69) On 10 February (Monday night), the Chief Minister, V. P. Naik, who was out of town when the riots had broken out, broadcast an appeal on All India Radio, Mumbai, asking citizens to bring peace to the city by forming neighbourhood peace corps to resist hooliganism and destruction of public property. (Mrt. 11.2.69)

The next day Shiv Sena leader, Thackeray, made a statement from jail, announcing the withdrawal of the Sena's border agitation; he too, made an appeal to his followers to bring peace back into the city. The news that the Shiv Sena volunteers had begun to clear up the debris-cluttered roads also followed. (Mrt. 12.2.69)

Riots and Political Parties on the Scene

How did the various political parties and personalities in Mumbai deal with the riot situation? What were their reactions? The following account is primarily based on reports from *Maratha* which opposed the Shiv Sena.

The first statement reacting to the incident was probably that of the PSP leaders. This was not unexpected, since the PSP was to support the Shiv Sena in the border agitation. Madhu Dandavate, Dr. V. P. Mandalik, G.G. Parikh and Sadanand Varde, brought out a statement in which they stated:

'The protesting demonstrators had obtained an assurance from the Deputy Commissioner of Police, Dafley that they would be allowed to present their memorandum to the Deputy Prime Minister Desai, at Mahim. However, Desai's car, instead of slowing down or stopping at Mahim, speeded up, knocking down the approaching demonstrators, which incited them to anger, giving a bad turn to the situation'.

The statement further condemned the police officials' indiscreet action of driving the car ruthlessly, past the waiting crowd, and demanded an enquiry into the matter. (Mrt. 9.2.69)

Atre responded to the PSP leaders' statement with slight skepticism. In the *Maratha* (9.2.69), he commented:

'If it is really true that the police went back on their word of assurance given to the Shiv Sena demonstrators, they deserve to be condemned; in that case, we would support an enquiry into the matter'.

The secretariat of the Communist Party of India released a statement condemning the lathi-charge:

'The Government and the pary in power fooled the people by giving them false hopes regarding a solution of the border problem and also made every effort to break down the people's protest when the people turned desperate. The only hope for the solution of the border problem lay in the united effort of all democratic forces'. (Mrt. 10.2.69)

The secretary of the CPI (Marxist), P.K. Kurane, made the following statement:

'Under the pretext of protecting the Central Ministers from the protest-demonstrators, the Government of Maharashtra has let loose an oppressive regime, which we condemn. By irresponsible firing, arrests, lathi charge and tear gas, the Government has created an atmosphere of oppression. By clamping down prohibitory orders on meetings and processions, the Government was trying to suppress a popular movement, and, especially the voice of the working class'.

The statement further declared that 'the Mumbai branch of the Marxist-Communist Party protests against the oppressive rule of the Government' and demanded the withdrawal of Section 144 of the IPC, and the prohibitory orders on public assemblies. (Mrt. 10.2.69)

PSP spokesmen published a second statement, in which Madhu Dandavate warned the State Government that it would not succeed in suppressing the border agitation by arresting the leaders or by using coercive measures. Some other PSP members, Municipal Councillors and Members of the Legislature, condemned the Government for its high-handed action. (Mrt. 10.2.69)

Gulabrao Ganacharya (CPI) and the Mumbai branch of the Communist Party of India, gave a call to all textile workers of Mumbai to go on strike on the 11 February, to protest the police action. The statement, however, also condemned the looting, damage and destruction of shops belonging to the minority communities. (Mrt. 11.2.69)

On 8 February, the SSP was to felicitate their leader George Fernandes who had won a case in the Supreme Court against S.K. Patil. The *Maratha* reported that the scheduled meeting of the SSP would be held, if necessary, contravening the prohibitory order on assemblies. (Mrt. 9.2.69) The SSP held a meeting at Chowpatty by special permission, which was wound up quickly due to hostile slogan-shouting by the audience. (Mrt. 10.2.69)

On 10 February, George Fernandes and Dada Naik, the two SSP leaders, published a joint statement demanding that the Government release Thackeray unconditionally. The statement also contained four proposals connected with the border agitation including an indefinite strike in Mumbai (a Mumbai 'bandh') and a 'gherao' at Sachivalaya. The statement favoured an all-out intensive agitation to press for the demand and it called for all-Party co-operation and concerted effort to channelise the agitation in a proper direction. (Mrt. 11.2.69)

However, Atre's *Daily Maratha*, in its editorials, chastised the people for meaningless destruction which was a blot on Mumbai's fair name and warned that such destruction was suicidal. (Mrt. 11.2.69, 12.2.69)

The PSP leader, N.G. Goray, also released a statement from Pune on 10 February, condemning the riots in Mumbai and remonstrating that it was not a civilised way of solving the problem. (Mrt. 11.2.69)

Viewing these events with the detachment afforded by the passage of time, it appears that none of the political personalities (except, of course, those mentioned above) directly or indirectly involved with the events, were able to grasp the seriousness of the riot situation as it developed fast, going beyond the control of the initiators of the agitation. Leaders of all the opposition parties were apparently trying to exploit the situation and reap whatever benefit they could. These statements from leftist parties made during the period of the riots and immediately after, seemed to have led to abetment, rather than abatement, of the explosive situation. The very voices censuring the State Government for the use of 'oppressive measures,' later did a *volte face* and criticised that very Government for covert encouragement and support to the Shiv Sena.

Thackeray's Statement

On 12 February, the PSP leader, Nath Pai, released Bal Thackeray's statement, after having met him in jail at Pune. In his statement, Thackeray regretted the loss of life and property during the riots.

He further said, 'Had I not been detained in jail, I would have been able to bring peace to the torn city. I am sure the Shiv Sainiks would have responded to my call, but I was never given the opportunity. Those in the State Government who want to see the Shiv Sena wiped out, are responsible for giving a violent turn to the situation'. (Mht. 13.2.69)

Nath Pai concurred:

The Shiv Sena wanted to make a peaceful representation to the Central Ministers and carry out the agitation in a disciplined manner, but police indiscretions led to untoward developments and incited people to violent action. (Mht. 13.2.69)

About this time, Atre and Nath Pai both independently toured the riot-stricken areas, appealing to the people for peace and tranquility. Nath Pai laid the blame on the political leaders of the various parties in Mumbai for not having made any efforts to visit the troubled areas and establish communication with the common people in order to forestall deterioration of the situation. (Mht. 13.2.69)

On the 23 February 1969, the Shiv Sena leaders now out of jail officially withdrew the agitation. (Mrt. 24.2.69)

The Aftermath and the Clean-up

By Wednesday, 12 February, the riots had died down; the situation was under control; the police had begun operations to recover and restore looted property. The police recovered most of the looted goods from various hutment colonies spread between Mahim and Agripada worth three-and-a-half lakh of rupees and in this connection arrested seventy five persons from different localities in the city. (Mrt. 14.2.69)

The National Response

These riots once again focused the nation's attention upon the Shiv Sena, which was subjected to considerable criticism and censure from all quarters of political opinion. The opposition parties in the State, as well as at the Centre, censured the Maharashtra Government. The latter faced the brunt of the criticism for 'allowing the Shiv Sena menace to grow.'

In the State Assembly, the Governor, (P.V. Chapterian), in the inaugural address, condemned the Shiv Sena for its fascist methods. The members of the opposition parties, however, took the State Government to task and made a three-pronged attack against it for

(a) Its failure in anticipating and controlling the Shiv Sena's violent agitation;

(b) Its abetment to this organisation; and,

(c) Its failure to bring about any satisfactory solution to the Maharashtra-Karnataka border problem.

The Chief Minister, in his reply, denied any connection between himself, his Government or the MPCC, and the Shiv Sena; he strongly disapproved of the aggressive chauvinism of the Sena. He accepted the necessity of resolving the border dispute, but affirmed that the problem could not be solved in the streets, but only in the Lok Sabha. He denied that the Government had, in any way, helped the Shiv Sena, and promised that, if necessary, Thackeray would be prosecuted. Regarding the use of firearms by the police, he stated that the government used these measures with reluctance, only as a last resort. (Maharashtra State Legislative Assembly Debates; March 1969, Vol. 26-II, 2; Mrt. 12.3.69, 13.3.69)

The various shades of political opinion all over the country – leftist, rightist and others – were for once, unanimous in condemning the Shiv Sena. Hafizka, the Chairman of the BPCC, laid the onus of the riots upon the Shiv Sena, 'its aggressive regionalism and rhetoric of ethnic hatred.' (Mrt. 15.2.69; Nvk. 14.2.69) The Shiv Sena agitation generated a query from the Chief Minister of Karnataka (Virendra Patil), regarding the loss and damage caused in the riots to the Kannada-speading people of Mumbai. (Lks. 15.2.69) The Challuvalligar leader, Vaithal Nagraj, declared that the Challuvalligars would burn effigies of Chavan and the Shiv Sena demon in Mysore. (Mrt. 17.2.69) The leftist leader Namboodiripad, declared that he would discuss with the Prime Minister the threat posed by the Shiv Sena to South Indians in Mumbai. (Mrt. 17.2.69) In the Lok Sabha, Ramamurthi of the CPI blamed the Maharashtra Government for not taking sufficient cognisance of Shiv Sena attacks on South Indians in Mumbai. (Mrt. 4.3.69) Members of the opposition parties in Parliament (the SSP, the CPI, and the CPI-M) condemned the Shiv Sena, demanded a ban on it, alleging that the Maharashtra Government had sympathy for the Sena, and was in effect abeting its activities. (Mrt. 19.2.69, 20.2.69, 4.3.69; Lok Sabha Debates, Feb. 1969, Vol. 24, Nos. 2.3. and 4)

It is interesting to note that during the riots, the leaders of these parties in Mumbai had made statements which could easily be interpreted as inciting, provocative or at least empathic to the Shiv Sena's agitation. The SSP statement, in favour of contravening the prohibitory order on assemblies, and the declaration by the SSP leader, George Fernandes, asking for an unconditional release of Thackeray, the threat of an indefinite strike in Mumbai, and a gherao of the Sachivalaya, certainly supported the 'popular agitation'. Similarly, the CPI and the CPM statements, during the riots, had severely criticised the State Government for enforcing orders under Section 144 of the Indian Penal Code, and for the use of 'coercive' and 'oppressive' measures to suppress the 'people's struggle'. One of their statements had even given a call for a strike in support of the border agitation.

The PSP was an exception. In fact, it had supported the agitation from the beginning. While the PSP MP, Mulka Govind Reddy, condemned the Shiv Sena in Parliament, his party colleagues in Mumbai almost held a brief for Thackeray. Conciliation with the Shiv Sena at the provincial and regional level and condemnation of the organisation at the national level, were perhaps matters of political expediency. In order to reap benefits for their own parties out of the popular discontent ignited by the Shiv Sena, they seemed to have no other alternative but to play this kind of a game.

Who was Responsible for the Riots?

Certain broad observations are inescapable when we examine the development of the riots. The targets of mob fury, during the first two days of the riots, were invariably milk booths, police chowkies, buses and bus stops, post offices, railway ticket windows and railway stations. Occasionally, telephone exchanges, too, were attacked, and attempts were made to obstruct rail traffic. Was there an element of planning in this uniform choice of targets for attack?

Thus, there seems to be a method in the madness of the rioting. Whatever belonged to the State, whatever symbolised the State or Central Government and whatever symbolised the party in power became targets of mob ire. Even a branch office of the MPCC was subjected to vandalism. It was later, chiefly on 9 and 10 February that the crowds were reported to be attacking shops, restaurants and other private property.

The Shiv Sena chief at no stage, however, was known to have publicly remonstrated with the Shiv Sainiks over the stone-throwing aimed at the Central Ministers' vehicles on 27 January and 7 February 1969. When Thackerary declared, in his Shivaji Park speech on 2 February 1969 that the Shiv Sena would continue with its protest demonstration in front of the visiting Central Ministers he had also said 'If necessary we will break the prohibitory orders issued under Section 144 of the Indian Penal Code'.

Subsequent to the incident of the Deputy Prime Minister's visit on the 7 February, when the Police Commissioner enforced prohibitory orders, Shiv Sainiks apparently followed their leader's advice and tried their hand at protest-marches. (Mrt. 9.2.69) As the police lathi charged them, the angry crowds resorted to stone-throwing in retaliation in various industrial areas of Mumbai – Dadar, Parel and Byculla. (Mrt. 9.2.69; also see Appendix A-III 'Riot Reports') Consequently, the agitation on 8 February turned into a virtual hide-and-seek battle between the people and the police. Among the rioters, many were young boys and unemployed youths. These young men perhaps, for a while, were thrilled at the prospect of a fake battle with the police.

From the very beginning, the agitation seemed to have lacked foresight and self-discipline. The element of violence in what seemed to be planned attacks on milk booths, and in the acts of stone-throwing, was perhaps a consciously chosen ingredient for its agitational value. Thackeray asked the people to defy the ban and come out into the streets, but did not seem to have told them what to do next. As a reader's letter put it'Thackeray knew how to start a fire, but did not know how to control or quench it'. (Mrt. 20.2.69)

The agitation initiated on the evening of 7 February took a violent turn and seemed to have gone out of the leaders' hands even prior to their arrests on the dawn of 9 February, which was a Sunday. By then the agitation had deteriorated into mob frenzy, always a risk with agitations unless it is controlled tightly by its leaders or helmsmen. Once the agitation deteriorated into mob misbehaviour, a shift from public rampage to private destruction was only a step away. The targets easily shifted from milk booths to shops and restaurants and from public buses to private cars. When the agitation turned into a general free-for-all, it was natural and easy for anti-social elements to join in. Among those arrested there were a good number of 'dadas' from Mumbai's underworld. (Nvs. 15.2.69)

Riots and South Indians

However, the charge made by responsible leaders, that the Shiv Sena agitation and the consequent riots were directed against South Indian communities, hardly seems to hold good. The border agitation began with a protest-demonstration, and then deteriorated into violence against state and public property, a kind of hide-and-seek game between the Sena adherents and the police; it escalated into blind mob frenzy, but there was no explicit discrimination against South Indians. The areas of rioting were predominantly Maharashtrian localities.

I have earlier mentioned the loot discovered in various hutment colonies in North and Central Mumbai; some of the colonies housed a number of non-Marathi and South Indian migrants. Among the shops and establishments destroyed by rioters, there were some belonging to Maharashtrians. A well-known Maharashtrian goldsmith's firm located in Dadar was vandalised during the riots. (Mrt. ed., 12.2.69) A headline in the *Maratha* of 11 February 1969 ran 'Shops looted! Belonging to all ethnic and linguistic communities! No discrimination!'

Of the123 shops looted, 14 belonged to South Indians, and of the 63 restaurants looted, 43 were run by South Indians. (Mrt. 20.2.69; See Chavan's statement in the Lok Sabha) A probable explanation was that a majority of the grain and cloth shops in Mumbai belonged to Marwari, Gujarai and Sindhi communities, while the majority of middle-class restaurants, especially in the riot-stricken areas, were owned by those from 'Udipi' in South Kanara. The total number of South Indian restaurants in the city at that time, according to the *Maratha*, was about three thousand. (Mrt. 1.3.69)

It appears that there was some sort of understanding between the Shiv Sena and the police that the Shiv Sena representatives would be allowed to present their memorandum to the arriving Central Minister provided that the Shiv Sena carried out its demonstration peacefully, and in a disciplined manner. Though the Police Commissioner had denied at having come to any such understanding or arrangement, it was obvious that faced with 341 protestors (Bulsara J. 1970 Pg. 402) the police would be looking for some arrangement. The fact was conceded by V.P. Naik, the Chief Minister at a press conference soon after the riots

In an industrial metropolis like Mumbai, where the Government had to handle several protest-marches and demonstrations every day, any arrangement to prevent obstructions to traffic was useful; and, therefore, any understanding between the Shiv Sena Chief and the Police Commissioner was not against the spirit of the law. (Lks. 15.2.69)

At about the same time, the Deputy Home Minister for the State, Kalyanrao Patil confided to reporters at a press conference in Aurangabad that the car escorting Morarji Desai was not stopped because the Shiv Sena chief had not given an assurance of a peaceful agitation. Since the police apprehended a risk to the person of the visiting minister, his car was speeded up and did not halt to receive the memorandum (Mrt. 17.2.69)

The Police Commissioner, too, had mentioned, at an earlier press conference that in view of threatening rhetoric used by Thackeray at his Shivaji Park rally, the police could not place adequate confidence in the Shiv Sena's intentions of a peaceful demonstration. (Mrt. 10.2.69)

Beside the talk of defying prohibitory orders, Thackeray had said:

'If the Government uses police force to suppress our struggle, we warn that it would face serious consequences' and also, 'If the Government forces on us an extreme and long-drawn struggle, like that of Samyukta Maharashtra, then it will have to call for the army and tanks. Therefore, we warn that the police should use discretion, and try not to suppress any legitimate agitation.' He also asked the Shiv Sainiks to be prepared to face 'lathi charges, even police firing'. (Mht. 3.2.69)

Perhaps, the language employed by Thackeray was rhetorical and useful as a strategy; but his youthful and impressionable followers were obviously going to hang on to every word of his. If this speech was not one 'inciting' violence, it was tantamount to an indirect sanction to the Shiv Sena volunteers to make use of it.

In a statement, soon after the riots, Comrade Dange said:

'There was nothing worng in the Shiv Sena organising an agitation in connection with the Maharashtra-Mysore border problem. What was wrong was that the Shiv Sena did not act in co-operation with the other parties'. (Mrt. 19.2.69)

However the fault that lay with the Shiv Sena agitations was the Shiv Sena leaders' repeated failure to accept responsibility for the use of violence by their adherents. This was an indirect legitimisation of the Shiv Sainiks' violent behaviour in a professedly peaceful agitation.

Shiv Sena's Rewards

After the February riots, the Shiv Sena lay low for some time. It no doubt invited criticism for its violent behaviour. However it also reaped some rewards; it had drawn the attention of the whole nation to the 'injustice' to Maharashtrians meted out by the Mahajan report, as most Maharashtrians, irrespective of political affiliations, believed. The MES from Belgaum condemned the police excesses during the riots and paid homage to the martyrs of the agitation. (Mrm. 23.2.69) The Belgaum Municipal Council passed a resolution appreciating the Shiv Sena's efforts at solving the border problem. (Lks. 2.3.69)

The Shiv Sena agitation had captured the attention of nearly a million Marathi- speaking people living in the border areas and had earned their sympathy. This fact could not be ignored – especially in the context of the forthcoming 1972 General Elections – by political parties who were well aware of the border issue's potential as a vote-getter. The PWP, which had a foothold in the interior of Western Maharashtra, and some of whose leaders hailed from the border areas, could ill-afford to ignore the growing popularity of the Shiv Sena because of the agitation. After the agitation, we find a marked increase in news about measures at 'detente' between the PWP and Shiv Sena. (Mrt. 24.2.69, 10.3.69, 7.5.69; Mht. 2.5.69, 12.5.69, 13.6.69; Lks. 4.3.69) The Shiv Sena thus scored one over the SPMS which had lapsed into silence after its border conference at Kolhapur and the protest-demonstrations against MPCC leaders at Sangli.

Piqued at the publicity gained by the Shiv Sena due to the agitation, the Samiti turned active again. In an editorial, the *Maratha* stated:

'Not by violent riots, but by peaceful and democratic means by the Marathi people's Maharashtra-wide movement, would the SPMS mitigate the injustice'. (Mrt. 7.3.69)

In another editorial, the *Maratha* declared:

'We shall extend support to anyone who rises to fight for the border issue, but the struggle must not be polluted with politics of linguistic hatred.' In this editorial, the *Maratha* also gave a call for an all-Party conference to chalk out the programme of struggle'. (Mrt. ed. 5.5.69, 'Call for a Border Conference')

The Peasants and Workers Party (PWP) had already launched a month-long Satyagraha from 1 May 1969. Every day, batches of PWP volunteers from different parts of Maharashtra, offered Satyagraha in Mumbai and they were arrested. (Mrt. 2.5.69, 3.5.69, 29.5.69) The pressure on the SPMS to activate the border issue was growing.

About this time, H.V. Pataskar, the Vice-Chancellor of Pune University, and the erstwhile Law Minister at the Centre, prepared the draft of a bill outlining the principles and policy for resolving border disputes between linguistic provinces. He also put forward a proposition for resolving the Maharashtra-Karnataka border problem. This draft was presented to the Prime Minister, Indira Gandhi, during her visit to Mumbai in the third week of May. (Mth. 18.5.69; Mrt. 21.5.69) However, the Congress took little notice of these proposals. (Mrt. 23.5.69)

At this juncture, the SPMS planned to launch a full programme of protest-demonstrations, Satyagraha and gheraos at the State Legislature and the Government District offices on 16 June, the inaugural day of the State Legislature. All the member parties of the SPMS were to co-operate. (Mht. 22.5.69; Mrt. 22.5.69) The SPMS also decided to involve hawkers and slum-dwellers of Mumbai. (Mrt. 28.5.69) To follow this up, the SPMS, in its meeting on 29 May, passed a resolution to protect the hawkers and hutment dwellers against those 'who threatened them'. (Mrt. 30.5.69) A large number of hawkers, especially those in the Fort area, hailed from Kerala; the Hawkers' Union was controlled by George Fernandes. The SPMS was thus set to exploit the grievances of a section of population largely composed of migrants for its border agitation. As a prologue to the proposed agitation by the SPMS on 16 June, a large protest-march of hawkers led by S.M. Joshi was taken to the Mumbai Municipal Corporation on 10 June. (Mrt. 11.6.69)

In spite of all its efforts, the SPMS, however, could not steal the limelight in the border struggle. On 13 June 1969, Atre, the founder-editor of the *Daily Maratha*, passed away after a brief illness. He was the moving force behind the SPMS, which he helped to keep alive through his newspaper. In the moment of shock and grief at Atre's death, leaders of the constituent parties of the SPMS (SSP, CPI, PWP and CPI-M) led the Satyagraha on 16 June, in which five thousand Satyagrahis participated. (Mrt. 17.6.69)

After the demise of Atre, with the fire of the *Maratha* quietened, and the SPMS in the process of dissolution, there was no competition to the Shiv Sena in championing the cause of the Marathi community. The dissolution of the Samiti also seemed to have contributed to 'détente' between the PWP and the Shiv Sena. In June 1969, the PWP refused to go with the SPMS in passing a resolution censuring the Shiv Sena for the February riots. (Mht. 13.6.69, 23.6.69)

The Period of Transformation

The two years following 1969 were crucial in the life of the Shiv Sena. During this period, the Shiv Sena's major demands received wider recognition and some acceptance; a beginning was made in the direction of their fulfilment. In 1970, the Shiv Sena made an entry into the State Legislature. This period of achievement for the Sena, however also saw defection among its members. This was a critical period of its transformation from a movement into a political organisation and a prospective political party, as also a period of slow ebbing of its early popularity as a regionalist movement.

a) Shiv Sena's Revivalist, Belligerent Phase

After the February 1969 riots, the Shiv Sena earned a bad name as a violent chauvinist movement. The Shiv Sena's alleged involvement in the Bhiwandi riots sharpened this image. (Mht. 22.5.69) In 1970, the Shiv Sainiks' clashes with the Muslims of Mahad and Kausa in the Thana district, gave the Shiv Sena a belligerent, anti-Muslim image. (Nvk. 5.2.70)

Members of the State Legislature raised questions in the State Assembly accusing the Shiv Sena of fanning communal tensions in Mahad. (Nvk. 10.3.70, 27.3.70) A *Times of India* editorial censured the State Government for conniving at Shiv Sena's terrorism against the minority community, though a Muslim social worker, Hamid Dalwai, presented contrary evidence. (T. Ind. Ed. 13.370, T. Ind. Letters 28.3.70)

As a sequel to these events, there was a private bill tabled by some PSP legislators in the State Legislative Assembly which demanded an enquiry into the affairs of the Shiv Sena. (Nvs. 18.7.70, Nvs. 16.12.70) The bill was later withdrawn. The Maharashtra branches of the PSP and the PWP passed resolutions censuring the Shiv Sena's 'fascist' methods of intimidation and terrorism. (Nvk. 20.5.70, Nvk. 13.6.70; Mht. 17.5.70)

Besides these events, Thackeray's advice in 1970 to State Government employees to withdraw their state-wide strike, also contributed to the alienation of sections of the middle and lower middle-class Government employees from the Shiv Sena. (Nvs. 8.12.70; Mrt. 8.12.70)

b) The Parel By-election

An important event at this juncture, a landmark in the growth of the Shiv Sena, was its decision to contest the Parel by-election to the State Legislature on 18 October 1970. (T. Ind. 20.10.70)

In a sense, this was a natural and an expected step for the Sena after its victory at the civic polls. However, the decision meant a critical and definite move towards the transformation of the Sena, from a regionalist movement and organisation into a political party. The Shiv Sena's triumph in the Parel by-election reinforced this process of transformation. If the growing image of the Shiv Sena as a vociferous militant organisation brought a blot to its name, the Shiv Sena's victory at the Parel by-election and its success in installing Marathi as the official language of the civic administration in Mumbai were feathers in its cap.

The Shiv Sena's victory in this by-election was significant because of the background. V.S. Mahadik, the Shiv Sena candidate won the election in Parel – an industrial area – against his rival Sarojini Desai (widow of the murdered CPI worker Krishna Desai), who was sponsored by CPI and supported by the SSP, the PSP, the Marxists and the ruling Congress. The Shiv Sena had the support of the Jan Sangh, the Swatantra Party and the Congress (O), parties that had little or no hold on the working class population of the area. Political observers interpreted the contest as a confrontation between rightist and leftist forces.

Realistically, however, the success of the Sena candidate in this by-election was symbolic of the appeal that the Shiv Sena and its regionalist demands still held for the working class of Mumbai's traditional industrial district. In the eyes of Maharashtrian voters, according to a survey in 1971, the Shiv Sena stood for improving Maharashrians' lot rather than for fighting against Muslims or Communism. (See Katzenstein M., 1973, 396)

c) Defection in the Shiv Sena

In spite of the Shiv Sena's success in the by-election, there is no denying that a large number of Shiv Sena sympathisers and supporters were slowly turning away from it. Apart from the February '69 riots, the Shiv Sainiks' alleged acts of intimidation brought the Sena into disrepute. The indictment of a few Shiv Sena youths in the Krishna Desai (CPI) murder in 1969, the murder of a Shiv Sena member Sadanand Dhavan the following year (1970), and recurring news of Shiv Sainiks' clashes – these were perhaps factors that were responsible for the gradual disaffection with the Sena among the middle and working classes of Mumbai. The mid-seventies saw the birth of a splinter group, Prati-Shiv Sena, which never became popular. Several scheduled caste youths who were drawn to the Shiv Sena and were its members earlier, defected to form their own active organisation under the banner of Dalit Panthers during the early 1970's.

Hundreds of Shiv Sainiks joined the new Congress in 1970. This flow from the Shiv Sena to the Congress (R) continued before and after the mid-term polls in 1971 and well until 1972. (Nvs. 21.6.70; Mht. Ed. 23.6.70; Nvs. 19.7.70, Lks. 27.7.70; T.Ind. 16.2.71, 16.2.72) This defection was an indication of the Shiv Sena youths' growing disaffection with the organisation during the early 70's.

d) The Sobering Influence of the General Election (1971-72)

Before the Parel by-election, Thackeray had announced that the Shiv Sena would contest the general elections 'to seek justice from the nation for Maharashtrian grievances'. (Nvk. 26.8.70) The decision to contest elections for Parliament and the State Legislature was bound to influence the Shiv Sena's character in many ways.

It was essential for the Shiv Sena to tone down its extremist, aggressive language, its xenophobia and hostility to South Indians and other outsiders, if it wanted to be elected to the

State Assembly and Parliament. At the earlier civic poll, the small homogeneous and single-member constituencies of the Mumbai Municipal Corporation made the Shiv Sena's victory possible in about 40 districts of Mumbai with Marathi (speaking) peoples' majorities. The constituencies for the State Legislature and Parliament were much larger consisting of five or more municipal constituencies and therefore more heterogeneous in composition and less favourable to the Shiv Sena.

The Shiv Sena grasped this logic of electoral politics and attempted to modify its extremist attitude. For instance, several South Indian speakers addressed the Shiv Sena's Shivaji Park rally on the eve of the Shiv Sena's 'Mumbai bandh' of 2 March 1970 for the border problem and were lustily cheered. (Ram Joshi, 1970) Similarly, during the same year, the Shiv Sena's annual Dassera rally was addressed, among others, by Vyjayantimala, the well-known South Indian actress of Mumbai films, and was attended by several leading personalities from the Hindi film world. (Mht. 11.10.70) The language of persuasion and accommodation in Thackeray's public statements (See Ram Joshi, 1970), and the Shiv Sena's support to the candidature of General C.M. Cariappa for the North-east Mumbai constituency in the mid-term polls of 1971 (T. Ind. 18.1.71), were sure signs of the Sena leaders' eagerness to cultivate the non-Maharashtrians of Mumbai.

However, the transformation in the Shiv Sena's stand was perhaps too sudden to convince the non-Maharashtrian voters. The Shiv Sena did not have the advantage this time of single-member homogeneous constituencies of the civic polls. Also the Indira wave was strong and sweeping in 1971 and issues at stake for the state and parliamentary elections seemed different from those of the civic poll. Consequently the Shiv Sena failed to win a single parliamentary seat in the mid-term polls in Mumbai and could obtain only one seat (besides that of Mahadik) in the elections for the State Assembly in 1972.

The Shiv Sena's Achievements

(i) One of the Shiv Sena's long-standing demands was that priority in jobs be given to Marathi speaking people in their own State. In 1970, three years after the Shiv Sena held a protest march to the Council Hall to focus attention on this demand the State Government accepted it as a guiding principle of policy. It was a major victory for the Sena, though its implementation was held in abeyance pending sanction from the Central Government which anticipated Constitutional difficulties. The State Labour Minister (Narendra Tidke) announced at a press conference the State Government's approval of the policy of reserving 90% of jobs in the State for the 'local people' of the State and further he stated that the State Government was consulting the Central Government for obtaining legal sanction. The difficulties about the definition of 'Maharashtrian' were avoided by substituting it with the term 'Local'. A 'local' person was defined as one domiciled in the State for 15 or more years. (Nvk. 22.7.70)

It must however be noted that though the Shiv Sena most aggressively championed this demand, the Sena was not alone making it. Members of most of the opposition parties had been vocal in making this or a similar demand in the State Assembly within a few years of the birth of the Maharashtra State. (Maharashtra Legislative Assembly Debates, 1964, Vol. 12, No. 24; Vol. 13-I, 356-358; 1965, vol. 15, No. 6)

Earlier, during the discussion on budgetary grants in the State Legislature, the Minister for Industry, R.A.Patil, in response to the complaints of unfair representation to Marathi speaking people in jobs, articulated the State Government's policy in favour of 80 per cent of jobs for the local people of the State. He informed the House of the various measures planned by the State Government for the implementation of this policy. He further informed the House that (i) the Government has advised the owners and the management of the industries to see that the percentage of 'local' persons is increased at the time of the new recruitments (ii) the Government had directed the Regional Employment Exchanges accordingly (iii) the Government had made it obligatory for the industries that they give jobs on priority basis to those whose land was acquired for setting up the industry (iv) the Government was planning to introduce in the service rules, the knowledge of Marathi as an essential qualification and condition, for the posts of the Welfare and/ or the Personnel Officers. (Maharashtra Legislative Assembly Debates 9.4.70, vol. 29, No. 25)

In 1972, the Labour Minister of Maharashtra N.M. Tidke, defended on the floor of the State Legislature, his Government's policy in favour of 80 per cent jobs to the local persons of the State, on the basis that the State provided the basic resources, land, water and electricity to the industries. He also affirmed the co-operation of the industrialists with the Government's policy. (Maharashtra Legislative Assembly Debates 19.7.72, Vol. 35, No. 28)

The norm was being increasingly accepted. The National Labour Commission favoured the principle of priority for locals in lower cadre jobs (Nvk. 21.1.68; Kesari 20.1.68), and so did the Gajendragadkar Committee for National Integration. (Lks. 7.7.72) During the debate on the subject in the Lok Sabha, the Prime Minister conceded the principle of priority to local people in jobs with salaries of Rs. 500 or less in order to avoid tensions created by the socio-economic imbalance. (Mht. 14.12.72; Lks. 14.12.72; Lok Sabha Debate, 13.12.72, Vol. 22, 25-32)

(ii) Another achievement to the credit of the Shiv Sena during these years was the acceptance of Marathi as the official language of its proceedings and administration by the Mumbai Municipal Corporation. The Shiv Sena introduced the bill in the Corporation in April 1968 and it was passed in July 1971, after seven stormy meetings spread over three-and-a-half years. (Mht. 26.5.68; Lks. Ed. 31.7.71) Earlier in 1964, Vaman Bapat, the SMS member, had proposed the bill for the introduction of Marathi as the official language for the proceedings of the Mumbai Municipal Corporation. The bill was passed on 28 January 1964, with an amendment by a Congress member, Dr. B.P. Divgi, to the effect that English would continue to be allowed along with Hindi, Urdu and Gujarati, for the convenience of non-Marathi speaking members. (Mrt. 20.5.68)

Inspite of this resolution passed by the Corporation, the minutes of the meetings and the administrative records, however, continued to be kept in English (due to the absence of corresponding change in rules regarding administrative records) Shiv Sena councillors, therefore, brought in a new bill for introducing the change even at the level of the administrative record keeping. The move was initially resisted by Shanti Patel, the leader of the Congress Party in the Corporation in 1968. He suggested an amendment favouring both English and Marathi for official purposes. While permission to use English along with other Indian languages already existed for the convenience of non-Marathi speaking members, the effort to give English the standing of an official language by an amendment was rightly interpreted as a resistance to Marathi by Marathi speaking persons. (Mrt. 13.5.68, 23.7.68, 20.5.68)

After the split in the Congress in 1969, Shanti Patel joined the Congress (O) and though this group remained a dominant party in the Corporation, the Shiv Sena succeeded in obtaining majority votes in favour of its resolution. Marathi became the official language of the Mumbai Municipal Corporation in its proceedings, records and administration. English, Hindi, Urdu and Gujarati were retained as additional languages for the convenience of the members of the Corporation. (Lks. 31.7.71)

In this narrative, the socio-political processes and contextual social circumstances related to the emergence and development of Shiv Sena have been chronologically presented in the early years. Understanding the process of growth of the movement and of its characteristics is essential for understanding the sociological factors that contributed to its rise.

CHAPTER IV

PROBLEMS OF AN EXPLODING METROPOLIS

The Maharashtrian Perspective

The Background

When Maharashtra was formed in 1960, Mumbai was already a metropolitan city with a large population of over four million people.

The island city of Mumbai was set on the path of success as a trading centre and an international port when Captain Humphrey Cooke took charge of the islands of Mumbai in 1664 from the Portuguese and decided to build a town for English merchants. Two centuries later, when the textile industry took root here during the decade of 1860-1870, it put the city on the road to prosperity. The laying of the first railway tracks in India between Mumbai and its Deccan hinterland in 1863, and between Mumbai and Ahmedabad in 1864, the opening of the Suez Canal in 1869, and the establishment of the Mumbai Port Trust in 1870, contributed greatly to the growth of this metropolis as a major west coast commercial centre and an international port.

The first voluntary census of the city was conducted in 1864 when the population of the island city with an area of 18.62 sq. miles was recorded as 7, 83,980. Mumbai has continued to grow phenomenally ever since.

Continuous industrial investment and expansion after the Second World War and the attainment of Independence, and the correlated urban development, led to an uninterrupted flow of migrants and uncontrolled growth of population in Mumbai. The population of Greater Mumbai increased by 1.1 million in 1941-1951 and to 1.15 million in 1951-1961; and again, by 1.4

million in 1961-1971. The population thus doubled in the short span of two decades between 1951 (29, 94,444) and 1971 (59, 31,981)

To enable the city and its civic government to cope with this unplanned, incessant growth, the limits of the city were twice extended beyond the original island city, bringing several villages of the adjacent Salsette Island under the jurisdiction of the Mumbai Municipal Corporation to form Greater Mumbai with an area of about 169 square miles. The first extension of the limits to Jogeshwari and Bhandup in the north-west and the north-east, respectively, took place in 1950; the second, to Dahisar in the west, and Mulund in the east, in 1957. (Gadgil committee, 1965, 15)

This measure, however, could hardly achieve planned growth or curb the urban sprawl, especially since heavy migration continued to swell the population. It was a miracle that the civic services and the urban infrastructure of the city, originally meant for a much smaller population, coped with the needs of an enormously large number of people that the city continued to attract throughout the three decades between 1941 and 1971. It is in this context that I had to consider and interpret the content-data from the Marathi journals (1961-1970) presented later in this chapter. Here I shall complete this brief outline of the story of Mumbai's development which forms the backdrop to the main study.

In 1948, the Mumbai Municipal Corporation prepared a Master Plan for Mumbai. The Plan had a rather short life, and before it was fully implemented, the government of Mumbai State passed a new 'Town Planning Act' in 1954, which rendered the earlier Master Plan invalid. The Mumbai Municipal Corporation declared its intention, in 1958, to prepare a fresh Development Plan for Greater Mumbai in line with the Act of 1954. The Draft of the Development Plan was prepared on the basis of information obtained through essential surveys and suggestions received from various advisory committees specially set up for the purpose. It was submitted to the Government of Maharashtra in July 1964. In the meanwhile, work on the implementation of the

Development Plan had already begun with the publication of a tentative Development Plan (no date available).

The Mumbai Town Planning Act had envisaged the implementation of the Development Plan through a series of Town Planning Schemes. This enabled the Local Authority to recover from land-owners a major part of the cost of improvements contemplated in the Town Planning Schemes. Generally, the Municipal contribution towards the costs of the schemes came to be about 20 to 30 per cent of the total cost, the rest being shared by landowners by way of betterment charges. (Municipal Corporation of Greater Mumbai, 1964, 173) The landowners would diligently pass their share of costs and betterment charges on to the property owners, and they, in turn, to the tenants. The majority of the Maharashtrian tenants who belonged to the low and middle income groups could not afford to bear this burden and so were left with no other option but to move out from the island city wherever the development schemes operated.

The implementation of the Mumbai Development Plan immediately precedes the period of the rise of the Shiv Sena in 1966, and therefore appears to have relevance to the study, as does the fact of explosion of the city's population, as seen in the content data.

The Data

As mentioned earlier, the data consists of the content of newspapers and journals chronicling the Maharashtrian community's grievances during the 1960's, i.e. immediately preceding and following the rise of the Shiv Sena movement.

A section of these grievances consists of people's distress arising out of the hardships that they had to face in their daily life in an expanding metropolis, such as the shortage of basic civic amenities like shelter and water, the problems of overcrowding and of transport, and problems of law and order in urban life.

It so happens that a very large number of entries in this category, especially those related to the themes of dishousing and displacement of people from old quarters, are from the *Maratha*.

Entries from other journals on these subjects are comparatively few. Apart from the *Marmik*, the mouthpiece of the Shiv Sena, I selected for close scrutiny, the Maratha, it being staunchly opposed to the former. The *Marmik*, as a weekly, did not provide me with entries on day-to day events or happenings in the way the *Maratha* did. Founded as a journal for championing and propagating the cause of the Samyukta Maharashtra Movement, the *Maratha* continued to uphold the cause of the Maharashtrian community and play the role of watchdog of the interests of the poor and the deprived. A large number of entries in this section, therefore, are from the *Maratha*. Without the coverage of the *Maratha*, I would have missed significant content data, which consistently throws considerable light on a major factor linked with the frustrations of the members of the Maharashtrian community in the metropolis.

The entries covered in this Chapter begin to surface rather sparsely around 1962, slowly gain in strength and reach the peak of 48 entries during 1966, as against 40 entries in the previous year (1965); thereafter the number begins to dwindle, until, by 1969, the entries are reduced to a very negligible quantity if not to a total disappearance. Most of the entries covered here, thus fall between 1963 and 1968. (This is a recurrent pattern in respect of other areas of aspirations and grievances – economic and socio-economic – also. I shall discuss this point in the concluding chapter)

Civic Grievances
Distribution of Content Data Entries during 1961-70

Years	1962	1963	1964	1965	1966	1967	1968	1969	1970	Total
Letters	1	1	5	7	13	12	5	-	-	44
Editorials	-	-	9	11	7	-	-	-	-	27
Reports and Articles	6	12	32	22	28	21	12	-	-	133
Total	7	13	46	40	48	33	17	-	-	204

The breakdown of the entries according to the themes is as follows

	Letters	Editorials	Reports & Articles	Total
1. Migration and Displacement	8	5	24	37
2. Dishousing and Rehabilitation	7	8	40	55
3. Housing and Other Civic Amenities	11	10	44	65
4. Unlawful and Anti-social Activities (Law and Order Issues)	18	4	25	47
Total No. of Entries	44	27	133	204

The forty-odd letters that we have, voicing the grievances of the community about the civic conditions of metropolitan life mainly reflect the problems that the middle and lower-middle classes (representative of Mumbai's Maharashtrian community), had to face when Mumbai was in the midst of industrial and urban expansion in the fifties and the sixties. These letters and the supporting content data, from news reports, articles and editorials, unmistakably express the people's apprehension of being uprooted from their habitat and from the community's traditional shelters in which they had lived for generations. These entries taken together convey a sense of insecurity at the threat of being rendered homeless, a feeling of hopeless anger at being ousted from 'their' city (since now it was the capital of 'their' State), to far-off corners of the metropolis, only because they lacked the economic power to safeguard their interests. These letters complain of the fair claims of the Marathi speaking people being neglected in allotment of public housing of the Civic and State Governments, in spite of their being natives of the state; and this after being deprived of their rightful traditional shelters in the city.

The grievances voiced in these letters, editorials and news reports seem to be the inevitable concomitant of the extraordinary growth of Mumbai's population. The letters tell stories of extreme scarcity of water, of the vicissitudes of daily commutes by train and of the increasing menace of beggars and street-hawkers. However, a majority of letters and reports are concerned about the problem of housing, and often express an apprehension of being pushed out of the city.

Table IV – I
1. Exploding Metropolis
Distribution of Entries on the Affective Scale
Letters, Editorials, Reports and Articles (Consolidated)

Index Points	AS	GR	FR/IN	PR	DE	CA	Intensity Value	No.01
Year								
1960	-	-	-	-	-	-	-	-
1961	-	-	-	-	-	-	-	-
1962	-	3	-	4	-	-	22	7
1963	-	5	2	9	2	-	62	13
1964	1	15	17	16	3	2	173	46
1965	-	11	15	21	8	2	203	40
1966	-	11	15	25	9	3	226	48
1967	-	7	15	18	3	3	164	33
1968	-	2	5	7	2	1	63	17
1969	-	-	-	-	-	-	-	-
1970	-	-	-	-	-	-	-	-

Index Points on the Scale Total No. of Entries 204

Letters 44

AS=Aspiration GR=Grievance FR/IN=Frustration/ Insecurity

Editorials 27

Reports & Articles 133

PR=Protest DE=Demand CA=Call for Action

i) Intensity value of an entry is the same as the intensity value of the index-point under which the entry is placed on the affective scale.

ii) The sum of units classified under various index points of the affective scale does not tally with the number of entries for the particular year since some of the entries occasionally fall under more than one index point.

Content Data

1. Influx of Population and Displacement of the Native Community.

The fast-growing population of the metropolis, consequent overcrowding, the shortage of housing and displacement of the community from the main city, were the major problems that weighed heavily on the Maharashtrian community in Mumbai in the sixties.

We have 37 entries on the subject of which about a dozen letters and editorials, taken together, articulate people's anxiety and apprehension over these issues, while about an equal number, consisting of reports and articles, echo this concern.

Letters

i) A group of persons in a jointly-written letter complains of the Marathi community being displaced from Central South Mumbai (Lamington, Vithalbhai Patel and Tribhuvan Roads) and ejected to distant suburbs by trading communities like the Punjabi, the Sindhi and the Gujarati by their readiness to pay 'pugree'. The letter demands of the Municipal Corporation, protective measures for old tenants. (Nvs. 7.12.64)

ii) Another letter consists of almost an identical complaint of the old, middle-class Maharashtrian residential community of Malabar Hill and Walkeshwar being uprooted from the locality in the wake of accelerated construction activity of new blocks with ownership flats in those areas. (Nvs. 28.12.64)

In another rather elaborate letter, a reader expresses his fears that

iii) The Maharashtrian community would perhaps disappear from Mumbai. Would Maharashtrians be seen in areas like Lalbaug, Parel, Girgaon, when these Master Development plans are carried out? Will they get the place where they have lived for years or would they be forced to go out to distant corners of the metropolis? If this trend continued, perhaps within a few years one would have to ask where Maharashtra is in Mumbai. (Mht. 9.4.65)

A letter in the *Navshakti* admonishes Maharashtrians for having lost the opportunities of protecting their interests in the capital city of Mumbai, due to their belated awakening to their problems. (Nvs. 26.6.65)

A letter writer describes of a new feeling of being somewhere in the South – in Tamil Nadu or Kerala – when in certain districts of Mumbai like Matunga, Sion, Chembur, Kurla, Bhandup, Govandi and sometimes even when in Bandra and Dadar. He complains of Tamilians and Keralites getting priority in public housing, Maharashtrians being generally ignored. He expresses the need for a movement for protecting and safeguarding Maharashtrian's rights against such injustice in their very own state. (Sanj. Maratha 25.5.65)

Michael Gonsalves and Daniel Dhar from Vasai (Bassein) complain that the Manikpur area of Vasai is on its way to become 'Manikpuram' with South Indian migrants outnumbering the local population. (Mrm. 7.8.66)

Daniel Dhar mentions in his letter that even the Maharashrian Christian community was not free of the feeling of being overpowered by South Indian Christians. Mission Hostels for orphaned girls and widows were often dominated by Kerala Christians and Maharashtrian Christrians were finding it difficult to get accommodation in these. (Mrm. 26.2.67)

Editorials

About half-a-dozen editorials written in 1964-1965 raise the problem of the displacement of the Maharashtrian community from the city, under the impact of the incessant growth of Mumbai's population and due to absence of a correct policy or programme by the Municipal Corporation and the State Government, to safeguard the interests of old tenants and residents of the city.

All these editorials express apprehension of the Maharashtrian being displaced and thrown out of Mumbai by the incessant influx of outsiders, of being reduced to a state of a refugee in his own capital and of his being unjustly ignored by the State Housing Board. The editorials ask the Government to take urgent measures to immediately stall the encroachment by people from other States and adopt a policy that would safeguard Maharashtrian survival.

Reports and Articles

The entries in the category of reports and articles, like those in that of letters and editorials, express apprehension and alarm at the heavy influx of people into Mumbai, the consequent overcrowding, and the inevitable failure of the urban system to cope with the enormity of the problem. As is seen in these reports, prominent and not-so-prominent leaders of all shades of political opinion express alarm and insecurity and demand measures to check the addition to the city's population.

i) The ex-Chief Engineer of the Municipal Corporation (N.V. Modak) speaking in 1964 at a conference of hutment dwellers warned that the population of Greater Mumbai limit should not exceed 55 lakh if the authorities were to maintain the minimum standard of living conditions. (Mrt. 23.3.64)

ii) Members of the socialist and leftist groups, speaking at a seminar, called upon the Government to stall the growth of Mumbai's population. Failure to do so, they warned, would render the development plans into projects for the deterioration of living conditions. (Mrt. 12.12.64)

iii) A municipal councillor belonging to the Opposition feared that the problems of providing basic civic amenities in Mumbai could never be solved with the unending influx of migrants. (Mrt. 19.1.65)

Another responsible councillor G.D. Pusalkar, the Chairman of the Medical Relief and Public Health Committee expressed concern at the incessant flow of migrants from other provinces to Mumbai – and warned of the failure of all public and health schemes and welfare plans under such pressure. (Mrt. 21.1.65)

iv) A columnist in Navshakti comments: In the wake of the inundation of Mumbai by people from all over India, the percentage of the Marathi community in the city is dwindling. Along with the growth of hutment colonies, bootlegging and the goonda element are on the increase in Mumbai. In this process, the Marathi man is being ousted from the capital of Maharashtra. (Nvs. 19.3.67)

v) In another column, the commentator observed that a large percentage of Southern migrants existed in the newly-sprung hutment colonics of Greater Mumbai and called for measures to stall the incessant flow of migrants to Mumbai. (Nvs. 26.3.67)

vi) A report of the Assembly Debates, States that during 1968, the State Government, forced to take note of these grievances, was considering possible measures to curb the flow of migrants to Mumbai from other States, as suggested by the Maharashtra Economic Development Council. (Mht. 20.3.68; Mrt. 20.3.68)

2. Development Plans and Dishousing

Besides the influx of migrant population and correlated shrinkage of civic amenities and housing, a related contributory factor that gave an edge to Maharashtrian frustration was the ruinous state of housing in the older localities that accommodated the community, and the resulting dishousing of people, a process especially augmented in the wake of various town planning and development schemes either proposed or under implementation in the early sixties.

In the wake of the Development Plan and Town Planning Schemes of 1964, the price of land began shooting up. In addition to this, with the shortage and high cost of construction material, housing became extremely expensive. The Maharashtrian community, the majority of whom belonged to the low and middle-income groups, could not afford to bear this burden and were left with no option but to move out of the city and beyond.

Thus, around 1964, Mumbai was undergoing considerable change in its physical structure, in its land-use pattern and also in the layout of the city. This process of developmental change was further complicated by the migration from other provinces that started during the post-War decades and was accelerated by the economic forces of the late 1950s and the 1960s. These processes affected the urban population and had their repercussions on the social life and group-relations of the city. Our entries are preoccupied with these changes as they impinged on individual and community life.

Letters

Seven letters between 1964 and 1967 reflect the Maharashtrian community's reaction to far-reaching changes enveloping them in the process of unprecedented growth and the 'planned' development of Mumbai during the mid-60s. Taken together, the letters express a feeling of resistance to these changes and give the impression that the Development projects were apparently for the rich and the upper-class of the city and not for them, the Maharashtrians from the middle and lower-classes.

i) Two letters detail the harassment of tenants of old buildings by affluent landlords wanting to construct new buildings on the plot without caring to accommodate the old inhabitants. One letter is a plea to tenants of old buildings in the Malabar Hill area to unite to fight the injustice done to them by the landlords. (Mrt. 24.6.64)

ii) The second is an open letter of complaint against the (non-Maharashtrian) landlord by tenants of Angrewada – 95 per cent of who were Marathi persons. (Mrm. 7.8.66)

iii) A letter by a representative of the fishing community in Mahim expresses apprehension at the threat of demolition of the community's traditional quarters for generations, under the town Planning and Development Schemes. The community could not afford to pay the high rents in Government or Municipal Housing and besides this would be inconvenient for their occupation. If instead, the Government helped the community to improve its present housing through loans and other measures of assistance, the community would respond cooperatively. (Mrt. 8.10.67)

iv) Another letter from a fishing community further north in Vesave (Versova) demands urgent remedial action to protect the sea-front at this fishing port, which was being eroded by high tides consequent to the filling up of the creek between Juhu-Andheri and Vesave. It complains that similar erosion in the posh area of Marine Drive was speedly checked while the woes of a fishing community fell on deaf ears. (Mrt. 31.1.67)

v) A letter in 1966 complains that Municipal tenements, newly-built to house families displaced due to the Town Planning Scheme under implementation in the old area of Khetwadi in 1964-66 in Santacruz, were infiltrated forcibly by 'outsiders' with the support of corrupt officials, unjustly leaving the older Maharashtrian tenants shelterless in their own capital. (Mrt. 28.12.1966)

The tales narrated in these letters are to an extent corroborated by similar accounts presented in the corresponding news reports and editorials.

Editorials

Six editorials in the *Maratha* during 1964-66 were given over to problems of displacement of people from old localities and the growth of slums and hutment colonies.

Early in 1964, an editorial in the *Maratha* points to the farcical Town Planning and Development Schemes conducted by the authorities.

i) The editorial states that during 1952-60, 4,826 one-room tenements were demolished under various schemes while in contrast only 1,500 new tenements were built for the poorer sections. On the other hand 435 flats were replaced by 9,214 new ones. In the process, the poorer sections living in chawls were being thrown out into the far-off suburbs of Govandi, Malvani, Mankhurd etc. and the affluent alone were allowed to reside within the city. The editorial prescribes the remedy of freezing land prices to do away with speculation and black marketing in land in order to provide people with public housing. (Mrt. 28.2.64)

ii) Several editorials criticise the speculative prices of land and the lucrative business of ownership flats which resulted in tall modern structures for the rich while the poor remained devoid of a place even to stretch themselves. (Mrt. 28.2.64, 26.9.64, 31.3.66)

iii) The occasion for these editorials are either the demolition of a hutment colony, for instance, that of Subhash Nagar at Worli, accommodating about 5,000 families, the majority of whom were neo-Buddhists, or that of a protest-march of hutment dwellers of the city like the one to the Council Hall led by Nana Patil, the erstwhile leader of the underground movement of 1942.

iv) The editorials make a stinging criticism against the policy of rehabilitating middle and working class people – clerks, teachapters and industrial workers of Central and South Mumbai, to distant places like Malwani or Mankhurd. (Mrt. 1.5.64, 28.2.64, 31.3.64, 30.10.66)

Editorials from other journals also make this point; for example, an editorial from the *Navakal* observes:

v) The Maharashtrian is being pushed out of the city from every aspect of urban life including matters of residential accommodation. Because he cannot afford ownership flats he is driven to the suburbs; and when he cannot afford the rental of the tenements in the suburbs, he is forced to seek shelter in hutment colonies. (Nvk. 15.5.64)

These editorials unanimously criticise the excessive concentration of economic opportunities in Mumbai which caused the heavy influx of large populations from other States. They ask the Maharashtra Government for dispersal of industries into a wider region and demand priority in housing for the Maharashtrian to protect him from being displaced from the growing metropolis. They call upon the State Government to brave the charge of parochialism likely to be leveled against it; for it was the bounden duty of every state to provide its natives with the minimum standards of living, and if needed, to take firm measures to protect native interests.

Reports and Articles

Several entries (reports and articles), between 1962 and 1967, carry accounts of old chawls and hutments of various neighbourhoods in the island city being demolished and people being uprooted under the development or clearance schemes of the Mumbai Municipal Corporation.

i) In 1962, the Town Planning Scheme No.4 (Mahim) was

announced. It covered the area along the seashore from Worli to Shivaji Park, which was earmarked for industrial estates and offices in the new scheme. This meant the demolition of 3,203 dwellings, old buildings, chawls and huts along the road. No plan was envisaged for the rehabilitation of the thousands of persons adversely affected by the scheme. (Mrt. 19.3.62, 23.3.62, 25.3.62, 23.6.62)

A citizens' conference held in March 1962 demanded immediate suspension and cancellation of the Town Planning Scheme No. 4 which it labelled as an 'anti-people' scheme. Stalwarts like Atre and even the-then Mayor of Mumbai (Worlikar) were associated with the conference. (Mrt. 26.3.62)

Another report speaks of the consequences of the Development Plan No. 6 (Sion-Matunga) on the economically backward sections of the Koliwada, Agriwada and Bhandarwada villages - named after Koli, Agri and Bhandari, the original native communities of Mumbai covered by the Plan.

ii) A report states that the native communities were deprived of their original lands for a very cheap price during 1908 and 1912 by the City Improvement Trust (i.e. Mumbai Imporvement Trust - see BMC Report on the Development Plan for Greater Mumbai 1964, PP XXVI-XXVII - under the-then Land Acquisition Act.) They were promised at that time that their right to accommodation would be protected. The entry is a narration of the grievances of the native fisher-folk who complained that the 124 newly-built tenements of the Municipal Corporation in the area accommodated 'newcomers' and 'outsiders', while members of the economically-backward native communities continued to live in hovels. (Mrt. 12.12.62)

iii) There is another story of the woes of hundreds of families settled in Raoli Camp, being threatened with removal to far-off Vikhroli. The colony consisted of 800-odd families, the majority of whom were neo-Buddhists and a few were refugees of Partition. 288 tenements built under the Corporation's 'Improvement Schemes' initially housed as many families of the neighbourhood. However, 'newcomers' and 'outsiders' infiltrated in the next lot of 224 tenements leaving many older resident families deprived of a roof over their heads and under threat of removal to distant northern suburbs.(Mrt. 1.11.63)

The story of the struggle between people trying to preserve their shelters and the Corporation trying to implement its 'Development Schemes,' continued through the mid-sixties.

iv) The Tenants' Association from the Prabhadevi-Dadar-Mahim area which was affected by the T.P. Scheme No. 4 demanded that the Corporation should provide substitute housing in the city itself to the seven thousand families which were to be dishoused in the Town Planning Scheme. (Mrt. 23.7.66)

Our data contains an open letter to the Mayor of Mumbai by the Socialist leader, Madhu Dandavate, reminding him that:

v) Town Planning and Development Schemes were meant for the people's welfare, not vice-versa. The controversial scheme No. 4 covered several very old buildings between Prabhadevi and Mahim which had housed three to four generations of poor and middle-class families. They were now threatened with being uprooted. The letter requests the Mayor to cooperate with the Minister for Urban Development in providing substitute housing for the affected people. (Mrt. 6.4.67)

vi) A month-and-a-half later, we come across the news of about 200 families from two chawls (Dabak and Shroffwadi) on Tulsi Pipe Road, being thrown out of their houses, since the place was required for a stadium under the new Town Planning Scheme. (Mrt. 20.5.67; Mrm. 2.7.67)

vii) Earlier, there was a report of the proposed clearance of a large number of chawls – 75 per cent of those in Tardeo-Mahalaxmi area. (Mrt. 21.4.64) A year later there was a report of about 800 huts being marked out for demolition in the Wadala Hutment Colony. (Mrt. 24.5.65)

viii) There are complaints and grievances about how the proposed plans were distorted to serve vested interests (generally perceived as non-Maharashrian) unless the people were vigilant and united in safeguarding their interests. Where the people failed to unite in time, vested interests would have their way. (Sanj. Mrt. 26.5.65; Mrt. 2.4.67; Mrm. 22.5.66)

Having demolished an old building under the slum clearance project a man of affluence planned a manoeuvre to build a cinema house on the vacant plot. The people, however, resisted unitedly and demanded inexpensive housing to accommodate the dishoused of the area. (Sanj. Mrt. 26.5.65)

Struggle and Resistance

Simultaneously there is news of resistance by people who were affected adversely by the clearance and development schemes. Atre, editor of *Maratha* championed the cause of these shelterless people through his paper.

ix) Several leaders of the erstwhile Samyukta Maharashtra Samiti jointly with other opposition (CPI) leaders, organised residents of the old chawls, hutments and old buildings to protest against being driven out of the city and demand rehabilitation of the affected. (Mrt. 19.3.62, 5.10.63, 24.2.64, 23.3.64, 25.4.65, 24.5.65, 23.7.66, 30.10.66)

x) A tenant-residents' association for Greater Mumbai was organised under the erstwhile SMS leadership. It became an active instrument for voicing the protest and demands of the victims of the clearance and development plans and for safeguarding their interests. A memorandum of its demands was sent to the Corporation and the State Government. (Mrt. 22.1.63, 26.2.63, 14.6.63)

The demands included possession of all the vacant land in the metropolis by the Government, freezing of land prices and passing of a law to limit the maximum floor space available for living accommodation. It further demanded that private builders should be barred from constructing residential buildings. (Mrt. 2.3.64)

The Municipal Commissioner promised the members of The Tenants' Association of the Garamwada neighbourhood in Parel that the Government would build inexpensive housing for them at their current place of residence so that they would not have to shift to the faraway suburbs. (Mrt. 23.3.64)

An article written by the chairman of an association of a slum neighbourhood in Tardeo, made the following significant observations about the Mumbai Development Plan of 1964

xi) The survey of the slums of Mumbai, made by the Municipal Corporation in 1956-1957, revealed the existence of 144 slums with a population of about 4 lakh in the island city of Mumbai (between Colaba and Mahim and Dharavi and Sion) Making allowance for the growth of the slum population since that time the writer puts the figure at one million (10 lakh) during the mid-60s. He criticises the Development Plan for its wrong priorities and for its failure to include either rehabilitation of the dishoused or a programme for slum improvement. Instead of focusing on the major problem of minimum housing for a vast majority of people from low-income groups, the Development Plan, according to the writer, spent large sums for those who were relatively better-off. The writer further claims that 75 per cent of the persons in the blighted section were members of the Maharashtrian community. The absence of allocations and programmes for their rehabilitation was tantamount to driving them The writer criticises the Development Plan as a plan of destruction rather than one of development for Maharashtrians. He strongly protests against a plan-proposal for a school building for upper-middle class children on the plot to be vacated in his particular neighbourhood under the proposed slum clearance programme. (Sanj. Mrt. 5.5.65)

Another article dubs the new Development Plan as a plan for the expulsion of the poor and middle-class Maharashtrians from the main city and gives a call for struggle against this injustice under the banner of the 'Zopadpatti Sangram Samiti' (The Front for the Struggle of the Hutment Dwellers) (Mrt. 29.3.66)

According to a *Maharashtra Times* report, a Legislative Councillor reiterated in the State Assembly debate, the fear that Maharashtrians were getting driven out of the city in the process of town planning and development of Mumbai. The native Marathi speaking residents living in the old quarters of the city were being forced out of the metropolis. They did not have enough money to buy or rent the expensive flats in the new buildings that were coming up in the city. (Mht. 22.2.68)

An article in 1968 points out that post the implementation of Town Planning Schemes No. 2, 3, and 4 (Mahim), a large number of native residents from this area had disappeared from the place for good. The article claims that the three schemes displaced a total of 10,500 families from their residences. The writer holds the opposition party responsible for the failure to visualise, even as late as 1962, the need for substitute housing and the failure to rehabilitate the victims of these 'plans'. (Mrt. 20.3.68)

Problems of Old Buildings and Response of the Authorities

xii) There are stories of landlords of old, dilapidated buildings and chawls, who instead of spending on repairs, preferred to wait for their eventual collapse, for vacant plots would fetch them enormous prices. In the process, poor tenants suffered. (Mrt. 5.4.65; Mrm. 5.6.66)

Often the landlord would be non-Maharashtrian and the tenant Maharashtrian! It is thus easy to perceive the situation in terms of group-distance.

xiii) Responding to the matter of housing conditions of the poor and the middle classes, the Mumbai Municipal Corporation passed two resolutions in 1964:

(1) To set aside a quota from cement available to the Corporation towards repairs of old buildings (Mrt. 5.10.64); (2) For the housing proposed for the dishoused, sanction to be given only to those plans of new buildings within the city, which were for one and two-room tenements. This was meant to protect the economically weaker sections from being pushed out of the city. (Mrt. 18.10.64)

At last, in response to the clamour from all quarters for remedial measures to protect tenants of old houses, the State Government appointed a committee at a ministerial level to which the Municipal Commissioner presented his suggestions. The suggestions were that (1) a fund of a crore of rupees be raised for purposes of loans for repairs to indigent landlords and tenants of old buildings. (ii) a repairs tax Several members of the opposition parties took keen interest in the problem and made useful suggestions with a view to present a bill in the state legislature. The State Government, which had already appointed a committee to consider the problem and its remedies, from various angles, decided to bring out a broad Rent Control Bill which would rationalise rents along with the raising of funds for repairs of old buildings. (Mrt. 21.6.67)

The question continued to be repeatedly discussed in the State Legislative Assembly. (Mrt. 21.6.67, 22.4.68, 13.5.68)

At last in June 1968 the State Government published a draft bill for establishing a Buildings Repairs Board for Mumbai and invited comments from the members of the Legislative Assembly as well the members of the public. (Mrt. 12.6.68, 29.6.68)

The bill was passed with a few amendments in 1969 and the problem of old housing which had adversely affected the Maharashtrian community of Mumbai city during the sixties, was at last on way its way to a solution. (Maharashtra Legislative Assembly Debates, 1969, Vol. 27-II, no. 44)

Tenants in Slums and Unauthorised Structures

Our data includes a letter describing the conditions of life in a slum of Mumbai. It is a document of bitter frustration at the inhuman living conditions.

xiv) The writer invites readers to the Majaswadi, slum in the distant western suburb of Jogeshwari (East) to have a first-hand experience of living in hell. The water had to be carried in pots from a distance of one mile and the slum did not have a single latrine. The writer mentions that a large number from the slum worked in offices in the Fort Area but had to reside in far-off Majaswadi, all for want of accommodation they could afford in Mumbai proper. (Mrt. 15.3.67)

The writer's frustration expressed in the letter was not unfounded.

In 1967, a member of the opposition (Datta Samant, SMS, had raised the issue of living conditions of suburban slums in the Legislative Assembly. He stated that there was only one latrine per 700 persons and only one tap for 2500 persons in these hutment colonies. (Mrt. 22.3.67, 18.7.67)

There was no exaggeration in these descriptions (See Desai and Pillai, 1972, 89-100) Majaswadi was a slum colony of chawls and huts in east Jogeshwari, a suburb of North Mumbai. In the early sixties, especially during 1963-1964, Majaswadi along with its neighbouring slums of the Janata Colony and Koldongri in Andheri-Parle (East) had become a hotbed of serious tensions and occasional clashes between unlawful landlords who raised hundreds of unauthorised chawls and huts to make quick and easy money and helpless tenants who were exploited in their dire need of a roof over their heads. By and large, it appears that the landlords were from the Ahir community from Mirzapur district of U.P. and had links with the cattle-breeders of the Aarey Colony.

The tenants in the slums included in a large percentage of Marathi speaking people (90 per cent according to the *Maratha*, 26.12.65), somc Christians from Karnataka and a small percentage of people from other States of the South. Some of the chawls were built even on top of the Jogeshwari caves. Reports said that the unlawful landlords had collected very large sums as depost and 'pugree' money from the tenants.

xv) In 1964, there began to appear news of threats by the landlords, of killing and of the burning of tenant's houses. There were reports of the residents being beaten up by the landlords, of harassment of women-folk by the toughs of Aarey Colony and even of attempts at murder of the tenant-leaders. (Mrt. 26.6.63, 11.1.64, 14.1.64, 19.2.64, 20,2,64, 21.2.64, 22.2.64, 8.3.64, 13.5.64)

The *Daily Maratha* complained to the Government that the police in charge of law and order in the Majaswadi area had taken bribes from the unlawful landlords and it warned that the events would reduce thousands of Maharashtrian tenants to a state of vagrancy. When the Home Department moved in the matter and made inquiries, it became clear that the landlords, enraged by the increasing demand for basic amenities in the chawls, had begun to resort to intimidatory measures. (Mrt. Ed. 17.1.64; Mrt. 11.3.64)

Ultimately the question of riots in Majaswadi and other slums was raised in the State Assembly.

The members of the Opposition reiterated the request of the Tenants' Association to the Government to take possession of unauthorised structures in these slums and to collect the rent from the tenants to provide them with alternative accommodation with needed amenities. Another important suggestion was for the establishment of a police chowky in the slum to protect tenants from harassment by enraged landlords. The Home Minister provisionally agreed to consider the suggestion after an appraisal conducted jointly with the Mumbai Municipal Corporation. (Mrt. 26.2.64, 12.3.64)

Soon after, the Government appointed a broad-based committee to invite suggestions to remedy the problems of unauthorised structures on Corporation and Government land, and of occupants of these structures. (Mrt. 23.4.64)

3. Housing and Civic Amenities

a. The Maharashtra State Housing Board

To cope with the demands of urban housing in the context of the fast-growing population of the city, the State Government had already established a Housing Board which with the aid of public funds undertook to construct and make inexpensive housing available to various middle and lower income groups, since private builders were not interested in investing capital in a business which brought them little profit. Unfortunately, there were a large number of complaints from the general public regarding the operation of the Housing Board, of its policies, method of allotment of accommodation, the corruption in its offices, etc. Also, the common complaint levelled against the Board was that it treated Maharashtrians unfairly while non-Maharashtrians were getting a greater share of its tenements.

Letters

Of the seven letters in our data, on the subject of the Housing Board, two are critical of its general policy while three specially allege that it indulged in acts of favoritism towards South Indians.

i) Writing in 1963, a letter-writer complains that some of the Government Housing Schemes, meant for low-income groups, were, in fact, beyond their reach; the instalments towards the cost of tenements were too high for them. Consequently, tenements fell into the hands of executives or persons of the high-income group; and the lower middle-class was left high and dry. (Mrt. 28.10.63)

Another letter-writer observes that the Government's policy of eradicating slums by providing hutment-dwellers with substitute housing in Government tenements was a self-defeating proposition. Hutment-dwellers housed in these tenements found rent and living expensive and preferred to dispose of the tenements for monetary gain and then squatted again on some other open space. Most of these hutment-dwellers were from other States, usually from the South. Therefore the Government's policy of providing substitute housing to slum dwellers deprived the natives of the State, their due share in accommodation, contributing to their displacement. (Nvs. 17.1.64)

ii) Another letter in the *Navakal* observes that 75 per cent of the tenements of the State Housing Board at Goregaon and Ghodbunder Road were occupied by South Indian families because the State Housing Board was manned by South Indians. The writer declares that Goregaon was on its way to becoming another little Madras in Mumbai. The writer comments: It is a strange kind of hospitality extended by the State Housing Board to 'outsiders' that kept the natives of its own state roofless. (Nvs. 3.8.65)

A letter in the *Maharashtra Times* complains of the Housing Board's indifference to an application for accommodation which had been languishing for ten years. The application was from a cultural and educational organisation set up by the Marathi tenants of Tilaknagar (a Housing Board Colony) while a non-Maharashtrian organisation had been granted such accommodation. (Mht. 8.4.66)

Yet another letter published in the *Maratha* also complained of a high percentage of the non-Marathi people in allotments to the State Board's tenements. It further observed that merely a 15 years' residence in the State should not be an adequate condition for eligibility to state housing, because it could easily be fulfilled in devious ways. The letter further suggests that these tenements be reserved for the Marathi and the non-Marathi in certain acceptable proportions (say 91) The interests of the poor and middle-class Maharashtrians badly needed to be thus protected. (Mrt. 23.7.66)

Another letter criticises the State Government's apparent readiness to make land available at a cheap rate for a co-operative housing society of South Indians, while similar facilities were hardly extended to the natives (Marathi speaking) of the state. (Mrm. 31.7.66)

A letter in 1967, asks, 'For whose benefit is the Maharashtra State Housing Boards' communication and correspondence being carried out exclusively in English instead of in Marathi?' (Nvs. 24.3.67)

Editorials

There are seven editorials from various journals between 1964 and 1966, which unequivocally express the concern and apprehension felt by the Maharashtrian community being displaced from Mumbai by the heavy influx of 'outsiders'. Simultaneously, these editorials were critical of the State Government for the mismanagement of the State Housing Board's affairs. The editors believed that Maharashtrians had not received their due share in the State Government's Public Housing projects while 'outsiders', chiefly South Indians, had managed to get the better of the natives of the state. The editorials asked the Government to take urgent remedial measures both to check the influx of population to Mumbai and restore to the Maharashtrian community its rightful due share.

i) The *Maratha's* editorial on the State's anniversary on May Day, regretted, in a general review of the situation in Maharashtra and of Maharashtrians that the living conditions of Maharashtrians in Mumbai had deteriorated. The editorial complained that even 5 per cent of residences in Mumbai were not owned by Maharashtrians and those they owned or had hired were being sold away to non-Maharashtrians in the prospect of some monetary gain. It was saddened that in State Housing the non-Maharashtrians had outnumbered the Marathi people. The editorial asks the State Government to stall non-Maharashtrian encroachment on Mumbai, to safeguard the Maharashtrian community's survival in the city. (Mrt. 1.5.64)

The theme of an editorial in the *Maharashtra Times* was that of the eradication of slums. The State Government at that time was considering construction of tenements to accommodate hutment dwellers following demolition of their dwellings. The editorial strongly protested against any such policy which involved expenditure running into astronomical figures. It also observed that the majority of hutment dwellers, especially in the newer suburbs outside the island city, were from other States. Maharashtra State could ill-afford to go on draining its exchequer to accommodate a continuous influx of migrants. In rehabilitating hutment and slum dwellers the Government owed priority to those who had been natives of the state and did not constitute the floating population of the city. Similarly, in public housing 'outsiders' i.e. those who had recently migrated to Mumbai were to be considered last. Otherwise in spite of all the Government expenditure upon public housing and rehabilitation, the Marathi people – the natives of the state – might still remain shelterless. The editorials reminded the Government that its primary duty was towards the natives of the state and went on to censure the Corporation and the State Housing Board for their failure in fulfiling their obligations towards the people of the State. (Mht. 31.5.65)

A *Marmik* editorial expresses almost identical views. According to it, among the million hutment-dwellers of Mumbai, about 300,000 were Marathi speaking, while the rest, 6-700,000 were non-Maharashtrians, 'outsiders'. In all fairness, the needs of the Maharashtrians had to receive priority in their own state, the editorial averred. (Mrm. 29.5.66)

ii) Another editorial in the same journal on the mismanagement of the State Housing Board, demands the resignation of the-then Minister for Housing and Construction, Homi Talyarkhan. The editorial observes that because of heavy criticism levelled at it from various quarters the State Housing Board had increased the tenure of domicile in Mumbai from 10 years to 15. However, it was quite easy for many a South Indian to meet with this condition by means of a false certificate of required domicile; whereas a Maharashtrian, inspite of being a native of the state, often failed to obtain accommodation in state housing for want of the right connections, influence or money. (Mrm. 31.7.66)

Reports and Articles

There are 14 entries, reports and articles, which are critical of the Housing Board and its mismanagement of Housing funds.

i) A lengthy article, in response to the *Maratha's* editorial on the Maharashtra State Anniversary Day, mentioned earlier reviews of various problems that faced the community and expresses grief at the injustice done to the Marathi people in allotments to State and Municipal Housing. (Mrt. 5.6.64)

ii) The Maharashtra Hitawardhini, an organisation established in 1964 to safeguard and promote Maharashtrian interests, presented a memorandum to the Chief Minister demanding that 80 per cent of the State Housing Board tenements should go to Marathi speaking people, considering the native community's lack of housing in its own state capital. (Mrt. 1.10.64)

In 1965, during an Assembly debate on the report on the State Housing Board, a communist member (Patkar, CPI) suggested that funds should be sought from the Central Government for housing Mumbai's enormous population, since it consisted of a large number of migrants from other States. (Mrt. 28.7.65)

The following year, during the budget session, another member of the Legislature, (Dr. Mandlik (PSP) criticised the State Housing Board's 'outsider-oriented' policy and administration. He demanded that 90 per cent of State Housing be reserved, in all fairness, for the natives of the state, the rest for outsiders. He also suggested that the officer granting the domicile certificate should also have fulfilled the same domicile conditions as the applicants. (Mht. 31.3.66; Lks. 31.3.66)

In 1966, again we have a report of the Maharashtra Hitawardhini presenting another memorandum to the State Government which included the following demands regarding housing (1) The minimum period of residence in Maharashtra required for eligibility to state housing should be 20 years. (2) While giving loans to co-operative housing societies the Board should stipulate that 75 per cent of the members of such societies be Maharashtrians. (3) Neither the State Government not the civic authorities should take upon themselves responsibility to provide housing to the migrant, floating population before housing the native citizens. (Nvs. 2.3.66)

The question of housing for Maharashtrians still continued to be discussed in the Assembly even in 1967.

In the spring session of the State Legislature, a member (Waman Bapat, SMS) pointed out to an advertisement by the Tamil Nadu government, which stipulated Tamil as the mother tongue, as a requisite for eligibility to its state housing. The member then asked the Maharashtra State Deputy Minister for Housing, why the Maharashtra Government could not take a similar step. In reply, the Deputy Minister referred to legal advice against such a policy. (Mrt. 31.3.67)

There were also reports of difficulties experienced by groups of people over obtaining housing accommodation in Mumbai.

iii) There is a news report of well-known Marathi stage actors seeking a meeting with the Chairman of the Housing Board to apprise him of their need for housing. (Mrt. 9.10.64) The Chairman of the Marathi Film Producers Association (V. Shantaram) made a similar demand for space for film studios and construction of cinema houses for Marathi films in the capital. (Mrt. 10.10.64)

The studios and cinema houses controlled by the Hindi film industry were generally not available to Marathi film producers at prices they could afford.

iv) Another news report complained that Maharashtrian demands for space for schools and educational institutions were neglected, especially since they could not compete with the rich institutions of other communities. There are news reports which grieve about the lack of accommodation for Maharashtrian schools and other educational institutions, whereas educational institutions and cultural centres of other communities had hardly any such difficulty, fortified as they were by economic strength. (Mrt. 25.1.65, 1.7.66, 1.10.66, 31.1.67, 13.5.67)

v) According to another new report, the Home Minister, B.D. Desai, accepted the principle of priority for Maharashtrians in both State and Municipal Housing. He admitted that the Maharashtrian in Mumbai was ill-served regarding his housing needs since the land for purposes of construction was already in the hands of non-Maharashtrian businessmen and speculators. He suggested cooperative effort and collective contributions to solve the housing problems of Maharashtrians. (Mrt. 5.5.65)

The point was reiterated in another article where the writer suggested loans and assistance may be given by the State to slum dwellers to improve their existing housing, instead of the state providing them with substitute housing. (Mrt. 26.12.65)

3.b) Water Scarcity

Water shortage became a persistent problem in Mumbai. As the metropolis expanded in the fifties, the problem became worse in the sixties, when the city entered an era of faster expansion, while the new schemes of water supply from the Upper Vaitarna and other sources in the adjacent hinterland of the Mumbai were yet to be completed. Even after the completion of the Upper Vaitarana project, water has remained a scarce commodity in Mumbai.

A letter from a reader in the evening edition of the *Maratha* is eloquent. The letter narrates the story of the Desai family.

i) Living in the Hindmata Lane of Parel, the Desais used to get water for 24 hours in their taps fifteen years ago. Now inspite of paying a water tax, they get only a small trickle between 6 and 7 p.m. (Sanj. 21.5.65)

ii) Earlier, in 1962, a letter-writer reacts with apprehension at the prospect of having to pay a small charge per glass of water served in restaurants as declared by the Secretary of the Hotel Owners' Federation at a press conference. (Mrt. 24.10.62)

iii) Two letters complain of the civic supply of water being discriminatory against the economically handicapped Maharashtrian community in the city. (Mrt. 4.4.64, 30.12.65)

Editorials

We have come across five editorials that discuss the subject of water scarcity, four from the *Daily Maratha* and one from the *Marmik*. Considering that 1964 and 1965 were years of drought in Maharashtra and that the monsoon arrived very late in 1966, it is not surprising that the subject received attention in editorial comments. Complaints in the letters against discrimination in supply of water are corroborated by editorials.

i) An editorial in the *Daily Maratha* describes the common man's ordeal in getting water in Mumbai and points out that the discrimination in water supply resulted as its distribution was made ward-wise with a total disregard to the variations in population on different wards. Consequently, localities comprising the lower-middle class and working class of the city often received a meagre supply. (Mrt. 19.5.65)

ii) Another editorial in the *Maratha* severely warns against the growth of Mumbai since the available resources of water supply to the city were limited. The editorial observes that unchecked growth of Mumbai had caused the water problem. It holds the civic and the State Governments responsible for abetting Mumbai's lop-sided expansion by reclaiming land from the sea, allowing the growth of industries and construction of skyscrapers in the metropolis. (Mrt. 12.7.66)

iii) A strong editorial by the *Marmik* written in 1965 fetched ten letters of appreciation from readers. The editorial held the unlimited industrial and economic growth of Mumbai and incessant flow of migrants responsible for the water famine. The wastage of water from water hydrants that were tampered with by the southern migrants in the new slums of Mumbai's northern suburbs was yet another point of editorial criticism. Restraining further industrial expansion in and around Mumbai and deterring the flow of jobless migrants to the city, were considered to be necessary measures to maintain Mumbai's water supply, since new water resources for the city were not available. (Mrm. Ed. 4.7.65)

Nineteen other entries in the form of articles and news items deal with the theme of water shortage in Mumbai city and most of these are from the *Maratha*.

The problem of water supply for the fast-growing metropolis was a constant headache for the Municipal Corporation and a matter of recurring debate, discussion and planning in the Municipal Council. The fortnightly columns of the *Maratha* on the Municipal Corporation were full of references to the problems of housing and water shortage from 1963 until 1968. Our data include 6 to 7 entries of these special columns on the water problem. (Mrt. 7.11.62, 10.9.62, 17.12.62, 1.7.64, 22.3.65, 13.7.66) The theme drew special articles and also comments in the form of cartoons in the *Marmik*. (Mrt. 23.7.66; Mrm. 17.7.66)

i) The newspapers often reported of the ordeals of people for water in different areas of the city, of women's and citizens' demonstrations and protest marches demanding water-supply some times under the aegis of well-known leaders of the opposition parties. (Mrt. 9.7.63, 1.1.63, 9.7.63, 7.12.63, 24.12.63, 29.10.63, 27.9.63, 31.7.64, 31.5.65) There were reports of the delayed departures of local coastal ships due to water shortage. (Mrt. 5.3.63) Common water taps in the tenements and slum quarters were often the venues of clashes and conflicts. One such clash even ended in a murder. (Mrt. 20.3.65)

ii) Legislators asked the State Government to look into the problem of Mumbai's water scarcity to find a permanent solution to it. Some of them also criticised the State Government for the continuation of its policy of industrial growth in Mumbai. (Mrt. 25.3.65) Questions of fair and equitable distribution of water were raised in the Municipal Council by the opposition parties (the SMS and CPI) but were rendered ineffective by the stalling tactics of the members of the ruling Party (BPCC), in the Municipal Council. (Mrt. 22.3.65)

In the smmer of 1966, Mumbai's water problem had become severe due to drought condtions in the preceeding two years.

iii) Since there was no sign of rain even until the second week of July (1966), the Municipal Commissioner of Mumbai publicly warned the citizens to be postpone reopening of schools and colleges. (Mrt. 9.7.66) The State Government, the manufacturers' and the labour representatives together, had taken the decision to curtail working days in the week to conserve water resources. (Mrt. 8.7.66)

The reservoirs supplying water to Mumbai had the storage to last for only 22 days more, according to the reports. (Mrt. 8.6.66) The *Maratha* columnist on the Municipal Corporation, commenting on the water situation, observed that out of the 250 million gallons' supply of water to Mumbai per day, 20 million gallons went to waste due to negligence, leakage, and pilferage from water hydrants. (Mrt. 5.7.66)

On the 12 and 13 July of the same year, the Corporation began preparations to face any eventuality. The Municipal Councillors engaged themselves in debate over the crisis. Several opposition members made various suggestions regarding measures to cope with the problem.

A lady councillor (M. Gore, SSP), complained that instructions for saving water and avoiding wastage, leakage etc., were not observed. Another councillor (R.G. Kharat of RPI) asked the Government to clamp down on unauthorised industries in Mumbai. He considered it essential to evacuate first the large non-Maharashtrian population in the hutment colonies of Mumbai. Another councillor (Pendse of SMS) demanded that anti-social elements like illicit liquor-brewers, and bootleggers whose population he estimated to be in the vicinity of 80,000, be first expelled from Mumbai and that those stealing water from hydrants be severely punished. (Mrt. 13.7.66, 14.7.66)

In the context of water shortage another Maharashtrian councillor (R.L. Belose, BPCC) suggested that there should be a restriction on the allotment of fresh ration cards to curb the influx of migrants.

Regarding the matter of evacuation of the citizens of Mumbai due to water shortage, Belose opined that non-Maharashtrians be evacuated initially. He further said that the city should be closed to fresh migrants from other States lest they came to occupy Mumbai while the Maharashtrian were evacuated from it. When confronted by the Press, belose explained that by 'non-Maharashtrian' he was referring to the recent migrants and that he never doubted that those who had lived in Mumbai for a few generations belonged to the city. (Mrt. 14.7.66)

However, Belose's remarks raised a hullaballoo in the BPCC and drew strong criticism from the English language press. The issue reverberated in the newspapers for quite some time, until the news of rains in the catchment areas of the lakes lulled the turmoil created by Belose's remarks.

4. Unlawful and Anti-social Activities

In addition to the rigours caused by the threat of being dishoused and by the shortage of civic amenities and the difficulties of communication etc., the common man also encountered new kinds of problems, hitherto little-known in Mumbai. The menace of hawkers, beggars, bootleggers and increasing anti-social activity (goondaism) penetrated to the older residential localities.

4.a) Hawkers

By 1964 the hawkers proved a sore problem for the Municipal Corporation. With a large number of unemployed youth migrating to Mumbai in search of a livelihood, the number of hawkers continued to swell and the system of Municipal licensing practically broke down under the pressure of increasing numbers seeking licences. The hawkers occupied the pavements of major roads in the business districts of Fort, as well of those adjacent to all important railway stations along the Western and Central suburban railways, obstructing pedestrian movement in Mumbai's crowded streets. Bribes were given to obtain licences from the Municipal Corporation and to elicit the connivance of the staff of the encroachment department. Occasionally however, under the pressure of councillors' criticism or due to the competence of an official of integrity, the Municipal Corporation woke up from its general attitude of lethargy and leniency to exercise a firm policy of restricting the number of licences and of fining those who were guilty of the breach of rules. However, on the whole, the general performance of the Corporation in this respect seemed to be an exercise in expediency under various kinds of pressures in the absence of any well-considered policy.

Six letters in our data refer to the nuisance of hawkers on the streets of Mumbai, between Victoria Terminus and the Museum, near Mahalaxmi and Dadar Railway Stations and other areas of the city. A majority of these letters also observe that the hawkers were from beyond the Maharashtra State, chiefly from Kerala and other parts of the South.

i) Most letters complain of the hawkers' rude and rough behaviour, of the nuisance caused by occupying pavements, of their bribes to the police and the Municipal Corporation's encroachment department's personnel (Sanj. Mrt. 28.5.65; Mrm. 22.5.66; Mrt. 1.10.66, 13.6.68) and at times even of eve-teasing. (Mrt. 1.10.66; Mrm. 22.5.66)

ii) Two letters by handcart pullers complain against the staff of the encroachment office for confiscating their handcarts parked on the roadside just for loading or unloading the luggage, while the unlawful encroachment on pavements and roads by non-Maharashtrian hawkers and by affluent car owners, was ignored. (Lks. 14.2.66; Mrt. 21.2.66)

Nearly a dozen major news items and comments between 1964 and 1968 cover the story of grievance against hawkers in Mumbai. Four major news reports underline the complaints made by readers against the hawkers. These reports are equally critical of the encroachment department of the Municipal Corporation for its abetment to hawkers.

i) The writers of the weekly column on Municipal affairs in the *Daily Maratha* agree that the Municipal department often turned a blind eye to hawkers on the pavements. The columnist observes that not a single district of Mumbai was free from unauthorised hawkers occupying the pavement and forcing pedestrians to walk on the main road. This often was a factor responsible for vehicular accidents in the crowded streets of the city. (Mrt. 20.12.65)

Instead of viewing the problem of hawkers as a matter of civic administration, political parties endeavoured to exploit it for Party interests.

ii) In 1964, the socialist leader George Fernandes in a press statement warned of a hawkers' agitation in case the Municipal Corporation failed to grant licences to one lakh hawkers of Mumbai. According to the leader, the hawker had a right to earn his livelihood and therefore, to claim a licence to hawk his goods. (Mrt. 11.2.64, 28.2.64, 7.3.64)

In March 1964, the Municipal Corporation, with the help of the police, confiscated the goods of unlicensed hawkers. The hawker problem was being exploited by political parties and was getting complicated, according to the *Maratha* columnist, (Mrt. 9.3.64)

iii) In reply to George Fernandes' warning of agitation for licences for a hundred thousand hawkers of the city, Waman Bapat, a Municipal Councillor, pointed out that the demand was based on a misconstrued concept of fundamental rights. The Municipal Corporation, which was responsible for civic administration and welfare, could not grant licences for hawking in a manner that could cause obstruction to traffic and pedestrian movement. A hawker's right to hawk for his living was liable to be governed by rules similar to those laid down by the civic government for other industrial, professional or business activities, while maintaining the civic order. The Councillor warned that a demand to give licences to a lakh of hawkers saying that it was their fundamental right was an invitation to anarchy and lawlessness and was inconsistent with socialist goals. The absurdity of the demand was apparent when stretched to a beggar's claim to practise begging in the city, in the name of a fundamental right. (Mrt. 17.3.64)

Following this, the problem of hawkers was referred to a special committee appointed by the Municipal Corporation (Mrt. 23.3.64)

Two reports in the *Daily Maratha* (1965-67) narrate about clashes between hawkers and the police in Dadar in North Mumbai.

iv) The first report was a story of harassment of pedestrians by unlicensed Malayali hawkers outside the Dadar Railway Station.

People had the impression that bribed by the hawkers, the police as well as the staff of the Municipal encroachment department, neglected the citizen's plaint. Thus emboldened, the hawkers tended to be insolent to pedestrians and even to those shop owners whose frontage they usurped to display their wares. Consequently, the Dadar Merchants' Association complained to the Home Minister of the hawkers' menace. A majority of hawkers reportedly were Muslims from Kerala who, by bribing the police managed to be forewarned of impending raids by the encroachment department or the police department itself. If occasionally an honest policeman did pull them up they banded together to intimidate the policeman by even brandishing a knife. The report appealed to the Police Commissioner of Mumbai to check these incidents before they deteriorated into group clashes. (Mrt. 28.12.65)

In spite of the complaints to the Home Minister, the hawker menace continued.

Another report two years later, tells how hawkers in Dadar attacked two policemen who forbade them from occupying the pavement in the market area. Members of the public supported the police and a clash ensued between them and the hawkers. The police ultimately sent 41 unlicensed hawkers to jail. (Mrt. 27.9.67)

Earlier, complaining about the insolence of hawkers in the Fort area and the harassment faced by pedestrians, a report in *Sanj Maratha* had made the observation that these hawkers were selling smuggled goods for the past few years, in the very vicinity of the Council Hall housing the State legislature and the seat of the Government. (Sanj. Mrt. 23.3.66)

This report was followed by a sudden raid on hawkers by the police and the Municipal encroachment department. The *Daily Maratha* attributed the diligent action by the police and the encroachment department to the report in the *Sanj Maratha* (Mrt. 2.7.66)

The year 1968 saw demonstrations and marches in support of, and in protest against hawkers, abetted by interested political parties.

v) The Shiv Sena took out a protest march against hawkers, which resulted in clashes between the Shiv Sainiks and the hawkers in the Fort area. (Mrt. 27.5.68)

The tussle between the hawkers and the political parties patronising them on the one side and the civic administration and the common man on the other, continued unresolved throughout the sixties and even later.

4.b) Beggars

i) In 1966, in reply to a question in the State Legislative Assembly, the Maharashtra Minister for Social Welfare (Nirmala Bhonsale) admitted that the beggar population of Mumbai was on the increase and that the majority of beggars in the city were migrants from other States; their exact number, however, was not available. (Mrt. 16.4.66)

ii) In reply to another question about the increase in the beggar population and related criminal activity, the Minister stated that other States were reluctant to accept the repatriation of beggars or of criminals hailing from those States. (Mrt. 22.7.66)

iii) A reader's letter expressing exasperation at the increase in beggar population of the city, asks for measures to stall the flow of beggars into Mumbai from other States. The letter states that the addition to the existing beggars' homes in the city could spur further inflow of migrant beggars (Lks. 2.12.68)

Similar letters appeared in the newspapers even in the seventies.

4.c) Anti-social Activities

i) Six letters in our data (1966-68) complain against the increasing menace of bootleggers and the rackets in smuggling rice into Mumbai for the black market from other States through the agency of female lepers. The common complaint in these letters is that the majority of people engaged in these unlawful activities are migrants from the Southern provinces of Kerala and Tamil Nadu. (Mrm. 12.6.66, 26.6.66, 15.1.67, 26.3.67; Mrt. 24.2.68; Lks. 2.12.68)

Reports and Articles

The report on prohibition by the Study Team appointed by the Government of India (Tekchand Report) was published in 1964. It presented its findings about the illicit liquor trade and of the areas and the people involved in related activities in Mumbai. The *Daily Maratha* ran excerpts of the report and criticised it for its support to the policy of prohibition even in the face of its own findings, which clearly pointed out how prohibition encouraged bootlegging and other criminal activities in the underworld. The excerpts from the Report incidentally focused on the role of Southern migrants in these activities in Mumbai (Mrt. 2.5.64)

ii) Another report in the *Daily Maratha* narrated how group tensions developed in Dharavi (a slum district of Mumbai) between the Marathi speaking fisher-folk and other communities on one side, and a group of Tamil-speaking toughs on the other. (Mrt. 11.11.66)

The news of major clashes around illicit liquor dens and among bootleggers continued to find place in the newspapers. (Mrt. 15.12.65, 11.11.66)

This kind of news became infrequent when prohibition was scrapped for all practical purposes by the end of 1968.

iii) A commentator grieving about the increase in crime in Mumbai observed that it was an aspect inevitably related to Mumbai's heterogeneity – to its so-called 'cosmopolitan' character. The commentator described this state of affairs as devoid of social norms and values – a state of anomie, which failed to bind together the total metropolitan society (Mrm. 29.5.66)

Editorials

A number of editorials and articles complain of increase in crime and anti-social activities in Mumbai. (Mrt. 9.4.64, 29.10.64, 5.6.65, Sanj. Mrt. 6.5.65, 26.5.65; Nvs.12.3.67)

The Editorials in the *Daily Maratha* attributed the increase in anti-social activities to the policy of prohibition, pursued by the Congress Government in the State, which resulted in a flourishing underground blackmarket in alcoholic drinks and in bootlegging. This, in turn, attracted anti-social elements from all over India especially from the Southern States. (Mrt. 1.5.64, 4.9.64, 8.11.64, 5.6.65)

It was in the context of the increasing menace of goondaism that the editor of the Maratha (Atre), in 1964 had declared in the newspaper his intention to establish Shiv Sena, a youth organisation, to fight the menace of anti-social elements in Mumbai and to further the non-political cultural interests of Maharashtra. (Mrt. 27.1.64, 17.2.64, 29.10.64)

A lengthy article in the *Navashakti*, in early 1967, written against the background of the Barve-Menon election, reiterated the complaint of crime being on increase in Mumbai, along with the growing heterogeneity of the city's population.

The article described as mischievous an allegation in circulation that Maharashtrians indulged in acts of intimidation and goondaism to obtain votes for Barve. All communities including the Maharashtrian had their black sheep, the writer conceded. However on the basis of 'responsible observation,' the article asserted

(i) that there was a high percentage of South Indians compared to that of Maharashtrians, among the anti-social elements of Mumbai's underworld, and that such Maharashtrian elements played only a second fiddle to the South Indian leaders of the gangs. (ii) that there existed a large percentage of boys from the southern States, among the juvenile delinquents confined to institutional care in correctional schools at Dongri and Matunga in Mumbai. (iii) that the North Indian toughs specialised in unlawful occupation of land while the South Indian elements specialised in bootlegging and (iv) that the Keralites dominated the business of hawking smuggled goods on pavements in the Fort area while the Tamil goondas were the brains behind burglaries and raids on railway and dock-yard goods.

These anti-social elements from the southern States were responsible, according to the article, for creating an atmosphere of intimidation and violence in election campaigns during the Barve-Menon election. These facts, unspoken until then, were revealed only in self-defence, says the author of the article. (Nvs. 12.3.67)

II

The grievances voiced through the content-data presented in this Chapter were echoes of a factual situation which was an inevitable concomitant of the fast expanding metropolis. Tremendous growth of population in Greater Mumbai has been the basic problem from which emanated other problems of the city. It was unavoidable that the sections of society which were lower down on the economic ladder suffered most the misery and the inconveniences caused by overcrowding and shortage of basic civic amenities in the exploding city. The Marathi speaking community happened to be the largest single group of the city which was among the economically poorer sections of the society (see Lakdawala et al. 1963, Tables V-13, V-21) and had to bear the brunt of the inconveniences as the civic crisis deepened.

Growth of Population

Mumbai has been allowed to grow to a sise which inevitably creates miserable living conditions for a very large number of its citizens. Of the four metropolitan cities of India, Kolkata and Mumbai have grown most rapidly. Between a short span of twenty years from 1951 to 1971, Kolkata added nearly 2.7 million while Mumbai added 2.97 million – nearly 3 million people to its population of 1951. Delhi and Madras added only 0.7 and 0.2 million people to their respective population of 1951.

During the thirty years since 1941 the population of Mumbai grew nearly 3 times and the city added to its population, on an average, 1.55 million persons per decade.

Growth of Mumbai's Population

Year	Population (lakh)	Rate of Growth over the Previous dcade
1941	18, 01,356	
1951	29, 94,444	66%
1961	41, 52,056	40%
1971	59, 31,981	43.7%

Source Census of India, Census Tables for Mumbai

On the other hand, the decennial growth rate of population of Maharashtra has been only 23.6 per cent in 1961 and 27.4 per cent in 1971.

Migration

As in the case of other metropolitan cities migration has been a major factor responsible for the rapid growth of the population of Mumbai. While the net increase in Mumbai's population in 1961 was 11.5 lakh, the gross migration to the metropolis during the previous decade was found to be 13.84 lakh. In 1961, more than 60 per cent of population was born outside the metropolis. Among the 26.67 lakh 'migrants' to the city, enumerated by the 1961 Census, those who came during the previous year were no less than 2.9 lakh. It was estimated that about 300 rural families arrived daily in Greater Mumbai region, during the 1960's (Bulsara J. F. 1970, 12) Both push and pull factors – the colossal pressure on land in rural areas and the attraction of the city for employment and other opportunities – simultaneously operated in this situation.

Strain on Civic Services

Such a heavy influx of people made any adequate provision for housing or basic civic services not only difficult but almost impossible. The civic services originally meant for a much smaller population could not but fail to cope with overcrowding on such an enormous scale. The incessant migration, combined with the limited land available in the island city of Mumbai, have led to terrible congestion and housing conditions. In the 1960's the density in some of the areas in Mumbai had reached the record mark of 1, 15,000 to 1, 20,000 persons per sq. mile. (Bulsara J. F. 1970, 337)

The growth of population also strained the water resources available to Mumbai. Water became an increasingly scarce commodity for the citizens of Mumbai during the fifties and throughout the sixties. According to the Report on the Development Plan of the Mumbai Municipal Corporation in 1964, the average per capita consumption of water for daily domestic needs in Mumbai was only about 29 gallons, while the consumption of 75-80 gallons per day is considered as the per capita optimum requirement in tropical cities. Even the average of 29 gallons per capita was, however, a misleading indicator since it did not show the variations in the actual consumption of water in different areas of Mumbai, which varied from 100 to 120 gallons per capita for Malabar Hill, Marine Drive and other posh localities of Mumbai, to per capita 10 gallons or even a smaller quantity, in some of the suburbs and over-crowded localities of the main city. (Bulsara J. F., Marg, June, 1965) Quarrels for water from the public taps in the poorer localities have been a familiar phenomenon in Mumbai. The poorer sections of the city thus bore the brunt of the strains on the civic services of the metropolis.

Economic Growth and Concentration of Population

There exists an inevitable relation between economic activity and population. Basically, the growth of economic activity in Mumbai and the job opportunities created by it attract and maintain the migrants within it. The large-scale migration and fast growth of population in Mumbai, thus were related to the continuous industrial investment and expansion in the city during the fifties and early sixties. The growing industrial activity further afforded a base which invited additional growth of subsidiary and tertiary activities in the island city adding to the city's population. (Gadgil Committee, 1965, 22) According to the *Study on Economic Activity Profile for Mumbai*, employment in Mumbai increased on an average from 16 thousand per year between 1911 and 1951 to 47 thousand per year between 1951 to 1971 (Operations Research Group, Mimeo., 1972, 4-5)

According to the Gadgil Committee Report, the policy of giving licences for establishments of industrial concerns in large numbers within a very small area and stimulating economic activity on the island in other ways has been largely responsible for congestion of population and shortage of housing and civic amenities in Mumbai. (Gadgil Committee, 1965, 21) In other words absence of a well-guided policy for land-use and industrial location combined with the laissez-faire attitude to development of industries during the 1950's, was responsible for congestion, urban sprawl and severe civic problems in Mumbai.

After the formation of Maharashtra State, the new State Government, recognising the need for industrial dispersal from Greater Mumbai and to speed up development of backward areas, set up the Maharashtra Industrial Development Corporation (MIDC) in August 1962. It also introduced elaborate monetary incentives and industrial assistance programmes to promote the dispersal. However, the industrial agglomeration in Greater Mumbai, built up through decades could not be rapidly reversed. Inspite of the efforts of Government organisations like MIDC and SICOM, the location of industries were still overwhelmingly in large metropolitan areas. Consequently though the MIDC achieved dispersal of the new larger industrial units to the Thane-Pune belt by 1970, the smaller industrial establishments continued to expand in the area of Municipal Corporation of Greater Mumbai. (Bhattacharya and Nalapat, Mimeo. March, 1972)

The growth of Mumbai and gravitation of population thus continued even during the seventies.

Housing

The incessant large-scale migration coupled with the geographical features limiting the land available in the city, created complex problems of housing in Mumbai. Simultaneously, the rent control, high prices of land and of building materials etc., restricted the supply of new dwellings to only the better-off, creating a desperate situation for economically weaker sections. (Gadgil Committee, 1965, 18-20; Ramachandran and Pillai, 1972, 2-3)

Ever since the mid-1940s when the city began to expand at a fast-pace, Mumbai has been deficient in housing, especially for the working and the poor classes. With further enormous growth in Mumbai's population, all efforts at providing housing to the city's population were futile. The State Housing Board established in the 1950's and believed to be the biggest agency for social housing in India, with the record construction of 95,000 tenements to its credit, provided housing for 6 lakh persons (Institute of Town Planners, Dec. 1975, 24-26) Inspite of this, the agency failed to cope with the colossal need for adequate shelter in the wake of continuous growth of the city's population.

The scarcity of land coupled with no measures introduced for freezing land prices, added to speculation in real estate. The high cost of building material and labour made it uneconomical for the builder to build for the middle and low income groups who formed a large proportion of population, but had little purchasing power or the power to pay the market rents. With the growth of the city and expansion of the tertiary sector in the late fifties and the sixties, demand for office accommodation increased. Consequently the city suffered the paradox of acute shortage of housing for the middle and low-income groups in the midst of a building boom. During the late sixties there were 17000 ownership flats vacant, while many could not get an adequate roof over their heads. (Ramachandra and Pillai, 1972, 2-3; Desai and Pillai 1972, 47)

The landlords were not interested in repairing and maintaining old buildings. A vacant plot after the collapse of a dilapidated building especially in the main city fetched astronomical prices and it was far more profitable for the landlord to allow the building to go to ruin. A large number of buildings especially in the central city stood in precarious condition due to deliberate neglect by landlords. The cumulative effect of several factors –migration, growth of population, high cost of land, labour, building material, Rent Control Act etc – was the increase in the blighted area of the city and a series of house collapses in every monsoon in the early sixties. During 1956-1971, on an average one hundred and thirteen buildings collapsed each year causing several deaths and injuries. (Mayur R., 1975, 45)

The Mumbai Municipal Corporation conducted a survey of old buildings in the city in 1956-57. The brief 'Report on the Survey of Old Buildings in the City' informs that the old buildings built before 1905 constituted 48.6 per cent of 36,000 residential buildings of the original city with its seven municipal wards. The report presented the ward-wise concentration of old buildings with varying lifespans. The highest percentage of residential buildings with less-than-15-years lifespan was found in G Ward (81.8%) Next in order were D (73.6%) and F (67.5%) wards. Within the city, the G and F wards along with E ward had the largest slum areas. The highest number of families (28,886) likely to be dishoused due to demolition of old houses was in G ward (BMC Survey Report, 1957, Statement XII and Appendix B, pp. 39 and 40)

G, F and D wards happened to be localities with a high percentage of Marathi speakers.

Percentage of three major communities of the most affected wards

	Ward	Community	% of population of the Ward
1.	G Ward	Marathi	58.0%
		Hindi	0.9%
		Gujarati	0.7%
2.	D Ward	Marathi	45.0%
		Gujarati	29.0%
		Urdu	11.4%
3.	F Ward	Marathi	55.0%
		Gujarati	10.7%
		Hindi	0.7%
4.	E Ward	Marathi	42.0%
		Urdu	29.02%
		Gujarati	9.0%

[Source: Census of India, Vol. X, Part X (1-B) Greater Mumbai Census Tables, Table C-V Mother Tongue, p. 185.]

The tales of woe related by the dishoused and displaced residents from the older quarters of the metropolis found in the content data presented earlier, thus are consistent with the objective facts about the housing shortage in the mid-sixties in Mumbai. In the new State of Maharashtra with Mumbai as its capital, the Marathi speaking citizens found this situation extremely intolerable. Their expectations of the kind of life that their capital city should have been able to provide them were sky-high.

When the problem of housing and rehabilitation became very acute it was repeatedly voiced in the Municipal Council and the State Assembly. (Maharashtra Legislative Assembly Debates, 1965, Vol. 17, pp. 205-206, 564-68, 1088-91, 1320, 1476-78; 1966,

Vol. 18 – II, no. 16, no. 18) Ultimately the government took some remedial steps in the matter. The State Government passed a bill in 1969, proposing formation of a Buildings Repair Board to stall the dishousing and 'ejection' of the older residents of the city. (The Mumbai Buildings Repairs and Reconstruction Board Act, 1969) The Building Repair Board began its work in early 1970's. The Board started repairing older buildings giving them a new lease of life. Later it encouraged the tenants to form their own co-operative housing societies to build new buildings in place of older buildings which were beyond repair. (Mht. 22.1.77; T. Ind. 24.1.77)

Slums and Squatter Population
Hutment Colonies

The unchecked influx of population into the city led to a mushrooming of slum dwellers and squatters in the sixties. Hutment colonies emerged and multiplied on vacant lands and the number of pavement dwellers increased. The Study Group on Greater Mumbai and its Housing Panel in fact had cautioned against this desperate situation. (Barve Committee Reports of the panels, 1959, 3)

Using the data of the BMC survey of old buildings in the city, the Study Group on Greater Mumbai mentioned 144 slum areas with a population of 4.15 lakh in the island city (between Colaba and Mahim-Sion), during the late 1950s. (Barve Committee, 1959, appendix V, P. 158; BMC, 1957, Appendix B, p. 40) However, within a decade after that i.e. by 1968, there were 180 hutment colonies in Greater Mumbai according to the data given by the Mumbai Municipal Corporation. Of these, 69 hutment colonies were in the city proper. (Desai and Pillai, 1972, 49) As the Gadgil Committee observed, the hutments became a law and order problem in mid-sixties. (Gadgil Committee, 1965, 20-21)

Pavement Dwellers

According to 1961 Census Report for Greater Mumbai, the metropolis had 62, 000 thousand homeless persons of whom 50, 000 were estimated to be in Mumbai city proper. (Ramachandran

p. 1972, 2-3) This perhaps was a conservative estimate. According to another estimate in the late sixties, there were about two lakh pavement dwellers in Greater Mumbai. (Khanna K.C. T. Ind. 13.2.68) Nearly one-third of the homeless population of Mumbai was concentrated in the municipal ward A in the southern part of the island city. A sample survey of the pavement dwellers conducted during the late sixties (by the Tata Institute of Social Sciences and the Mumbai Civic Trust) found the following percentages of various linguistic-regional groups among the pavement dwellers. Migrants from Maharashtra 19 per cent, Hindi-speaking people from Uttar Pradesh and Madhya Pradesh 19 per cent, from Gujarat 11 per cent, from Tamil Nadu 15 per cent, from Andhra Pradesh 11 per cent, from Mysore 8 per cent and from Kerala 5 per cent. (T. Ind. 24.7.73; Ramachandran p. 1972, Table 17) Together the migrants from the four southern States accounted for 39 per cent of the total pavement dwellers.

Combining the populations of old slums, hutment colonies and pavements of Greater Mumbai, it was estimated that about 10 lakh people were living in Mumbai's slums by the end of 1960s, besides the daily influx of hundreds of families into the city. (Bulsara J.F. 1970, 353) The Maharashtra State Housing Board had constructed 90,000 tenements in the urban areas of Maharashtra. Of these 60,000 were located in Greater Mumbai. In spite of this, Mumbai was short of 3, 85,000 housing units in 1971. (Mht. 2.7.73; Mayur R., 1975, 45) A large number of rural migrants to the metropolis had no option but to live in hutments.

What was the percentage of migrants from various States in this slum population? In the absence of specific data it is difficult to arrive at any conclusion. Desai and Pillai (1972, Tables 4 and 5) found in the population of the hutment slum of Golibar Maidan on Western Express Highway in North Mumbai, about 40 to 45 per cent dwellers from Maharashtra, about 30 per cent dwellers from Hindi speaking States, about 4 per cent from Gujarat and about 13 per cent from the southern States. However, the non-Marathi speaking communities together were in a higher proportion than Marathi speakers in this slum, as in most of the other slums.

It is this large proportion of migrants from outside the state that made Thackeray and his Shiv Sena call for a halt to migration to Mumbai. This proportion of the Marathi speaking among the slum dwellers during the sixties, seemed to be consistent with the proportion of the Marathi speaking (nearly 44 per cent), in Mumbai's total population by 1961 Census. (See Ch. VI) The number of Maharashtrian slum dwellers, however, seems to have increased disproportionately in the seventies.

The Growth of Slum-Population during the 1970s

The severe famine conditions in Maharashtra during 1972-73 seem to have caused an increase in the percentage of Maharashtrians in the slum population of Mumbai. During these famine years large numbers of landless labourers arrived in the city with their families and settled in Mumbai in hutments, on pavements and by the side of the railway stations. (Mht. 20.7.73, 23.2.75; T. Ind. 30.9.74, 2.11.75)

In 1976, the Maharashtra State Government jointly with the Municipal Corporation carried out an ambitious survey of Greater Mumbai's 847 hutment colonies, before the launch of a slum improvement programme. (T. Ind. 5.1.76) The survey covered unauthorised structures on Municipal, State and private land in Mumbai, excluding those on the vacant plots owned by the Central Government. In other words the survey covered 97.4 per cent of the hutments in Mumbai. The huts were numbered and families were registered. In this survey, it was found that these hutments included 2, 62,629 tenements in 1, 10,312 structures which housed 2, 55,795 families with a total population of 11, 10,448. (Mht. 16.1.76; T. Ind. 16.1.76) Among these hutment dwellers, 20 per cent were migrants from Hindi speaking States. Percentage of migrants from Southern States was not available. Migrants from Maharashtra were found to be 47 per cent, one-third of whom came from Ratnagiri district alone. The percentage of the Marathi speaking among the hutment dwellers thus suggests an increase.

Under the mounting pressure of population and the growth of hutments, the Maharashtra Government initiated legal measures for improvement of slum conditions in Mumbai and other cities.

It passed the Maharashtra Slum Areas (Improvement, Clearance and Re-development) Act (1971), Slum Improvement Board Act (1973), and Slum Areas (Improvement, Clearance and Re-development, Amendment Act (1976) Apart from undertaking slum improvement programmes, the State Government passed in 1973, an amendment to the Rent Control Act which had added to the complexity of Mumbai's housing problem. (T. Ind. 3.3.73; Maharashtra Government Gazette Extra. 31.3.73 p. 68) Following the lead given by the BPCC Seminar on developmental needs of Mumbai in August 1974, the State and the Municipal Governments adopted a firm policy regarding the problems of hawkers and beggars which had by then acquired a threatening proportion and created a law-and-order problem.

The Maharashtra Government's Minister of State for Housing (Prabhakar Kunte) in his detailed note on slum improvement presented at a BPCC Meeting, pointed out that the colossal problem of hutments in Mumbai, could not be solved without Central Government's sumptuous financial aid. Referring to this in an editorial, a prestigious Marathi newspaper (Maharashtra Times) demanded of the Central Government a larger share in the financial responsibility of Mumbai's slum improvement programme. The crisis of housing in Mumbai was an inevitable result of the continuous large-scale migration of population into Mumbai from all over the country; the editorial argued that housing in Mumbai was therefore, a national problem, which needed the Centre's attention and financial aid. (Mht. Ed. 25.1.75)

Scale of Migration, the Root Cause of Mumbai's Problems

During the 1970's the call to put a check on the influx of population to Mumbai did not come only from Bal Thackeray and his followers. Alarmed at the fast expanding population of pavement and hutment-dwellers in Mumbai, responsible persons from various walks of life including Central Ministers began to caution about the pace of migration to Mumbai and asked for urgent measures to put a check on it. (T. Ind. 24.3.73; 1.8.76, 26.12.76; Mht. 26.6.74, 25.1.75, 12.04.75, 19.6.75, 26.12.76)

In 1975, the Maharashtra Government appointed a high-level

committee to find out ways to stall the influx of beggars to the city. (T. Ind. 21.3.75) The Committee was to examine the possibility of issuing work-permits to newcomers to the metropolis. (Mht. Ed. 25.1.75) The proposal followed the recommendations of a seminar on beggars' problems, held in 1974.

Migration and the Beggar Problem

An important seminar on 'The Prevention of Begging and Rehabilitation of Beggars' sponsored by the Indian Council for Social Welfare, Mumbai, and the Central Bureau of Correctional services, Government of India in 1974, suggested a work-permit for entry to Mumbai for controlling the beggar population.

It was revealed during the seminar that more than one-third (65,000) of the total estimated beggar population of the Maharashtra State (1, 50,000), was found in Greater Mumbai alone. Of the total beggar population of the State, nearly 60% or 90,000 beggars had migrated from other States and the number of beggars coming from 'South India' far exceeded that of the beggars from 'North India'.

Maharashtra had 21 beggars' homes and very limited funds that could take care of about 5,000 beggars only. This provision was inadequate in the face of the colossal nature of the problem. The participants at the Seminar suggested that a legal provision for repatriation of the large number of out-of-state beggars could help reduce the enormously heavy load on the city and a proposal for a work-permit for new entrants to the city was mooted.

The seminar in its concluding session made recommendations for a uniform national policy for eradication of beggary and framing of a model act by the Central Government. It suggested the inclusion of a clause in the Prevention of Begging Act that would empower the Court to transfer the convicted beggars from the State where they were found begging, to the State of their origin. (Report of the Seminar, ICSW, Mumbai, Nov. 26, 1974, pp.11, 22-25, 33, 45)

Nearly one-third of the total number of beggars in Mumbai – i.e. 20-25,000 - were said to be lepers. (Mht. Ed. 9.1.76) In 1974, the Maharashtra Minister for Health informed the State Legislature that the number of leprosy-afflicted persons in the State had increased by 20,000 within a span of two years between 1971 and 1973. (Mht. 11.4.74) The use of lepers for carrying contraband rice and illicit liquor was well-known. (T. Ind. 22.8.75, 14.12.75; Lks. 10.12.75; Mht. Letters 17.6.76) Earlier in the sixties, the Study Team on Prohibition appointed by the Government of India, also had drawn attention to the employment of lepers for transporting illicit liquor and had observed that majority of these lepers came from Salem District of Madras State. (Report of the Study Team on Prohibition, 1964, Vol. 1, 139-140)

This was the context of the appointment of a high-level committee to consider the proposal for introducing work-permits to new entrants to the city. The proposal and the Shiv Sena's vocal support to it were severely criticised in the national English press. (T. Ind. 2.7.73, 22.3.75) A *Maharashtra Times* editorial on the other hand justified the appointment of the Committee. It even mentioned the support of the BPCC for the proposed measures. (Mht. Ed. 25.1.75)

In March 1976, the State Government launched 'Operation Beggars' to round them up and send the able-bodied beggars to work centres run by the State Government. In the following month, it passed the Mumbai Prevention of Begging and Mumbai Police (Amendment), Act, to provide adequate legal sanction to the measures adopted by the Government to counter the beggar problem. (T. Ind. 2.4.76, 5.3.76 and 12.3.76; Mah. Government Gazette extra – 18.4.76, p. 108) The proposal for work permits, however, was never put into practice.

Both push-and-pull factors were responsible for the heavy flow of rural migrants to the metropolis. In the absence of planned programme for rural development and improvement in agriculture and other primary occupations to create economic opportunities in rural areas, mere curb on entry to the metropolis through the work-permit cannot be a proper or final solution to the problem nor is it easily implemented. However, in the desperate situation of Mumbai, issuing work-permits perhaps may have proved useful to curb heavy migration to the city and to check the flow of beggars and vagrants. It could at least have served to pressurise the Central Government to frame a national policy and a planned programme of urbanisation. It could have spurred other States and the Central Government to launch large-scale rural development programmes which alone could halt the heavy flow of migrants from all over the country to Mumbai.

The Rural Employment Guarantee Scheme of Maharashtra State

During the mid-70s, the Maharashtra Government was forced to take notice of the famine conditions in Maharashtra, which rendered thousands of agricultural workers destitute. Rural migration to the metropolis in the wake of 1972-73 famine in Maharashtra, added to Mumbai's poorest sections of population. The State Government at this stage had to take some remedial steps. It evolved and introduced the Employment (Wage) Guarantee Scheme in the rural areas of Maharashtra State experimentally in 1972 to control the uprooting of the rural population and to curb the city-ward migration of the rural population and landless labourers. Two years later, the scope of the scheme was extended to smaller towns. (See Sadhu A., T.Ind. 7.5.75; Khanna K.C. T.Ind. 20.9.76) The implementation of the Employment Guarantee Scheme was a pioneer effort in the right direction - the first necessary step both for rural development and planned programme of urbanisation in India.

The Hawker Problem

The hawker problem was only a part of the larger problem of Mumbai's exploding population due to migration.

The hawker population of Mumbai was estimated to be 100,000 in 1970. A majority of these hawkers were without licences. During 1973, only 15,000 hawkers were licencees, while nearly 1, 35,000 carried on their 'businesses' without licences. (T. Ind., Ed. 29.6.73) With unemployment looming large even Mumbai with the average annual increase of 47,000 jobs from 1951-1970, was unable to provide employment to a large number of incoming migrants. In the absence of jobs, many of them turned to self-employment. Hawking goods was one of the easier ways for a migrant to earn a livelihood.

When the Shiv Sena was elected as the second largest party in the Municipal Corporation in March 1968, it pressurised the administration into adopting a firmer policy of licensing and into activating the Encroachment Department to take action against those without licences. The hawkers reacted aggressively to the Civic Government's campaign to remove them from pedestrian areas. In South Mumbai the hawkers gheraoed the Magistrate of the Mobile Court which looked into encroachment cases. The police then had to resort to a lathi charge. (Ind. Exp. 4.3.74; Mht. 15.6.74)

In a sequel to the police eviction of hawkers from the Fort Area, the hawkers filed a suit in 1974 against the Municipal Corporation for refusing to renew their licences and sought a mandatory order compelling the Corporation to issue licences to hawkers. The Court however dismissed the suit and pointed out that the hawkers had no 'right' but only 'liberty' to sell their goods and that the hawkers could not claim as a matter of right under the Mumbai Municipal Corporation Act, either the renewal of their licences or a hearing. (T. Ind. 4.9.76)

In mid-70s, the Civic Government experimented with demarcated zones for hawkers in Dadar during evening peak hours (after 5 p.m.) for a short period of time.

CHAPTER V

ECONOMIC ASPIRATIONS

The demand of Thackeray's Shiv Sena was 'eighty per cent of jobs for Maharashtrians – the sons of the soil'. It caught people's imagination and earned the Shiv Sena a large following in its early days. But it was this demand which also stamped it as 'parochial' movement. Where lay the secret of the Shiv Sena's popularity? Was it the large-scale unemployment which made it popular? Unemployment was a widespread phenomenon in India not particular to the Maharashtrian community in Mumbai. Why was such a demand not articulated in other metropolitan cities – at least in the cities with cosmopolitan populations – like Bengaluru or Kolkata? The rise of the Shiv Sena in Mumbai throws up these and many more questions.

Material success is very important to people everywhere. Revolutionary theorists have often seen in economic values, a crucial potential for social unrest – rebellion, revolution or a protest movement. A study based on a cross-national survey of human concerns by H. Cantril, covering 863 million people of twelve nations has borne this out. The survey found that material values were the most salient of values to most people. For example, hopes and fears about standards of living, health, technological advances, economic stability and owning a house or land, were the material values, the survey found, of greatest concern to most people. ('The Pattern of Human Concerns', G.V. Ted R. Gurr, 1970, p. 69) In a poor country like India, job and employment opportunities along with housing, would weigh most heavily on people's minds.

Our data from six journals consists of a total of 399 entries in the category of Economic Aspirations. These entries are distributed in the following sub-themes. (i) Jobs and Employment (ii) Entry to Business and Industry (iii) Educational and Professional Training Opportunities (iv) Food and Related Issues (v) A small number of entries which express the regional community's grievances over the Central Government's financial allocation to the State. These entries are put under Centre-State Grievances. The number of entries in this category is however, very small - only twelve.

Apart from the large number of entries in the first two categories, there are a good many entries including letters, which express serious concern regarding educational and training opportunities for the youth, in preparation for employment or a career. Most of these letters are from urban areas. The entries under 'Food and Related Issues' articulated grievances relating to more basic needs like the shortage of foodgrains, water scarcity, deprivation of land, etc. The break-up of the entries in the content-data is as follows

	Letters	Editorials Articles	Reports and
1. Jobs and Employment	39	23	123
2. Entry to Business and Industry	15	11	33
3. Educational and Professional Training Opportunities	34	6	48
4. Food and Related Issues	14	8	34
5. Centre-State Grievances	--	2	10
	102	50	247
	Total No. of Entries		399
	(Entries from *Marmik*)		66

In addition, there are sixty-six entries from seven issues of the *Marmik*, which, if included, would make the total number of our entries in the section of Economic Aspirations, 465.

These sixty six entries are part of the *Marmik's* survey of the executive cadres in Mumbai's offices, in support of its complaint against clan-nepotism of the outsiders and injustice to the locals. Though we have taken note of the content of these entries, to avoid bias we did not put these on the affective scale.

The most important items of the data are letters, as in the previous chapter. The editorials and the news reports and articles mostly follow the issues raised in the letters or issues related to them.

A glance at the table showing the distribution of entries on the affective scale shows that the highest number of entries is from the years 1965 to 1967. The number of consolidated entries from three genres of writing letters, reports, articles and editorials (see Table v.1), is the highest for the year 1965; so also is the number of entries in the category of reports or of editorials. The number of letters however reaches a peak in 1966. Could it be that the letters were written in response to the *Marmik's* propaganda and the call of the Shiv Sena? Many of the letters, however, are from other journals. All the letters from 1966, except seven, actually precede the birth of the Shiv Sena in June 1966. Most of the letters which fall in the second half of the year are from journals other than the *Marmik*.

Along with the number of entries, the intensity responses on the Affective Index Points of As (Aspiration), Gr (Grievances), Fr/In (Frustration-Insecurity), Pr (Protest), De (Demand) and Ca (Call-for-Action) also rise fast in 1965 and then upto 1967. However, both the number of entries as well as the intensity responses begins to fall 1967 onwards.

While collecting the data, I had no clear idea of the pattern that might emerge when the data was classified theme-wise and distributed on the Affective Scale. However, the pattern is unmistakable. The pattern clearly indicates the widespread dissatisfaction of the Maharashtrian community with their economic status, which rose to a crescendo around 1965-66. The close parallel between the grievances and frustrations reflected in the content-data from the press and the Shiv Sena's demands, is striking.

When the Shiv Sena raised the slogan of 'priority for the sons of the soil in jobs in Mumbai' its contention was that the large influx of people from outside Maharashtra, especially from the Southern States, was responsible for the shrinkage of economic opportunities for the local people. It brought about a rapid fall in the percentage of Maharashtrians in employment in Mumbai, even as it placed Maharashtrians at a disadvantage in getting residential accommodation.

Surprisingly, similar fears and doubts were found expressed in the five score letters in our data during the decade (1961-70), the majority (62) of which date prior to the birth of the Shiv Sena. Many a letter finds a corresponding voice in reports, articles and editorials.

The Shiv Sena's voicing of 'injustice to the locals' and 'priority for the sons of the soil', was apparently a crystallisation or articulation of the already simmering frustration and resentment of the community. The *Marmik's* strident propaganda might have aggravated it, but does not seem to have created it.

Table V – 1
Economic Aspirations
Distribution of Entries on the Affective Scale
Letters, Editorials, Reports and Articles (Consolidated)

Index Points	AS	GR IN	FR/	PR	DE	CA	Total Intensity Value	No. of Entries
Index Value	1	2	3	4	5	6		
Year								
1960	5	3	-	-	-	-	11	4
1961	4	3	-	-	-	-	10	4
1962	2	2	2	4	-	-	28	4
1963	7	17	2	2	1	1	66	24
1964	6	13	9	11	4	-	123	37
1965	8	30	36	26	7	2	327	90
1966	6	24	17	23	7	6	268	71

1967	8	24	19	24	14	5	309	82
1968	2	2	5	13	11	2	140	31
1969	2	7	1	3	-	-	31	15
1970	4	7	2	5	3	1	65	22

Total No. of Entries		399
Letters	102	
Editorials		50
Reports and Articles		247
Additional Entries from		
Marmik	66	
	165	

I

Content Data

1. Jobs and Employment

Letters

Several of the letters published between 1964 and 1968 voice a common complaint, that of the 'injustice' to the 'local' man i.e. Maharashtrian in recruitment to jobs. These letters complain of a disproportionately large number of appointments of South Indians in offices allegedly through nepotism and clan-favouritism, and of a disproportionately small number of Marathi persons, who as the natives of the State ought to get a major or at least a fair share of jobs at all levels, especially in their own State and *in their own State capital.*

The letters also complain of infiltration of workers from outside Maharashtra. The management and recruiting officials being non-Maharashtrian, gave preference to non Maharashtrians.

(Mht. 17.12.64, 30.7.66; Nvs. 20.7.65, 6.12.65; Lks. 14.8.65; Mrm. 22.8.65, 6.3.66, 5.3.67, 2.7.67, 28.1.68, 7.3.68, 12.8.70)

There are also some letters with more specific grievances about recruitment mal-practices in certain industries and offices.

(Mrt. 10.9.66, 22.4.67, 28.6.68; Mht. 21.4.70; Mrm. 29.8.65, 5.6.65, 16.1.66, 19.6.66, 17.7.66, 17.9.67, 8.10.67, 9.6.68, 11.10.70)

Reports and Articles

A number of reports and articles speak of incidents of malpractice in recruitment to jobs and of injustice to the local man in certain industries and offices, chiefly in and around Mumbai. These included the grievances of Marathi dock workers, of goods transport workers, infiltration of workers from outside Maharashtra in private industries like National Rayon and Sandoz and favouritism in recruitment in public sector offices and factories like Hindustan Antibiotics in Pimpri, MIG, Hindustan Aeronautics in Nasik and the office of the State Electricity Board. Most of these entries are from the mid-sixties, chiefly between 1965 and 1967.

The *Marmik* survey already referred to, had covered (the *Marmik* claimed) 1500 executive posts in various establishments of private industrial houses and several public sector offices. According to the *Marmik*, only 5 per cent of the executive posts went to Maharashtrians. The *Marmik's* lists were only rarely challenged and appeared to be objective. However, we have not included these entries for our analysis of the Affective Scale.

Reports (Mrt. 29.7.62, 30.9.62, 24.9.64, 4.11.64, 15.10.64, 1.12.64, 15.1.65, 21.2.65, 10.4.65, 15.4.65, 1.7.65, 2.8.65, 16.8.65, 9.12.65, 13.4.67, 9.10.67, 13.11.67, 4.5.68; Nvs. 3.6.65, 4.6.65, 16.10.65, 10.12.65; Mrm. 5.1.69)

Apart from these reports of specific complaints, there is a large number (42) of reported statements and speeches by the community leaders of various persuasions - leaders of political parties, of trade unions, of social and political workers, members of the State Legislature etc. - which corroborate or voice these and similar grievances. It is clear from these entries that the question of injustice to the 'local' and lack of priority for him in employment in Maharashtra was reportedly raised by members of both the opposition (including CPI) and the ruling parties in the State Legislature, as early as 1964. The Sampoorna Maharashtra Samiti, which supported Menon in the 1967 elections and staunchly opposed the Shiv Sena, also had included in its election manifesto, the demand for 70 to 80 per cent of jobs for Marathi people in Mumbai.

Reports (Nvs. 11.4.67, 12.4.67, 13.4.67, 14.4.67, 15.4.67, 10.8.67; Nvk. 20.2.65, 10.8.67, 5.5.70, 22.2.70; Mrt. 26.3.64, 31.7.64, 20.2.65, 1.3.65, 4.3.65, 25.3.65, 31.3.65, 14.4.66, 21.3.67, 3.8.67, 7.8.67, 9.8.67, 10.8.67, 11.2.68, 13.3.68, 21.3.68, 12.4.68; Mht. 3.8.67, 6.12.68, 7.1.70, 7.3.70, 14.12.72; Mrm. 2.7.67, 1.5.66 Lks. 8.7.67, 24.1.68; Kes. 1.10.68. Also see appendix a. V- a, 18-19)

A good many editorials and a few articles and letters evince interest in the theoretical and constitutional aspects of the question of priority for the natives of the State in jobs and other economic opportunities. These editorials are also concerned about the factors responsible for the increasing grievances of the Maharashtrian community.

Letters (Mrt. 3.4.65; Nvk. 25.5.66; Lks. 28.3.67, 1.6.67)

Editorials (Nvs. 29.4.61, 4.6.65; Nvk. 23.5.64, 4.8.67, 11.8.67, 21.1.68, 23.7.70; Mrt. 20.3.67; Mht. 21.11.68; Mrm. 11.4.65, 15.6.65; Kes. 20.1.68; Lks. 15.12.72)

Articles (Mht. 2.5.64; Mrt. 21.12.66, 20.4.67; Nvs. 9.4.67; Mrm. 5.6.66, 20.4.67, 20.8.67, 3.9.67; Nvk. 29.5.70, Kes. 20.10.66, 1.10.67, 7.5.67, 31.1.68)

Besides these entries directly related to the question of employment, a few entries of the period are related to the issues like closure of industries in Mumbai. These entries, mainly editorials (10) and reports and articles (40), are concerned with the closure of several of the textile and engineering units and growing unemployment in Mumbai in the mid-sixties. A number of reports and a few articles also deal with the question of shifting of some of the public sector production units like the Electronics Division of the Atomic Energy from Mumbai and the Vehicle Research and Development from Ahmednagar to outside the State. This news had given rise to considerable resentment in the minds of the people. These grievances hardly found expression in letters from readers, perhaps because of the institutionalised channels of trade unions, already available for ventilating grievances in these areas. The majority of the entries in these sections are from the *Daily Maratha*.

Editorials (Mrt. 22.12.64, 15.4.65, 22.11.66, 15.12.66, 30.12.66, 20.6.67, 25.5.63; Mht. 1.12.66; Kes. 15.1.68)

Reports and Articles

Closure and Flight of Industry

(Nvs. 14.7.68, 21.7.68; Nvk. 27.5.65, 30.4.70; Mrt. 28.8.64, 7.9.64, 9.9.64, 21.1.65, 22.11.66, 14.12.66, 19.12.66, 30.12.66, 12.1.67, 13.1.67, 6.3.67, 13.3.67, 3.4.67, 7.4.67, 11.4.67, 21.5.67, 2.6.67, 20.6.67, 3.6.67, 25.3.69; Mrm. 15.1.67, 26.3.67, 17.9.67; Lks. 10.2.67)

Unemployment and Recession

(Mrt. 4.3.64, 2.12.65, 8.12.65, 16.12.65, 7.11.65, 8.11.65, 12.11.65, 15.11.65, 25.11.65, 16.4.68; Mrm. 9.1.66; Kes. 1.1.60, 8.1.60)

In the midst of these stories of unemployment and malpractice, a few entries are people's reactions to the vital issues affecting their lives. A few letters appeal to the community leaders to redress these issues before attending to any other matter. Some other letters evince greater self-reliance and declare plans and programmes to fight the evils of unemployment and injustice through organised efforts. Some announce establishment of centres for guidance to job seekers.

There are reports of efforts also at the level of political parties. The Peasants and Workers Party had announced its plans to start a youth organisation as well as an agitation to press the question of unemployment of Maharashtrian youth, two years after the rise of the Shiv Sena.

Letters (Mrt. 17.2.66, 7.9.66, 29.5.67, 8.6.67; Mrt. 15.7.66; Nvk. 3.9.65)

2. Entry to Business and Industry

About a dozen letters discuss the absence of Maharashtrians in business and industry of the metropolis or of the State. Most of the letters in this section express concern over the low economic status of the community and the community's reduced share in the control of the city's economy. However, simultaneously, the letters express the hope that Maharashtrian entrepreneurship would carve out a niche for itself with co-operative effort and Government assistance. This articulation of new aspirations had a special context, as the letters reveal, that of the formation of the linguistic community's own State of united Maharashtra with Mumbai as its capital. Five years after the birth of the new State, was apparently the right time for assessment of the community's limitations and for defining new goals.

Letters (Nvs. 26.1.64, 21.12.64, 1.6.65, 27.7.65, 6.12.66; Nvk. 29.5.62, 21.5.64; 3 Letters, 3.9.65, 22.9.66; 2 Letters, 3.12.66; Mrm. 2.7.67, 5.5.68; Lks. 28.5.69; Nvk. 13.5.74; 2 Letters)

Reports and Articles (Nvk. 28.4.60, 20.6.60, 19.3.61, 17.1.63, 26.7.64, 6.10.67, 10.10.68, Mrt. 26.4.64, 9.6.65, 20.6.65, 8.2.69; Mht. 6.12.66, 1.10.67, 8.10.67, 10.12.67, 13.1.70; Mrm. 12.6.66, 8.7.67, 4.5.70)

Editorials

The editorials also discuss the possibilities and programmes of building up business and industry through Maharashtrian effort, entrepreneurship and co-operation. These are also dilations on and exercises in self-assessment and self-criticism.

Editorials (Nvs. 10.10.61, Nvk. 21.4.61, 20.11.63, 27.7.64, 6.10.67, 5.5.70, 14.2.70; Mrt. 18.1.65, 2.12.65, 21.8.68; Mht. 12.7.67)

Reports and Articles

The reports and articles cover a wider range of subjects. Some of the reports, for example, speak about the various instances of how the existing Maharashtrian businessmen or new aspirants to the field, had to face handicaps due to lack of capital, lack of community support and keen competition from the large, well-established non-Maharashtrian enterprises in the world of commerce and industry.

There are articles which severely criticise the concentration of commercial and industrial development in and around Mumbai to the exclusion of other regions of the State. These articles hold this disparity responsible for the growing sense of deprivation among Maharashtrians.

A majority of these reports and articles are from pre Shiv Sena days.

Reports and Articles (Mrt. 21.3.64, 14.3.65, 12.5.65; Sanj. Mrt. 22.5.65; Mrt. 18.8.65, 18.3.68, 8.8.68; Mrm. 8.5.66, 24.7.66)

3. Educational and Professional Training Opportunities

A large number of entries, nearly a hundred, next only to those on the question of employment, reveal the concern of the community about the educational and professional opportunities available for its youth, these being valuable means of realising economic aspirations.

i) Nearly one-third of the entries on this vital subject, are letters from readers of the journals. The readers' letters are concerned with both the opportunities available and the performance of the youth. Many of these letters express dissatisfaction over lack of a 'fair' share for the Maharashtrian community in the opportunities for specialised and higher training available in the State. A majority of these appear to voice concerns of the urban-educated middle class.

ii) Another complaint was that Marathi youth had fewer opportunities to enter professional courses subsidised by the State, such as nursing, technology, medicine and engineering.

Letters repeatedly complained about the absence of training facilities outside metropolitan Mumbai and undue emphasis on the English language as the medium of examination, which practically excluded Marathi girls from training and job opportunities in the nursing profession. (Nvs. 11.8.65, 27.1.66; Nvk. 16.10.68, 11.4.70)

Readers complained against the reservation of a disproportionately large share of seats for youth from outside Maharashtra that deprived the Maharashtrian youth of his fair share. According to some of the letters the opportunities available in the State were far too few in relation to the total population of Maharashtra. The reservation of seats for students from other provinces and even from other countries was therefore totally unfair to candidates from the State.

Letters (Mrt. 1.2.63, 18.6.65, 22.7.66; Lks. 4.7.66; Mrm. 16.6.68, 1.12.68)

Editorials (Nvk. 4.2.63; Mht. 18.1.63; Mrm. 8.8.65; Lks. 1.4.69)

Reports and Articles (Nvs. 1.5.66; Mrm. 11.9.66, 24.3.68, 21.6.70; Mrt. 28.11.64, 8.3.65, 24.3.65, 8.4.65, 17.5.65, 18.6.65, 6.8.65, 2.12.65, 2.9.67, 29.4.68; Mht. 16.1.69)

iii) The sore points voiced in letters, reports and articles as well as editorials were many. One of them was the small percentage of Maharashtrian candidates in the Indian Administrative Service. Many letters and reports allude to this theme. Another was the small proportion of Marathi cadets in the national Defence Academy established in 1960 in Maharashtra. In 1962, the State Home Minister drew attention to the fact that in spite of the Maharashtrians' conception of themselves as great warriors and freedom-fighters, there were only 3 Maharashtrian (Marathi speaking) cadets among the 900 cadets in the National Defence Academy at Khadakvasla, near Pune. (Mrt. 23.7.62) This continued to be a point of recurring concern and debate, as evidenced by a number of entries on the subject in our press data.

Letters Nvs. 31.7.62, 1.1.64; Nvk. 30.7.62, 12.2.63, 3.3.66 (5 letters)

Mht. 24.1.63, 25.1.63, 19.2.63, 26.3.63, 8.3.63, 4.2.69, 14.2.69 (2 letters) 1.5.69, 15.5.69

Mrs. 3.3.63; Mrt. 20.4.66; Lks. 17.7.70

Editorials Lks. 9.6.70, 11.7.70

Reports and Articles Nvk. 1.2.60, 27.1.63, 23.2.65, 3.5.65

Mrt. 23.7.62, 13.3.62, 1.1.63, 8.1.63, 17.3.63, 29.7.63, 8.5.67, 18.7.67, 26.3.69

Mht. 11.2.63, 19.2.63, 30.1.65, 3.5.65, 20.4.69, 27.5.69

Lks. 20.10.65, 12.5.66

Lack of proper command over the English language and higher minimum age requirement for entrance to primary schools in Maharashtra, were considered to be the obstacles in the way of Maharashtrian boys aspiring for success in these careers.

iv) Yet another grievance voiced by some of the letter-writers and a few reports was about the gradual disappearance or closure of Marathi medium schools in various parts of Mumbai including older residential localities of the city. According to the reports, the Maharashtrian educational institutions were finding it difficult to obtain accommodation either for starting new schools or for expanding the older established ones. High cost of land and the affluence of other communities who could afford to buy land at higher prices, was forcing a retreat of Marathi educational and training institutions in Maharashtra's capital.

Letters (Mht. 26.3.63, 9.4.70)

Reports (Mrt. 1.7.66, 11.7.66, 1.10.66, 13.5.67)

The Marathi community's outward movement from old residential localities of South-central Mumbai, in the wake of changes in the city, mentioned earlier, seems to have affected these schools also.

4. Food and Related Issues

The years 1964 to 1967 were drought years in various districts of Maharashtra. The year 1965-66 was the worst. These famine conditions hit mostly the peripheral and backward regions of the State such as the Konkan, which even otherwise suffered from chronic food shortage due to poverty, and indifferent communication and transport services. This situation is reflected in the fifty-six entries on the theme of 'Food and Related Issues.'

Reports and Articles (34)

The news from the hinterland, during this period, consists of reports of scarcity and famine conditions, especially in the rural areas of Thane, Kolhapur, Solapur, Nasik, Vidarbha and Ratnagiri districts, of long queues at fair-price foodgrain shops and of the poor subsisting on leaves and roots in the tribal tracts of Thane district adjacent to Mumbai.

Editorials

The editorials echo the grievances of the people already conveyed by the reports and letters from readers. One of the editorials consisted of a story of a Warli (a tribal) driven to sell his child to save its life ('Rama Sukha Warli sells his child for five rupees.' Mrt. Ed. 6.7.66)

These editorials criticised the State Government for not taking sufficient precautionary steps to avoid inconvenience to people. However, the editorials hold the Central Government responsible for insufficient allocation of foodgrains to Maharashtra, which was known to be lacking in self-sufficiency in food supplies and which had to face simultaneously the formidable problem of providing food to the vast urban population of Mumbai consisting of a large number of migrants from other States.

Letters

The letters from the rural and backward areas of the Konkan and other districts speak of extreme scarcity conditions; lack of food stocks in shops, shortage of fair-price grain-shops, of the threat of starvation deaths in the region and urge speedy help from the State Government and other agencies. The year 1967 also saw the Bihar famine. A letter from the Konkan complains that the far-off Bihar famine received much more attention and financial help in Mumbai while the extreme famine conditions in the nearby Konkan remained relatively unnoticed. (Mrt. 30.3.67)

Letters from urban centres also express intense grievance at the meagre supply of foodgrains especially of rice, at the fair price shops in Mumbai. The abundant food supply available in neighbouring States inevitably led to the charge that the Central Government had discriminated against Maharashtra.

Another issue written about, both in the letters, reports and articles, was the restriction imposed by the Central and State Governments on inter-state movement of foodgrains and edible oils which were in short supply in Maharashtra, while sugar produced in Maharashtra was available all over the country without restriction. (Mrt. 10.6.63, 31.5.65, 20.5.67, 21.5.67)

Another group of entries, small in number but significant in content, consist of people's reactions and responses to the disparity in the prosperity of the urban areas and the poverty in the under-developed backward areas of the State.

Among these are reports of protest by villagers about a scheme for water supply to metropolitan Mumbai.

A letter also lambasts the neglect of the development of the railways in Maharashtra, especially in the Konkan. This was in spite of the fact that the first train in India ran between Mumbai and Thane, hundred years ago. (Mrt. 7.2.64) There is also an article which notes that the devastation in Ratnagiri caused by a terrible typhoon that hit the Konkan coast in November 1966, remained unnoticed both in Mumbai and in Delhi.

Reports and Articles (Mrt. 23.2.63, 2.4.64, 5.12.64)

Letters (Nvs. 15.7.75; Mrm. 8.5.66, 19.6.66, 21.8.66; Mrm. 8.6.63, 7.2.64, 14.1.66, 6.2.66, 25.3.66, 30.3.66, 8.7.66, 10.9.66, 30.3.67, 8.4.67)

Editorials (Mrt. 24.12.64, 15.6.65, 28.6.65, 2.7.65, 12.8.65, 6.7.66, 16.4.68; Mrm. 22.5.66)
Reports and Articles (Nvk. 1.2.60, 27.1.63, 23.2.65, 3.5.65, Nvs. 1.5.66; Mht. 11.2.63, 19.2.63, 30.1.65, 3.5.65; Lks. 20.10.65, 12.5.66; Mrm. 29.1.61, 31.3.63, 11.9.66, 24.3.68, 21.6.70; Mrt. 19 reports)

5. Centre-State Grievances

In the federal structure of India, the tug-of-war between the Centre and the States for greater share of financial resources seems inevitable. Twelve entries on the subject in our data are drawn from two editorials and ten news reports. Although there is not a single letter on the subject, we included these entries in our analysis because they seemed closely related to the various problems of Mumbai – the basis of the regionalist movement.

Editorials

The editorials, as well as the reports, articulate a common grievance in relation to the Central Government. The grievance concerned non-recognition of the special needs of Maharashtra and inadequate financial allocations to the State by the Central Government.

Editorials (Mrt. 29.3.62, 7.7.65)

Reports and Articles

According to the reports, the grievance was voiced as early as 1962 and repeatedly echoed throughout the sixties by various spokesmen of the State Government in the Central Legislature.

Mumbai, which is a source of a great deal of India's industrial and commercial wealth, also accounts for a large share of revenue to the Central Government through direct levies like income, corporate, wealth taxes and excise duties. According to the Minister for Urban Development of the State (R. Zakaria), Mumbai's contribution was nearly one-third of the Centre's total revenue through these taxes. The grievance expressed by the Minister was that, of the total revenue collected in Mumbai, Maharashtra State received only a very small percentage. (Mrt. 17.5.65)

Maharashtra's Finance Minister had also complained earlier in 1962 that the State received a share of only 5.73 per cent of the total revenue resources of the country while the State's population was 9.16 per cent of the nation's total population. (Mrt. 28.3.62; also Maharashtra Legislative Assembly Debates, March 1962, Vol. VI, Pt. II, No. 9, pp. 281-285)

It is true that, upon the recommendations of successive Finance Commissions, Maharashtra's proportionate share in direct taxation was becoming a progressively reduced proportion of the total budgetary resources. Also, being considered a rich and a progressive State, Maharashtra was not entitled to the Central Government's grants-in-aid, available under the provisions of Federal Finance. On the other hand, the accelerated growth of Mumbai's population due to large-scale migration, threw an additional burden of expenditure on the Municipal and State Governments.

Administration, Law and Order, Health, Sanitation, and most importantly, Housing for the large population of the city, claimed a considerable amount of the State resources. Introducing statutory rationing (at the direction of the Central Government in 1965) in fast-growing Mumbai constituted a formidable problem. Maharashtra State was deficient in foodgrains, as stated by the Chief Minister of the State (V.P. Naik) at a press conference. (Mrt. 4.7.65, 8.8. 65, 17.5.65)

The rest of Maharashtra outside the capital city, was underdeveloped and deficit in food production due to inadequate irrigation and chronic drought. The aggrieved State's demand, therefore, was for greater financial assistance from the Centre, for additional costs involved in tending to the needs of the metropolis. (Mrt. 17.5.65, Ed. 7.7.65)

Reports and Articles (Mrt. 28.3.62, 12.6.64, 9.7.64, 17.5.65, 28.6.65, 29.6.65, 30.6.65, 4.7.65, 8.8.65, 26.2.66, 20.3.69)

II

What do all these grievances summed up in Section I signify? What credibility do they carry? What could be the factors responsible for such recurring and vehement expression of grievances?

It is the metropolis of Mumbai where these grievances chiefly originate, find expression, and where their redressal is sought for. Here we note that a large number of these letters in our data make it clear that their demands for priority in jobs or in educational opportunities, for special considerations and concessions for entry into commercial and industrial enterprise, are specifically hinged upon the fact that Mumbai is the capital city and part of their native State. Their emotions are understandable if one considers that the State of Maharashtra was formed in 1960 after a five-year-long agitation and an organised movement (the Samyukta Maharashtra Movement) by the Marathi people. The SMS also sought the inclusion of Mumbai city – geographically, a part of the Konkan coast of Maharashtra – in a united Maharashtra. This was granted after a bitter struggle mainly due to resistance by the affluent Gujarati community and certain influential sections of Mumbai society. (Stern R., 1970; Phadke Y.D., 1973)

It is a well-known fact that Maharashtrians, by and large, are not a business community; control of trade not only in Mumbai city but in most of Maharashtra as well, has been in the hands of non-Maharashtrians. Mumbai's commerce and industry has been controlled by the Bhatia, the Bania, the Parsi and the Bohra – all from Gujarat, and by Sindhi and Marwari merchants and industrialists. These industrialists and merchant communities voiced their demands through the Indian Merchants' Chamber, the Indian Manufacturers' Association and through the BPCC which they once dominated. The Indian Merchants' Chamber is the largest of the Chambers of Commerce, the most powerful and representative arm of big business, where non-Maharashtrians hold a dominant position. (IMC Diamond Jubilee Souvenir, Mumbai, 1967)

The local Marathi community not only did not control Mumbai's commercial or industrial wealth, but economically too it was one of the poorer communities of the city. An economic survey of metropolitan Mumbai conducted in the mid-fifties, 'Work, Wages and Well-being in an Indian Metropolis'

(Lakdawala D.T., 1963), found that the Sindhi and the English-speaking families of the city, were economically speaking, in the most secure position compared to all other communities, while Maharashtrian families, along with the Urdu-speaking, had the lowest per capita income in the city; the Gujarati and the South Indian groups stood between these two extremes. (Pavement dwellers and persons living in boarding houses were excluded from the purview of the study) The average family income, as well as the average per capita income of the Marathi community, was thus found to be the lowest and less than the average for Mumbai.

This position seemed to hold good even in the sixties. The 1961 Census data available for industrial classification or occupational divisions supports the findings of the 'Economic Survey' (Lakdawala, 1963). The census data reveals that the percentage of the Marathi community in the categories of trade and commerce, in administrative, executive and managerial positions and as sales-workers, is noticeably less than the percentage of other non-Marathi communities taken together. The percentage of the Maharashtrian, however, was much higher in the category of manual workers and labourers.

If we contrast this low economic position of the Maharashtrian with the fast rise of his new economic aspirations – almost like a sudden release of a pent-up emotion – upon the formation of Maharashtra State in 1960, we get a fairly accurate picture of the situation. During the controversy over Mumbai's inclusion in Maharashtra, those who resisted the move claimed that the city's prosperity was largely the result of non-Maharashtrian effort and enterprise. (The Mumbai Committee, Memorandum, n.d. 9) The leaders of the Samyukta Maharashtra Movement, on the other hand, saw the city as a para-colonial enclave which exploited the resources of its Maharashtrian hinterland. Their demand, therefore, for inclusion of Mumbai city in the proposed State of Maharashtra was one for recognising the integral relationship of the city with the Maharashtra region. Mumbai city could not be separated from its Maharashtra hinterland to be an independent or 'free' city, or to play the role of an exploiting overlord of the surrounding rural area. (See Stern R., 1970, P.47; Sam. Maha. Parishad, 1954, Pp. 68-74)

A large number of economic grievances articulated in the Marathi press from 1963 onwards can be understood and analysed only in the context of the points made above. A Maharashtrian who now indentified himself more closely with the new State Government (1960), expected the Government to protect his interests and assist him in the keen economic competition to be at par with the other better-off communities of the city. The Maharashtrian looked upon this as a legitimate and fair expectation from his 'own' Government, in his 'own' State capital. A number of entries in our content data, especially the letters by readers in the newspapers, articulate this point. The expectation appears to be all-pervasive. The demand for priority, greater concession in economic opportunities for the 'locals' and the grievances against an alleged or real greater share in jobs and positions of authority by others, needs to be perceived in this context.

The worry that 'outsiders' were usurping the jobs of the 'local' man in Mumbai goes back to the days of the Samyukta Maharashtra Movement. T.R. Naravane, the leader of the dissident Congress, the Jan Parishad, claimed that there was a letter in circulation advising the city's industrialists to reduce their hiring of Maharashtra labour, although Babubhai Chinai, a prominent businessman and Congress M.P. from Mumbai had denied this. (q.v. Stern, Robert, p.48) During the Samyukta Maharashtra Movement, it was believed that Mumbai industrialists, afraid of trouble from disaffected Maharashtrian labour organised under the militant labour unions formed by the SMS leaders, quietly pursued the policy of recruiting non-Marathi labour either from the north or the south.

Even before the Marmik began publishing – as a mark of protest – its lists of appointments of South Indian and non-Maharashtrian officials and executives in private and public sector firms of Mumbai, members of the legislature and responsible leaders of the community, of various parties, including those of the CPI, had made complaints of injustice and ill-treatment to 'local' labour.

(See Maharashtra Legislative Assembly Debates, 1964, Vol. XII, Pt. II, no. 8, Pp. 234-238, no. 24, Pp. 852-864, 886-888, Vol. XIII, Pt. I, Pp. 356-358; 1965, Vol. XV, Pt. I, Pp. 106-109, Pt. II Pp. 170-177, 183-184)

The Question of Nepotism and Contacts

The grievances summarised in Section I, relate to two major points (i) the large number of appointments of South Indians in office jobs in Mumbai through contacts and nepotism (ii) the relatively small share of educational and training opportunities and of office jobs for Maharashtrians in Mumbai due to discrimination against them. It is generally believed that the Shiv Sena emerged in response to the keen job competition between the 'locals' and the 'outsiders' which found articulation in the above grievances.

It is difficult to define nepotism and corruption in the Indian context. What is seen as nepotism by one may be considered as a clan obligation or an obligation to co-villagers or the joint family members by another, even by the urban and the educated.

'There could be such finely graded shades of give-and take-between the various strata and categories of the political party, the politician, the official hierarchy, the businessman and his agents and such narrowly differentiated types of indirect or direct transactions among them that it would be difficult to isolate and bring home a corruption charge except in the case of the specially inept'. (Gadgil D.R. 1972, P. 309)

In this context, therefore, we have to explore the processes and mechanisms of recruitment to jobs in a metropolitan city. How do migrants come to the city and find a job? What role do contacts and influence play in getting jobs and appointments at various levels?

Studies of migration and recruitment reveal that contacts and clan considerations, among other mechanisms of recruitment, do play a part in the employment market of a metropolitan city. Gore's survey of migrants provides evidence that some migrants to the city have jobs arranged for them in advance. He mentions that 74 per cent of the Marathi speaking and 82 per cent of the Hindi and Tamil speaking people came to Mumbai for reasons other than routine transfer. (Gore M.S., 1970, Pp. 36-37)

This shows that while some migrants came to the city in the hope of getting a job, a few of them came to the city with jobs already arranged for them. The 'fixing' of a job can take place as much in the unorganised sector as it can in the organised sector. In Gore's sample, informal contact played a more marked role among the Hindi-speaking especially among those working in an old established private sector factory. 'Many of the workers in unskilled jobs felt that they could bring 'cousins' and friends as 'substitutes' when they proceeded on home leave. Gore found that more formal channels of recruitment tended to be used in a public sector factory.

We may note that Gore's sample included groups of both white-collar and blue-collar workers. There is evidence from other quarters which also suggests that informal channels of contact are not altogether absent at the level of white-collar and managerial jobs. Nair, in his study of the South Indian community in Pune city, (Nair K.S. 1975), states that members of the community migrated to Pune in search of employment. He also observes: 'About two-thirds of the migrants (66.5 per cent) were very sure of finding employment in Pune before they migrated. Around 64.5 per cent of the migrants found their first job in Pune, 24 per cent the second and the rest, their third or fourth.'

'The majority of migrants are employed in white-collar occupations; 79 per cent of the migrants are employed in Central Government service either in junior administrative technical or clerical jobs. Of the migrants employed in Central Government service, 66 per cent are employed in the office of the Controller of Defence Accounts'. (Nair K.S. 1975, p. 80)

Formal channels of recruitment to the organised sector jobs through the Employment Exchange were utilised only to a small extent. According to a survey of 67 large private sector firms employing more than 500 workers carried out by the Directorate of Employment of Maharashtra State in 1964-65, 7 per cent of the recruits were provided by the Employment Exchanges, 60 per cent by direct recruitment, 20 per cent through present employees and 13 per cent through other sources. The average picture differed only slightly in four of the public sector factories under survey. In general, the public sector is more likely to use the Employment Exchange than the private sector. (The Mumbai Labour Market, P. 84, Government of Maharashtra, November 1966; also see Nair P.A. 1968, P.17)

The effect of an informal network of contacts in placing people in the city's labour market is seen in the creation of differential corridors of migration from a few places on the one hand and, on the other, of a significant degree of specialisation within the overall industrial structure of workers from different States. (Visaria P.M. 1969, Mimeo) The existence of such migration corridors and the importance of clan-contacts seem to have been confirmed by cross-section econometric studies of migration relationships. (Anand S. q.v. H. and V. Joshi 1976, Footnotes on Pp. 42 and 182) When there was an overall shortage of employment, the tendency was to exploit informal networks of contacts in spite of the risk of being accused of nepotism and injustice. The alarming pressure of migrant manpower in the labour market for the limited job opportunities seems to be a crucial factor in the growing resistance of the natives of the State to 'outsiders'.

Problem of the Educated Unemployed

It is generally believed that the regionalism of the Shiv Sena is a response of the native population of Maharashtra to the keen competition for middle-class jobs in Mumbai. Devoid of investment capital, lacking in commercial and industrial skills and a tradition of enterprise, Maharashtrians were proverbially said to prefer the safety of a salaried job. With the increasing concentration of economic opportunities in fast-developing Mumbai, and with the accelerated inflow of migrants from all over India, Maharashtrians faced the threat of keen competition from South Indians who had better secretarial skills. The post-independence spur in education and the fast rise in the number of high school certificate holders or matriculates, only contributed further to the competition. The rise of the Shiv Sena, according to this theory, was in response to the situation in Mumbai's employment market.

The theory seems to present a plausible explanation not only of the emergence of the Shiv Sena but also of the choice of South Indians as the target of its antagonism. The Shiv Sena's demand of '80 per cent of jobs for the sons of the soil,' lent further credibility to this explanation based on a combination of demographic and economic factors. However, M. Katzanstein (1973) rejects this theory of middle-class job competition on the following grounds

i) Katzenstein points out that the number of educated unemployed in Mumbai increased only modestly when compared to other major cities in India. The unemployment statistics of Mumbai City for the period of 1956-66, does not show either a high or sudden increase in the number of the educated unemployed registered with the Employment Exchange of Mumbai. (M. Katzenstein, 1973)

ii) On the other hand, there was tremendous growth of the tertiary sector resulting in expansion of white-collar jobs in the mid-sixties.

iii) The data on the relative occupational status of different linguistic communities in Mumbai, according to 1961 Census, indicates that the Maharashtrian population was almost proportionately represented in clerical positions, over-represented in manual jobs and under-represented only in professional and managerial positions. It is not only the South Indian communities but the Gujarati community that had a slightly large proportion of clerical positions, as may be seen from the following table

Table V-7

Estimates of the Percentage of Positions in Selected Occupations Held by Maharashtrian, Gujarati and South Indian Male Workers living in Mumbai, 1961

Census	Classification	Maharashtrian	Gujarati	South Indian
Professional	...	35	23	19
Administrative	...	35	25	21
Clerical	...	41	31	15
Labourers	...	50	11	13
Percentage of Mumbai Population	...	43	19	9

Source M. Katzenstein, 1973, Asian Survey, vol. XIII, No. 4 computed from the Census Tables, Tables B-V, C-V; Census of India, 1961, Vol. X, Part X (1-C), Tables V, VIII; K.C. Zachariah, 1968, Tables 10.1, 13.5, 13.25.

Note The row percentages do not total 100, since all linguistic groups are not included in the table.

However, a close scrutiny of this data, with some other information available, suggests a slightly different picture than the one seen by Katzentein.

The overall rate of unemployment is higher for Mumbai than for other metropolitan cities. Greater Mumbai had little more than 10 per cent of the total unemployed in India while Kolkata and Chennai had about 9 per cent and 4 per cent. The rates of unemployment by various educational levels for Mumbai, with the exception of the graduate level, were higher than for the rest of urban India. The following table should make the point clear:

Table V-8

Rates of Unemployment Mumbai and All Urban India, 1961 Census, by Education

	Mumbai	All Urban India
Unemployed as a percentage of Labour Force		
All Educational Levels	4.6	2.9
Without Education	3.9	2.0
Primary Education	6.0	4.7
Secondary Education	5.3	5.9
Graduate	2.3	3.3
Unemployed as percentage of All Educational levels	5.9	5.5

Source Joshi H. and V., 1976, Surplus Labour and the City, Table II-8, P.30; Census of India 1961, General Economic Tables and Greater Mumbai Census Tables B-VIII-A, B-III-A, VI-A and B.

Unemployment rates for those without education and those with primary education are much higher in Mumbai than similar rates for similar educational levels in the rest of urban India. On the other hand, unemployment rates for those with secondary education, and especially for graduates, are much lower.

These facts made Katzenstein reject the theory of middle-class job competition to explain the rise of Shiv Sena which had received vocal support from the educated Marathi middle-classes.

The job competition of the educated in Mumbai (seen by Katzenstein as a factor of doubtful validity), however, was not altogether an insignificant factor. In spite of the lower rate of educated unemployment in Mumbai and the corroborating data presented by Blaug, et at, (1969, Table A-9), the competition between job seekers from Maharashtra and those from outside the State for all categories of middle-class jobs in Mumbai, appears on closer scrutiny, to be keen.

Employment Exchange registers, because of several limitations, are not very accurate indicators of employment situation in India. This fact is noted by Katzenstein also. The 1961 Census recorded 80, 416 unemployed persons in Mumbai of whom 14208 were educated unemployed. However, the Employment Exchange Live Register for 1960-1961, reported 44, 037 job seekers among whom 18, 412 were registered educated unemployed. (Joshi H. and v., 1976, Pp. 79-80) Even after making an allowance for the little inaccuracies inevitable in Employment Exchange figures, the fact suggests that some of the registrants with the Employment Exchange were either already employed, seeking better jobs and/or that some of the registrants were not residents of Mumbai. That many registrants at the Employment Exchange in Mumbai came from outside the State of Maharashtra is confirmed by 'A Survey of Educated Unemployed in Mumbai', by P.A. Nair (1968)

iv) Blaug, et al (1969, Table A-9), have observed that among the educated unemployed registered with the Employment

Exchange, the ratio of matriculates to those with higher education, was very high, especially in Mumbai, when compared to a similar ratio in other metro-centres. These ratios were as follows:

Delhi	4.6	Chennai	5.5
Kolkata	5.1	Mumbai	7.6

Among the educated job seekers (over 19, 000 in 1964) registered with the employment exchange in Mumbai, nearly 80 per cent were matriculates most of these (i.e. nearly 70 per cent of the total job seekers and 80 per cent of the matriculates), came from the home state of Maharashtra. Among the rest of the matriculates (20 per cent), Kerala and Gujarat had a predominant share. (Nair, 1968, p. 12) Distribution of the Registrants with the Regional Employment Exchange in Mumbai as on 30.9.64 was as follows:

Table V-9

Distribution of Registrants from Maharashtra and Other States at the Employment Exchange in Mumbai

	Maharashtra	All other States
Matriculates	13284 (81%)	3297 (19%)
Undergraduates and Graduates	1773 (65.6%)	931 (34.4%)
Post-Graduates	68 (59.7%)	46 (40.3%)

Source: Abstracted from Table 2 Registrants by States of Origin, P.A. Nair, 1968, *Employment Market in an Industrial Metropolis A Survey of Educated Unemployment in Mumbai.*

Nearly 38 per cent of the college educated registrants at the regional employment exchange in Mumbai came from States other than Maharashtra. The percentage of the migrant registrants from other States thus rises with the level of education.

Among the migrant educated unemployed, persons from the eastern States of Bengal, Bihar, Orissa and Assam hardly account for one per cent, while job seekers from Jammu and Kashmir are conspicuous by their absence. The data, by Nair, based on a survey of Live Registers from the Employment Exchange in

Mumbai between 1961 and 1964, shows by mother tongue the following major groups of job seekers in the employment market of Mumbai in the sixties

Marathi	46.14%
Gujarati, Kutchi and Sindhi	25.42%
South Indians	21.21%
Rest	7.23%
	100.00%

Source: Abstracted from Table 16 Number of Unemployed by Mother Tongue, P.A. Nair 1968, p.47

Sindhis have a large share of 19.76 per cent among the total number of educated job seekers in Mumbai. The Sindhi, Gujarati and Kutchi are communities with local moorings in Mumbai and their large share is to be expected. The percentage share of job seekers of the South Indian group (21.21 per cent) appears to be disproportionately large in relation to the percentage of their population (8 per cent) in the total population of Mumbai. (The Malayali, among the South Indian job seekers, has a large percentage of 15.01). This share of percentage of the job seekers from the South is larger than the percentage of workers (in all categories), from the four southern States (14 percent), in Mumbai's total male labour force, by the 1961 Census. The percentage of the migrant population from four Southern States in Mumbai was 15.6 in 1961. (Joshi, H. and V. 1976, Table V.4, Pp. 142-143; also K. C. Zachariah, 1968; Census of India 1961, Vol. X, Pt. X (1-c) Table V)

Nair observes that of the educated job seekers registered at the Regional Employment Exchange in Mumbai more than 15 per cent came from the States of Kerala (7 per cent), Gujarat (4 per cent) and Uttar Pradesh (4 per cent) From outside the home State, the number from Kerala and Gujarat was predominant. 'There was a large flow of graduates from Tamil Nadu, Uttar Pradesh and Kerala while post-graduates came mostly from Uttar Pradesh and Tamil Nadu'. (P. A. Nair, 1968, Pp. 12, 10-11)

The survey by Nair allows us to analyse the data from the Employment Exchange. It reveals the growing competition for the local educated job seekers from non-Marathi groups of whom the South Indian group forms a formidable section. Thus, in spite of the lower rate of educated unemployment due to the expansion of tertiary-sector jobs in Mumbai in the decade of the sixties, we cannot ignore the possibility of middle-class job competition as a contributing factor to the growing disaffection of Maharashtrian youth. It is the unemployment of the educated which is open unemployment and an urban phenomenon that is more likely to get politically exploited.

The Educated Job Seekers from the Southern States

Two non-competing streams of job seekers flow to the city of Mumbai: the educated and the uneducated. The uneducated at best can aspire to get jobs in the civic and administrative services, in trade and commerce, or for the 'white-coated' jobs as technicians, consultants or assistants in modern industry.

A significant sociological factor which in this context seems to have given an edge to the competition between the 'local' and the 'outsider' – the South Indian job seeker – is the differential composition of the two groups. Among the educated job seekers from the South, evidence from different quarters suggests a preponderance of higher caste persons. The composition of the local job seekers is inevitably more heterogeneous with a cross-section of castes including a significant percentage of neo-Buddhists and other scheduled castes.

This is seen in Gore's study of 'Migrants and Neighbourhoods' of Mumbai. (1970, TISS) There is a greater preponderance of Brahmins and other upper castes in the Tamil sample, compared to the sample of the local Marathi community. Though this difference is not brought out sufficiently in the analysis by Gore, it, however, is present and observable if probed a little deeper. (See S. Gogate, July-August 1971) Gore's survey of migrants found that the Tamil sample had 38 per cent Brahmins and 20 per cent Christians among whom there was a high percentage of the educated. The sample had 42 per cent of low-caste Hindus. The Marathi sample, on the other hand, had 22 per cent Brahmins, 66.6 per cent non-Brahmins and 11 per cent Hindus, half the number of whom were neo-Buddhists. In the Tamil sample, among those in white-collar jobs, 83 per cent were Brahmins and 17 per cent non-Brahmins. In the Marathi sample, among those in white-collar jobs, 57 per cent were Brahmins and 43 per cent non-Brahmins including some neo-Buddhists. Very high occupational polarisation by caste difference and disproportionately high percentage of Brahmins in white-collar jobs were the marked characteristics of the South Indian sample in Gore's Survey of migrants. The Gore Survey need not be taken as definitive; but it serves as a pointer to the trend.

Three studies of South Indian migrant communities in the three major cities of Maharashtra – Mumbai, Nagpur and Pune – also confirm the above observation. (K.L. Mythili, 1959; R. Jayaraman, 1964, K.C. Nair 1975) Among the migrants studied Mythili discovered 93 per cent to be Brahmins, Nair found 84 per cent to be Brahmins and 7 per cent to be of other high castes and Jayaraman speaks of the majority being Brahmins. The picture that emerges from these studies of the migrant South Indian community is that a large number of its members were Brahmins and upper castes, educated, more urban than rural, and holding white-collar office jobs. These findings are consistent with the well-known observed fact that long-distance migration generally involves inter-urban migration of the educationally better-equipped.

Maharashtrians and Middle-Class Employment

In the light of the characteristics of the educated migrant South Indian group, it is not surprising that the group held a higher percentage-share of the professional, administrative and clerical positions in Mumbai, compared to the group's proportion (8 per cent), in Mumbai's population according to 1961 Census. The group's percentage share in each of these three categories of jobs was also higher compared to the group's share (14 per cent) in the total male labour force of the city. It meant that the group was chiefly concentrated in these three categories, rather than any other, of the city's economy.

Relative to their proportion in the population, the Maharashtrian community was under-represented in both the professional and administrative categories and over-represented in manual labour jobs (50 per cent) The community's share in clerical jobs, however, matched more or less with its share in the metropolitan population. By the criterion of the community's proportion (43 per cent) in the city's population, the Maharashtrian group thus lagged behind by about 8 per cent in high-status administrative and professional positions, while the South Indian community was in the front by almost equal or greater percentage (7 to 12 per cent) in the share of these status-positions.

That a keen sense of socio-economic disparity was part of the Maharashtrian community's experience and awareness is recorded in the content data from the Marathi press predating the birth of the Sena. The lower socio-economic status of the members of the community in contrast to the better positions held by the members of other communities, particularly the new migrant groups, was a cause for a strong sense of disparity and frustration especially in the context of heightened economic aspirations upon the formation of Maharashtra State.

The tertiary sector in Mumbai expanded at a higher rate during the sixties and the number of middle-class jobs increased from 1962 onwards – the period of fermentation prior to the emergence of Shiv Sena. In spite of the easing of the situation, due to the tertiary expansion, unemployment of the educated still remained a problem in the mid-sixties. (P.A. Nair 1968) Besides, the growth of the tertiary sector seems to have strengthened the heightened economic aspirations and corresponding sense of frustration, as is observed from the increasing number of entries on the index points of frustration-protest in1964-65. (See Table and also from the articulation of grievances in letters from readers. See Appendix A.V-a no. 2 and 3) On the other hand, the position of the Maharashtrian community in employment, especially, in the matter of high-status positions did not seem to have improved.

'The means of wealth were vastly increasing', but the economic and social benefits of those means seemed to be narrowly escaping the community's grasp. The 'demonstration effect' of other groups to whom the benefits seemed to accrue and whose situation seemed to improve, appears to have given an edge to the community's expectation levels and consequent frustrations. The situation appears to be a case of a mixture of aspirational and progressive deprivation. (See Chap. 1, Pp. 16-18) This sense of deprivation regarding the status-positions in administration and professions appears to be a crucial factor contributing to the disaffection of the Maharashtrian community with new groups of migrants to the city.

However, the competition for middle-class jobs or the sense of deprivation regarding high-status positions could directly affect only a relatively small proportion of the city's Maharashtrian population – the middle classes. The emergence of a popular movement, however, is possible only with wider support from a broad cross-section of the community. That the Shiv-Sena received large popular support during the sixties, is amply evident from the facts (See Chapter 3) Like its sweeping success in its first-ever election-contest in Mumbai, its emergence as the major opposition party in the Municipal Corporation in March, 1968 and the success of the Shiv Sena candidate in the by-election to the State Legislature in 1970 in a straight contest with the CPI candidate in Parel-Naigaum (a working class district and a CPI stronghold).

The factor of the middle-class job competition of the educated, proves inadequate to explain the large support that the Sena received from the traditional working-class in Mumbai during its heyday (1966-1971) To understand this phenomenon, we have to look elsewhere.

The Changing Structure of Economic Activity and Employment

The structure of economic activity of the city and so also the structure of employment in the organised sector of this developing metropolis was changing. (Operations Research Group, Mimco., 1972, Introduction Pp. 7-8; Joshi H. and V., 1976, Ch. 3) These changes seem to have affected significantly the job opportunities of the traditional Maharashtrian working class of Mumbai.

The data now available from various quarters, regarding the growth of economic activity in Mumbai during the decade 1961-

71 brings to light certain salient features of this growth. 'A Study on Economic Activity Profile for Mumbai' (Operations Research Group, Mimeo., 1972), observes that 'there is a clear shift in emphasis in the decade 1961-71, in Mumbai's economic activity from manufacturing to non-manufacturing sector.' (p.8) Another study of economy and employment of Mumbai, observes the following noteworthy features of changes during the decade:

(1) A slow rate of growth of the organised sector employment in proportion to Mumbai's work-force, during 1961-71;

(2) Stagnation of the textile industry within the organised sector employment after 1961; and

(3) Relatively fast growth of skill-intensive industries and of the public sector, in the organised sector.

(Joshi H. and V., 1976, p. 57-63, Table III.6)

Elaborating the first point, the Joshis point out that after a fairly steady growth in the organised sector till 1965, 'there was a period of stagnation and recession which hit employment in private manufacturing particularly hard'. (p.57) The data collected by the Operations Research Group also corroborates those points. (ORG, 1972, Ch. 2)

2) Apart from the several measures of control on further expansion of manufacturing activity in Mumbai, a reason for the indifferent performance of the 'manufacturing' group during the sixties was the stagnation in the cotton textile industry. As the oldest established factory industry of Mumbai, textile mills accounted for half of all the workers in the manufacturing sector of the city. During the three decades preceding 1961, textiles were a growing industry; however, the trend began to reverse during the late fifties and turned into an absolute decline by the sixties. The average number of workers per factory in the cotton textile industry was 1772 in 1957; by 1964 it was reduced to an average of 504 workers per factory. (Committee for Regional Plans, 1965, Tables 4.2. and 4.3. Pp. 115-116) There was stagnation in output as well as rationalisation of the industry. The replacement of men and women workers by machinery was a response not only to high wage costs but also

to changes in the techniques of manufacture needed by new types of textile products. As a consequence the textile group, which accounted for 49.4 per cent of the total employment in the manufacturing division in 1961, had a share of only 41.9 per cent in 1970. The absolute number of workers employed in registered factories of the textile industry fell by 10,000 in 1966 and never picked up after 1970. (ORG, 1972, Table 2.8 D, p. 63-65) In fact, the trend continued in the seventies. According to a State Government publication, the number of workers in the textile industry declined by 26,000 between 1961 and 1974. (Directorate of Economics and Statistics, Government of Maharashtra, 1976, p. 28).

3) a. The growth of employment was much faster in newer industries like chemicals. Pharmaceuticals, accounting for half the decade's increase in this industry, more than doubled. Other branches of manufacturing like non-metallic mineral products, basic metal alloys industries, manufacture of metal products, of electrical machinery, apparatus, appliances, of transport equipment and parts, etc., expanded in employment. The Joshis, however, point out that the 'skill-intensity' of the expanding industries like pharmaceuticals, petro-chemicals, electronics, etc., is significantly higher than that of the older textile industry.

3) b. The fastest-growing industry during 1961-70, was, however, the 'services' sector. (ORG, 1972. p. 57-58) The private sector of the manufacturing industries bore the brunt of recession and employment fell in 1966-68 and did not regain the 1966 level till after 1971. On the other hand, the public sector in Mumbai continued to have an upward movement of growth throughout the decade. In fact, during the first half of the decade the public sector grew very fast.

The public sector included Public Services, Medical and Health Services, Educational and Scientific Services. Jobs in government administration grew fast, and so did employment in health and education. (ORG, 1972, 58-61)

Employment Growth of Major Groups of Economic Activities in Mumbai

Group		Per cent 1961-71	Growth 1961-65	during 1965-70
Manufacturing	...	26.5	15.3	5.8
Trade	...	37.8	18.1	14.8
Business and Commerce	...	34.3	13.1	17.2
Services	...	61.6	25.8	25.5
Transport	...	28.6	23.6	2.0
Utilities and Construction	...	38.2	27.7	5.9
	Total	34.2	18.7	10.3

Source: ORG, Mimeo, 1972, Table 2.8-A, p.58, Ch. II.

These newly expanding industries and the public sector services in the city were avenues of employment for the more educated. The new job opportunities were thus in the 'white collar' jobs inclusive of administration, finance, education and in manufacturing. (H. and V. Joshi, 1976, Table III.6, 64-66)

The Uneducated Job Seekers and the Changing Economic Structure

Of the two streams of job seekers in the city, the educated and the uneducated, the the latter's chances of getting organised sector jobs were thus fast decreasing in the changing structure of the city's economic activity. Increasingly, recruitment to organised sector jobs required educational qualifications, even if the performance of these jobs did not necessarily require formal training. (Peons in offices formerly used to be primary-educated; peons in organised sector offices now required secondary education as a minimum). The prospect of graduating into organised employment now applied more to the people who came to the city for education or with education, than those who went to work in the unorganised sector. Consequently, during the sixties the educated seemed to be displacing the uneducated in Mumbai especially in the organised sector of its economy.

These changes had significant implications for the Maharashtrian population which held a share of 50 per cent of the city's manual labour force in 1961. Fast expansion of the tertiary sector combined with a slow movement of the secondary sector in the developing metropolis, had unforeseen consequences for the working class from Maharashtra. The relative stagnation of the manufacturing industry, especially the textile sector mentioned earlier, hit the Maharashtrian workers hard during the sixties.

Traditionally, Maharashtrian labour in Mumbai was concentrated chiefly in the textile, chemical and engineering industries. The textile industry had been the oldest and the biggest, accounting for (nearly 2, 30,000 workers in 1961) half the number of workers in manufacturing industries.

The industry being located in Mumbai, the largest proportion of millhands came from Maharashtra, from the Konkan coast and the districts of the Deccan plateau, such as Satara, Pune, Ahmednagar and Solapur. The biggest share was that of Ratnagiri district and Konkan. This pattern existed from the beginning of the industry's history though with the passage of time, other regions like Uttar Pradesh began contributing a rising proportion of workers to the industry. However, according to the survey of millhands in 1955 by the Mumbai Mill Owners' Association, the percentage of Marathi workers in the industry was still almost 70 per cent; the next major group of workers being from Uttar Pradesh with a percentage of 22.40. (M.D. Morris, 1965, Pp.62-75; 229-Appedix IV)

With the recession setting in, industry laid off 10,000 workers during the first half of the decade (1961-65) and another 10,000 by 1974 as mentioned earlier. Though the recession became more pronounced in the sixties, the trend began in the late fifties. (Joshi, 1976, p. 63)

A ward-wise distribution of the city's unemployed, by the 1961 Census, seems to reflect the deterioration of the city's biggest industry - textile. The 1961 Census for Greater Mumbai (Vol. X, Part X (1-B), Table B-II; also see Naik, R.D. 1971, 17) locates a large number of the unemployed in the traditional working-class districts of Mumbai. By the 1961 Census, Wards G, E and F hold the 1st, 3rd and 4th ranks by the number of the unemployed. (The dubious distinction of the second rank went to the sprawling Western suburbs of Mumbai, where identification of the unemployed by community was more difficult) Ward G which had the largest number of the unemployed also happened to have the largest concentration of the industrial workers in Mumbai. Both Ward G and F were homogeneous and predominantly Maharashtrian in composition in the early sixties. These two wards together covered, along with Dadar, Mahim, Matunga and Sion, the traditional industrial, chiefly textile millworkers' districts of Prabhadevi, Worli, Chinchpokli, Love Grove, Parel, Naigaum and Sewri. Ward E, though not predominantly Maharashtrian, had a large Maharashtrian labour class population in the neighbourhoods of Kamathipura, Gadge Chowk (former Jacob Circle), N.M. Joshi Marg, etc. These facts suggest that the Maharashtrian working-class was adversely affected by the structural changes in the economy of Mumbai during the sixties.

In the midst of the growing opportunities offered by a metropolis poised for changes in its economy, the Maharashtrian worker, however, was faced with hardship from all quarters. With the increasing rationalisation of the textile industry and the increasing emphasis on skill and training in the newer industries, the traditional Marathi worker had no easy or alternative avenues of employment. Even those of the Maharashtrian labour force who worked as casual and contract labour – the 'Mathadi' and the 'Lokhandi Jatha Kamgar' groups – were facing trouble over wages and other problems. (Report of the Mathadi Labour Enquiry Committee, 1965) Together with coolies, porters and the celebrated tiffin-carriers of Mumbai, the Mathadis and the Lokhandi Jatha Kamgar of the city accounted for more than 20,000 workers.

All these facts suggest that there was a strong ground for the Maharashtrian labour class to feel dissatisfied with their lot, especially when the others by comparison, seemed to be doing better. This dissatisfaction could make them susceptible to the persuasions of a new ideology that promised them better prospects.

The Shiv Sena demand for 'eighty per cent of jobs for the local people' could not fail to appeal strongly to them in the circumstances.

Economic Variables and the Regionalist Movement

Having considered the various relevant factors in the situation, we are now in a position to assess the role of economic variables in the rise of the regionalist movement of the Shiv Sena. The job competition from the educated or the recession in the textile industry do not appear to be factors sufficient in themselves to explain the rise of the Shiv Sena. The job competition from new ethnic groups from other States, however, is significant because it made the regional community more keenly aware of its own deprivations. Though job competition at various levels might have provided some provocation, the reasons for the emergence of the regionalist movement of the Shiv Sena, seem to lie deeper in the totality of the particular situation of the Maharashtrian community, apart from the community's increased self-awareness and heightened aspirations after 1960.

Besides competition for jobs, the cause could have been the Maharashtrian community's educational backwardness and the failure of the State Government to remedy the situation. Such a theory, though vindicated by facts up to a point, is also inadequate to explain the emergence of the Shiv Sena.

Disparity and Imbalance

The relative deprivation of the Maharashtrian community, which finds articulation in the demand for priority in economic opportunities for the 'local people' is rooted in the pervasive socio-economic disparity between the Marathi and the non-Marathi communities, than in just the competition for jobs. This socio-economic disparity seems to be closely linked with the regional or spatial economic imbalance. Economic opportunities were excessively concentrated in metropolitan Mumbai to the exclusion of other parts of the State and this had its repercussions on the life of Maharashtrians in Mumbai.

We shall first research the educational backwardness of the Maharashtrian community in Mumbai, before exploring the problem of regional economic imbalance and its social repercussions. We draw attention here to certain relevant characteristics of the Maharashtrian community, observed earlier (i) The percentage of the Maharashtrian community in the city's population had slowly declined over the decades and was about 44 per cent in the sixties, (ii) The low level of its income compared to that of most other non-Maharashtrian communities, and (iii) The high proportion (50 per cent) of the Maharashtrians, in the total manual labour force of the city and a relatively low proportion of the members of the community in the higher cadres of professional, managerial and executive positions, until the seventies.

A closer scrutiny of these facts reveals the different levels of education found in the migrant communities to the city as a significant variable related to economic factors. (Sehgal, Kuldeep Chunder, September 1969) By the 1961 Census, 64 per cent of Mumbai's population was migrant, i.e., born outside the city. Compared to non-Marathi migrants, migrants from Maharashtra reveal lower levels of literacy and education.

Educational Level of Marathi and Non-Marathi Migrants in Greater Mumbai, in Terms of Percentages

	Educational level Percentage among Marathi and Non-Marathi migrants to Mumbai	
	Marathi	Non-Marathi
All educational levels	100.0	100.0
Illiterate	37.9	31.7
Literate without educational level	25.5	26.0
Primary or Junior	26.2	13.5
Technical or non-technical diploma	0.3	0.6
University Degree (technical or non-technical)	2.4	5.1
Educated (secondary of higher levels)	10.4	19.2

Source: Census of India, 1961, Vol. X, Part X (1-C), Abstracted from Table VI

It is an oft-observed phenomenon. Long-distance migrants are likely to educated and urban, while short-distance migrants tend to be rural and uneducated. (Lee, E.S. 1969) We therefore may look into the ratio of rural-urban migration for elucidation of the lower levels of literacy and education among the migrants from Maharashtra. The rural-urban ratio for the worker population from Maharashtra, in Mumbai was as high as nearly 4 to 1 (41), while for workers from all other States, it was about 3 to 2 (32), by the 1961 Census. Significantly, nearly sixty per cent of workers from rural Maharashtra came from the Konkan districts, chiefly from Ratnagiri.

Migrant Workers from Maharashtra in Mumbai by Rural-Urban Division

Place of Origin

(in lakhs)	Konkan	Other Districts	Workers from Maharashtra
Rural (78.83 %)	2, 83,945	7, 76,480	4, 60,425
Urban (21.17%)	64,295	59,199	1, 23,594
Total (100%)	3, 48,340	2, 35,699	5, 84,019
	(64.7%)	(35.3%)	(100%)
Percentage of Workers	Rural	78.83%	
	Urban	21.17%	

Source: Census of India, 1961, Vol. V, Part X (1-C), Table III.

Of the total migrants from Maharashtra 45 per cent i.e. nearly 5, 00,000 persons came from Ratnagiri (7 per cent urban), one of the most backward districts of Maharashtra. Another large block of migrants came from the Satara district of western Maharashtra. Almost an equal number came from the mainland districts adjacent to Mumbai - Thane and Raigad (Konkan) These four districts together made up 70 per cent of migration, nearly 75 per cent of the migrant labour from Maharashtra and 25.7 per cent of the total labour force of Mumbai by the 1961 Census. It was therefore not surprising that the educational levels of workers from Maharashtra was low and that a large number of them were in the manual labour force.

Migrants from Maharashtra in Mumbai

Place of origin	Percentage
Ratnagiri	44.45
Satara	12.66
Pune	10.60
Kolaba	9.73
Thana	4.06
Other districts	18.50
	100.00 (1961 Census)

The dependency ratio (the young and the old dependent on the economically active) was high in Ratnagiri. It increased from 89.9 in 1951 to 96.7 in 1961. The sex-ratio (females per thousand males) increased from 1224 in 1951 to 1237 in 1961. By the figures available from the 1971 Census, the sex-ratio in Ratnagiri was one of the highest in the country, 1250 females per thousand males. These ratios are indicative of backwardness and absence of economic opportunities in the area.

Under-development in Maharashtra - The Question of Spread Effects

All these facts are pointers to the measure of under-development in the rest of Maharashtra excluding Mumbai. The fast growth of the metropolis of Mumbai and its increasing affluence during the two decades of 1951-71, tended to camouflage the backward conditions in the rest of Maharashtra. Though the most urbanised State of India (with the highest percentage of urban population 28.22 by the 1961 Census and 31.20 by the 1971 Census), Maharashtra had paradoxically remained rural, since its urbanisation had been extremely concentrated in Mumbai and a couple of other pockets like Thane and Pune. The spread-effects or benefits of urbanisation of Mumbai had not reached the surrounding areas, not even the area on the mainland just across the harbour, even until the seventies, in spite of the developmental efforts of a twin city under progress in the area.

Unfortunately, there are very few studies which can tell us more specifically about the extent of and reason for under-development in the region surrounding Mumbai, or about the relationship between the concentrated metropolitan development and the under-development in the adjacent areas. The Palghar-Tarapur area just outside the Mumbai Metropolitan Region in Thane District had only 6 per cent of urban population which was less than the national norm or even by Ratnagiri standards. Greater Mumbai heavily drew upon the vital resources of this area, like water and electricity, for maintaining Mumbai's vast population and concentration of industries. The plans of future metropolitan development also counted upon these resources from beyond the metropolitan region while it was a matter of common knowledge and general observation that people in the area suffered from acute water scarcity, poor employment opportunities and very low standard of living.

Ellefsen's study of the city-hinterland relationship in the India of the fifties, pointed out that the rural areas surrounding industrialising cities participate if at all, only to a very limited extent in the expansion of the urban economy. This was found especially true of Mumbai. Compared to other major cities like Chennai, Delhi and Hyderabad, Mumbai showed the lowest degree of spread effects and steepest fall from the city to interstitial villages in the vicinity (beyond the 'belt' and 'ribbon' developments of the city), by three out of four indicators of urbanisation such as density of population, sex-ratio (per cent male), non-agricultural livelihood (per cent of total population) and livelihood from commerce. Only in literacy rates, did Mumbai, compared to other cities, show a less steep drop. (See Ellefsen, R.A., 1962, Pp. 94-116)

Thus, while a metropolis absorbs resources from all over the State for its maintenance and further development, those left out of the development stream are relegated to an increasing state of backwardness.

Another study in connection with Mumbai points out that the total community cost for growth and maintenance of a large metro is considerably higher than that required for the growth of smaller centres. (Kulkarni G.S. and Kulkarni A.P., 1968) The total expenditure on metropolitan areas is not only large, but it also cuts deeply into outlays badly required for development of backward regions. In the case of Mumbai, the resources available to the State were often found inadequate for the minimum outlay required for the existing population of Mumbai city. (Gadgil D.R., 1972, P. 306) On the other hand, since it was considered a progressive state, Maharashtra's proportionate share in direct taxation was reducing as a result of the recommendations of successive Finance Commissions. Also Maharashtra was not entitled to any grants-in-aid under the-then provisions of federal finance. (Dhekney B.R., 1973, p. 77)

Urbanisation and Regional Imbalance in Maharashtra

Maharashtra is considered to be the most progressive and the most urbanised state of India. It is supposed to hold a premier position in the country on the basis of indicators like per capita income and per capita output. The third largest state in India in terms of area, population and 'national' income, it had, in 1970 the average daily employment of 10 lakh workers in nearly 10, 000 establishments. It led other States in power generation, with bulk of the installed capacity (2030 mw of power), being consumed by industry within the state. About 32 per cent of the State income was contributed by industry and mining while the national percentage was only 19 per cent. These and similar statistical averages and percentages conveyed the image of Maharashtra as an economically developed state of India. However, such a picture was extremely deceptive and hid the excessive economic disparity that existed between metropolitan Mumbai and the rest of Maharashtra.

Economists were increasingly becoming aware of the scale of under-development that co-existed with the concentration of development in the metropolitan areas of Maharashtra. The Planning Commission classified as backward, as many as thirteen of the twenty six districts of Maharashtra State, covering 54 per cent of the area and 43 per cent of the population. Some of the backward areas in Maharashtra emerged as the poorest in India on indicators like per capita income, per capita electricity consumption, road and rail mileage and contribution of industry and mining. (Pendse, D.R., 1973, Pp. 450-459) Practically all the industrial investments in Maharashtra had been in the private sector. The investments in the public sector were less than 5 per cent and the share of the State Government as well as of the Central Government in industrial investment was not significant till 1967. Although reputed for being an industrially advanced State, Maharashtra had nearly 72 per cent of the labour force engaged in the primary sector. The secondary sector or industry contributed only about 12 per cent of employment in the State. (Sahasrabudhe V.G., Nov. 1967 Pp. 4-5, 126)

Agriculture which was the major economic activity outside Mumbai remained undeveloped and had very low productivity. Maharashtra had one of the lowest average rates of foodgrain production. This was the only State that had negative growth-rate of foodgrain production excepting sugarcane, between 1961 and 1971. (Maharashtra Economic Development Council, 1976. Pp.14-15) Of the total gross cropped area in the State, Maharashtra had only 6.7 per cent in 1964-65 and 8.3 per cent in 1970-71, under irrigation. Compared to this, the national average of irrigated land under cultivation was 18 per cent in 1964-65 and 22 per cent in 1971. Of the total workers of Maharashtra nearly 22 per cent were landless labourers compared to a similar percentage of 16.72, for India. (Bureau of Economics and Statistics, Government of Maharashtra, 1965, Pp. 7 and 42; 1974, P. 16)

According to official sources, the per capita income in Maharashtra in 1969-70, was Rs. 750 at the-then current prices (for India it was Rs. 598), and Rs. 424.7 (for India it was Rs. 339.4) at the 1960-61 constant price level. (Bureau of Economics and Statistics, Government of Maharashtra, 1974, Table 5, Chart 2, Pp. 9-10) However, available data also revealed that per capita income for Mumbai for the year was two and half times that of the rest of Maharashtra including urban areas. In 1964-65, per capita income in Maharashtra was Rs. 524; while in Mumbai it was Rs. 1500. There was similar disparity in the consumption-expenditure levels. The data collected by the National Sample Survey confirmed that the per capita consumption-expenditure in urban areas of Maharashtra was 50 per cent higher than that of the rural areas. Ten years later, it was 55 per cent higher. (M.E.D.C., 1976, 9-10)

Except Greater Mumbai and the industrial pockets of Thane and Pune, other areas of the State remained economically backward. The economic progress of Maharashtra therefore was very deceptive. An illustration may make the point clear.

Maharashtra operated the largest number of banks in the country; the number was 50 in 1969. It had the largest number of bank branches. The share of Maharashtra in total deposits and credits was again highest among all the States at 23.8 per cent and 30.4 per cent respectively. However, this buoyant picture of Maharashtra's banking condition was considerably deceptive. The figures were skewed by a disproportionately large share being from Mumbai city. See the following table:

Table V.13
Banking in Maharashtra
Rs. in Crores

		As at the End of 1970		
		Branches	Deposit	Credit
India	...	11,184	6,051.15	4,590.38
Maharashtra	...	1,408	1,453.32	1,320.94
		(12.58)	(24.02)	(28.77)
Greater Mumbai	...	485	1,151.65	1,121.73
		(4.32)	(19.03)	(24.43)
Maharashtra	...	924	301.67	199.21
(Excluding Mumbai)		(8.26)	(4.99)	(4.34)

(Note: Figures in brackets indicate percentage share in the all-India total)
Source: Shah A.C. and Kulkarni M.V., 1973, *Development of Banking*, Economy of Maharashtra, p. 378, Pune, Samaj Prabodhan Sanstha.

Consequently, Maharashtra lagged behind many other States on the various parameters of economic and social development. Some of the basic amenities were very inadequate in rural Maharashtra. This could be seen in the following table

Table V. 14
Percentage of Villages having Particular Facilities – State-wise

	Bus Stop	Railway Station	Market Centre	Post Office	Radio	Doctor
Maharashtra	13.6	1.1	7.5	20.5	30.1	6.9
States with Good Facilities						
Andhra Pradesh	25.6	4.2	5.4	52.3	50.6	11.8
Kerala	54.5	2.1	27.3	43.9	23.3	20.9
States with Poor Facilities						
Madhya Pradesh	9.7	0.5	3.4	8.4	23.5	1.8
Uttar Pradesh	5.0	0.8	3.5	8.4	16.2	4.2

Source: Programme Evaluation organisation (Planning Commission), 1968, Regional Variations in social Development and Levels of Living – A Study of the Impact of Plan Programmes, Vol. II, Pp. 34–35.

The Scale of Imbalance

The disparity between metropolitan urban Maharashtra represented by Mumbai and the rest of Maharashtra was glaring. The following table gives an idea of the measure of concentration of economic development in Greater Mumbai during the sixties.

Table V-15

Percentage share of (Sub-) regions of Maharashtra In Employment, Gross Output and Value Added by Manufacture

Sr. No.	Region	Employment 1961	Employment 1969	Gross Output 1961	Gross Output 1969	Value added by Manufacture 1961	Value added by Manufacture 1969
1.	Greater Mumbai	65.91	66.20	72.81	61.70	77.73	66.40
2.	Mumbai Division excluding Greater Mumbai	8.96	13.60	8.77	15.70	7357	17.30
3.	Pune Division	14.25	13.60	11.30	18.90	10.19	13.40
4.	Aurangabad Division	2.04	0.80	1.15	0.30	0.66	0.10
5.	Nagpur Division	8.84	5.80	5.97	3.40	4.35	2.80
6.	Maharashtra	100.00	100.00	100.00	100.00	100.00	100.00

Source: Table No. 7, Regional Imbalances in Maharashtra, P.26 M.E.D.C., Mumbai; 1976.

This extreme imbalance in the regional spatial economy of Maharashtra, due to concentration of opportunities in Mumbai, was reflected in the whole socio-economic life of the region and regional society. It reflected in the rural-urban ratios, in educational levels in terms of literacy, schooling facilities, enrolment in secondary schools and distribution of institutions of higher education. In brief, the spatial economic imbalance reflected itself in the total opportunity structures of the metropolis and the rest of the region as seen in the following tables.

Table V.16

Division-wise percentage of Urban and Literate Population and Schooling Facilities (1961)

Division	% of Urban Population Census '61	Literacy % of Population (According to Census '61) Gen.	Male	Female	Villages without Schools With School Nearby	With No School Nearby		Total
I Greater Mumbai	100	58.5	64.9	48.8	-	-	-	
II Mumbai Division	43.1	37.4	44.4	24.4	850	373	1223	
III Mumbai Division Including Mumbai	17.6	28.13	39.9	15.7	850	373	1223	
IV Pune Division		22.2	29.2	41.9	16.0	256	100	356
V Nagpur (Vidarbha Division)	22.3	27.8	40.9	14.1	2151	1375	3526	
VI Marathwada Division	12.6	16.1	26.2	5.7	504	420	924	
VII Maharashtra Excluding Mumbai	19.23	25.57	37.2	12.85	3761	2268	6029	
VIII Maharashtra		27.9	29.7	41.8	16.07	3761	2268	6029
India	18.0	24.0	34.5	13.00	-	-	-	

Sources: 1. Education in Maharashtra Statistical Epitome, as on 31st March 1966; General Table 1, Pp. 2 – 5; Directorate of Education, Maharashtra State, Pune, 1969

2. Figures for India are according to 1961 Census data. See Ashish Bose, (1973), Studies in India's Urbanisation 1901 – 1971, Tables 8 and 24, Pp. 280 and 291, Tata – McGraw Hill Publishing Co. Ltd., Mumbai.

3. Mumbai division includes Nasik, Dhulia and Jalgaon Districts apart from the three Konkan districts.

4. Figures for Maharashtra and Mumbai Division excluding Mumbai are not in the original table but are computed on the basis of data for the districts. (See Table V. 17)

Higher Education in Maharashtra (As on 31st March, 1966) Distribution of Institutions and Enrolment by Number of Institutions and Pupils

Greater Mumbai	Pune Vidarbha	Nagpur and and Marathwada	Aurangabad Maharashtra	Total for State
3	3	2	1	9
2815	2300	696	436	6247
	(45%)	(36.81%)	(11.14%)	(100%)
645	-	1	-	2
645	-	434	-	1079
	(50.9%)			(100%)
1	-	1	-	2
1569	-	221	-	1790
		(87.6%)		(100%)
2	-	-	-	2
682	-	-	-	682
(100%)				(100%)
2	-	-	-	2
75	-	-	-	75
(100%)				(100%)
6	4	1	1	12
2834	1916	959	430	6139
(46.16%)	(31.23%)	(15.45%)	(7.10%)	(100%)

Source: Education in Maharashtra Statistical Epitome March 1966, Directorate of Education, Maha. State (Pune, 1969)

Table V.20

Distribution of Some Socio-Economic Indicators of Disparity between Greater Mumbai and Other Divisions of the State

Table V.20

Distribution of Some Socio-Economic Indicators of Disparity between Greater Mumbai and Other Divisions of the State

Sr. No.	Indicator	Greater Mumbai	Mumbai Division excluding Gr. Mum.	Pune Divn.	Nagpur Divn.	Aurangabad Division
1.	Advances by Commercial Bank (1970-71)	87.1%	1.9%	8.3%	2.1%	0.6%
2.	Industrial Electric Consumption (1973-74)	63.2%	25.3%		10.4%	1.1%
3.	Number of Goods Transport Vehicles per lakh of Population (1970-71)	402	69	130	45	32

Source: Data from Regional Economic Imbalance in Maharashtra, Pp. 19-25 (Maharashtra Economic Development Council, Mumbai)

Information on various socio-economic indicators clearly shows the excessive economic and spatial disparity that divided Mumbai from the rest of Maharashtra. Nearly 20 per cent of the investment capital of the nation was concentrated in Mumbai city alone, and created not only an inter-State economic imbalance but also a more acute intra-State economic imbalance. This spatial economic disparity was reflected in the economic disparity mentioned earlier between the Maharashtrians and the non-Maharashtrians of Mumbai. (See Table V.5)

The data presented previously amply indicates that a variety of socio-economic opportunities continued to be concentrated in the capital city. Mumbai became a powerful magnet that attracted migrants to the city. However, this excessive concentration of opportunities in a single centre like Mumbai deprived the large majority of the natives of the State of a fair share in them. Mumbai's percentage share in the population of Maharashtra was only 10% according to the 1961 Census and 11% according to the 1972 Census. The concentration of opportunities in Mumbai therefore, theoretically speaking, meant that only 10 per cent of the State's population could have access to them. This heavy balance of economic and other opportunities in favour of only 10 per cent of the population of the State deprived 90 per cent of what should have been their due. Mumbai's population was only 43 to 44 per cent Maharashtrian. In other words only 4.4 per cent of the total Marathi speaking population of the state had an access to and a share of the opportunities that this metropolis offered. It is not surprising, therefore, that this disparity and the consequent deprivation of people, found expression in the form of a movement that focused exclusively on regionalist demands.

Our content data records that a number of organised groups were formed to voice regionalist grievances and were planning organised efforts to redress them. It is a possibility that if Thackeray's Shiv Sena was not born some other group or movement might have emerged to take its place.

CHAPTER VI

THE MAHARASHTRIAN COMMUNITY

Interaction in the Metropolis

The Shiv Sena arose, claims an official publication of the Sena, in the mid-1960s, 'in defence of the rights and privileges of the sons and daughters of Maharashtra soil'. (Kapilacharya, 1967, p.3) While 'eighty per cent of jobs and of tenements in Government housing for the sons of the soil' was the more well-known of the demands of the Shiv Sena, a familiar refrain in the speeches of the Sena leaders was that the Shiv Sena was born ostensibly 'to regain for the Maharashtrian, his lost status in Mumbai'. However, this claim seems to have been either ignored or dismissed by others as mere rhetoric on the part of the Sena leaders. But empty rhetoric is not capable of mobilising people, unless the people themselves find in it echoes of their own responses and reflections of their own perspectives. As discussed in the first chapter, leaders of popular movements cannot fabricate motivating goals without a base of relevant frustration and deprivation.

An oft-repeated gibe current among Maharashtrians during the sixties and the early seventies was 'Mumbai is in Maharashtra but Maharashtra isn't in Mumbai', suggesting the fast disappearance of the Marathi community and its culture from Mumbai. The expression was in imitation of a statement attributed to Hare Krishna Mahatab, the Governor of Mumbai in the early sixties. While on a visit to the National Defence Academy at Khadakvasla, he was reported to have remarked upon the minuscule percentage of Maharashtrian cadets in the National Defense Academy (NDA) 'Khadakvasla is in Maharashtra but Maharashtra is not in Khadakvasla!'

Since then, the community leaders quoted it by way of self-criticism and also as an expression of the community's frustration.

In the previous chapter we have mentioned the survey conducted by Thackeray's *Marmik* to assess the percentage of Marathi speaking-persons in white collar jobs. It is worth noting that the survey conducted by the *Marmik* covered executive positions in Government and private establishments, rather than the employees of Class III and IV categories. Thus, although the more vehement of the demands of the Shiv Sena were related to jobs and living accommodation, the status of the Maharashtrian in Mumbai continued to be an oft-used question to evoke Maharashtrian response. This concern for the status of the Maharashtrian in Mumbai could not be expressed as a concrete demand, so except for a persistent demand that the Marathi language be used for social interactions in Mumbai, it remained more an inarticulate aspiration. However, from our data it seems clear that this concern was very much present in the minds of the members of the Maharashtrian community which later propelled, or for a while at least, supported the Shiv Sena agitation.

This concern for the status of the community was for the status of the Maharashtrian community as a whole, represented by the status of its individual members.

The focal point of a vast number of entries in the data, to be discussed in this chapter, is the 'status' of the Maharashtrian community vis-à-vis the other communities in Mumbai. These entries, touch upon (1) the status of the Maharashtrian community, its identity and culture in metropolitan life (2) the status of Marathi, the language of the Maharashtrian community in Mumbai (3) the Maharashtrian community's political equations with other communities and (4) the Maharashtrian community's definition of, and response to, its total situation.

A total of 1198 entries are considered in this chapter. Attention is focused on 645 of these, which have a direct bearing on the community's status in its various aspects. These include 53 readers' letters concerned with boundary disputes. Since the community's 'status' is inextricably related to its regional identity, the related problem of the boundary disputes becomes relevant (this point will be discussed later in its context.) However, I have excluded the reports, articles and editorials on the theme of boundary disputes from the qualitative content analysis in this chapter.

The relative intensity of various concerns can be assessed from the number of entries in different categories of themes. Of the 645 entries directly bearing on 'status' as many as 322 i.e. 50 per cent, consist of letters from readers - an indication of the intensity of people's feeling in the matter.

The distribution of the entries considered in this chapter is as follows:

Content Data

1. The Apprehensions of Maharashtrians in an Expanding Metropolis Encroachment of 'Outsiders'

We have noted in the earlier chapters the Maharashtrian community's apprehension of being pushed out of their capital city. A combination of several factors discussed earlier contributed to the migration of the middle and lower classes from the central city, which included a large number of Maharashtrians, towards the suburbs and far-off satellite towns.

This inevitable, but unwelcome outward movement of the Maharashtrian population was resented by the community for two reasons, besides the community's displacement from the centrally located residential area. Firstly, they saw in this a threat of their turning into a numerical minority in Mumbai and that too when they had just managed after a long struggle, to get Mumbai included in the linguistic state of Maharashtra. Secondly, with the fast development of Mumbai's industries and offices and with the burgeoning influx of migrants from other states, Mumbai's population was growing in leaps and bounds.

Within the migrant population there were two streams. One stream was of poor rural folk who, upon entering the city, were more or less condemned to a life in slums and shanty towns for want of better accommodation within their means. The second stream was that of the educated urban people who flocked to the city in search of jobs or hoping to seek their fortune in *urbs prima in Indis.* This upper class educated migrant not only added an edge to the economic competition faced by the native Maharashtrian, but was also better-placed to get housing in the districts of the central city from where the Maharashtrians were being increasingly pushed out to far-off places. In a city like Mumbai with a mixed population it was easy for the better-placed migrants to have a share in the control of the economic and political life of the city.

The fear of a fall in the numerical strength and the status of the Maharashtrian community in the city and the resentment at the perceived factor responsible for this situation – the heavy influx of 'outsiders' – were articulated in a number of letters by newspaper readers.

Encroachment of Outsiders

There are twenty-six letters in the data, thirteen of which are mainly concerned with encroachment on 'their' city by 'outsiders'; almost an equal number of letters are chiefly preoccupied with the community's reduced numerical strength and its falling status in the fast-growing metropolis. These letters, by and large, perceive a threat in the situation to the community's aspiration to assert its identity and leave its mark upon the city.

Surprisingly a number of letters reveal considerable introspective evaluation of the community's strength and weaknesses. Some self-critical letters warn the Marathi community that it could never entertain hopes of asserting its identity in Mumbai, its own State capital, unless it could have a share in the control of the trade and commerce and the economic activity of the city.

Some of these letters censure Maharashtrian complacency and absence of group solidarity. The community spirit evinced by the migrant communities is held up as a pertinent ideal, a prerequisite for safeguarding one's community interests.

Corresponding to these letters, in almost equal numerical strength are reports and articles that appeared between 1964 and 1966. The grievance seems to be publicly voiced by community leaders at various levels, prior to its gaining currency in print.

Dwindling Maharashtrian Population

Several Maharashtrian leaders from various fields publicly expressed their feeling of apprehension at the fast growth of Mumbai and the relative fall of its Maharashtrian population. As early as 1964, these forebodings were expressed in the State Legislative Assembly by members of both the ruling and opposition parties, as noted in the earlier chapters. In the late sixties, the *Maratha* as well as some other papers reported that the State Government was considering a bill to control the influx of migrants. (Mrt. 20.3.368; Mht. 20.3.68; Nvs. 22.2.68)

Leaders' Apprehensions

Even outside the State Legislature, the call for restraining the stream of migrants from other States was often repeated by various leaders and party spokesmen, in different contexts.

As mentioned in the earlier chapters, representatives of the Municipal Corporation publicly said that it was impossible to solve Mumbai's civic problems without maintaining a check on its fast-growing population. (Mrt. 23.3.64, 12.12.64, 19.1.65, 21.1.65)

N.V. Gadgil, an eminent Congress leader from Maharashtra and once a minister in the Central Cabinet, warned the Marathi community at a public speech, that the fast growth of the city and the explosion of its population would upset the population balance in Mumbai, much to the disadvantage of Maharashtrians, their life and culture in the city. This would deprive the Maharashtrian of his representative role in the city, he complained. (Mrt. 11.4.64)

Apprehensions were expressed from public platforms that with the rapid increase of the non-Maharashtrian population of the city, the Marathi speaking citizen's chances of being elected to public bodies and representing the citizenry, thereby safeguarding his own community's interests, were fast dwindling.

The large out-of-State migrant population displacing Maharashtrians in all walks of city life was seen as a threat to Maharashtrian identity and its bearing upon the city. (Mrt.21.9.64)

Even a newspaper like the *Maharashtra Times* which generally subscribed to a balanced opinion, published articles criticising the State Government's apathy and ineptitude regarding the problems arising out of the excessive urban and industrial expansion in Mumbai and its failure to safeguard the interests of the native Maharashtrian community. (Mht. 2.5.64)

Occasions for Tensions

Some of the reports carry stories of incidents contributing to the resentment against migrants or 'outsiders'. This vast metropolis of Mumbai where people of diverse languages and cultures - both from the North and the South - encountered one another (as perhaps nowhere else in India) easily escalated tensions between various groups.

Some reports complained of forcible occupation of land by members of certain North Indian communities.

In Chapter IV, there were reference to reports of clashes between tenants of chawls and landlords who had built unauthorised structures on illegally-occupied land.

Irrespective of their validity, these reported incidents reveal how a feeling of distance and resentment was imperceptibly building up in the minds of the native community regarding the 'outsiders' whose population was incessantly increasing. In some of these reported incidents, the 'outsiders' consist of South Indian communities.

Editorials

Apart from these reports, several editorials in Marathi journals during 1964 and 1965 consistently complained of the excessive migration to Mumbai and the consequent worsening of its civic and social situation. Also they warned against the effects of these forces on the position and proportion of the Marathi community in Mumbai's population.

These editorials refer to the alienation, frustration and feeling of harassment among Maharashtrians in Mumbai. They pointed out that the Maharashtrians, composed of the middle and working classes of the city, were being fast driven out of the main city and out of white collar and industrial jobs. The Maharashtrian situation had taken a turn quite contrary to Maharashtrian expectations and aspirations prior to the formation of Maharashtra State.

The *Marmik* took a more extremist and alarmist position regarding the explosion of Mumbai's population due to the yearly influx of 100,000 persons and its effect on the Maharashtrians' situation.

Commenting on its success in family planning, (Maharashtra State ranked first in the country in the early 1970's), the *Marmik* observed that Maharashtra, already less populated compared to many other States, because of its success in controlling its population, was going to draw increasing numbers of migrants from all over the country especially from more populous States like Kerala. This meant more and complex problems for Maharashtra. The Marmik editorial cautions the Marathi community and directs its criticism to uneven implementation of family planning in different States. (Mrm. 14.2.70)

A number of editorials were concerned with the problem of the proliferation of hutment colonies all over Mumbai and observed that a majority of people in the hutment colonies in the Northern suburbs with a few exceptions were poor migrants from outside Maharashtra. On the one hand, there was displacement of the members of the native and older residents belonging to the middle and working classes by the better-off upper middle class migrants. On the other hand, simultaneously there was a growth of slums in the new suburbs and satellite towns, due to the influx from the southern States of Tamil Nadu and Kerala, who could not afford better housing. Most of the editorials criticised the State Government for its failure in protecting native Maharashtrian's interests.

A *Marmik* editorial pointed out that once hutment colonies came up they tended to get established and were allowed to grow on humanitarian grounds under popular pressure. The slum dwellers under slum improvement schemes received financial aid from the Municipal Corporation and the State Government. While access to Government Housing Colonies required a domicile certificate of 10 to 15 years, the migrant slum-dwellers received financial aid from the Mumbai Municipal Corporation and the State Government under slum improvement schemes. In other words; the poor migrants were encouraged to join

Mumbai's slums and were allowed to add to the pressure on civic amenities, without having to pay taxes for them. They in fact were financially aided by the Civic and State Governments! If the State allowed this proliferation of slums in Mumbai the editorial warned, people would have to protest and agitate against it. (Mrm. 15.2.70)

2. Maharashtrian Identity and Culture on the Retreat

In our data about 35 letters and 80 reports voice their distress at the status of the Maharashtrian (the Marathi speaking person) The general complaint was that Maharashtrian identity, language and culture did not receive due recognition and respect from the non-Maharashtrian communities of Mumbai. These communities, although individually in a numerical minority, together tended to ignore the Maharashtrian in his own State capital, because of his weaker economic position.

The Maharashtrian Ignored in the Metropolis

The complaint that the Maharashtrian was being ignored and isolated in his own State capital was oft-repeated in different contexts. They expressed the Maharashtrian's many-sided frustration and his growing alienation. These expressions of frustration, unlike the entries on the other themes, begin to appear soon after 1960, the year of the formation of Maharashtra State. A letter complains that in the new State's first cabinet, from among the five seats from Mumbai, only one went to a Marathi speaking person although Maharashtrians formed the single largest community in Mumbai. (Nvk. 4.5.60)

Letters express anguish that Maharashtrian identity was not recognised and respected in various walks of life by the non-Maharashtrian communities of Mumbai, even after Mumbai had become the capital city of Maharashtra and no more belonged to a bilingual State.

A letter complains (referring to a relevant editorial in the *Maratha*, 11.4.62) that the High Court in Mumbai still continued to be referred to as Mumbai High Court even by Supreme Court judges, in spite of the Government Gazette having decreed that it be called Maharashtra High Court. (Mrt. 25.4.62)

Another letter complains that Tarapore, which was clearly within the borders of Maharashtra, was referred to in a report by the *Times of India* of 21.8.62 as being in Gujarat. A letter pointing out the mistake was ignored by the *Times*, says the *Maratha* letter. (Mrt. 1.9.62)

The state of Maharashtra was still referred to as Mumbai State and described as bilingual in school textbooks (including those prepared by the State Government!) even four years after the formation of the unilingual Maharashtra State. (Mht. 2.6.64)

Anglicised distortions of place names in and around Greater Mumbai, the subtle non-recognition or even suppression of Marathi culture, for example, when presenting items as representative regional cultures of India to foreign visitors, newspaper articles critical of Maharashtrian heroes (Heroes and Hysteria, Ind. Exp. 3.7.66), letters by non-Maharashtrians, especially by South Indians (T. Ind., Readers' Letters' 1.7.66) against introduction of Marathi in the state administration in Mumbai – all these instances were interpreted as disrespectful to the Marathi community in Mumbai and the Maharashtrian identity of the metropolis. The English press, which repeatedly voiced these examples of non-Maharashtrian resistance and subscribed to a so-called 'cosmopolitan culture', came to represent an anti-Maharashtrian attitude.

Reports and Articles

These tensions and resentments voiced in letters and the Maharashtrian community's tussle with other communities for a position of status and authority, find an echo in many a report, article and editorial. They throw further light on various aspects of Maharashtrian aspiration and frustration.

A report in early 1960 conveys the Marathi community's aspirations as well as financial limitations.

C.D. Deshmukh (acclaimed by the Maharashtrian community for his resignation as the Finance Minister in the Nehru Cabinet over the issue of Mumbai's inclusion in Maharashtra) while laying the foundation stone for a building to house an auditorium etc., for multifarious literary and dramatic activities of the Mumbai Marathi Sahitya Sangh, advised the sponsors to collect Rs. 10/-

from every Marathi family in Mumbai to overcome paucity of funds for the project. (Mrt. 8.1.60)

The desire to assert Marathi culture in Mumbai seems to be a reaction to the perceived non-recognition of it by non-Maharashtrians.

In 1962, the *Maratha* writing on a resolution passed in the Municipal Council to re-name Girgaum Road after one of the founders of modern Mumbai – Jagannath Sunkersett - on the occasion of his centenary commented that the resolution was stalled and ignored for long by the Mumbai Pradesh Congress Committee. (Mrt. 21.2.62)

Similarly, the *Maratha* reported that a film made by the Films Division showing the unveiling of the Martyr's Column (raised to commemorate 105 lives lost during the Samyukta Maharashtra Movement) at Flora Fountain in Mumbai, was quashed by the Film Censor Board. The *Maratha* saw in this, the hand of non-Maharashtrian authorities who seemed to have viewed the event as an expression of Maharashtrian 'chauvinism'. (Mrt. 8.8.63)

Mumbai's Integration with Maharashtra

One of the grievances of the Marathi Community was that Mumbai, in spite of being a part of Maharashtra and also connected to the hinterland of Maharashtra, was looked at as separate from Maharashtra and that efforts were made to keep it so.

An early editorial refers to the tendency to look upon Mumbai as separate from Maharashtra and observes that this disposition was symbolic of the absence of integration of Mumbai with Maharashtra and of its distance from the hinterland. (Nvs. Ed; 15.11.61)

In 1965, Atre, the editor of the *Maratha* and a member of the State Legislature, brought to the notice of the Home Minister that the Greater Mumbai Police were using a separate flag from the one used by the Maharashtra Police. The Home Minister promised removal of this differential practice. (Mrt. 2.3.65)

There were other occasions on which differences of opinion, attitude and perception caused tensions to run high. An example was the centenary celebration of Mumbai High Court and the commemorative volume published at that time.

The *Maratha* reported: The Committee appointed by the State Government for writing the history of the Mumbai High Court brought out a volume in which it quoted Hon'ble Justice Chagla at the unveiling of Lokmanya Tilak's portrait in the High Court premises. Mr. Chagla observed that history had proved that Tilak's cause was right and just while the verdict of the High Court on Tilak was proved unjust. However, the Advocate-General of Maharashtra (Mr. Seervai) objected to the inclusion of these remarks on the grounds that they were disrespectful to the High Court. This became an issue of controversy, the opposition parties criticising the Advocate-General's stand as non-national to say the least. Ultimately when the State Government decided to bring out only an abridged version of the history to avoid controversy, it was criticised for lacking self-respect and courage of conviction. (Mrt. 27.3.62 and 1.4.62)

Soon after grievances regarding appointments of judges to the Mumbai High Court and other small-causes courts surfaced.

According to the report in the *Maratha* these appointments were manipulated by the-then Law minister (Shantilal Shah) and were not in accordance with the rules for selection by the Public Services Commission of the State Government. The report alleged that Marathi persons were subtly eased out or denied positions of high office in various fields in Mumbai and demanded that the appointments of the two judges be made through the Public Service Commission. (Mrt. 28.11.64)

Two years later, the *Marmik* published, after its survey of executive and similar positions in Mumbai's establishments, a list of people in judicial and legal positions in Mumbai and Maharashtra State. This included the Law Minister, the Chief Justice of the High Court, the judges of the civil and criminal courts, the Advocate-General of the State, his assistant, the solicitors of the Mumbai Municipal Corporation, the Coroner and the Inspector-General of Police. It observed that it was rather strange that not a single Marathi name was on the list. It further commented that non-Maharashtrians who did not know Marathi were supposed to give justice to the common man in Mumbai and Maharashtra. (Mrm. 11.9.66)

Occasionally, community leaders also voiced grievances and warned against injustice to the members of the native community. (Mrt. 3.5.62; Nvk. 22.4.62)

At a large meet of the 'head-load carriers'or Mathadi workers (most of whom came from the rural districts of Southern Maharashtra) the Home Minister of the State, the Chief Guest on the occasion, declared that the exploitation of the Maharashtrian in Mumbai would no longer be tolerated or allowed. (Mrt. 1.3.65)

Two years later, the President of the Maharashtra Pradesh congress Committee, speaking at an inaugural function in Mumbai observed that the Maharashtrian was not yet (even after Mumbai had become the State capital) a first-class citizen of Mumbai. He added that he was interested in bringing about a change in the situation through co-operative banks which would supply capital to Maharashtrians for small scale industries and business. (Lks. 8.7.67)

Maharashtra's Heroes and 'Others'

In the mid-sixties an editorial in *Loksatta* referred to an incident over the Shivaji Jayanti holiday in a business firm in Mumbai.

The editorial observed that the Marathi man, even after the formation of Maharashtra State, had no status in his capital city. The firm had refused to give holidays on the 1st and the 3rd May which happened to be Maharashtra Day and Shivaji's birth anniversary respectively, but insisted on granting the holiday on 2nd May, a Sunday. The workers were willing to work on that Sunday partly to compensate for the second holiday in the week. The editorial observed that this kind of incident revealed a total lack of sensitivity to peoples' sentiments about their idols and heroes. To call this lack of sensitivity and understanding as 'cosmopolitanism' was a travesty of the term and it shielded vested interests. (Lks. 14.5.65)

In 1966, an equestrian statue of Shivaji was installed at Shivaji Park in Mumbai for which part of the funds were contributed by

Mumbai's textile workers. The act of installing the statue was in a sense, symbolic of asserting the Maharashtrian identity in Mumbai. Any criticism of the 'Shivaji cult' especially coming from the non-Maharashtrian was unwelcome and interpreted as an affront to Maharashtrian identity.

The *Maratha* reported a speech appealing for funds by the-then Home Minister who asserted that there was nothing parochial about the 'Shivaji cult' but it is pertinent to the time. (Mrt. 24.7.66)

Around the mid-sixties the feeling that the Marathi community was imperceptibly pushed out of its capital city and that its identity and culture was being ignored and treated with indifference and disrespect by others in the city, was so strong and pervasive that even popular literary and dramatic works bore references to it. A popular farce in the tradition of folk-plays had for its title, an eloquent and pithy Marathi saying, 'The blind one mills the flour, and the dog laps it up'.

According to a review of this popular farce in the *Maratha*, the play depicted a realistic picture of the position of the Maharashtrian in Mumbai, who 'inspite of being the master of the house' and the native of the land, was often looked upon as a thief and culprit. The review appreciated the tragi-comic presentation of the theme. (Mrt. 31.8.66)

Another review of the same play in *Navashakti* observed with satisfaction that the farce had been able to focus on the shortcomings of the Marathi community itself rather than on the others' drawbacks. That it avoided a 'hate campaign' was also to its credit. (Nvs. 5.9.66)

Marathi Educational Institutions on Decline

Marathi Schools

A persistent grievance was that the demand for more Marathi Primary Schools in various parts of Mumbai was consistently ignored by the Mumbai Municipal Corporation and its Educational Department. Consequently Marathi speaking children were occasionally forced to attend Gujarati and Hindi medium schools in their own state capital. (Mht. 26.3.63 Lks. 4.6.65, 2.7.65) Another complaint was that the existing Municipal

Schools were neglected by the Education Department while more attention was paid to Gujarati and other language schools. Marathi medium schools received less funding. (Nvk. 11.9.60; Mrt. 19.2.66, 17.2.68)

As late as 1970, a letter rued the decision to substitute English for Marathi as the medium of instruction, at one of the oldest and well-established Mission high schools for girls in Central South Mumbai. The letter referred to the inconvenience that the new decision was likely to cause to the young pupils and their parents and pointed out that the decision was quite inconsistent with the Government's professed policy to encourage the regional language. (Mht. 9.4.70)

Municipal Marathi Schools

Readers' letters also mention the absence of Municipal Primary (Marathi) schools even in areas with a fairly large Maharashtrian population. These letters are consistent with reports and comments on the Municipal Council debates. It appears that in spite of the demands of parents and a large number of potential pupils, many a district of the city did not have primary schools for Marathi speaking children.

The press reports of the Municipal Council meetings show that the opposition party aired the grievance that the Party in power consistently neglected the Marathi schools of the Municipal Corporation. These reports thus corroborate the grievance voiced in the readers' letters.

The opposition leader in the Council observed that certain areas (Mumbadevi, Imamwada, Mahim, Borivali, Andheri, Kandivali, Vileparle East), inspite of their having a large number of Marathi speaking pupils, did not have Marathi schools. While more than two-thirds of the 23,000 students of the 7th standard in the Municipal schools were Marathi speaking, the number of Marathi schools in relation to this was very small. The opposition party members hoped for the rectification of this lack by the opening of additional Marathi schools. (Mrt. 16.8.68, 15.5.65; Sanj Mrt.)

Reports and complaints from several Municipal Councillors, of grossly inadequate and ill-served buildings for these schools, especially those in the far-off suburbs, continued to appear even after the mid-sixties. (Mrt. 2.5.64, 2.8.65, 13.9.66, 5.8.67, 21.8.67)

Several other entries allege discrimination against Marathi schools and favouritism towards Gujarati schools by the Corporation's Education Department.

An article appearing in the *Marmik* throws some light on the situation.

It observed that relatively lesser proportion of the Corporation's grant-in-aid was expended on Marathi pupils than on pupils from other linguistic communities. Only thirty-two private Marathi primary schools (with 6939 pupils) compared to 65 similar Gujarati schools (with 24,196 pupils) were recipients of a share in grants to the tune of Rs. 6 lakhs, disbursed by the Mumbai Municipal Corporation. This happened, according to the article, because the condition stipulated for the receipt of grant was that the recipients raise a fund of matching amount. Few Marathi schools could fulfil this condition. Consequently the biggest share of grants went to Gujarati schools. The article warned that unless the Marathi community was more careful, the other communities would reap the fruits of opportunities available in Mumbai, to the disadvantage of Marathi community. (Mrm. 15.5.66)

The fact was that the number of Municipal schools was inadequate for the growing number of Mumbai's school-going children. This affected the Marathi community most, it being numerically the single largest, but economically poorest community. The percentage of Marathi speaking children attending Municipal schools was much higher that these attending private schools, compared to children of other language groups in the city.

Marathi (medium) Schools on the Retreat

As referred to in the fifth chapter, some of the entries suggest that Marathi secondary and higher secondary schools and other educational institutions began to disappear in Mumbai when it became the capital city of Maharashtra State. It naturally was seen as another danger signal that the Maharashtrian community was 'disappearing' from the metropolis. (Mrt. 1.7.66, 1.10.66, 31.1.67, 13.5.67)

Secondary schools and the Language-media in Mumbai - A Note

It probably was true that Marathi medium schools were facing a threat of reduced financial support and consequent falling standards and/or closure in Central and South Mumbai.

The cause for this situation however, was not the decline in absolute numbers of secondary school scholars among the Marathi community in Mumbai. A major factor responsible for this situation in Central and South Mumbai seems to be the movement of the community from the city to northern suburbs. The extreme shortage of living accommodation and high prices of apartments, and stiff rents in the city forced the growing families of residents of old quarters to move out. This outward movement of the community affected the Marathi medium schools in Girgaon and Grant Road in Central-South Mumbai. The late sixties saw the institutions in the city reducing in strength while the new ones in the suburbs were yet to reach the standard and build up a sufficient reputation.

Another relevant factor was that although the number of Marathi medium schools and their student population had grown in absolute numbers during the decade, their growth was not fast relative to that of schools and student population of other language media. It is not surprising therefore that Marathi medium secondary schools appeared to be shrinking in number and standard in the sixties.

With the fast expanding tertiary sector in Mumbai and consequent increase in the educated urban middle class composed of migrants from various linguistic regions, English gained popularity as the medium of instruction and the number of English (medium) schools - both primary and secondary - increased.

Marathi Cinema

During the 1960's Marathi cinema was passing through a difficult phase. It had already left behind the golden days of Prabhat Film Company, Hans Pictures and Atre Theatres. Operating on relatively small capital and working by different values from that of the Hindi film industry in Mumbai, Marathi cinema had already lost a lot of ground in the competition with Hindi cinema in the fifties.

A letter in the *Maratha* by a person connected with the cinema complains that the celebration of the golden jubilee of Indian cinema in Mumbai was conspicuous by the absence of well known Maharashtrian film personalities like V. Shantaram, Baburao Pendharkar, Durga Khote, Acharya Atre, etc. Thus the organisers of the function had failed to recognise the important contribution made by Maharashtrians to Indian cinema.

Another letter grieves that well-known Marathi films made by the Prabhat Film Company were with a South Indian mortgagee and were in danger of being damaged by the sheer ravages of time. The mortgagee in whose custody the films were would not permit fresh prints of these to be made.

A third letter requests the State Government to reduce taxes and give financial help to the Marathi film industry which was in bad shape. It regrets that the exorbitant rates charged by the theatre owners were beyond the capacity of Marathi film producers who made films on shoestring budgets. As a result, Marathi films had all but disappeared from Mumbai's film market. (Nvs. 21.9.67)

The first Marathi film festival was held in Mumbai in April 1963, after the formation of Marashtra State. High hopes were expressed for Marathi cinema both by those connected with Marathi films and the Chief Guest, Gopal Reddy, the Minister for Information & Broadcasting. (Mrt. 24.4.63)

The market for Marathi cinema was limited compared to that of Hindi cinema. As a result, Marathi cinema both as a profession and as an art had lost its prime place in Mumbai and was driven out of competition by Hindi films which had a wider market and could afford higher investment. The Information Minister's hope that Marathi cinema would become a symbol of prestige for Indian cinema was ironic considering the reality. (Mrt. 17.11.63)

Reporting on the opening of the third Indian International Film Festival held in Mumbai, the *Maratha* commented upon the conspicuous absence of the well-known Maharashtrian personalities who were the pioneers of Indian cinema. (Mrt. 31.1.65)

The grievance expressed in the report was similar to the one earlier articulated by a letter.

The frustration and alienation of Marathi film makers is reflected in the entries in our data. Simultaneously, there are reports, articles and an occasional editorial, which perform critical self-assessment and discuss the problems encountered by Marathi cinema, especially in Mumbai.

Although beaten in competition with the Hindi cinema of Mumbai, the Marathi film makers, critics and audience expressed confidence that their films, given the limitations of the small investment, were qualitatively better, had better thematic values and projected a world true to life.

However, in a more introspective and evaluative mood, they also admitted that the Marathi film had got into the habit of indulging in rural imagery and stereotypes and its failure to reflect life and problems of changing rural and urban Maharashtra was responsible for its failure both as an art and as a commercial venture. (Mrt. 11.2.63, 17.11.63, 22.1.67)

The Prabhat Studio, where some of the best Indian films were produced by the Prabhat Company, was taken over in the sixties by the Central Government to start the Film Institute of India for training young people in the art and craft of the cinema.

The entries in our data point out that the fees at this Film Institute were beyond the reach of Maharashtrian families and most of the students as well as instructors at the Institute were non-Maharashtrians coming from the upper crust of Indian society.

The establishment of the Film Institute on the premises of Prabhat Studio contributed little to the interest of Maharashtra or Maharashtrians, except conferring on Maharashtra and Pune, the dubious prestige of having an All-India Institute. Those who passed out from the institute did not easily get absorbed in the film industry in Mumbai. In such a situation, the Maharashtrian community which characteristically had little financial security, was unlikely to encourage its youth to train at the Film Institute. (Mrt. 22.7.66, 2.9.66)

Here again, the old jibe seemed to ring true. The Film Institute was in Maharashtra but Maharashtra was not in the Film Institute!

The major difficulty faced by the Marathi film industry was regarding capital investment. Co-operative effort was recognised as the only alternative available to Marathi film makers for building up capital. (Sakal 8.5.60; Mrt. 8.12.63; Sanj. Mrt. Ed. 8.5.65)

However, more important than capital were well-equipped studios and theatres for exhibition. It was a long-standing and uniform experience of those connected with Marathi films that Marathi films did not get theatres for exhibition; and when they got the theatres they found their rates to be exorbitant. The well-equipped Prabhat Studio was bought by the Central Government and the other studio in Kolhapur was too far away from the main film centre and market of Mumbai. Faced with this tough situation, the Marathi film industry which was already finding it difficult to compete with Hindi cinema was thrown completely into the doldrums. (Mrt. Art. 17.11.63, 10.10.64)

The Marathi film-makers, at this stage, appealed to the State Government to make available to them, film studios and cinema-houses for production and exhibition of Marathi films, instead of limiting State patronage to distributing annual prises. (Mrt. 10.10.64; Mht, 24.11.69)

Leading Marathi film-makers approached the State Government and met the Central Ministers to seek help. (Mrt. 10.10.64, 12.9.66) Questions were raised and debated in the State Legislature. Chief Minister Naik promised to persuade the theatre-owners to exhibit Marathi films in their cinema houses. (Mrt. 22.7.65) It apparently did not work. The State Government ultimately issued an order directing every theatre in Mumbai to exhibit Marathi films at least for four weeks every year. (Mrt. 2.3.68, 12.4.68) This raised a hornet's nest and the Government was criticised severely both by the cinema owners and the non-Marathi press. Rigorous implementation of this rule, in the face of stiff opposition by cinema-owners, was thus difficult. (Mrt. 19.3.69)

The regular exhibition of Marathi films in Mumbai was still limited to about 4 to 6 cinema houses in areas like Dadar, Parel and Girgaum which have predominantly Maharashtrian populations. Hindi cinema dominated the Mumbai scene completely.

3. Marathi Language in the Metropolis

Of all the sub-themes if there is any single one which merits the highest number of readers' letters, then it is that of 'the Marathi language' - with 134 letters.

What is distinctive about these letters on the theme of use of Marathi language is that the demand for wider use of the regional language seemed to originate from the people themselves and was not brought to their notice by the press.

These letters by common people demand the use of Marathi in various walks of life in the metropolitan city, particularly in the civic and the state administration.

These letters, more than those on any other theme, are found across all the journals under review.

Marathi in Social Intercourse

In Mumbai, the regional language had to contend with twin rivals. Firstly, Marathi had to face the stiff competition from a universal language, English, which had come to serve as the 'link language' among the elite and the educated. Secondly, it had to contend with other regional languages like Gujarati, (the language of the dominant business community), and with Hindi, (the national link language) which had already found acceptance among the Maharashtrians.

There are about two dozen letters which appeal for making a beginning in the use of Marathi in the public life of the metropolis especially in matters concerning people at large. English could still continue to be employed in the exclusive areas of academic learning and at higher level of commerce and industry.

A letter in 1962 advocates that though it may not be possible to eliminate English altogether, especially in higher education it should be possible at least to get rid of its unnecessary use in facets of our daily life, such as in schools, cinema houses, public institutions, the Secretariat and in Government offices. Name plates and signboards in offices could function with the Nagari script (currently used for Marathi) and the seats in auditoriums could be arranged in Indian alphabetical order. The letter maintains that the making of even a modest beginning was necessary so that the use of Indian language and script become self-propagating. (Mrt. 4.1.62)

The other letters make a demand for making a beginning in the use of the regional language and the Nagari i.e. Marathi script which was familiar to a large number of people and therefore could be introduced with hardly any inconvenience to any one. For example, signboards, bus, train and lottery tickets, names of public buildings, of Government and other establishments, cinema houses etc., could easily employ the Marathi (Nagari) script.

Reports and Articles

During 1965, at a public meeting, when the-then Home Minister of the State (N.D.Desai) began his speech in Marathi, he was heckled by a crowd demanding that he speak in Hindi and not in Marathi. The Minister however firmly refused to speak in any other language but Marathi, in the capital of Maharashtra and the hecklers were told that they were free to leave the meeting if they could not follow the speech. (Mht. 29.3.65; Mrt. 29.3.65)

The incident received lot of publicity in all Marathi papers.

The struggle for Samyukta Maharashtra had made the Maharashtrians hypersensitive to the reluctance and resistance of non-Maharashtrians to the use of Marathi language.

The disregard for Marathi in public announcements on the Railways and over radio; screening documentary films in languages other than Marathi while showing Marathi feature films, as against the usual practice of showing short films of the same language as that of the feature film in theatres; the use of English, Hindi, Gujarati and South Indian languages instead of Marathi on signboards intended for public information; these were all subtle sources of annoyance for the members of the Marathi community. (Mrm. 8.5.66, 22.5.66; Mrt. 10.12.66; Mht. 23.4.70)

The predominance of English, Hindi and even Gujarati at prestigious functions and public gatherings of mixed communities, even after the formation of Maharashtra, was seen as demeaning to the status of the Marathi language.

The *Maratha* reported in 1967, that according to an earlier announcement, the citation of civic honour to be presented by the Mumbai Municipal Corporation to Dr. Zakir Hussain, the President of India, was to be in Marathi. However, at the actual ceremony, complained the Maratha, the Congress mayor read only the English translation of the original citation. (Mrt. 23.8.67)

Maharashtrians were not only touchy about the silent, unspoken non-recognition of Marathi in Mumbai's public life; they also felt hurt at the resistance shown by non-Maharashtrians in Mumbai to the use of Marathi.

In an issue of the *Indian Express* (9 May 1966), a South Indian criticised the proposed measure of introducing Marathi in the State administration and complained that this would affect non-Marathi employees' prospects adversely. The letter suggested that the measure should be recommendatory, not compulsory.

A columnist in the *Marmik* reacted to this letter strongly. He observed that it was the lenient attitude of the Maharashtra State Government which had encouraged the migrants and visitors to consider it their birthright not to learn the local regional language even after living in Maharashtra for a number of years. (Mrm. 22.5.66)

An incident in the Maharashtra State secretariat received considerable coverage. A highly-placed non-Maharashtrian State Government official connected with Government warehousing was approached by a Maharashtrian journalist from a small town. The journalist submitted an application in Marathi on behalf of employees of certain Government warehouses. The official reportedly threw the application away as it was in Marathi, a language he could not understand. The non-Maharashtrian official's action was perceived as not only rude, but also an insult to Marathi, the language of the State. (Mrt. 29.10.66)

Marathi in Civic Administration

Letters demanding that Marathi be introduced in the Civic and the State administration began to appear in the press early in 1960s.

A letter in 1961 urged that the Mumbai Municipal Corporation had until then ignored the popular demand for Marathi; it was high time that it took steps for conducting the administrative activities of the Civic Government through the regional language. (Nvk. 24.1.61)

Another letter demanded that the various forms brought out by the departments of the Municipal Corporation be filled in by the general public in Marathi.

Letters suggest that instructions to the general public from the Municipal Corporation and the bus tickets of the B.E.S.T. be printed in Marathi. (Lks. 16.7.69, 30.7.69)

A few letters complain that the general communications sent out to primary Marathi schools of the Municipal Corporation were often in Gujarati and occasionally in Hindi or English; they question the propriety of such a practice.

A letter observed that the progress reports of pupils in the Municipal primary Marathi schools, which used to be in Marathi prior to the formation of Maharashtra State appeared now rather curiously, in Hindi. The letter writer was upset by the Corporation's scant respect for Marathi. (Nvk. 28.4.63)

Letters demanded that the correspondence conducted by the Corporation's education department with their primary Marathi schools, or the health and other information bulletins that it issued for parents should be in Marathi instead of Hindi or Gujarati. (Nvs. 2.4.67, 26.7.67)

Another letter made a somewhat curious complaint A new Municipal school building in a suburb, Kandivali East, housed primary schools which taught in different languages including Gujarati, Hindi, Marathi and Urdu. Each primary school had its signboard displayed on the school building except the Marathi school. A number of representations by responsible citizens and social workers in the area to the school authorities and Municipality's Education Department to put up the signboard in Marathi proved futile. (Nvs. 2.9.67)

As late as 1968, a letter pointed out that the admission forms to Municipal primary schools in Mumbai were printed in English. The writer of the letter complained that persons like him not familiar with English found it quite an ordeal to fill in the admission form. The letter strongly opined that the Municipal Corporation of the capital city of Maharashtra had to conduct its affairs in Marathi - the language spoken by 4 crore people in Maharashtra - if democracy had to have any meaning. (Nvk. 18.5.68)

Reports & Articles

Marathi in Corporation Schools

An effort to introduce Marathi as a compulsory subject in the Corporation's non-Marathi schools, initiated by the opposition parties, was not successful due to the resistance by the BPCC according to press reports.

The BPCC representing the non-Marathi communities in Mumbai continued its resistance to the move initiated by the opposition parties of introducing Marathi in all Municipal Schools. (Mrt. 16.8.64, 15.5.65; Sanj Mrt. 13.7.67, 11.8.67)

The question of compulsory Marathi in non-Marathi Municipal primary schools continued to be discussed and debated even after and in spite of the State Government's order to introduce Marathi language as a compulsory subject in the school curriculum in Maharashtra. The Education Department of the Municipal Corporation resisted the move according to reports in the *Daily Maratha.* (Mrt. 13.7.67, 11.8.67)

The resolution for introducing Marathi as a compulsory subject in Municipal primary schools tabled by the opposition parties could not be passed due to the BPCC's vote against it. (Mrt. 21.8.67)

Marathi & Corporation Administration

Twenty-six out of thirty-two reports and articles were preoccupied with the problem of the introduction of Marathi in civic administration.

The Mumbai Municipal Corporation, representing the citizens of the city had on its body members from various communities of the city. The biggest single community was Marathi speaking. The suggestions that Marathi be used in the affairs of municipal administration, which till the sixties, were conducted entirely in

English provoked protest and resistance. The decision about it was not as smooth as the decision by the state legislature for the introduction of Marathi in the state administration. While the State Government had taken a decision in this respect by the mid-sixties, the Corporation debated this decision for over a decade (1961-70)

The majority of reports and articles narrate a long-drawn struggle during the decade by various opposition parties including the SSP, CPI, CPM and ultimately the Shiv Sena for recognising and introducing Marathi in the Civic Government's affairs, with the BPCC trying hard to resist. The story ends with a measure of success for Marathi in civic affairs.

After the formation of Maharashtra a demand for the use of Marathi in Municipal administration was made by the SSP members George Fernandes and Mrinal Gore. The resolution was however, resisted by the members of the ruling Party, BPCC, and therefore could not be passed. (Mrm. 23.4.61; Nvs. 19.10.61; Mrt. 29.1.64)

Again in 1963, the opposition parties jointly pressed for the use of Marathi in civic administration. The demand initially, was for use of Marathi for presenting the agenda and maintaining the minutes of the meetings of the Municipal Council. It was expected that eventually Marathi would be introduced in the rest of the administration. A number of Marathi speaking members of the BPCC disregarded the norms of Party discipline and voted in favour of Marathi. (Mrt. 20.12.63, 23.12.63)

In a meeting of the Municipal Council held on 28.1.64, a resolution in favour of Marathi as the language of the municipal administration, moved by the leader of the opposition (Waman Bapat) was passed unexpectedly with a thumping majority. (Nvk. 29.1.64; Mrt. 29.1.64, 3.2.64, 23.5.64; Mht. 30.1.64)

Prahlad K. Atre published an editorial in *Daily Maratha*, welcoming the momentous decision, as 'The Triumph of Mother Marathi.' (Mrt. 31.1.64) In spite of the resolution being passed in 1964, it came to be actively implemented only from 1970 onwards.

Slowly, however, the winds of change were blowing. The question of administration through Marathi was revived again in

April 1968. The Shiv Sena by then had entered the civic council.

In 1968 the Municipal Commissioner made a statement to the effect that some knowledge of Marathi would be required for eligibility to get jobs in the Municipal Corporation. The statement was welcomed by a majority of members of the Municipal Council. (Mrt. 10.4.68)

When the Shiv Sena member, Manohar Joshi, demanded that minutes of the meetings of the Council be kept in Marathi, Mrs. Ahilya Rangnekar (CPI-M) pressed for an amendment that the administrative records should also be kept in Marathi. However, Shanti Patel, the leader of the ruling Party (BPCC) in the Municipal Council tried to thwart the passing of the resolution and the amendment, by pressing for both English and Marathi for keeping the minutes of the meetings and the records of the corporation. At this stage, all the opposition parties staged a walk-out in protest. (Mrt. 26.4.68)

The Shiv Sena that emerged as the strongest of the opposition parties in the 1968 civic elections threatened non-operation with the ruling Party of the Municipal Corporation over the issue of Marathi language. (Nvk. 21.1.70) However, a resolution favouring the use of Marathi not only for the minutes of the council meetings but also for other administrative records was ultimately passed in 1970.

Marathi and the State Government

In current data, eighteen letters from six journals appeal to the State Government for the use of Marathi in its public announcements and correspondence with the people at large. The letters regret the slow pace of the introduction of Marathi in State administration.

Some of these letters demand that various government circulars and instructions be printed in Marathi rather than in English. A letter demands that the State Public Services Commission Examination should be conducted in the regional language. (Mht. 6.2.65; 14.5.65; Lks. 10.6.65, 4.8.65)

Other letters demand that the regional language Marathi be accepted as a language for court applications.

A letter narrates the story of a tribal whose application to the Government in connection with his land, did not reach the higher authorities as it was in Marathi and not in English. (Mrt. 2.4.63)

Another letter complained that the new land reform law which affected the lives of the rural people was unavailable in Marathi. (Lks. 3.7.68)

A number of letters repeat the demand that various official forms that people have to fill in for the Government Departments should be made available to them in the regional language (Marathi), instead of English which was an alien language for a majority of the people.

The content data includes letters demanding that the regional offices of the State and Central Governments conduct their correspondence with the people in the people's language i.e.the regional language (Marathi)

The State Housing Board and the English Language

Letters spanning the decade repeatedly complained against the English language being used in the State Government's Housing Board in Greater Mumbai. The letters protest against the persistent use of English by the Housing Board in its correspondence, its application and other forms, its information bills, its instructions to the tenant-residents, its rent-receipts, and even the signboards indicating locations in the Housing Colonies - all of these meant for people of the lower-middle, middle and working classes. The letters complained that this caused considerable inconvenience to applicants and the residents of the housing colonies, especially those of the working class who had little or no familiarity with the English language. The letters strongly criticised the use of English as inappropriate for the purpose and asked why Marathi, the language of the State of Maharashtra, had no place in the administration of the State Housing Board. (Letters Mht. 2.8.62, 16.12.64; Nvk. 3.7.63; Nvs. 7.9.65; Mrt. 20.3.67; Lks. 31.10.69)

Reports & Articles

The demand for Marathi in Government administration was

rooted in the aspirations stimulated by the formation of the linguistic State of Maharashtra. At the start of the decade, the aspirations and the expectations of fulfilment were strong and unsullied.

An editorial in the *Loksatta* in 1962 in response to the complaint that the Marathi language was being treated as a second-class citizen's language, had advised patience. It assured that the Marathi language would assert itself in Mumbai once it had evolved and developed sufficiently to deal with modern industrial life. (Lks. Ed. 10.4.62)

With the passage of time, however, hopes began to dissipate inspite of the assurance by the State Government of its intention to introduce the regional language (Marathi) into administration at various levels. (Lks. 21.11.63)

Maharashtra's Chief Minister (V.P. Naik), during the question hour in the State Legislature, stated that his Government was making serious efforts for the introduction of Marathi, since the Indian Constitution included the directive favouring replacement of English by regional Indian language by January 1965. (Mrt. 10.3.64)

Towards the end of 1964, the State Legislature, following the unanimous decision of the State Cabinet, resolved to introduce Marathi in the State Government's administration by the Indian Republic Day (26th January) 1965. (Mrt. 1.11.64, 3.12.64, 17.1.64, 30.3.65) However, the implementation of this resolve was a difficult and slow process. It was in 1966 that the State Government, by a special notification, declared Marathi as the State's official language. The reports of the State legislature were also to be maintained and printed in Marathi. (Mrt. 22.2.66, 1.5.66; Mht. 1.5.66)

However, the Governor's speeches at the opening of the budget session continued to be in English, even after this declaration.

Several members of the opposition parties voiced the demand that the Governor make his speech in Marathi. In 1965, Mr. Dhulup, a member of the opposition (PWP), strongly criticised the Governor (Mr. Cherian) for speaking in English. (Lks. 19.2.65)

In 1968 the opposition members were still making the same

demand for the Governor's speech in the regional language. The opposition parties sent a letter to the Governor, asking him to make his inaugural speech either in Marathi, Hindi or even Malayalam (the language of the Governor's native State) The Governor, however, declined to use any of the languages suggested, on the ground that he was not sufficiently conversant with any of them, and made his speech in English. (Mrt. 4.2.68)

In 1969, the opposition parties again repeated their request with little success. (Mrt. 26.2.69)

According to a report in the *Maratha*, in spite of the Government's efforts to introduce Marathi in administration, there was only a limited and half-hearted implementation of the Government's orders. This came to light in the State Government's enquiry. (Mrt. 11.5.68)

Marathi in the Railways

A good number of letters (15) complain of the neglect of Marathi by the Central and Western Railways which run suburban rail networks apart from having the terminal of their main lines in Mumbai. Letters demand the use of Marathi by these two railways in Mumbai.

Ten letters from1960-67 air the grievance that Marathi was systematically ignored by the railways especially by the Western Railway 'with its terminal office in Mumbai, the capital of the Marathi speaking area.' These letters refer to the disappearance of Marathi on the Western Railway signboards in the very area of the Marathi-speaking i.e., in metropolitan Mumbai and its immediate environs and complain that the signboards appeared only in Gujarati, Hindi and English. This, according to the letters, was absolutely unfair and against the accepted norm of the railways that place names of each linguistic region and state would be indicated in its particular language and script. The letters demand that instructions to passengers in compartments ought to also be in Marathi along with Hindi and Gujarati.

Another oft-repeated complaint was that announcements to passengers on the public address system on suburban and other stations on the Western Railway, in Mumbai and adjacent areas in Maharashtra, were often in Gujarati, Hindi and English to the exclusion of Marathi. The letters complain that even after repeated requests and complaints to the Railways, the situation did not change.

A letter in the early sixties observed that Marathi was gradually being replaced by Hindi in the Central Railway inspite of the announcement that Marathi would receive an important place on that Railway network spread over large areas of Maharashtra. Instructions to passengers at the Victoria Terminus which were in Marathi in earlier times, had given way to those in Hindi and English. Whereas the G.I.P. Railway, the predecessor of the Central Railway, brought out its timetables in Marathi, the Central Railway did not. Marathi was often excluded even from the announcements to passengers on the public address system at the Victoria Terminus. (Mht. 20.6.62)

Letters demanded that announcements at the railway stations be made in Marathi and that the timetable be also made available in Marathi. (Mht. 20.6.62, 10.7.63; Mrt. 7.2.67; Lks. 18.2.70, 17.3.70)

A few letters said that signboards on roads, railways and post offices in Mumbai and its vicinity were often in English, Hindi, Gujarati, often even in South Indian languages but rarely in Marathi. (Mht. 27.8.65; Mrm. 6.3.66, 24.7.66; Nvs. 30.6.67; Nvk. 26.2.67)

Similarly there was a demand that small suburban and village post offices should have facilities to accept telegrams in Marathi since it employed the Nagari script. (Mht. 11.12.62; Lks. 28.2.63)

Marathi and All India Radio

There are in all 59 letters that complain about the unfair treatment to programmes in Marathi, both on the regular general broadcasts or on Vividh Bharati Commercial section. The chief grievance was that a meagre amount of time was given to Marathi programmes at Mumbai's broadcasting centre. Keeping in view that the Marathi community was the single biggest community of Mumbai and that Mumbai was the capital city of their state, the letters strongly demanded that A.I.R. Mumbai ought to give greater broadcasting time for Marathi programmes. These letters do not ask that programmes in other languages be excluded on Mumbai's rador station; what they did ask for was to reserve one powerful transmission wave-length exclusively for Marathi (a demand more or less fulfiled by the mid-seventies) These letters began to appear in 1962, at least four years before the birth of Shiv Sena and continued almost throughout the decade.

Marathi and Vividh Bharati

A repeated common complaint was that Vividh Bharati, Mumbai, gave very little time for Marathi recorded music. The constant referent for comparison in these complaints was the period of one and three-fourth hours reserved for recorded songs in South Indian languages under the 'Carnatic Sabha' programme. The rest of the broadcast time, complain the letters, was used for recorded music in Hindi interspersed with a song or two in other languages including that of an occasional one in Marathi. The letters expressed disbelief that the A.I.R. should find it difficult to reserve the same amount of time for songs in Marathi, the language of the transmission region.

In fact, there was no justification for the 'Carnatic Sabha' programme on Vividh Bharati from Mumbai since Mumbai's South Indians could surely listen to programmes in South Indian languages relayed by the powerful southern broadcasting station, argued the letters. The major share of time for songs on Vividh Bharati other than those in Hindi should appropriately go, according to the letters, to Marathi songs on a radio station situated in Maharashtra.

The letters, therefore, considered the arrangement grossly unjust, frustrating and subtly insulting to the native community of the State. The readers' letters further said that their repeated complaints and communications to the A.I.R. fell on deaf ears, without bringing about any change in the situation even after the formation of Maharashtra State.

An occasional letter drew the conclusion that this happened because the A.I.R. administration in Mumbai was dominated by South Indian officials. (Mrm. 19.6.66) An occasional letter also complained that South Indian film actresses were invited (from the South) to inaugurate special Vividh Bharati programmes in Mumbai but similar courtesy was never accorded to Marathi actresses in the capital of Maharashtra. (Nvk. 8.5.66)

All these instances were looked upon as covert ways of not giving proper status to if not aiming deliberate insults at the Marathi language and the Marathi speaking people. These letters were mostly from 1964-70.

Demand for more time for Marathi programmes

In the sixties, Marathi programmes were broadcast from 5 centres – Mumbai, Nagpur, Pune, Goa and Sangli. Of these Mumbai alone had a powerful transmission. The readers' letters maintain that the capital city of each State is the chief broadcasting centre for programmes in the language of that particular State except in the case of Mumbai where the language of the State did not get the prominence it should have. Demand for more time and an exclusive wavelength for Marathi programmes was made in these letters.

Another point of irritation was that announcements were made in Hindi even for Marathi programmes on Mumbai-B. The announcements continued to be in Hindi even when the quantum of Marathi broadcasts was increased. The announcement in Hindi (for Marathi programmes) was perceived as a (systematic) denial of the prospect of reserving the wavelength Mumbai-B exclusively for Marathi. It also meant a symbolic supersession of Marathi by Hindi; in short, it was seen as an affront to the regional language of the State.

The letters questioned

For whose benefit were the announcements made in Hindi? If they are for non-Marathi listeners, these listeners, surely, could understand Marathi announcements in case they could understand the programme; but if they were meant for Marathi listeners, they should appropriately be in Marathi.

The only explanation for this anomalous situation offered by the A.I.R. was that of 'technical difficulties.' (Lks. 1.9.67) Most of the complaints remained unanswered, according to these letters. (Mrt. 24.3.67; Lks. 2.6.67; Mht. 1.2.68)

Letters occasionally made comparisons between the situation at Mumbai and at centres in the South.

In the South, a letter observed the Tamil Nadu Government even changed the name Akashvani into its Tamil equivalent. Obviously, the people of the Southern States, Tamil Nadu and Kerala well knew how to enforce their demands by resorting to violent agitations. Would the Central Government, letters enquire, like Maharashtra to follow suit, for the redressal of their grievances and fair demands? (Lks. 1.9.67; Mht. 1.2.68; Nvs. 24.11.67; Nvk. 31.1.68)

By and large, the letters opined that Akashvani at Mumbai and the Ministry of Information & Broadcasting at the Centre, were being very unreasonable, a situation they found to be frustrating and annoying. K.K. Shah, the Minister for Information & Broadcasting, had promised that the Mumbai-B channel would soon come to be exclusively reserved for Marathi broadcasts. However, since the promise was not fully implemented by 1968 it brought in a spate of angry letters. (Nvs. 14.9.67, 17.10.67, 21.11.67; Lks. 1.9.67; Mht. 1.2.68)

Some of these letters spoke of organising agitations and demonstrations.

A letter writer offered to organise and lead a protest demonstration to A.I.R. Mumbai, for the redressal of the grievances of Marathi listeners. (Nvk. 31.1.68) Another letter repeated the necessity of taking out a protest march to A.I.R. Mumbai. (Mrt. 29.6.68)

A reader enunciated that merely reserving channel Mumbai-B was not really enough unless its transmitter was more powerful. Mumbai-B, according to the letter, was much weaker than Mumbai-A and Mumbai-C which broadcast non-Marathi programmes. (Mrt. 296.68)

Demand for Marathi Programmes from other Centres

Besides a demand for an increase in Marathi programmes from Mumbai, the letters also asked for programmes in this language from other centres like Baroda, Ahmedabad, Indore, Delhi and Hyderabad which had a siseable Maharashtrian community.

Letters from readers in Gujarat pointed out that about 2 lakh Maharashtrians lived in Gujarat and that the Municipal Corporation of Baroda, a city which had a large Marathi population (Baroda being a former Maratha princely state) made its public announcements in both Gujarati and Marathi.

The letters demanded that the transmission centres in Gujarat should broadcast some programmes in Marathi. The letters observed 'If Mumbai could regularly broadcast programmes in six different languages, it should not be impossible for the transmission centres in Gujarat to introduce a quota for Marathi programmes.'

A.I.R. Publication

Yet another grievance voiced by the letters in the mid-sixties was regarding A.I.R. publications. Letters question why the A.I.R. fortnightly was not being published in Marathi as was done in English and other Indian languages like Hindi, Urdu, Bengali, Assamese, Telugu and Gujarati.

Reports and Articles

The few entries under the genre of reports and articles in the data on the subject fully concur with the large number of readers' letters voicing grievances about All India Radio. Most of these reports trace the origin of the developments to the policy and programming of the Mumbai radio station.

A detailed article based on a two-week fact-finding survey and observation of A.I.R. programmes broadcast from Mumbai and other State-capitals, concurred with the grievances in the readers' letters, Recorded music in four Southern languages was gradually being added to regular broadcasts in eight languages from Mumbai Radio Station. Besides the question of listeners' interests, the question of patronage to artists of various linguistic groups was also involved, said the article. In Mumbai, of the total programming of nearly 5500 minutes during the two weeks, 3055 minutes were reserved for programmes in languages other than Marathi while 2355 minutes were given to Marathi, the language of the surrounding region. This was grossly unfair according to the article. (Mrt. 2.6.63)

Early in the decade, the State Government had complained to the Central Minister for Information & Broadcasting, regarding the inadequate representation for Marathi programmes in radio broadcasts from Mumbai. The State Government had asked for one more powerful transmitter to be exclusively deployed for Marathi programmes. Pune then was already a broadcasting centre with prospects of further fortification while two more broadcasting centres were to start functioning in Western Maharashtra and Marathwada. (Mrt. 19.10.62)

The Marathi Literary Conference at its session in Hyderabad passed a resolution repeating the demand for a wavelength exclusively meant for Marathi programmes over the Mumbai radio station. The conference, besides asking for autonomy for All India Radio, made pleas to the Chanda Committee for transmission of Marathi programmes from broadcasting centres at Indore, Baroda, Hyderabad cities which had large Marathi speaking populations. (Mht. 28.12.65; Mrt. 28.12.65)

A conference of Marathi speaking persons representing 20 lakh Maharashtrians living outside Maharashtra, made a demand for a more powerful broadcasting transmitter and a greater number of Marathi programmes for Mumbai, Nagpur and Goa. (Nvk. 25.5.65)

Two years later, the Marathi Literary Conference held at Bhopal reiterated the earlier demand for due recognition to Marathi by reserving Mumbai-B wavelength for Marathi programmes. The-then information and broadcasting minister (K.K. Shah) who inaugurated the poets' meet at the Conference, promised to look into the Marathi community's grievances. (Mrt. 14.5.67)

From 1st of August 1967 Mumbai-B began broadcasting Marathi programmes exclusively. It meant that all the announcements which were earlier made in Hindi (a practice which annoyed the Marathi community) now came to be made in Marathi, though non-Marathi programmes in Sindhi, Kokani and Hindi continued to be broadcast on Mumbai-B as before. Mumbai-B however, technically became an exclusive transmission service for Marathi programmes. (Mrt. 2.8.67)

The Information and Broadcasting Minister, aware of the irony of the situation, promised to solve the technical difficulty and to all appearances, Mumbai-B would be entirely for Marathi programmes by October 1967. (Mrt. 31.8.67)

Marathi in Higher Education
Marathi and the University of Mumbai

A few letters discuss the place of Marathi in university education in Mumbai. The demand for the introduction of Marathi as an alternative medium of instruction and examination in various subjects at the university level had raised its head in the early sixties, when the question was being debated all over the country. In the mid-sixties the Maharashtra Government declared Marathi the official language of the State and introduced it in the state administration. The Central Government introduced the official languages (Amendment) Bill in the Lok Sabha in 1967; this gave rise to a countrywide debate on the subject of language in higher education.

Letters

A letter written in 1966, welcomes the State Government's step of introducing the regional language for state administration and suggests that this good step for its success, needs to be followed by another, that of stipulating minimum knowledge of Marathi as a requirement for eligibility for examinations conducted by universities in Maharashtra (Mht. 12.12.66)

About the same time there arose the demand for introduction of Marathi as the alternative medium of instruction and education at the University of Mumbai, as in other Universities in Maharashtra. Letters articulating this demand refused to make an exception of the Mumbai University in this matter.

Two letters observed that 'Mumbai's cosmopolitan character had often been overplayed' and was likely to be used as an excuse to stall introduction of Marathi as an alternative medium of instruction and examination at the University. Some non-Maharashtrian members and the English press in Mumbai had already started a mild campaign against this thought. However, University of Mumbai, like the universities in other state capitals

- Kolkata, Madras, Ahmedabad, Allahabad and Chandigarh - cannot escape giving recognition to the regional language. (Nvk. 28.7.67; Nvs. 9.8.67)

One of the letters averred that the status of the official national language of the University of Mumbai should be given to Marathi rather than Hindi. The University was located in Maharashtra whose people's language was Marathi. Besides, Marathi being one of the 14 national languages of India, recognition to it as the official language was not parochial. (Nvs. 20.3.65)

Reports and Articles

The formation of Maharashtra, following the break-up of the bilingual Mumbai state, stimulated considerable debate about the place of the regional language in higher education and institutions of higher learning.

At the time of the bifurcation of bilingual Mumbai state, to allay the fears of the non-Marathi communities (regarding the dominance of Marathi), the-then Chief Minister Y.B. Chavan, in his statement in the State Legislature, gave an assurance that the medium of instruction in the Mumbai University would continue to be English, to be replaced by Hindi at a later date.

However, it seems that the natural course of events could not be contained by political assurances. By the mid-sixties, a demand for the use of Marathi in the administration and at the University became increasingly vocal. There was considerable tug-of-war between the opposing demand and a continual debate raged.

An article in early sixties discusses the need and the significance of the use of regional language in higher learning while analysing the odds against it. It points out that the real difficulty in introducing the regional language at the higher education level is not so much the lack of developed vocabulary; vocabulary develops with the expanding use of language. The real obstacle was the prejudice against such use. If the regional language could be used at other universities and centres in the State, there was no reason why it could not be used at the University of Mumbai. The article suggests that Marathi should be given an experimental trial as an optional medium of instruction and examination at the University. Lack of will and prejudice on the part of the University were according to the article, real hindrances to the development of the language. (Lks. 20.4.62)

From Maharashtrian quarters, there was considerable criticism of the Mumbai University for its resistance to the introduction of Marathi as the medium of instruction and learning at the College and University levels and also, for the University's reluctance until then to establish a department of Marathi in spite of it being a well-developed modern Indian language.

Reports of discussions on the budget of the University point out that the University Library had less than 5 per cent books in Marathi. A member of the senate remarked that the state of affairs at the University compared with that of a colonial University. (Mrt. 13.10.63, 21.3.65)

In the Marathi Literary Conference in 1967, Dr. Kolte, Vice-Chancellor of the Nagpur University and president of the Conference, complained that Marathi was being suppressed in the State capital. He criticised the reluctance of the University of Mumbai to introduce Marathi, the language of the people of the state, as the medium of instruction at the college level. (Mrt. 14.5.67)

Madhu Limaye, MP (SSP), advocated use of Marathi at the University as well as in the State administration including the courts of justice at a public meeting. (Mrt. 3.9.67)

Mumbai Marathi Granth Sangrahalaya, a leading cultural institution of the Maharashtrian community, invited University teachers to participate in a seminar on introduction of Marathi as the medium of instruction at the College and University levels. The seminar participants unanimously agreed to request the Vice-Chancellor of the Mumbai University to arrange for the introduction of Marathi as the medium of instruction at the University. (Mrt. 17.2.68)

Soon the news followed that Justice Gajendra Gadkar, Vice-Chancellor of Mumbai University had begun to move in the direction of introducing Marathi at the Mumbai University, following the decision at the All India Vice-Chancellors' Conference. (Mrt. 24.2.68)

Simultaneously, however thinkers and community leaders through their writing and speeches drew attention to the fact that the English language was likely to dominate the cultural scene in India besides the field of higher learning as long as it carried extraordinary prestige with the Indian elite. The bureaucracy's hold on the Government and other jobs perpetuated the importance of English in the job-market. This was a real obstacle to the propagation of the regional language. The change to the regional language therefore needed caution at the State level and coordination of efforts at the Central and State levels. (Lks. 21.4.62; Mrt. 17.9.62, 6.11.64; Mht. 17.8.66)

4. Maharashtrians in Interaction in the Metropolis

The BPCC and Marathi Community

The Mumbai Pradesh Congress Committee (BPCC) was an important Congress Committee in the structural organisation of Indian National Congress ever since the 1920's. It dominated the civic and political life of the city. The Congress movement in pre-independent India and the Congress Party in independent India were strong forces both in Maharashtra, Gujarat and in Mumbai where the people of these two provinces met, lived and worked together. However, increasingly the BPCC came to represent the interests of the business community and entrepreneur class which was chiefly from Gujarat. It dominated the BPCC especially during the post-independence period and the bilingual phase of Mumbai State.

The Maharashtrian community made up of the middle and working class of Mumbai came to be slowly alienated from the BPCC, though, in the rest of Maharashtra the Congress Party dominated the scene through another independent Committee – the Maharashtra Pradesh Congress Committee (MPCC) During the active period of Samyukta Maharashtra Movement beginning 1954 and lasting up to the formation of unilingual Maharashtra State, the distance between the BPCC and the MPCC widened. The Congress in Mumbai i.e. the BPCC viewed peoples' aspirations for a unilingual Maharashtra as a threat to its interests. It could not identify itself with the aspirations and goals of the people of the surrounding region of Maharashtra. The content data on the relevant theme is to be interpreted in the context of the background presented above.

Letters

There are more than a dozen letters critical of the BPCC, considered to be the arch-enemy of the Maharashtrian community ever since the Samyukta Maharashtra Movement. S.K.Patil, the leader of the BPCC described as the uncrowned king of Mumbai during the 1950's and 1960's, was rather unpopular with the Marathi community because of his anti-Samyukta Maharashtra stance. Rather, he was looked upon by the Maharashtrians as a spokesman of the capitalist class and the rich merchant community of Mumbai, who dominated the Mumbai Pradesh Congress Committee.

During the Samyukta Maharashtra Movement, S.K. Patil had incurred the wrath of the Marathi community, by declaring in a Mumbai public meeting, that Mumbai would never be included in Maharashtra State, 'as long as Sun and Moon shone in the firmament.'

For all practical purposes the Marathi community never really forgave Patil for his statement.

In 1962, however, Patil was felicitated for his work for the Mumbai Marathi Grantha Sangrahalaya (a well-known Marathi library) In his speech on the occasion, Patil stated that it was he who persuaded Nehru to give consent to the formation of unilingual Maharashtra State inclusive of Mumbai which was what the Marathi community wanted.

A letter in *Maratha* ridiculed Patil for his attempt to reinstate himself in the eyes of the Maharashtrian community. According to the letter, the only work Patil did in his life was to collect funds for the Congress Party from the rich of Mumbai in recognition of which, he was appointed treasurer of the All-India Congress Committee. The letter remarked 'The mutually close ties between the capitalists of Mumbai and Patil, perhaps made Patil oppose the formation of a unilingual Maharashtra including Mumbai.' (Mrt. 23.5.62)

Another letter highly critical and suspicious of the BPCC, in the early sixties, warns the Maharashtra State Government against following the footsteps of former Congress Governments in Mumbai, dominated by the BPCC and therefore under the sway of the rich communities and the capitalist class of Mumbai. (Mrt. 1.5.63)

A letter in the *Marmik* holds the BPCC responsible for Maharashtra's misfortunes and comments that Maharashtra would march forward only when the BPCC's separate identity merges in the Maharashtra Pradesh Congress Committee. (Mrm. 24.7.66)

Another episode which threw light on the tension between the BPCC and the Marathi community, took place when the Sampoorna Maharashtra Samiti staged a *bandh* in September 1966 to protest against rising prices and a few Ministers from the BPCC in the Maharashtra cabinet resigned to censure the Chief Minister and his MPCC colleagues.

Following this *bandh* by the SPMS, there was also a revival of the demand for a centrally-administered Mumbai by five hundred non-Marathi members of the BPCC (refer to Ch. III)

In the wake of these events, letters in the Marathi press came out with strong disapproval and criticism. These letters considered such a demand unjustifiable, and viewed the whole matter as a conspiracy against the Marathi community.

Editorials

The relationship between the BPCC and the Marathi community received attention in 14 editorials – the largest number of editorials on a sub-theme in the present chapter. A majority of these are from the *Maratha*, the mouthpiece of the opposition in Maharashtra. The views expressed in these editorials are not very different from those voiced in the letters. We explore these editorials in the hope of throwing further light on the relationship between Maharashtrians and the BPCC which claimed to represent a cosmopolitan community consisting of different ethnic groups of the city.

Of these 14, ten editorials deal more directly with the subject of the BPCC, its activities and policies and express their resentment in varying degrees.

An editorial of the early 1960's in the *Navakal* – the pro-Congress independent paper - discusses the place given to Maharashtrians by the BPCC in its distribution of candidature for the-then impending Municipal Corporation elections.

The prickly fact about the selection of candidates by the BPCC, the editorial complained, was that the BPCC list had largely ignored Marathi speaking candidates in the capital of Maharashtra, revealing its shortsighted, callous attitude towards Maharashtrians. According to the editorial, the Marathi community had been given only 48 candidates, when the community's proportionate share ought to have been 60. Also many of these candidates were selected for their capacity to blindly support the BPCC policies which in all likelihood, were to further the plurality of Mumbai. The editorial observed that Marathi members were in a minority in the Congress Party of the Municipal Corporation even under the leadership of S.K. Patil. Consequently the Marathi members in the BPCC were always forced to play second fiddle and carry the burden of the opinion of the dominant community.

The editorial further observed that the Maharashtrians often let their Party loyalty ride over their community loyalty. On the other hand members of other communities were bound by loyalty to the community. Consequently Maharashtrians often helped members of non-Marathi communities to get elected even in constituencies predominantly Maharashtrian in population. On the other hand all non-Marathi communities often united in a common interest; that of maintaining Mumbai's 'cosmopolitan' and plural character. They would, therefore, keep away from the members of the Marathi community even of their own political Party, over the question of Mumbai.

As a result, inspite of Maharashtrians being the single biggest community of Mumbai, the city always remained a pocket of non-Marathi vested interests. (Nvk. 26.1.61)

The Daily *Maratha* was generally a harsh critic of the BPCC and often described it as the arch-enemy of Maharashtrians. (Mrt. 10.12.64, 12.12.66)

The *Maratha* repeatedly pointed out that the industrialists and the business communities of Mumbai, who together controlled the economic activity of the metropolis, also held the reigns of the BPCC Through the BPCC, they could exercise their power in the political affairs of the State. The Marathi community, on the other hand, representing chiefly the middle and the working classes of the city who lacked entrepreneurship and remained away from business activity, had no voice in the BPCC and therefore in the civic government of the Mumbai Municipal Corporation as well. In the civic government of the capital city of Maharashtra, the non-Maharashtrians predominated as the representatives of the BPCC, the *Maratha* observed. (Mrt. 10.12.64)

Editorials in the Marathi press often pointedly articulated their disapproval of the existence of the BPCC as a separate entity of a Pradesh Congress Committee.

Referring to the news that V.A. Patil, the President of the MPCC, forbade its members to raise the issue of the merger of the BPCC with the MPCC, the *Daily Maratha* in yet another editorial observed that the existence of Mumbai Pradesh Congress Committee as an independent body was not only unnecessary and against the norm, but that it also was a threat to Maharashtra's identity and interests. However, the independent entity of BPCC was allowed to continue, the editorial commented, only to humour the capitalist and business community in Mumbai who contributed to Congress coffers. (Mrt. 26.6.65)

Several editorials of the *Maratha* air their criticism and censure the BPCC, its policies and programmes as 'pro-capitalist, pro-big-business, anti-proletariat and therefore anti-Maharashtrian.' One of these editorials written in the context of the 1967 elections gave a call for the 'demolition of the BPCC' (Mrt. 12.12.66)

The *Marmik* also spared no criticism of the BPCC. In its editorial written upon the formation of the Sampoorna Maharashtra Samiti (for the integration of Belgaum Karwar with

Maharashtra), it had appealed that all parties in Maharashtra including the MPCC be united to resist the BPCC's anti Maharashtra machinations.

The editorial observed that it was not sufficient that the opposition parties in Maharashtra united themselves for the resolution of the Goa and Mysore problems. It insisted that the SPMS should skillfully win over the support of the MPCC which represented the majority in the districts of Maharashtra. After all, the editorial pointed out that the interests of the MPCC and the BPCC were far from being identical. According to the editorial, it was necessary that the opposition parties raise a united voice together with that of the MPCC (for the inclusion of Goa and Belgaum in Maharashtra) Such a united effort alone could resist the anti-Maharashtra stance of the BPCC, especially in the case of Goa (Mrm. 12.6.66)

When the BPCC elected Madhavan Nair as the candidate for Mumbai's mayoralty in 1966, the *Daily Maratha*, in an outspoken editorial, observed that 'even after the formation of the linguistic State of Maharashtra with Mumbai as its capital, the BPCC was unwilling to work under the guidance of the Maharashtra Pradesh Congress and that it continued with its anti-Maharashtrian attitude under the garb of 'cosmopolitanism.' An aspect of this anti-Maharashtrian attitude was to keep the mayoralty of Mumbai away from Maharashtrians, if possible. It was time that Maharashtrians, irrespective of their Party loyalty, raised their voice against such a practice. The *Maratha* further observed that the BPCC candidate, Nair, had staunchly and actively opposed the Samyukta Maharashtra Movement. The BPCC chose him because the South Indian community in Sion (Nair's constituency), was an important vote-bank for the BPCC in the general elections of 1967.

The editorial observed that from 1947-57, the only Marathi mayor elected by the BPCC was S.K. Patil, the person who built up Mumbai's reputation as a 'cosmopolitan' city and did everything to thwart the people's demand for Samyukta Maharashtra. During 1957-60, when the Samyukta Maharashtra Samiti was in power in the civic government, Mumbai had three Maharashtrian mayors. However, during the next five years of 1961-65, when the BPCC was again in power, Mumbai saw three non-Marathi mayors. The editorial asked why the BPCC should often choose non-Marathi mayors in Maharashtra's first city. (Mrt. 1.4.65)

Reports and Articles

Following the formation of Maharashtra State the Marathi community desired the merger of the BPCC with the Maharashtra Pradesh Congress Committee, while the Gujarati and non-Marathi communities opposed such a move. This clash of interests was reflected in the tussle between the Marathi and the non-Marathi in the BPCC, and gave rise to the complaint that Maharashtrians did not receive due representation in the BPCC and its bodies.

Inadequate Representation for Maharashtrian Members in the BPCC

A report in the *Maratha* in the early sixties corroborates the grievances voiced in this context by the *Navakal* editorial (Nvk. 26.1.61) Commenting on the elections of the BPCC for its various executive offices, a report in the *Daily Maratha* observed that only ten of the 49 elected positions went to Marathi speaking persons. This rendered the BPCC a non-Marathi organisation. (Mrt. 14.7.63, 29.7.63)

Reports in 1965 narrate incidents of rebellion by Maharashtrian Congressmen in the BPCC

The *Maratha*, in May 1965, reported of a memorandum presented by Maharashtrian Councillors of the Congress Party in the Municipal Corporation, Mumbai, to the Congress President, Kamaraj. These rebel Congressmen, according to the report, complained to the Congress President that the Maharashtrians did not get adequate representation on the various municipal bodies of the Council. They demanded a 50% representation as their proportionate due.

Among the Congress Party Corporators, 24 were Marathi, 21 Gujarati and 30 of other communities. And yet, according to the rebels, between 1960 and 1966 only once was a Maharashtrian member of the BPCC given the mayorship and only twice did they play the role of the leader of the House. They were inadequately represented in the various Municipal Committees, according to the statistics presented in the memorandum.

The *Marmik*, reviewing the position of Maharashtrians in the Municipal Corporation, in 1966, provided statistics regarding the distribution of Municipal Councillors by their Party and linguistic community. The picture was identical with the one given by the *Maratha*. The *Marmik* complained that even though the number of Marathi speaking councillors was larger than that of any other group, they were not given due representation on the various municipal bodies by the BPCC (Mrm. 17.4.66)

One of the grievances in this context was regarding the prestigious position of the first citizen of the metropolis, as noted earlier.

In 1964, the *Maratha* complained that the BPCC totally ignored leader of the MPCC and Chief Minister Naik's suggestion regarding selection of the candidate for the Mayorship, in the special context of the Goa-Maharashtra merger issue. According to the BPCC the selection of the candidate was totally a matter of the BPCC's discretion. (Mrt. 23.3.64)

During the mayoral contest in 1965, the opposition party (SMS) in the Municipal Council, fielded its own candidate (Waman Bapat) During the counting of the votes, it became clear that seven Marathi Congressmen had voted for the Maharashtrian candidate of the opposition. (Mrt. 29.3.65, 6.4.65)

In 1966, in the contest for the two Municipal representatives in the State Legislature, two members of the SMS (the opposition party), Harris (a Muslim) and Bapat (the leader) were elected with 46 and 39 votes respectively, while the Congress member Belose lost the election. This was in spite of the Congress' 73 members, and the opposition's 40. It was obvious that a few Congressmen preferred to vote for Harris – a minority community man from the opposition party – rather than a Maharashtrian of their own Party. (Mrt. 11.4.66)

These reports seem to support the grievance voiced by the *Navakal* editor earlier in the decade (26.1.61) Non-recognition of the due claims of the Maharashtrians and domination by the non-Marathi communities in the Congress Party in the Mumbai Municipal Council continued to be the twin plaints of the Maharashtrians during the sixties.

Alientation between the BPCC & the Maharashtrians

The Goa Issue

After the liberation of Goa, the Marathi community expected the merger of Goa with Maharashtra. The hope receded because of the factional politics in Goa. However, in 1965, the State Legislature of Goa passed a resolution favouring early merger of Goa with Maharashtra. (Nvk. 23.1.65; Mrt. 23.1.65 In response to this, the State Legislature of Maharashtra (also in March 1965) passed a resolution demanding urgent steps for such a merger. (Mht. 11.6.65)

Against this background the leader of the Samyukta Maharashtra Samiti in the Municipal Council Waman Bapat, tabled an adjournment motion, to support the demand for immediate merger of Goa with Maharashtra. The motion was not successful because it fell short by three votes. However, the voting made it clear that six leading Marathi councillors from the BPCC (D'Souza, Toraskar, Sawant, Pusalkar, Loke and Kalgutkar) supported the adjournment motion tabled by the opposition party, while another Maharashtrian from BPCC, Mirashi, abstained. Loke, one of the secretaries of the Congress Party in the Municipal Council, was said to have resigned his secretaryship to enable himself to vote in favour of the adjournment motion. (Mkt. 17.11.64)

The incident was indicative of the distance between the Marathi and the non-Marathi members of the BPCC This clash of interests of the Marathi and non-Marathi communities came to a flash point in 1966.

Two episodes during which this rift became conspicuous, were (1) the water-crisis in Mumbai in June 1966 and (2) the resignations by the BPCC ministers and legislators following the Mumbai *bandh* (organised by the Sampoorna Maharashtra Samiti) in August 1966.

Water Crisis in Mumbai & Storm in the Municipal Council

The years 1965 and 1966 saw severe drought in Maharashtra, which affected the catchment area of the lakes providing water to Mumbai. The expansion of the city had already put a strain on Mumbai's limited water resources.

In April 1966, the Hydraulic Engineer of the Corporation had given a warning of a severe water famine, in the case of a delayed monsoon. (Mrt. 22.4.66)

As feared, there were no rains until the second week of July, and a water famine appeared impending. The Municipal Commissioner suggested a temporary migration of citizens as the only solution possible and closure of schools and colleges as a crisis measure. (Mrt. 9.7.66)

The State Government, the Municipal Corporation and the industrialists, together decided to cut down working days of the industries. (Mrt. 8.7.66)

There were heated discussions on the suggested measures in the Municipal Council. The opposition leader, criticising the measure remarked that the Government was causing inconvenience to the common man while sparing the rich. Another member of the opposition (A. Pendse-SMS) demanded that the lakhs of migrants engaged in illicit distillation of liquor and bootlegging, be deported immediately. He also asked for measures to stop pilferage of water from hydrants by anti-social elements. A Republican member (R.G. Kharat) suggested that the non-Marathi settlers in suburban hutment colonies must first be asked to leave the city in case of evacuation operations. (Mrt. 13.7.65)

During these discussions a Maharashtrian member of the BPCC (Belose), also pleaded for evacuation of the non-Maharashtrian migrants on priority basis and called for measures to stall further migration to Mumbai. Shifting the city's older population without halting the incessant influx of migrants from other states would not solve the problem, he observed. (Mrt. 14.7.66)

Belose's remarks, similar in spirit and in content to those made by others, however, raised a hornet's nest for his 'parochial' views in the city's English and non-Marathi press.

To be able to provide the basic amenities to the city's existing population, Belose answered, the incessant influx of newcomers had to be stalled. By 'non-Maharashtrian' he was referring to the new migrants and not to old residents of the city, Belose explained. (Mrt. 14.7.66)

The storm soon subsided upon the arrival of the monsoon in the catchment area of lakes. (Mrt. 14.7.66)

The incident was, however, indicative of the gulf dividing the Marathi and the non-Marathi communities in the BPCC

The second episode included 'Ghera Dalo' and 'Mumbai Bandh' programmes on 24th and 25th August 1966, organised by the alliance of opposition parties under the banner of the Sampoorna Maharashtra Samiti. (Mht. 24.8.66, 25.8.66, also refer to Ch. III)

Fifteen thousand *satyagrahis* from the Mysore-Maharashtra border areas and interiors of Maharashtra and about ten thousand demonstrators from Mumbai reportedly participated in the 'Ghera Dalo'.

The following day, 19 members of the State Legislature (including two ministers), from the BPCC, resigned protesting the State Government's leniency towards the demonstrators and its failure to maintain law and order. (Among these 19, five were Marathi speaking persons)

The letters of resignation, though they received publicity in the press, however did not reach the Speaker of the Legislature. The opposition parties therefore, described these resignations as a political stunt. (Mht. 25.8.66)

The episode clearly indicated the rift between the Pradesh Congress Committees in Maharashtra.

S.M. Joshi, the opposition leader and the President of the Sampoorna Maharashtra Samiti said the dramatic resignations were a publicity stunt to spoil the name of Maharashtra which had made its demand for a democratic solution to the border dispute by way of a peaceful *bandh*. (Mht. 25.8.66)

Those who resigned accused the State government of lenient treatment to the demonstrators and protest marchers. (Mht. 28.8.66)

The Home Minister however pointed out that 3000 anti-social elements were already rounded up as a precautionary measure a day before the demonstrations while 350 more were held on that particular day. The police had to open fire twice and lathi charge and tear gas the crowds several times for which the opposition parties had accused the Government of the use of suppressive measures. The Home Minister added that there were limits to use of force in the face of a popular demonstration supported by the masses and greater use of force would have led to deterioration of peace and order in the city. (Mht. 28.8.66)

By and large, however, the Maharashtra Government received kudos for handling the situation deftly. (Mrt. Ed. 30.8.66; Mrm. 18.9.66)

The resignation issue was followed by a demand by a large number of BPCC members of the minority communities of the city, for a centrally-administered Mumbai distinct from the rest of Maharashtra.

Several reports published the news of a telegram being sent to Kamaraj, the Congress President, by five hundred Congressmen from 'A' ward, regarding the demand for a centrally-administered Mumbai. The leader of the move, Puthran denied that the demand was a reaction linked to Maharashtra's demand for Belgaum area. (Mrt. 31.8.66; Nvs. 16.9.66)

However, the Marathi speaking members from the BPCC declared that they would resist a move for the separation of Mumbai city from Maharashtra. The BPCC also, by this time declared that it was no Party to such a demand. Soon after, the 'A' ward Congress committee reportedly asked for the ouster of those demanding a separate Mumbai State. (Mrt. 31.8.66, 9.9.66)

These incidents – of the collective resignations and of the signature campaign for a centrally-administered Mumbai – seemed to have stimulated, within the Congress Party, new demands vocalising Maharashtrian grievances.

Maratha reported in September '66 that the MPCC leaders demanded that 50% of the candidates from Mumbai for the seats in the State Legislature must be Marathi speaking persons. The MPCC also claimed that it was the Pradesh Congress Committee with wider jurisdiction and authority in the State, so it should be treated as a senior Pradesh Congress Committee and its advice treated with respect by the BPCC (Mrt. 15.9.66)

Following these events, a move was initiated by the rebel members of the BPCC for the merger of the BPCC with the MPCC, for creating a single Pradesh Congress Committee for the whole region of Maharashtra including Mumbai, as in the case of other States. The issue became urgent in the context of the impending general elections of 1967.

A resolution favouring the merger of the BPCC with that of the MPCC in the interests of effective and homogeneous working of the organisation was passed at a special meet of the rebels from the BPCC under the Chairmanship of S.B. Mahadeshwar. (Mrt. 28.11.66)

This meeting held at Dadar also voiced its dissatisfaction over the BPCC's resistance to socialist policies and lack of guiding principles in selection of candidates for the general election. The chief complaint was that the middle and working classes were not given due representation in the selection.

The meet reiterated its faith in the Maharashtra Government's policies and administration and in the MPCC as a body capable of handling minority problems and safeguarding their interests in Mumbai. The meeting also passed a resolution favouring merger of Goa. This meet was attended, according to the newspaper reports, by 16 executive members of the Ward Committees of the BPCC including two chairmen, along with other rebels.(Mrt. 26.11.66, 28.11.66)

Maharashtrians and Others

In a city like Mumbai, where people of different communities came in contact with each other, close friendships were struck across the communities, as often as there were ethnic tensions between the linguistically and culturally divergent groups.What were the occasions for inter-community contacts and relationships, as well as tensions? How did the Maharashtrians (who considered themselves as the native and host community)perceive these relationships or occasions that sparked the tensions?

Letters

The content data consists of ten letters that articulate readers' reactions to 'others' and to what they perceive as parochial behaviour of 'others'. These letters touch upon various areas of life, such as recognition of the Marathi language in the social life of Mumbai, resistance to or adoption of local habits and ways, or the events linked with the DMK's politics in the South.

Parochialism and 'Others'

A letter from a reader in Baroda (Gujarat) criticises a Gujarati minister of the bilingual Mumbai State (Dr. Jivraj Mehta), for his statement in the State Legislature that Hindi, the national language, instead of Marathi, be the future medium of instruction at the University of Mumbai, after the formation of Maharashtra State with Mumbai as its capital. This arrangement was proposed to safeguard the interests of the Gujarati and other non-Marathi communities of Mumbai.

The letter regrets that the minister did not show similar concern for the safeguarding of the interests of the Maharashtrian community in Gujrat which had a siseable population in Ahmedabad and especially in Baroda. (Nvk. 9.4.60)

As noted in the previous Chapter, since the turn of the decade, letters had been appearing in journals pointing out that recruitment had become a matter of group-membership and relationship and that office jobs were becoming a preserve of South Indians.

A letter in 1965 observed that the nepotism and parochial attitude of the members of the South Indian community were chiefly responsible for large-scale recruitment of South Indians in Mumbai's offices and complained that even the usual norms of recruitment were often set aside to appoint relations or friends hailing from the same 'native place'. (Nvs. 20.7.65)

The *Maratha* had voiced a similar grievance regarding Udipi eating-houses; this was before *Marmik* began its campaign against them. The *Maratha*, through its columns, had criticised the Udipi and Kanara restaurant-owners for bringing over waiter-boys from their native Karnataka districts while a large number of unemployed boys were locally available for such a job. (Mrt. 15.2.65, 14.3.65)

The grievance against the outsiders was not only that they deprived the members of the local community of jobs, but also that they held high social positions and political offices.

A Tanjore Maharashtrian in his letter to the *Marmik* pointed out that Tamilians had accepted Gujarati and Marwari businessmen on Madras's Mint Street and that the Malayali and Kannadiga flourished in Madras's film industry and this proved that Tamilians were not parochial and narrow-minded on their home ground.

The *Marmik* in reply to the letter pointed out that the South Indians in Mumbai were not only well-settled and made a good living and were in no way harassed by any one, but they often held high social position or political office (like Madhavan Nair becoming Mumbai's mayor or Krishna Menon getting elected as the M.P. from Mumbai.) The *Marmik* asked if Maharashtrians were welcome in high social or political offices in the Southern States; and if not, who then, could be called parochial. (Mrm. 10.7.66)

Two letters from women readers react strongly to what they perceived as narrow and parochial behaviour on the part of migrants from other states. The grievance voiced was that similar behaviour on the part of the native community was invariably labelled as parochial or narrow.

A letter commenting on Jan Sangh leader Jagannathrao Joshi's advice to Maharashtrians to curb their parochialism, said that the advice first needs to be implemented by South Indian migrants to the city, who tended to use community grapevines to obtain jobs and then live exclusively community-centred encapsulated lives in the metropolis. (Mrm. 17.7.66)

The second letter, written against the background of the General Elections (1967), observed that by and large members of all the South Indian communities, irrespective of their language or State of origin, education or political loyalties, cast their vote for Mr. K. Menon in which the major consideration was that he was a 'South Indian'.

On the other hand, the letter commented, many Marathi speaking persons, workers and leaders were assisting the election campaigns of non-Marathi candidates like Krishna Menon, Harish Mahindra and Shantilal Shah. The letter rued that in spite of this the members of the Marathi community were labeled as parochial and narrow. (Mrm. 12.3.67)

Others and 'Native' Ways

The vocal resistance on the part of the migrants to adopting local ways and languages invariably seemed to generate resentment from the members of the native community. This was for obvious reasons, truer of the South Indian communities, especially the Malayali and the Tamil people who linguistically and culturally were more divergent from the Marathi community, than the neighbouring and long-domiciled Gujarati community (one of the city's oldest communities)

Others and 'Native' Language

All those who settled in Maharashtra regarded it as their homeland and adopted the language of the region for social intercourse within a generation or two. They thereby integrated and identified themselves with the Marathi speaking people of Maharashtra. Thus the Gujarati, Marwari and Sindhi carrying on their trade or business in the interiors of Maharashtra came to adopt Marathi for social life while employing their mother tongue within the confines of their homes. Bene Israeli Jews of the Konkan coast consider Marathi as their mother tongue in the manner Parsis in Gujarat treat Gujarati. The Christian population in Bassein, Ahmednagar or Nasik districts of Maharashtra are Marathi-speaking even as the Muslims in Western Maharashtra or Vidarbha are.

In other words, those who looked upon Maharashtra (and not Mumbai city alone) as their homeland, came to accept, as a natural course, the regional language – Marathi – for social communication. For all practical purposes they were Marathi-speaking even in case they retained their mother-tongue for communication within the family and kin.

This process did not take place in Mumbai for two major reasons (i) the numerical strength of the migrant community permitted its members to lead their life within the community without having to intergrate or identify themselves with the larger regional linguistic community; and (ii) Mumbai's isolation from its surrounding region especially prior to independence, encouraged this to happen. Consequently, the migrant communities of Mumbai who looked upon the city as their homeland simultaneously came to treat it as if it was independent and separate from the surrounding region of Maharashtra; in other words, they considered Mumbai in isolation, rather than Maharashtra, as their homeland.

On 1 May, 1966, Marathi was recognised as the official language of the Maharashtra State and was introduced in State administration.

In this context, a South Indian reader's letter in the *Indian Express* (9.5.66) complained that knowledge of Marathi as the condition for promotion in State Government jobs was very hard on the non-Marathi people. The letter drew a strong reaction from a Marathi speaking reader.

The latter felt that learning the language of the region where a person expected to work, was the least that he could do without complaint and that there was nothing parochial or unfair in setting up this condition. The letter-writer complained that the English version of the letter sent to the *Indian Express* was not published by that paper and therefore sought the columns of the *Marmik*. (Mrm. 24.7.66)

The grievance in this context, particularly, was that when 'knowledge of the regional language of the State' was an accepted condition for eligibility to jobs in a relevant state, 'others' objected, in case of Marathi, in Mumbai. More specifically the grievance was that 'others' in Mumbai did not give due recognition to Marathi as the regional language of the State and therefore as a precondition to avail of the opportunities available in the city.

Both the *Maratha* and the *Marmik* complained that advertisements from private and public establishments in States than other Maharashtra, often stipulated the condition of knowledge of the local (State) language as a requirement for eligibility to particular jobs in the State. However, often, there were no such stipulations in the case of jobs in Maharashtra State. This discrepancy was advantageous to the non-Marathi seeking jobs in Maharashtra, especially in Mumbai, which was one of the biggest job markets of India. (Mrm. 14.8.64; Mrt. 4.11.64)

Some of the editorials voiced similar views as expressed in the letters.

Editorials

An early editorial in the *Navakal* had complained that members of the non-Marathi communities including the minority communities were very insular and parochial in their voting behaviour and that they invariably voted for a member of their own community or its political ally but never for a Maharashtrian candidate. On the other hand the Maharashtrian perhaps being of the majority community showed a tendency to vote by Party loyalty rather than by community loyalty. However, the combination of these two patterns of behaviour proved disadvantageous to the Maharashtrian community. (Nvk. 26.3.61)

A *Loksatta* editorial in the mid-sixties had complained that the so called 'cosmopolitanism' of certain communities, people and parties, was nothing but a garb to cover their own parochial, narrow tendencies and anti-Maharashtrian attitude. It was lack of a real broad and genuine cosmopolitan outlook which made them disrespect Marathi, the language of the region as also Maharashtra's heroes adored by the regional masses. (Lks. 14.5.65)

Reports and Articles

These letters, editorials, reports and articles, reflecting a cross-section of incidents and related attitudes, suggest that the behaviour of the native community was a cumulative response to the behaviour of Mumbai's migrant communities.

In the mid-sixties, regional languages were being introduced in state administration.

In 1964, the *Maratha* reported that the Governor of Mysore addressed the inaugural session of the Mysore legislative houses in Kannada.

Commenting on this news, the *Maratha* observed

In spite of the repeated requests from members of the State Legislature in Maharashtra no Governor of this State has ever addressed the two houses of the Legislature in Marathi. No wonder that Marathi is not received with respect elsewhere. (Mrt. 26.3.64)

The *Marmik* in 1966, referred to the news that the Mysore Government evicted encroachers from the neighbouring state of Kerala, who had illegally occupied the forest lands of the State. Approving the firm hand with which Mysore Government dealt with the problem, the *Marmik* columnist contrasted it with the situation in Mumbai

In Mumbai, illegal occupation of the municipal and state lands by migrants coming from other states in search of employment was greeted with protection to such occupants in the name of the citizen's right to free inter-state movement. Consequently, the *Marmik* complained, Mumbai had become a free and open house to a variety of migrants including vagrants, beggars and other anti-social elements. (Mrm. 29.5.66)

Boundary Disputes

The unilingual State of Maharashtra was formed on 1st May, 1960. Earlier, it was part of the bilingual State of Mumbai. Before 1954, Mumbai State consisted of three major linguistic regions Gujarati, Marathi and the Kannada speaking districts of North Karnataka. Belgaum town, like parts of Karwar district with their largely Marathi-Konkani population, was a part of the old Mumbai State. When Mysore* State of Kannada speaking people was formed, the border districts of Belgaum and Karwar,

*Later renamed as Karnataka

parts of which were Marathi speaking and bilingual and parts Kannada and bilingual, were allotted to Mysore.

Since Marathi speaking people did not then have their own State, the problem of including these Marathi speaking areas in it was not a pressing one. However, after the formation of unilingual Maharashtra, the problem of defining its borders and including all the Marathi speaking areas in it became an urgent matter. Strange as it may appear, this problem of unsettled disputed boundaries was a factor which contributed to arousing people's consciousness of linguistic regional identity and consolidating a movement which tried to assert the demands of this linguistic regional identity.

Why should the border grievance contribute to an issue the centre of which was the city of Mumbai and the Maharashtrian community's place in it? The answer lies in the fact that Mumbai, besides being a national centre for industrial and commercial activity, was also inevitably the chief centre of Maharashtra's socio-political and cultural life (as of no other province – not even of Gujarat) As the nerve centre of the social, political, economic and cultural life of this linguistic region, Mumbai played the lead role in all the major activities in the surrounding region of Maharashtra. It was inevitable that this urban centre provided the leadership for Maharashtra's political activities including the agitation for inclusion of disputed border areas in Maharashtra. The MES from the districts of Belgaum and Karwar was well-equipped to carry out the protest movement and its programme in these areas and fought the elections on this issue. However, the Samiti looked for leadership, for press publicity, for economic aid and popular support from other major cities of Maharashtra like Nagpur, Kolhapur, Pune and Aurangabad and especially from Mumbai, the capital city.

We have in our data a total of 53 letters voicing grievances and demands related to the boundary disputes of Maharashtra. Eighteen of these letters are concerned with the Maharashtra-Mysore border. Twenty-three discuss the Goa merger issue in all its aspects while 12 focus on the northern borders of Maharashtra.

If we are to judge solely by the number of letters on a given theme, the issues concerning Goa's language and its integration with Maharashtra appear to be comparatively strongly felt issues, more than the dispute regarding Belgaum and Karwar. Grievances regarding the Goa issue were related to the question of regional identity and prominently added to the Maharashtrian community's misgivings between 1962 and 1967. However, it was the Mysore-Maharashtra border issue that was more directly connected with the Shiv Sena movement; attention therefore is focused on this issue in the present analysis.

Maharashtra-Mysore Border

The earliest letter on the theme of the Mahrashtra-Mysore dispute in our data is from 1963.

In this letter the Chairman of the MES (Maharashtra Ekikaran Samiti) of Karwar district, perhaps rather naively pronounced that the border dispute was almost resolved. People from the disputed area had given a clear verdict in favour of union with Maharashtra, by electing the MES's members at all levels of democratic machinery - from Gram Panchayats and local boards to the State Legislature. Since in a democracy, the people's verdict was to be treated as sovereign, the letter hoped that the official resolution of the problem was only a matter of time and formality. (Lks. 4.5.63)

Four years later, letters no more evinced the confidence that the people's verdict would be honoured by the Government although they reiterated the claim that the MES had won all the elections, Gram Panchayat upwards, in the disputed border area. (Mrt. 30.1.67; Mrm. 22.10.67)

Referring to the rumours floating around that the Mahajan Commission had retained Belgaum (claimed by pro-Maharashtra people) in Karnataka, a letter in the *Marmik* grieved that the Mahajan Commission, apart from ignoring the linguistic principle of the reorganisation of States, ignored the popular verdict of three general elections in favour of union with Maharashtra.

The letter reflected disillusionment and disaffection with the Commission when it admitted that the democratic ways and methods of seeking solutions to people's problems were futile. The letter observed that the only hope left for the people of the area was in the news that Senapati Bapat, the veteran leader of Samyukta Maharashtra Samiti, had proposed a fast unto death for the cause and that the Shiv Sena had declared its intention of starting a stir in the matter of the border problem. (Mrm. 22.10.67)

Another letter appealed to the editors of the *Maratha* and the *Marmik* to join hands to lead the border agitation and said that the youth were looking to them for guidance in resolving the long-drawn border dispute. (Mrm. 22.10.67)

A letter had appealed earlier to the editor of the *Marmik*, urging him to organise the proposed Shiv Sena, to carry out an agitation for resolving the border dispute, since the Maharasthra Government had proved incompetent to resolve the problems of the State with the Centre. (Mrm. 12.6.66)

A letter by an ex-leader of the District Youth Congress, complained in the *Maratha* that the Central Government and the High Command of the Congress, had always consistently ignored Maharashtra's problems and had been unjust to it. The State Government and the MPCC were weak-kneed and failed to assert their genuine opinions in a frank manner. The need of the hour, therefore, was that the Marathi people unite and press their point through democratic non-violent agitation, fasts, etc. (Mrt. 12.5.66)

When the report of the Mahajan Commission came out, it immediately provoked people's anger. Letters complained that parts of Belgaum and Karwar districts were unjustifiably included in Mysore by the Mahajan Commission. (Mrm. 17.9.67; Mrt. 24.10.67; Nvk. 28.2.70)

Letters from Benadi village in Belgaum district claimed that the majority of Benadi's population was Marathi speaking, unlike the claim of Mahajan Commission; the oldest school in Benadi, established on 1st May 1879, by the British, was a Marathi-medium school and local records in the village were maintained in Marathi. One of the letters claimed that Benadi had of late provided Belgaum district with two hundred Marathi language teachers. (Mrt. 24.10.67, 5.11.67)

A letter from Karwar grieved at the talk in some quarters that if Belgaum was included in Maharashtra, the people of Maharashtra were willing to give up their claim on Karwar and observed that such talk was unfair to people of Karwar who wanted unification with Maharashtra. The letter asserts that people of Karwar had firmly indicated their choice in favour of Maharashtra by electing the candidates of the MES in every election in the area until then. (Nvk. 28.2.70)

An occasional letter from the disputed border area complained of ill-treatment or mischievous and maligning propaganda against Maharashtra. (Mrt. 3.8.66; Lks. 28.10.67)

Some of the letters expressed doubts that the Central Government and the Congress High Command genuinely wanted to resolve the border.

Though there was no movement or agitation in Mumbai for merger of Goa in Maharashtra, till the referendum poll of Goa the verdict of which want against the merger in 1967, there had been constant debate in the Marathi press over the issue of Goa. During the mid-sixties the questions regarding the future of Goa and its language were still burning questions capable of arousing people's emotions. All parties in Maharashtra including the Sampoorna Maharashtra Samiti and the Shiv Sena supported the Maharashtrawadi Gomantak Party and its pro-merger stand. The Shiv Sena leader, Bal Thackeray, had blessed a pro-merger front of Goans organised under Melatio Fernandes.

Though the merger of Goa and the language of Goa were not issues for which the Shiv Sena agitated, unlike their passion over the Maharashtra-Mysore border issue, these were important political issues in Maharashtra. The Shiv Sena could not ignore them, since these issues emphasised and underlined the fundamental linguistic-regional principles which the Shiv Sena exploited for building its front. These issues then contributed to strengthen the Shiv Sena's stand, however indirectly.

Like the Maharashtra-Mysore border issue, the Marathi community's expectations (justified by the success of the Maharashtrawadi Gomantak Party in the elections), and later frustrations over the issue of Goa's integration with

Maharashtra, perhaps indirectly pushed the Maharashtrian towards a vociferous aggressive regionalist movement.

This is the justification for taking into consideration the content data on the Goa issue for analysis. However, since the issue is not directly connected with the Shiv Sena movement, only a few letters have been included in the content data.

Language and Identity of Goa

Ever since the liberation of Goa in December 1962, the Goa issue repeatedly came up in the Marathi journals throughout the sixties. A large number of these letters discuss the language issue of Goa's merger in Maharashtra.

As early as 1962, soon after the liberation of Goa, letters from Goa complained about the All India Radio's policy of curtailing Marathi programmes broadcast from Goa radio. The letters pointed out that Marathi had a prominent place on Goa radio even during Portuguese rule. Did the Government of India think that Marathi was not an aspect of Goa's distinctive culture? The people of Goa had always used Konkani for speech and Marathi for writing. Goan culture was not different from Maharashtrian culture, but only an aspect of it. (Lks. 6.1.62, 31.1.62)

Another letter from Goa observed that the debate about the language of Goa did not exist before the liberation of Goa because traditionally Goans had accepted Marathi as their language. Even the Portuguese regime could not drive out Marathi. Marathi served as the standard language with the help of which Goans retained their identity and links with India. So there was no need for a debate on Goa's language. (Lks. 9.3.62)

One more letter from a Goan wryly commented that if Marathi was not the language of Goa, more than three hundred Marathi schools would not have flourished in Goa despite being under foreign rule. The writer compared this to the total absence of Konkani schools.

Another letter observed that the people of Goa considered themselves to be Maharashtrians. Unification with Maharashtra, therefore, seemed a natural destiny for Goa. (Mrt. 16.4.62)

Maharashtra's Northern Border

When the erstwhile bilingual Mumbai State was divided into Gujarat and Maharashtra in May 1960, the district of Dangs, a tribal tract of forest area and parts of Umbergaon Taluka of Thana district (18 Marathi villages) as also 156 villages in Dhulia district, went to Gujarat according to the settlement worked out between the Congress leaders of the two regions of Gujarat and Maharashtra. In Maharashtra, this arrangement was seen as a special consideration to Gujarat as a compensation for inclusion of Mumbai city in Maharashtra State. (Phadke, 1973, Pp. 586 – 605, G.S.Singh, 1966, p. 70-71) However, people raised questions about the propriety of allotting the villages to Gujarat, when, according to their claim, the language spoken in these areas was Marathi and its dialect.

Soon after the formation of Maharashtra, letters began to appear in the press complaining and protesting against the proposed arrangements regarding transfer of villages from Umbergaon and Dhulia in Maharashtra to Gujarat.

One of the letters complained that Maharashtra's grievances about its borders between Maharashtra and Gujarat in the north and Mysore in its south remained unheeded by the Congress High Command and the Central Government and that only an organised movement might wake them up from their lethargy. (Mrt. 2.5.63)

Letters also complained about the ad hoc manner of resolving border disputes as politically expedient rather than on the basis of some definite principles and their consistent application.

Letters from the Dangs speak of the troubles and trials upon their inclusion in Gujarat State. Some of the letters demand that Maharashtra leaders raise the issue of the Dangs either through the State legislative debates or through organised movements.

Some of the letters complained that after inclusion of their villages in Gujarat, Marathi schools even in those villages which had a majority of Maharashtrians were being closed down.

The letters complained that people's grievances regarding the border areas in Mysore, Gujarat, Madhya Pradesh and Karnataka, could not be redressed except by an organised movement, since the Central Government or the Congress Party were unwilling to discuss the issue of disputed border areas.

Maharashtra Mysore Border Dispute

Editorials

The Maharashtra-Mysore border dispute, especially the problem of Belgaum often provoked Maharashtrian protest, voiced in the press through letters, comments, as well as editorials. The editorials on the theme invariably refer to the inclusion of the disputed areas in Karnataka against public opinion. They point out that in all the elections since November 1956, the members of the MES who were demanding merger with Maharashtra had been repeatedly elected. Yet, public opinion vindicated by election results was repeatedly ignored. The demand by the people that the dispute be settled by the application of some fundamental rational principle as the one evolved by H.S. Pataskar to solve the Madras-Andhra border dispute had also been repeatedly ignored.

This treatment was seen to be unfair to Maharashtrians whose demands were reasonable and tested by democratic support. A people's struggle, therefore, seemed to be the only way of forcing the rulers to be more responsive. One of the editorials was written on the eve of the MES's declaration to reopen the struggle, while some others were in support of the agitations already undertaken by the MES.

In 1966, the Maharashtra State Legislative Assembly unanimously passed a resolution demanding the merger of disputed border areas where people had by democratic procedures clearly indicated their opinion through election verdicts. (Mht. 8.9.66, 15.9.66)

Written in this context, a *Maratha* editorial believed that the Central Government's decision would be influenced by political pressures and expediency. The editorial expressed distrust in the Centre's sincerity and its ability to resolve the issue justly. (Mrt. 10.5.66)

In the meanwhile people from Belgaum and Karwar areas carried out a protest march on foot from the border area to Mumbai to present a memorandum voicing their demand for merger of these areas with Maharashtra to the Chief Minister. (Ref to Ch. III)

A *Marmik* editorial of the time observed that the Central Government's treatment to Maharashtra was discriminatory. The demand for the Punjabi Suba, the agitation and the demand of the South Indians against Hindi, were conceded by the Centre, while Maharashtra's reasonable and long-standing demands supported by democratic verdicts, continued to be ignored for ten long years. The Centre seemed to be moved only by public protest while agitations alone seemed to bring desired results for the people. (Mrm. 15.5.66)

In response to Maharashtra's repeated and long standing demand, at last the Central Government decided to appoint the one-man Mahajan Commission to look into the problem and give recommendations. The response to this was divided among the Marathi people. Some welcomed it. (Mht. Ed. 19.10.66) Some looked at it with suspicion. Some of the militant journals expressed distrust about the appointment of the Commission without defining the guiding principles for its work while others criticised the appointment of Mahajan whose opinion on linguistic States was well-known.

A little before the Commission's report was out, it was rumoured that Belgaum, the city which was the subject of the major demand of Maharashtrians (and which was the cause of the controversy necessitating the appointment of a Commission), was retained in Karnataka. Large protest meetings were held both in Belgaum and Mumbai, in anticipation of the recommendations in the report. (Mrt. 27.8.67, 8.10.67) By September 1967, copies of the Mahajan report were submitted to the respective State Governments. (Mrt. 28.9.67)

A *Marmik* editorial criticised the Mahajan report as an ad hoc report, devoid of any basic principle. (Mrm. Ed. 1.10.67) *Marmik* warned in its editorial that the implementation of the Mahajan report, would lead to violent protests all over Maharashtra. (Mrm. 17.12.67) The Sampoorna Maharashtra Samiti executive board meeting resolved to prepare for a struggle with the Central Government to ensure justice to the people of border areas. (Mrt. 26.8.67)

The *Maratha* almost daily published a militant editorial on the Belgaum issue.

News Reports and Articles

The Mahajan Commission Report was published in Delhi on 4.11.67. Very soon the 'report' was burned at several places in Mumbai. The Chief Minister of Maharashtra (Mr. Naik) admitted that the report was unacceptable to Maharashtra. (Mrt. 5.11.66)

There was news of burning of the report from several small places in Maharashtra. The report was severely criticised by several public personalities and leaders in Maharashtra. (Mrt. 6.11.67)

The heightened tension was followed by news of the use of repressive measures against the Marathi population and the Marathi language in Belgaum and other areas on the Maharashtra-Mysore border. (Lks. 6.5.67; Mrt. 6.11.67, 9.11.67; Mrm. 19.11.67)

The Sampoorna Maharashtra Samiti held a Border Conference at Kolhapur in December 1967, in preparation of a long-term agitation on the Mysore border issue. The conference called for 'people's struggle' for the border area. (Mrt. 18.11.67, 20.11.67, 24.11.67)

The Maharashtra Congress also rejected the Mahajan report. To take the wind out of the sails of the Sampoorna Maharashtra Samiti's militant programme, the Chief Minister, Naik, tabled a resolution rejecting the Mahajan report. The resolution was passed in the State Legislative Assembly. Naik urged the necessity of winning over the support of the Parliamentary members. (Mrt. 1.12.67; Sakal 7.1.69; Mrt. 15.2.68)

The people of Mysore, on the other hand, threatened a stir if the Mahajan report was not implemented. However, the Central Government seemed to have put the report in cold storage. The Home Minister told the Lok Sabha on 2nd August that no decision was taken regarding the implementation of Mahajan report. (Mrt. 3.8.68)

In the month of May, outside the venue of the annual meet of the MPCC in Mumbai, members of the MES from the disputed border area went on a hunger-strike for 24 hours to draw the attention of the Congress leaders to their grievance (Mrt. 23.5.68)

The Sampoorna Maharashtra Samiti, being preoccupied with the wrangles of the unit-parties took little notice of the event.

Criticising the Samiti's lack of interest in mustering up sufficient support for the M. Ekikaran Samiti, the *Daily Maratha* declared that it would go alone, if necessary, to support the Ekikaran Samiti. (Mrt. 23.5.68)

Shiv Sena and Mysore Border Dispute

In November 1968, Bal Thackeray of the Shiv Sena presented to the Prime Minister, a statement urging her to solve the border problem by conceding the demand of the people of the border area for merger with Maharashtra. (Mrm. 7.11.68)

In Belgaum, in the Municipal elections in Feb. 1969, the MES's candidates were elected in a majority, and Mrs. Khade, a Marathi lady, became the Chairman of the Municipal Corporation. (Mrt. 20.3.69, 23.2.69)

While the Shiv Sena was being criticised all over the country for the violence in Mumbai during the Mumbai *bandh* the MES's extraordinarily large meeting at Belgaum paid homage to 'martyrs' of the February agitation and tributes were paid to the Shiv Sena's support to the border people's lonely struggle for their rights. (Lks. 2.3.69)

The M.P.S. from Mysore was insisting on the implementation of the Mahajan Report. Prime Minister Indira Gandhi, however, favoured decision by consensus between various parties (Mht. 25.2.69, 27.2.69)

Call for Action

The State of Maharashtra was born on 1st of May 1960 with Mumbai as its capital. Even after this, however, there still lurked doubts and apprehensions in the minds of the members of the Maharashtrian community regarding the inclusion of Mumbai in Maharashtra, as it was rumoured that the capital of the state will be moved from Mumbai to elsewhere in Maharashtra. (Mrt. Ed. 2.2.65)

These apprehensions were not altogether without basis as was seen from the recurring demand from non-Marathi quarters for a centrally-administered Mumbai. One of the earliest letters giving a call for united action by Maharashtrians was in response to this apprehension, an appeal to vote unitedly for the candidates representing the interests of the community.

A letter written in the context of the coming elections of the Municipal Council of the Mumbai Municipal Corporation, appealed to the readers to vote only for those who had been loyal to the cause of Maharashtra; that was the only effective way according to the letter, to prove beyond doubt that Mumbai was part of Maharashtra and belonged to it. (Nvk. 24.3.61)

Except for a stray letter like this, we do not come across entries giving a call for united action till almost the mid-sixties (1964-1966) Only in 1964 did letters demanding an organised action for redressal of the community's grievances begin to appear in good number. In the same year we come across editorials in popular Marathi dailies articulating Maharashtrian plaints. It could be that the letters were in response to the editorials. It seems that the editorials cogently articulated the feelings and thoughts which perhaps were uppermost in the minds of a large number of people, and naturally enough were received with enthusiasm. In spite of the plausibility of this explanation, the question still remains as to why these entries are found concentrated in 1964.

Editorials

The only explanation of the mystique of 1964 seems to be that the newly-formed State completed four years of its existence. It was therefore perhaps seen as the proper time for stock-taking and assessment of the State's progress in the previous four years.

An editorial in the *Maratha* (Mrt. 1.5.64) on the occasion of the fourth birth anniversary of Maharashtra State fetched dozens of appreciative letters in response. As the *Maratha* put it 'letters kept pouring in' (Mrt. 6.5.54) It also spurred discussions in the State Legislature (Mrt. 5.6.64) A similar response was seen in the case of a *Marmik* editorial a year later. (Mrm. 4.7.65)

What did the *Maratha* editorials contain that they were received with such excitement and welcome?

The *Maratha* editorial on the fourth anniversary of Maharashtra State was an assessment of Maharashtrians' situation in Mumbai and in the four-year life of the State.

Referring to the staunch opposition of the non-Marathi capitalist and business communities of Mumbai and of the central leadership (Nehru and others) of the Congress High Command, to the inclusion of Mumbai in Maharashtra, the editorial reminded its readers that Maharashtra State was formed only after 105 persons had laid down their lives during the struggle for Samyukta Maharashtra. This sacrifice of the people seemed futile, the editorial contended, because Maharashtrians in their own capital city were in no better condition than they were earlier.

Business and Industry were always controlled by non-Marathi communities. Houses and estates also were owned by them on the basis of their economic power. Even small businesses like Hair Cutting Saloons, Bidi and Tobacco Shops, Toddy Shops, small restaurants etc had now slipped out of Maharashtrian hands with the entry of the non-Marathi who could invest bigger capital required for modernisation of these businesses.

In the offices of private and central Government establishments, non-Maharashtrians, especially the South Indians, outnumbered Maharashtrians. Even in the State Government offices and specifically in the Housing Board and its tenements, the South Indians fared better than the local people. The editorial observed Even among the jailbirds, nearly 65% were migrants from the North and the South.

Maharashtra, as a linguistic State, was a State of Marathi speaking people and it was to be expected that they control the political authority and economic power here. Unless the State Government successfully stalled the continuous influx of population and encroachment of outsiders on the economic opportunities available here, and protected and safeguarded the Marathi community's interests in Mumbai at all costs, Maharashtrians would become outsiders in their own State capital. (Mrt. Ed. 1.5.64)

The *Maharashtra Times*, relatively sober in tone, although not giving a call to people for an agitation or a struggle, expressed very similar views in its editorial and called upon the State Government to adopt effective measures to protect Maharashtrian interests in Mumbai.

Referring to the remarks made by the-then Defense Minister, Y.B. Chavan (ex-chief Minister, Maharashtra State) that Mumbai should carry an impress of Maharashtrian culture, an editorial in the *Maharashtra Times* (May 1964) commented The issue for Maharashtrians was no more how to retain or make an impact of Maharashtrian culture on Mumbai, the issue was that of Maharashtrians' survival in Mumbai, the city which he had all along considered as his mother city, which nursed him and provided him with a livelihood.

The editorial complained that in the process of the development of Mumbai, land and houses of the native community were often acquired by the new industries; these industries however recruited as a rule, cheap labour of migrants from other states or people from the industrialist's province, leaving the members of the native community deprived of land, housing and even of employment. The editorial warns that this needed urgent rectification with stringent measures regarding the development of industries in Mumbai as well as protection and priority to the local people regarding jobs and housing.

The editorial observed When a State and its people provided land, water and electricity – the three basic resources for any industry – the demand for priority to natives in jobs and housing could not be described as parochial. These norms needed to be universally implemented to protect local people's interests and to ward off their getting uprooted. The editorial pointed out that fair-play and justice demanded such a rational arrangement in the given situation. Since every State owned its duty first to the natives, the people of the State, the Central and State Governments, the industrialists and the non-Marathi citizens of Mumbai needed to co-operate in implementing a rational arrangement which would ward off uprooting of Maharashtrians from Mumbai (Mht. 14.5.65)

Letters

The enthusiastic response that the *Maratha* editorial got was beyond imagination.

One of these letters says, 'We very enthusiastically welcome, support and propagate your resolve that the Maharashtrian in Mumbai must secure his due status in his capital city and that encroachment by people from all over India in Mumbai must be stalled. This was necessary to safeguard Maharashtrian interests.' (Mrt. 6.5.64)

Another letter hailed the editor as a courageous spokesman who dared to voice the unpleasant truth. (Mrt. 6.5.64) A third reader appealed to the editor to provide leadership to the people in their struggle for their rights. (Mrt. 6.5.64) This appeal to the editor to accept the role of leadership continued to be expressed off and on.

A letter in the *Maratha* in 1960 observed that though the Maharashtrians often enough voiced their grievances through the letters to the press, this measure of articulation was far too inadequate to solve the problem. As in the struggle for Samyukta Maharashtra, the letter maintained that all political parties and personalities and social organisations in Maharashtra join hands to solve the problem of the Maharashtrian in Mumbai, who lacked social status in his own capital city. The letter observed The people of other regions and States enjoyed in Maharashtra (Mumbai) privileges denied to members of the Maharashtrian community. While the State Government, under pressure from the Central Government, refused to give protection and reservation of employment opportunities to the local community, several other State Governments had unhesitatingly implemented the rule of priority in 80% or even 100% of jobs for the 'locals'. The letter ended with an appeal to Atre, to give his lion-call to lead another agitation for asserting Maharashtrians' rights in their capital city. (Mrt. 15.7.66)

The *Marmik* editorial (Mrm. 4.7.65) drew a similar response in the form of letters. A majority of these letters called for organised effort to improve the situation of the Maharashtrians who faced increasing competition and encroachment upon his opportunities – land, housing and employment – in Mumbai by the non-Marathi outsiders. The letters call for restoring his status in Maharashtra. (Mrm. 18.7.65; 10 letters in response to Mrm. Ed. 4.7.65)

Several of these letters to the editor in various journals evince keen interest in the Maharashtra Hitwardhini Sabha – an organisation established in 1964 to protect and further Maharashtrian interests. One of the letters urges the organisation to act urgently before the whole of Maharashtra became 'cosmopolitan' like Mumbai.

A letter in the *Navakal* (an independent pro-Congress paper) in the mid-sixties, welcomes the coming of the Shiv Sena. The letter considered that the organisation was needed for asserting Maharashtrian rights in the metropolis of Mumbai where non-Maharashtrians were becoming predominant. (Nvk. 10.7.66)

Reports and Articles

In all 24 entries consisting of reports and articles, give a call to people for action, urge them to change their situation through organised effort and popular struggle against the injustice done to them in Mumbai. All these entries are from a period close to the mid-sixties and fall between 1964 and 1966-67. On 19 June 1966 the Shiv Sena claiming to represent the voice of 'the sons of the soil' was born. However, the first clarion call for organised effort against injustice came from the *Daily Maratha* in early 1964.

Thereafter, between 1964 and 1966, the call for action to redress Maharashtrian grievances was repeated by many, from different quarters, till one day in June 1966 Thackeray's Shiv Sena saw the light of day and began to grow quickly.

These various calls for action to redress the Marathi community's grievances, though coming from different quarters stemmed from a common ground of (i) a sense of frustration and alienation – a feeling of being a stranger, without control in one's own capital city, (ii) a sense of being subjected to injustice and (iii) an increasing sense of a need for united action to fight against this faceless injustice against the Marathi community in Mumbai. This is amply testified to by our content data.

As early as 26 January 1964, the Indian Republic day, the editor of the *Maratha* declared at a private meeting at Shiv Shakti, from where the *Maratha* was published, his resolved to found a youth organisation of 100, 000 youths from Maharashtra, which was to devote itself to the interests and the services of Maharashtra. On 27 January 1964, the *Maratha* carried a front-page banner

Acharya Atre to found Shiv Sena in Maharashtra

Atre's Shiv Sena, according to the report, was to be a voluntary organisation of young men below the age of 21. A quotation by Samarth Ramdas, the 17th-century poet saint 'Let the Marathas unite! May the Marathi spirit grow!' formed the motto of the proposed Shiv Sena of Atre. The organisation was to work towards furthering the welfare of Maharashtra by peaceful means and within the framework of the Constitution. The report declared that the details about the structure of the organisation would be announced at a later date after consultation with the leaders of Maharashtra. (Mrt. 27.1.64)

Atre's proposed Shive Sena did not however materialise.

In the context of Jogeshwari riots and prolonged tensions thereafter between the (non-Marathi) landlords and the tenants of unauthorised chawls in that suburb, the *Maratha* had declared on 17 February 1964 'The tenants must unite under the banner of Shiv Sena.' (Mrt. 17.2.64)

Atre, in a number of his public speeches during these years referred to the plight of the Marathi community in Mumbai, spoke of its alienation and frustrations in its own State capital and pleaded for an organised effort by Maharashtrians to remedy the situation. According to him, it was a depressing situation that inspite of the success of the Samyukta Maharashtra Movement and the inclusion of Mumbai in Maharashtra State, the Marathi man was increasingly losing his place in Mumbai.

He was keen to establish 'a Maharashtra Samiti', an organisation of Maharashtrians 'to protect and further Maharashtrian interests' and 'to stall encroachment of others on Maharashtra's capital city'. Shiv Sena as a youth wing of the proposed Maharashtra Samiti was Atre's brainchild. (Mrt. 17.10.64)

On several occasions till as late as 1967 and 1968 Atre voiced the demand for priority and reservation for Marathi persons, in jobs, housing and licences for small businesses in Mumbai as measures to protect the Marathi community from the encroachment of powerful vested interests of non-Marathi outsiders.

Even before the *Maratha* published its Maharashtra and May Day article in 1964, (which eventually drew enthusiastic popular response), articles written anonymously as well as under specific names, were published in the *Maratha* which voiced and discussed Marathi grievances and considered at great length possible remedial measures. The predominant mood of these writings was to appeal to the State Government for remedial measures, although they voiced demands for priority and protection. These articles, on the whole, appear as a prelude to the mass organisational efforts that followed soon after.

The need for a mass organisation to safeguard the Marathi community's interests in Mumbai was felt by many and voiced from different quarters, even as noted in the earlier chapters.

For instance an article in the *Navakal*, published in July 1965, voiced such a need for a non-political front, 'to stall the suppression of Maharashtrian interests in Mumbai'. The article referred to the retrenchment of Marathi workers in Mumbai's industries and recruitment of non-Marathi persons in Mumbai's offices. It refers to the heavy influx of people into Mumbai from all over the country. It refers to the large scale migration of the unemployed coming in search of jobs, migration of the poor, the slum dwellers, the beggars, the vagrants, the anti-social elements, from all over India, whose responsibility however had to be shouldered by the State Government with funds inadequate for the task. The article demands priority for the natives of the State in jobs and housing. The article ends with an appeal to Maharashtrians to unite and put a struggle against the suppression. (Nvk. 3.7.65)

Much before Thackeray's Shiv Sena appeared on the scene or Atre's Shiv Sena could materialise, an organisation named 'Maharashtra Hitwardhini' was established with similar goals, in October 1964. It presented its memorandum of demands to the Chief Minister of the State on 30 September 1964. (Mrt. 1.10.64)

The chief was regarding reservation of 80 per cent of jobs and tenements in the State Housing, for the natives of the State. The Hitwardhini claimed that every State first looked after its own natives. Considering the extraordinary fact that a large number of Marathi-speaking persons i.e. natives of the State were houseless and jobless, the Hitwardhini pleaded, the State Government must protect their interests.

The Maharashtra Hitwardhini at its meeting in March 1966 articulated a statement of its policy and of its demands from the State government. It

i) Believed it was the duty of the Maharashtra Government to give priority to Maharashtrians i.e. the Marathi speaking persons, in jobs in Maharashtra.

ii) Demanded that in Maharashtra which was the linguistic State of Marathi speaking people, 75 per cent of all jobs should go to the Marathi speaking persons.

iii) Demanded reorganisation of the Employment Exchange in Mumbai under Maharashtrian officials.

iv Advised the State Government to favour Maharashtrian officials and workers in the State sponsored industries.

v) Recommended that 'knowledge of Marathi' be considered as a requirement for jobs in the industries, services or office establishments of the State or the Civic Government, including the Mumbai Telephones, the Mumbai Electric Supply and Transport Company and civic and government hospitals.

vi) Recommended that those deprived of their agricultural land or housing under various developmental schemes and projects be given priority in employment or business opportunities available in the region.

vii) Recommended stipulation of a domicile period for the non-natives or migrants from other states, for allotment of tenements in the State government housing colonies.

viii) Demanded that a minimum percentage of Maharashtrian members be stipulated by the State Government for the Co-operative Housing Societies seeking government loan for housing.

ix) Demanded that the beggars, vagrants and criminals from outside Maharashtra be sent back to their respective States, to stall the swelling of their numbers in Mumbai.

x) Demanded urgent provision of institutions of technical and industrial training for Marathi speaking youth.

xi) Recommended opening of a public relations office of the Government to provide information in Marathi to the natives of the State, regarding jobs, housing and educational opportunities available in the State.

The Hitwardhini also voiced its opinion that the State and the Civic Governments should not be responsible for rehabilitating the burgeoning number of slum dwellers due to constant influx of migrants from other states. It in fact recommended setting up of a vigilance committee to stall the growth of the hutment colonies in Mumbai. (Nvk. 2.3.66)

However, beyond holding public meetings and submitting the memoranda to the Chief Minister, the Hitwardhini did not do anything. It was not very active.

A reader's letter complained about Hitwardhini's non-action and wondered if this was because the BPCC brought pressure on Hitwardhini members and sponsors majority of whom were Marathi Congressmen from the city. (Mrt. Letter 10.2.66)

An article published in the prestigious *Kesari* from Pune, in October 1966, pleaded for an organisation, a 'Sampanna Maharashtra Samiti', to focus on and to resolve Maharashtra's major economic grievances and problems. The name 'Sampanna (Prosperous) Maharashtra Samiti' rhymed with the earlier 'Samyukta Maharashtra Samiti'.

Analysing Maharashtra's major economic problems, the article observed that heavy concentration of industries and related urban growth in Mumbai, the control of Maharashtra's economy in the hands of non-Marathi industrialists and class of businessmen in Mumbai and Central Government's unfair treatment to Maharashtra's and Marathi speaking people's needs and demands were the economic problems of Maharashtra State. The grievance against the Centre was that while the Central Government controlled the price of industrial products like sugar (amply produced in Maharashtra by the co-operatives of the Marathi speaking people), it had failed to provide foodgrains and cooking oil at controlled rates to the people of Maharashtra who always faced shortage of these items of daily use. This caused considerable hardships for people of Maharashtra. The article appealed for establishment of an organisation which could argue Maharashtra's case and fight against the Central Government's unfair treatment. (Kesari, 26.10.66)

In the meanwhile, the grievances and the pent-up frustrations of the Marathi community needed an outlet. Apart from the Maharashtra Hitwardhini, there are references to other groups and organisations born to remedy the situation, indicative of ferment in society as noted earlier. The Sampoorna Maharashtra Samiti was established in March 1966. In June 1966 the Shiv Sena was born to seek redressal of Marathi grievances in Mumbai. (Mrm. 12.6.66, 19.6.66)

Two articles in the *Marmik* on the 1 and 8 May 1966, pronounced an urgent need to organise a front of the Marathi people. (Mrm. 1.5.66, 8.5.66)

The following month the *Marmik* disclosed that it was organising the Shiv Sena. On 19 June Thackeray's Shiv Sena became a reality with thousands of young men registering themselves as Shiv Sainiks. (Mrm. 12.6.66, 19.6.66)

Atre's proposed 'Shiv Sena' was thus appropriated by Thackeray and was given the identity of a militant youth organisation with the limited objective of obtaining redressal of Maharashtrians' grievances in Mumbai.

Thackeray declared that his 'Shiv Sena was born to lead the struggle for obtaining justice for the Maharashtrians. (Nvk. 3.7.66; Mrm. 27.7.66) Within a couple of months its popularity started rising and it grew in strength till the end of the 1960's. The Shiv Sena held its first Dussera meet at the Shivaji Park, which was attended by an unusually large audience, as large as one seen during the Samyukta Maharashtra days.

The discussion of the grievances of the Maharashtrian community, their causes and remedies, continued to reverberate in the Marathi press for some time even after the birth of the Shiv Sena, especially until the general elections of 1967. (Nvk. 5.12.66; Mrt. 5.12.66; Nvs. 2.4.67, 9.4.67, 16.4.67)

The earlier themes of grievances gradually began to disappear after 1967. A marked fall in the number of entries on the higher scale points of our affective scale is noticeable from 1968 onwards. The coming of the Shiv Sena, perhaps, brought about a change in the situation, presumably by giving a voice to grievances in an organised manner.

The Shiv Sena

The call to remedy the injustice done to the Maharashtrian community, eventually turned into a call for support to Thackeray's Shiv Sena which claimed that its birth and existence was for the redressal of Maharashtrians' grievances. However, the Shiv Sena shot into prominence only during the 1967 general elections (see Chapter III)

When S.K. Patil selected a local man, a Maharashtrian, S.G. Barve, for the North Mumbai Constituency, it was perhaps a shrewd political move on Patil's part intended to checkmate two of his political opponents within the Congress Party the leftist Krishna Menon who intended contesting from North Mumbai, and Y.B. Chavan, the leader of the MPCC (See Ch. III)

In this tussle, Krishna Menon who decided to contest as an independent, received support from the leftist alliance of the Sampoorna Maharashtra Samiti which always directed its propaganda against the BPCC and its non-Marathi capitalist supporters. The Shiv Sena, known for its resistance to 'outsiders' and South Indians naturally gave support to S.G. Barve. The Sampoorna Maharashtra Samiti dubbed the Shiv Sena's support to Barve as support to the BPCC

However, the Sampoorna Maharashtra Samiti (SPMS), to keep its popularity with the Maharashtrian community intact, had to include in its manifesto Maharashtrian demands for reservation of 80 per cent of jobs and housing for the local man i.e. for the Maharashtrian, while it supported Krishna Menon for the parliamentary seat. In the contest, Barve and, later, (in the by-election due to Barve's death), his sister, Mrs. Sapre won the election; and Krishna Menon was twice defeated in the same constituency, in March 1967. In the process, the Shiv Sena which supported Barve and his sister emerged as a victorious popular front.

On the other hand, the SPMS which until then had Maharashtrian support in its battle against the BPCC, found its popularity on the wane. The Shiv Sena now could claim to be the real champion of the Maharashtrian cause. The mantle of the protector of Maharashtrian interests, which was earlier worn by the Samyukta Maharashtra Samiti, instead of falling on the SPMS, thus fell upon Thackeray's Shiv Sena. The critical event that was at the crux of this climatic result was the North Mumbai constituency contest.

The letters in the contest data shed some light on these developments related to the emergence of the Shiv Sena and its rise to popularity.

Politicisation of Call and Support to the Shiv Sena

So when the Shiv Sena actually came into being, it was received with enthusiasm and a sense of acclaim, notwithstanding disparagement and criticism by political and other leaders. In fact it enjoyed an anticipatory welcome prior to its very birth.

It was in this tone, that some of the readers' letters appreciate the *Marmik's* voice against 'outsiders'. Some of those letters mention a growing feeling among the Marathi speaking that they were 'outsiders' and 'strangers' in their home State capital. (*Marmik*, 2 letters 15.5.66)

A letter in the *Navakal* observes that the Maharashtrians' complacency with regard to themselves while being charitably disposed to others (i.e. non-Maharashtrians) alone had relegated Maharashtrians to a ranking of insignificance in Mumbai. The Shiv Sena which would set this injustice right was indeed welcome. (Nvk. 21.7.66)

The letters, however, also warn against extremism, violence and political stunt-making and suggest that the Shiv Sena should confine its endeavours to obtaining reservation for Maharashtrians in jobs and housing by legitimate and non-violent methods (Nvk. 21.7.66 four letters)

These letters also included occasional criticism of the Shiv Sena. For example

A letter welcomes the establishment of the Shiv Sena. However, it cautions the Sena that in order to be successful it must win the confidence of the non-Maharashtrian minorities and must not alienate them by its extremist words or deeds. (Nvk. 9.2.67)

Another letter asks the Sena to work on the non-political plane. The entry into the sphere of politics would distract it from the right goals.

Yet another letter asks the Shiv Sena to avoid entering into election politics and to concentrate on the agitation for reserving a certain percentage of jobs and housing for Maharashtrians. (Nvk. 9.2.67, 2 letters)

All these letters, even the critical ones, indicate the growing interest in the Shiv Sena and how the event of the 1967 general elections gave a further boost to its image. It was inevitable that a large majority of Maharashtrians were sympathetic to S.G. Barve as a candidate for elections. He had earned a reputation as a saviour of Pune where he worked as the Municipal Commissioner immediately after the tragedy of the Panshet Dam burst. Krishna Menon was not particularly popular in Maharashtra; earlier he had won the elections from Mumbai since he was Nehru's man. Some of the member parties of the SPMS and Atre, the editor of *Maratha*, supported Menon in 1967; though earlier in the 1962 general elections they had staunchly opposed him as a Congress candidate.

When Barve won the elections, many readers attributed to the Shiv Sena, the credit for the triumph, and conceded that they voted for Barve hoping that it would help improve the situation of the 'natives' in cosmopolitan Mumbai.

The general elections and the defeat of Krishna Menon in 1967 drew the attention of people at the national level, to the Shiv Sena. Soon after, the Shiv Sena also succeeded in capturing the Thane Municipality, to the north of Mumbai, beyond the Mumbai metropolitan area. But the Shiv Sena's aggressive stance attracted a considerable amount of criticism especially from the non-Marathi people.

Incidentally, it may be noted that several letters supporting the Shiv Sena are from female readers.

A woman writing from Vidarbha gave credit to the Shiv Sena for awakening Maharashtra's sense of identity and self-respect to battle against the injustice done to it and opines that when other States installed measures to safeguard the interests of their native population, no one protested. Then why were demands by the Shiv Sena for similar measures in Maharashtra regarded as parochial or anti-national? (Mrm. 12.3.67)

Another woman referred to the news that Members of Parliament from the Southern States intended to come to Maharashtra for an inquiry into the disturbances allegedly instigated by the Shiv Sena.

She wrote During the anti-Hindi agitation the DMK followers in Tamil Nadu burned even the Constitution, but no N.P.S. from Maharashtra interfered with what belonged to the jurisdiction of the State Government. How and why should Maharashtra then brook this self-appointed Commission of representatives of a State where the ruling Party allowed its followers to set fire to the Constitution? The letter declaimed that the 'mothers, sisters and Maharashtrian women in general would support the Shiv Sena.' (Mrm. 10.9.67)

The visit of the MPs from the Southern States irked many readers. The Southern States, they said, often evinced separatist tendencies. The readers described it as highly ironical and expressed bitterness at the initiative of the Southern MPs. (Letters. Mrm. 10.9.67, 17.9.67, 22.10.67; Mht. Ed. 25.9.67)

A letter from a female reader observed that confronted with an incessant flow of people from the Southern States into Mumbai, Maharashtra's lead in family planning would achieve very little success for Maharashtra. Explaining the popular support to the Shiv Sena, the letter averred that Maharashtrians did not want favours from others but only wanted was rightfully due to them. The letter ended with a demand for the use of Marathi in Mumbai on the signboards of Government and public undertakings like the Railways, the Municipality, Government Transport Service and Government offices. (Mrm. 10.9.67)

However, by 1968, letters of disillusionment with the Shiv Sena begin to appear. They mention that support to the Shiv Sena was given in the prospect that it would weed out injustice towards the Maharashtrian and obtain for him his rightful minimum due, but the Shiv Sena was getting involved with anti-communist politics rather than being concerned about the achievement of its professed goals. (Nvk. 4.1.68)

Reports and Articles

An article in *Marmik* in early 1967 during the election campaign, appeals to the readers to give their votes to those who would support and fight for the Maharashtrians' cause and therefore, not to vote for those who were against the Shiv Sena. (Mrm. 22.1.67)

It is equally interesting to go through the major points of the election manifesto of the SPMS, which supported Menon for parliamentary elections while having its own candidates for Assembly seats.

The manifesto as presented in the *Maratha*, requests the voters to reject the Congress Party and vote for the Sampoorna Maharashtra Samiti for following reasons

1) The Congress Party's clearly anti-Maharashtra policies and behaviour as evinced in the delay in forming the unilingual Maharashtra State; in its partisan spirit favouring Andhra in Krishna-Godavari water dispute; Congress Party's deaf ears to the demand for Konkan railway; its discrimination in pricing the sugar and sugarcane in Maharashtra and Uttar Pradesh (lower prices for Maharashtra and higher in U.P.) etc.

2) Failure of the Congress Party Government to protect the Maharashtrian who was being driven out of Mumbai, using

priority measures and a policy of reservation of a percentage in Government housing and jobs both in public and private sector. According to the manifesto, the fact that even the unskilled jobs in the MIG factory at Nasik and ordnance factory at Varangaon, in Maharashtra went to the non-Marathis on a large scale (in spite of Maharashtrian Y.B. Chavan being the Central Defense Minister in whose purview these factories came), was sufficient evidence of the Congress Government's indifference to Maharashtrian interests.

The manifesto distinguishes between the SPMS and the Shiv Sena and their respective stands.

The SPMS though it stood for safeguarding Maharashtrian interests by measures of priority and reservation of percentage, categorically rejected directing its propaganda against outsiders or South Indians and avoided making scapegoats of them. Because, according to the SPMS, the culprit responsible for injustice to the Maharashtrian was the Mumbai Pradesh Congress Committee. The defeat of the BPCC candidate and the victory of the SPMS, were therefore imperative for change in the Maharashtrian situation, according to the statement.

The manifesto also included the demands of the SPMS. Besides the 'socialist' demands like nationalisation of banks and of export-import trade etc., the statement focused on the following

(i) The demarcation of the borders of Maharashtra State on the basis of village as the basic unit of demarcation.

(ii) The merger of Goa with Maharashtra.

(iii) Removal of injustice to Maharashtra in respect of the share of river waters, road and rail facilities, in case of the State's share in the taxes from the Centre etc.

(iv) Reservation of 70 to 80 per cent of jobs in the new industries and in the Government offices in Mumbai, for the native community of Maharashtra, i.e. for the Maharashtrians.

(v) Urgent development of the Konkan railway (Mrt. 11.2.67, 20.2.67)

The Shiv Sena had no election manifesto of its own since it was not a contesting Party in the election. However, Thackeray at an extraordinarily large meeting in Thane (part of the North Mumbai parliamentary constituency) spelled out in his speech in January 1967, the policy and role of Shiv Sena.

Thackeray in his speech, described the Shiv Sena as a militant organisation born for the Maharashtrian cause. He ridiculed those who dubbed the Shiv Sena as 'a separatist, parochial organisation' and those who tried to teach Maharashtra and Maharashtrians 'the national spirit'. He criticised the so-called national or Indo-English press for its anti-Maharashtrian attitude, as evinced in its censure of Maharashtrians, since the days of the Samyukta Maharashtra Movement.

Thackeray, at this meeting, staunchly opposed Menon's candidature from Mumbai on the ground that Menon took little interest in the people or problems of Mumbai. Menon never supported the vital movement of Samyukta Maharashtra; he never spoke a word for solving Maharashtra's border or water problems. Why should Maharashtrians then vote for Menon who did nothing for Mumbai, Maharashtra or Maharashtrians? (Deafening applause)

Would the people of Bengal or of Tamil Nadu elect a Maharashtrian leader from their constituency simply because he chooses to contest the election there, Thackeray asked rhetorically. Shiv Sena supported S.G. Barve, Thackeray declared, because Barve served the people of Maharashtra in many capacities. The result of the contest between Menon and Barve was therefore an issue of Maharashtra's prestige, Thackeray contended.

In his speech Thackeray defined Maharashtrian as one who identified himself with Maharashtra and its people and stood by them. Those who remained indifferent to Maharashtrians in their hour of need were 'outsiders'. (Mrm. 15.1.67)

Support to Shiv Sena

Even after the general elections, the Shiv Sena's popularity and support did not wane. The Shiv Sena soon launched a protest march to the Council Hall (venue of the State Legislature), to present a memorandum of its twenty-five demands to the Chief Minister of Maharashtra.

The prospect of the Shiv Sena's protest march had caused certain apprehensions and misgivings in Mumbai. However, the event, with about ten thousand participants passed off largely peacefully according to a report in the *Maratha* - the rival of the *Marmik.* (Mrt. 22.7.67)

The memorandum pressed for

(i) The reservation of 80 per cent of jobs in Maharashtra for Maharashtrians;
(ii) The reservation of 80 per cent of the Government Housing Board's tenements for Maharashtrians.
(iii) Knowledge of Marathi essential to qualify for Government service in Mumbai and Maharashtra.
(iv) Use of Marathi language and Nagari script in display of signboards on railway stations, roads and the offices.
(v) Check on influx of outsiders into Mumbai.

According to the memorandum, a large number of city's beggars, hawkers, slum-dwellers, bootleggers and anti-social elements, in addition to the multitude of white and blue collar migrant workers, came from the Southern States. The Shiv Sena complained The enormity of the population had made Mumbai, the capital of Maharashtra; a city predominated by South Indians. (Mrt. 22.7.67; Lks. 22.7.67)

There was little to distinguish between the programmes and policies presented by the Shiv Sena and the SPMS, in their respective manifestoes for the civic election. Both the parties promised clean administration. While Shiv Sena promised to introduce the Marathi language in the civic administration, to free the citizens of Mumbai from constant influx of beggars and the nuisance of roadside hawkers, the SPMS promised slum improvement and planned measures to fight and control the daily influx of three hundred families of migrants from other States contributing to Mumbai's slum growth. (Mht. 8..68; Lks. 9.3.68. Mrt. 9.3.68, 25.3.68)

The *Maratha* in its editorial while analysing the reasons for the defeat of the SPMS in the civic election, admitted that the SPMS had forfeited the confidence and the prestige it had enjoyed among the Maharashtrians in the heyday of the Samyukta Maharashtra Movement. Among the factors responsible for this loss of confidence, the editorial concluded, was the failure on the part of the Samiti to voice the Maharashtrian grievances and to build sufficient pressure to obtain their redressal, especially in respect of those related to employment and housing.

The editorial observed that the Marathi people especially the youth had forsaken the Samiti (SPMS) and turned over to the Shiv Sena due to the Samiti's failure to focus attention on the problems of the middle and working classes and to provide an active programme which would engage the people in the task of resolving their problems. (Mrt. 28.3.68)

According to an article in the *Marmik*, the success of the Shiv Sena at the civic polls was an indication of the Marathi community's slow disaffection with the BPCC which, for long, had ignored and suppressed Maharashtrian aspirations. It also was a pointer to the reluctance of Maharashtrians to wait indefinitely for the redressal of their grievances and restitution of their rights. In effect, when the Shiv Sena appeared on the scene solely to voice Maharashtrians grievances and retrieve the Marathi man's status, people voted for it. The success of the Shiv Sena in the civic council election was thus a measure of the Maharashtrians' growing confidence in the Shiv Sena as an organisation born to retrieve their self-respect. (Mrm. 7.4.68)

The Marathi community's sense of frustration over the increasing economic competition with migrants for jobs and housing, their decreasing numbers compared to outsiders and losing their respectable 'status' in the fast expanding metropolis, was quite strong during the mid-sixties and could be ignored by a political Party representing Maharashtrians at its peril. No wonder that the Shiv Sena and Sampoorna Maharashtra Samiti, inspite of their stiff ideological differences, were both competing to exploit the same grievances and to voice similar demands. Soon after the Corporation elections even the Peasants and Workers Party of Maharashtra joined in the chorus.

Support for the Peasants and Workers Party, which is a regional Party in Maharashtra, emanated chiefly from the districts rather than the metropolis; it could not, however, afford to ignore the unrest among the urban Maharashtrians. After all, the Maharashtrian job seekers and the industrial labour came from the districts of Konkan and Western Maharashtra, where the Party had a considerable stronghold.

A report in the *Maratha* early in the 1968, informed the readers of the intention of the Peasants and Workers Party to establish a youth organisation of its own (the Maharashtra Yuvak Sangh) for safeguarding Maharashtrian interests in Mumbai. (Mrt. 12.4.68)

These entries seem to suggest that the calls for action and for agitational policies were a natural and logical consequence of long-standing Maharashtrian grievances and frustrations, in the given situation of Mumbai. The group and political Party which responded to these grievances and frustrations could exploit and channelise them for better or worse and those groups or parties that happened to ignore or failed to respond to them with conviction could neither gain from them nor mould them. Thackeray's Shiv Sena appeared on the forefront, to an extent usurping the SPMS's position, boldly voicing the plaints and the sense of frustration pervading the Marathi community. It was therefore able to mould and channelise these grievances and frustrations according to the genius and light of its leadership.

II

The major apprehension and grievances voiced in the content-data presented in this chapter are

i) The continuous dwindling of numerical strength and consequent 'retreat' of linguistic identity and culture of the region, i.e. of the Marathi community, in the wake of expansion and growth of Mumbai.

ii) An attitude of indifference and resistance to Marathi – the language of the State – by the non-Marathi communities of Mumbai who, together made up a numerical majority combined with economic power.

iii) The lack of voice and the absence of fair and due representation to the Marathi community in the affairs of the metropolitan Mumbai Pradesh Congress Committee which then controlled the ruling Party and the Government in the State and thus symbolised political power.

Do these grievances represent an objective situation, or are they purely subjective perceptions? If the grievances represented an objective reality, what was that reality? In other words, what factors in the situation were responsible for the rise of these grievances? How far could these factors be controlled for the redressal of the grievances? These are some of the questions which we should try to seek answers for in this section.

What were the factors responsible for these apprehensions of the Marathi community? Were Maharashtrian identity, culture and language on the decline in Mumbai due to large-scale migration of people from different States? Corresponding to these fears, was there a large scale or sudden spurt in the migration from the South? Was this migration responsible for a general resentment against South Indian, especially against the Tamilians and Malayalis? And was it the cause of the emergence of the Shiv Sena?

Earlier, we have referred to the fast growth of industries in Mumbai and the correlated growth of Mumbai's population during the post-war years and in the fifties. That the large-scale migration spurred by this industrial growth caused an explosion of metropolitan population and that the heavy influx of population to Mumbai caused urgent problems of civic amenities and housing, is too well known to be repeated. However, this growth of Mumbai was not completely sudden within a span of two to three years as in the case of the influx at the time of Partition or at the time of birth of Bangladesh, but it was spread over a period of about two decades. Nor did it consist of only the South Indians population. Why then was the Shiv Sena successful in making South Indians the focus of its propaganda as 'outsiders'? Why was there more widespread resentment against South Indians than against the North Indians who too were 'outsiders' by Shiv Sena's definition? How far do demographic factors explain these phenomena?

The Demographic Factors and the Regionalist Movement

Studies of ethnic relations have occasionally identified certain demographic factors in the situations in which are obtained attitudes of antagonism and protest against ethnic migrants. (1) Sudden change in the demographic balance between groups in a population of region, and/or (2) Rapid large-scale migration of alien ethnic communities, is proposed as an explanation of antagonism against outsiders. (Williams A.M. Pp. 57-56; 1947, Katzenstein M. Dec. 1975) (3) Large-scale migration from other ethnic regions combined with low outmigration of the native community, in a particular region, also is seen as a complex factor responsible for provoking anti-migrant attitudes and for their occasional build-up into an anti-outsider movement. (See M. Katzenstein, Dec. 1975)

Constant large-scale migration implies a threat to the numerical strength of the native community and thereby to its economic, political and cultural position. The outmigration provides alternative opportunities for advancement, especially to the dissatisfied elements at home. Low outmigration on the other hand, means lack of or closure of (whatever may be the reasons) alternative avenues of betterment. When the absence of such openings outside is combined with high migration, the disgruntled native elements are likely to direct their resentment against the migrants for depriving them of locally available opportunities. The situation hypothetically thus contributes to the rise of political protest by natives against the outsiders (often described as nativist movements)

Migration and Growth of Mumbai's Population

Although Mumbai's population was continuously growing at a fast pace, it seems to reveal a consistent direction. The balance of population of the various communities in Mumbai did not seem to have undergone any major abrupt change. The percentage of the Gujarathi and Marathi communities from the adjacent regions of Western India slowly declined and gave way to increasing percentages of speakers of Hindi and the southern languages. The increasing proportion of migrants from beyond Western India, and the falling ratio of those born within or near the State, however was not a sudden development. Lakdawala et al (1963), in their survey of Mumbai carried out in the fifties, have noted the change in the pattern of migration increase in long-distance migration and fall in short-distance migration. The trend thus was set in the late forties during the Partition and post-war years and continued even later. Therefore the first two demographic propositions (i.e., a sudden change in demographic balance, or rapid migration) by themselves do not seem to be crucial to the rise of the regionalist movement.

However, the third demographic condition of high migration combined with low outmigration, seems to be an extremely plausible hypothesis in case of Mumbai. Both Mumbai and Maharashtra reveal a rate of outmigration which is low in the country (2.5 according to 1961 census.) (See also Katzenstein M.F.) The scale of migration to Maharashtra and especially to Mumbai is very high. According to the 1961 census, 64.2 per cent of Mumbai's population was born outside the district of Greater Mumbai and more than half the number of these migrants was from beyond Maharashtra. In 1961, 37.5 per cent of Mumbai's population came from other linguistic regions while only 26.5 per cent came from the districts of Maharashtra. Thus the demographic condition, suggested in the third proposition is clearly obtained in the case of Mumbai.

However, to consider this demographic combination as the crucial factor in the rise of the Shiv Sena movement would be an over-simplification of the problem. The demographic hypothesis by itself cannot explain why the Shiv Sena emerged, particularly in the mid-sixties. Mumbai has grown at a fast pace since the mid-forties and the combination of high migration and low outmigration has always held good for this metropolis since the post-war spurt in its industrial and urban growth. Nor can this theory explain why the Shiv Sena labelled chiefly the South Indians as outsiders when the migrants from the northern States had a slightly higher percentage than those from the South.

Therefore, to answer these questions, we have to look for other relevant factors in the situation. There can be no denying, however, that the demographic factors of high migration in

Mumbai combined with low outmigration of the native regional community had significant implications for the native community, its relations with others and its position in Mumbai.

Language in Metropolitan Life

An important and relevant factor in the situation is the language used in social life – a factor which has received very scant attention from social scientists. Multilinguality is a very special characteristic of India's urban life.

Metropolitan cities outside India also tend to be multilingual; however, with a significant difference. In these cities, there is rarely any doubt about what the main and effective language of the city is. Problems of multilingualism in these cities, therefore, recede to the background and other problems of race relations or religious tensions take priority. In India, on the other hand, multilinguality itself is a source of problems in communication and social relationships. These problems get further complicated by linguistic regional identities and economic and political rivalries. It is therefore essential to look briefly into the role, functions and place of language in social life.

Language and Group Identity

Language, besides being an instrument of communication, is an important means of sharing and transmitting cultural experience. It is in fact a vehicle of culture and as such is inextricably and intimately linked with culture and identity of a group or a community. It therefore serves as a potent symbol of group-identity.

As a means of verbal communication, language plays an important role in the complex process of socialisation, through which people become attached to their region, its culture, way of life and the language itself. Thus the language is not only a treasured heritage of the community and a means of regional socialisation, it also is an ingredient in people's identity – especially where a regional community has its own language.

Because language becomes a symbol and ingredient of group-identity, hearing one's language, the mother tongue – especially abroad, outside its home – can give a high degree of emotional satisfaction and an upsurge of emotional identification with one's own national or regional community and its culture. Again, because of this link between language and group identity, language conflict can be very 'painful and harsh in the most intimate sense' and 'touches people vitally and completely.' (Nels Anderson, 1969, p.2)

A factor that raises the intensity of one's awareness of self, or of a group's awareness of its regional/cultural/linguistic identity, is its contact with an alien group. 'It is in contact with the world outside that any social group differentiates and becomes conscious of its own self. Only against the stranger does its solidarity fully assert itself'. (Charles de Visschapter, q.v. Duchacek, I.D. 1970, p.43) This seems to work at various levels of group-identity.

Apart from the arousal of one's group-identity, people are confronted with serious communication problems whenever languages meet; and these make for tensions between groups and the wider society. With the increasing geographical and social mobility in the wake of industrialisation and urbanisation, it is inevitable that groups and communities living so far in mutual isolation would increasingly confront each other. In the face of these processes of rapid and radical change, language conflicts seem inevitable and as Nels Anderson observes, 'they cannot be wished away by anything less than realistic thinking'. (Nels Anderson, 1969. p.1)

Mumbai the Scene of Linguistic Heterogeneity and Changes

Mumbai and the adjacent Thane town and its surrounding area which is the scene of the rise of Shiv Sena, is one of the most heterogeneous of Indian cities. Its population is a multilingual and multi-ethnic conglomeration of people. Unlike New York – another of the world's most multilingual cities – there is no single language in Mumbai that is generally accepted as a medium of communication in all walks of life, including business, academics and Government. In spite of New York's large Italian and Spanish speaking minorities, English received unquestioned allegiance from all populations in the American metropolis.

There had been an absence of such a commonly accepted medium of communication in Mumbai, especially in the recent past. During the sixties national debates about the official language and the national language were still going on. The formation of the State of Maharashtra was a relatively recent event (May 1960) Mumbai's position as the capital of the Marathi speaking people's State, had yet made little impact on the use and currency of the Marathi language in the city. Marathi was yet to gain proper recognition and prestige.

The formation of the linguistic State of Maharashtra came only after the struggle for a Samyukta Maharashtra and for the inclusion of Mumbai in this State. The delay was chiefly due to the opposition of non-Marathi groups of the city to the Marathi language and to the inclusion of Mumbai in the Marathi speaking linguistic State of Maharashtra. (Phadke Y.D. 1973 Stern Robert, 1970) Against this background, the non-Marathi elite groups of the city were not in a mood to welcome or accept the regional language in the city's general administrative machinery. The mood of resistance on the part of non-Marathi communities to the introduction of regional language was further strengthened by the debate over official and national languages in the mid sixties and also by the Southern States', especially Tamil Nadu's, pro-English and anti-Hindi stance.

In the absence of a commonly accepted or acceptable medium of communication in Mumbai, even after Mumbai became the capital city of Maharashtra in the sixties, English continued to be the undisputedly prestigious medium of communication among the elite groups of the city. In fact, with the spread of education and the disappearance of the feeling of resistance to English as 'the language of the rulers', English gained both in currency and prestige with educated Indians after Independence all over India, including Mumbai. A combination of a few other factors in the situation of Mumbai furthered the use and prestige of English in Mumbai. The increased migration and multi-linguality of Mumbai is of course one of the factors. Besides, Mumbai and Maharashtra, geographically poised between North and the South India, became the arena where 'South India' met and confronted 'North India'. The South Indians' pro-English and anti-Hindi stance, and the concentrated growth of the tertiary sector in Mumbai, where the educated alone could survive, were some of the factors that indirectly contributed to the consolidation of English in Mumbai during the sixties. The weaker economic position of the Marathi community and the demographic factor of the steady fall in the proportion of the Marathi population of Mumbai deprived the Marathi community of an opportunity to fight in favour of the Marathi language.

In Mumbai, along with Marathi, Gujarati, English and Hindi have had currency, for business, education and mass-communication. Mumbai radio station of All India Radio broadcasts its news and programmes in eight languages Marathi, Gujarati, English, Hindi, Urdu, Konkani, Sindhi and Kannada. The Mumbai Municipal Corporation runs its primary schools in ten languages. The State Government and the Municipality give aid to primary and secondary schools of these ten languages. In India, no other city faces this measure of heterogeneity in its population – not even New Delhi, Kolkata or Bengaluru. Even among the metropolises of the world, perhaps very few face the challenge of multilinguality on the scale of Mumbai. This excessive multilinguality lends Mumbai its image as 'a cosmopolitan city'. However, it simultaneously creates problems of communication and provides ground for ethnic tensions. It is this prevalence of multilinguality that makes Maharashtrians regret that Mumbai is in Maharashtra but not of it.

Comparison with Other Metropolitan Cities

Of course, nearly all the metropolitan cities of India – the Union and States Capitals – are multilingual, with nearly 25 to 40 per cent of its population being migrants from other ethnic regions, speaking languages other than the local or regional language. Mumbai, because of historical reasons, is exceptional in having over 55 per cent of its population speaking languages other than that of its surrounding region. Bengaluru, in this respect, came close to Mumbai, with only 50 per cent of its population being Kannada speaking.

A broad comparison of the linguistic composition of the metropolitan cities of India provides an interesting and useful perspective. The percentage of the speakers of the regional language, Marathi in Mumbai had steadily fallen to nearly 42% in 1971, from approximately 54% (excluding Konkani speakers, and 56 per cent including Konkani speakers) in 1921, i.e. by 12 per cent in the previous five decades. The percentage of the local-regional community is much higher in other metropolitan cities and State capitals.

In Kolkata, Bengali speakers comprising nearly 65 per cent of the city population in 1961 dominated the metropolis. The next major linguistic group was of the Hindi-Urdu speakers (19 per cent Hindi and 9 per cent Urdu speakers) who together made up nearly 30 per cent of the population. The percentages of all other linguistic groups were negligible and together made up the remaining 5 per cent of the population. In Chennai, Tamils constituted 72 per cent of the inhabitants of the city while the next major linguistic groups were the Telugus (14 per cent of city population) and the Urdu speaking (6%) All other language groups had a population of less than 1 per cent each. Even in the Union capital Delhi, Hindi speaking people made up 76 per cent of the capital's population. Next major linguistic groups were Punjabis (13 per cent) and of the Urdu speakers (6 per cent)

The difference in the composition of the population of Mumbai and that of other metropolitan cities is notable. The local-regional language community makes an overwhelmingly large proportion of population in Delhi, Kolkata and Chennai, a situation absent in Mumbai. Besides, in Mumbai, of the fourteen major Indian languages at least eleven are represented by a population larger than ten thousand compared to seven or eight such groups found in other metropolitan cities. Another notable difference is that in Kolkata, Chennai and Delhi and even in case of Hyderabad and Bengaluru (the two other cities with the reputation of being cosmopolitan), the majority of linguistic groups belong either to the South Indian or North Indian language groups.

Mumbai differs in both respects. The local-regional language community makes up relatively a small proportion (42 per cent, according to the 1971 census) of Mumbai's population while the range of diversity of its linguistic groups is wider. As already mentioned, Mumbai being located midway between the north and the south, large populations both from the north and the south converged here. Apart from the large populations of central Indian groups of Marathi and Gujarati speakers, the Hindi and Urdu language groups in Mumbai together had a population of over a million, according to the 1971 Census.

The large-scale growth of South Indian population was a relatively recent phenomenon. In 1951, the share of South Indians in Mumbai's migrant population was 8.5 per cent while in 1961 it almost doubled to 15.3 per cent. In the Indian context, Mumbai had increasingly become a meeting point for the two groups of languages, the southern and the northern which differ considerably from one another. Their representative groups also differ in culture and especially in their attitudes to English and Hindi languages.

This created complex problems regarding meaningful communication and social relationships in the city. Even without language barriers, group relations tend to be complex; and the language distance adds to the difficulties. No other Indian city faces the problems of communication and social relationships that Mumbai does. Bengaluru, which, to an extent, draws migrants from all over India, seems a close parallel to Mumbai, especially because of the low percentage of its regional Kannada speaking community (50 per cent) (See M.S. Gore 1970)

To recapitulate our argument, we note that Mumbai differs from other metropolitan cities in two respects (1) the excessive heterogeneity or linguistic diversity of its population (2) a percentage less than 50 per cent, of its local i.e. linguistic-regional population. (This low percentage of the native-regional population was a major reason for opposition to including Mumbai in Maharashtra) Bengaluru appeared to share these characteristics with Mumbai. However, on a closer scrutiny, it became clear that the population of Bengaluru was less diverse linguistically. Though the percentage of those with the Kannada mother tongue i.e. of the regional community, was relatively low

(50 per cent), a considerable proportion of the two other major groups of the city was bilingual and knew and spoke Kannada. Kannada still held the position of the major language of social communication in Bengaluru. This situation was different from that of Mumbai.

Demographic Change and Language in Greater Mumbai

Greater Mumbai, in the three decades after independence, has continuously added about a million or more persons to its population. The post-war industrial boom, the influx of refugees during Partition and later, the acceleration of industrialisation and urbanisation, were responsible for this growth. Patterns of city-ward migration to Mumbai steadily underwent change during these three decades of growth. As could be expected, the long-distance migration increased while short-distance migration from Western India (Gujarat and Maharashtra) steadily declined in proportion (Lakdawala et al, - 1963, p. 93) The share of Maharashtra, among migrants to Mumbai, steadily fell from 54.2 per cent in 1931, and 44.3 per cent in 1951, to 41.6 per cent in 1961. With the acceleration of the pace of long-distance migration, the linguistic composition of the city underwent a slow but definite change.

During this process of change, the percentage of the Marathi community in the total population of Mumbai steadily declined by about seven to ten per cent. At the turn of the century and a few decades before that, the population of the Marathi-Konkani was a little over 50 per cent. However during the first two decades of the twentieth century, the proportion of Marathi-Konkani population rose to 56 per cent in the total population of Mumbai. In 1941, however, the proportion of the Marathi community in the metropolis was just enough (51.4 per cent) to balance the combined population of all other groups of Mumbai. By 1961 the ratio had declined to 47.2 per cent. According to the 1971 Census the percentage of the Marathi population in Mumbai dropped to only 41.9 per cent of the total population of Greater Mumbai.

Implications of Demographic Change

This steady but consistent fall in the percentage of the Marathi community in Mumbai meant decrease in its relative numerical strength. Moreover, while the city was growing, the community's strength seemed to decrease. In fact, the city's growth was responsible for this fall. In terms of absolute numbers, Mumbai's population increased by 1.1 million during 1951-61 and again during 1961-71, it increased by 1.8 million i.e. nearly by two million. This was the highest increase in the city's decadal growth so far, in terms of absolute numbers. In terms of percentage increase, Mumbai grew fastest by 66 per cent between 1941 and 1951.

i) The increasing loss of the community's numerical proportion in the context of the growing metropolis, when coupled with its weaker economic position, seemed to contribute to the community's apprehensions about its position and status in the city, as seen in our content data.

ii) Also, the loss of community's relative numerical strength meant further shrinking of the scope and use of the Marathi language in Mumbai. In the community's living memory, the city had a majority (56 per cent) of its population speaking Marathi-Konkani, and it was the most important centre of Marathi culture and language. All this was happening on the heels of the formation of the new State of Maharashtra (May 1960) an event which had raised expectations about the introduction of Marathi in the general administration of the State.

Altogether, it was a case of progressive relative deprivation to which demographic, economic and linguistic factors contributed. Though similar loss of percentage is noticeable in the case of the Gujarati community in Mumbai, the phenomenon did not have the same implications for that community. For further elucidation of these points, we may look into the relevant details of changing patterns of migration and linguistic composition of the metropolis.

Changing Pattern of Migration

i) While the share of migrants from Maharashtra decreased from 54.2 per cent in 1931 to 41.6 per cent in 1961, i.e. by 12 per cent; that of migrants from Gujarat fell from 19.6 per cent to 16.98 per cent i.e. by 2.7 per cent in 1961.

ii) The percentage of Hindi speaking migrants from the north, on the other hand, increased from 13.3 per cent in 1931 to 17.3 per cent i.e. by 5 per cent in 1961.

iii) The percentage of migrants from the Southern India leaped from 3.2 per cent in 1931 to 15.8 per cent in 1961 i.e. by 12.6 per cent. It almost doubled in the decade 1951-61.

Changing Linguistic Composition

These changes in migration pattern continued to affect the language composition of the metropolis slowly but significantly.

i) The Marathi community which had a share of 42.7% in the city's population in 1961 further got reduced to 41.9 per cent in 1971; the Gujarati community from 19.1 per cent in 1961 to 17.6 per cent in 1971.

ii) The Hindi and Urdu speakers who together made up 18 per cent of city's population in 1961, ten years later made up 20.7 per cent. The Punjabis who were 1.3 per cent of the 1961 population had a minor increase and became 1.4 per cent in 1971. The Sindhis, who had become a local group after the Partition and had a population of 2.3 per cent in 1961, came to have a share of 2.6 per cent in 1971.

iii) The number of speakers of southern languages who formed 8.1 per cent of the city's population in 1961 increased to 9 per cent in 1971.

Thus, during the decade of 1961-71, while the percentage of the Marathi and Gujarati speaking population decreased by about 0.8 per cent, that of the Hindi speakers rose by 2.8 per cent and that of South Indian group increased by one per cent.

The increase in the Hindi-Urdu speaking population, both in absolute numbers (nearly 5 lakh) as well as in their proportionate share in the total population during 1961-71, was higher than that of the population speaking southern languages. On the other hand, the numerical increase, (1.8 lakhs) in the South Indian population during the same decade, did not seem to warrant a provocation or resentment against them, especially when compared to the North Indian group. Why then, did the South Indian group become the target of resentment rather than the Hindi-Urdu group which outnumbered the South Indian in numerical terms? Is this resentment to be attributed entirely to the successful manipulation and skilled propaganda by Thackeray? Or were there any other factors which made the native community perceive South Indians as 'outsiders'? Were these factors absent in case of Hindi-speaking groups, so as to make the native community more tolerant towards them? Here it seems the language-distance combined with certain other socio-economic factors, made a crucial difference.

Growth of South Indian Groups

Of the South Indian language group, Tamil and Malyalam together made up 4 per cent of the city's population in 1961; by 1971, their numbers rose to nearly 4.8 per cent of Mumbai's population. Of these the Malayalis almost doubled their number (92 per cent increase i.e. about 61, 000) during the sixties, while the Tamil group gained by nearly 50 per cent (i.e. over 52, 000) On the other hand, the Kannada and Telugu speaking groups who together made up 4 per cent of the city's population in 1961, showed only a slight increase of 0.2 per cent to make up a 4.2 per cent share of the metropolitan population in 1971. The Telugus maintained their ratio of 2.1 per cent over the decade, while the share of Kannada speakers increased from 1.9 per cent to 2.1 per cent during the decade. The Tamil and Malyali groups together rose faster both in absolute number (by 1, 12,942) as well in their proportionate share in city's population, than the Telugu-Kannada group.

Socio-Economic Characteristics of the Southern Groups

Among the Southern language groups, the main targets of resentment of the native community and of the attack of Shiv Sena were Malayali and Tamil speakers rather than the Telugu and Kannada groups. Tamil and Malayali groups were relatively recent migrants and culturally and linguistically more alien than the neighbouring South Indian groups of Telugu and Kannada speakers.

The latter groups were part of the familiar scene in Mumbai as well as in Maharashtra. The Telugus were one of the oldest South Indian communities in Mumbai, settled in the city in mid-19th century in Central Mumbai in the locality of Kamathipura named after the Kamathis from Andhra. The erstwhile Nizam's State had a few Marathi-speaking districts and the Marathis and Telugus in that State together participated in the State's freedom movement. Similarly some of the Kannada-speaking districts were part of old Mumbai State and people of the border districts in Maharashtra were often bilingual. The incidence of bilingualism with Marathi as the subsidiary language was higher among these two groups than among the Tamils or Malayalis in Mumbai. (Bilingualism with Marathi subsidiary Telugu 7038/97993; Kannada 9161/82831; Tamil 2151/1, 04387; Malayali 944/65673) The Telugus were hardly mentioned in the Shiv Sena agitation. The provocation for resentment against the Kannadigas was limited to two contexts (a) The Maharashtra-Mysore border dispute over Belgaum and a few other areas; and (b) owners of Udipi restaurants bringing native unskilled workers for their business.

The chief focus of the regionalist protest and resentment was against the Tamil and Malayali migrants.

The migration stream from the far south began in the thirties, but accelerated only in the 'fifties and sixties. By 1961 the population of these two groups, Tamils and Malayalis had increased four times to what it was in 1941. We have noted that the Malyali population doubled in the troubled years of 1960's. The migration of these communities took place chiefly within the past two decades, relatively a very recent phenomenon. These two groups thus were linguistically and culturally alien on the Mumbai scene.

The distance between these communities and the native regional community becomes further marked due to the tendency of these groups to live an insular life within their own groups.

(See Ch. V; also refer to Mythili, 1959; Nair K.C., 1975) In its turn, language-distance seems to contribute to the tendency of the migrant communities to live an insular life.

The social distance due to language difference and related linguistic culture was accentuated by other socio-economic factors.

i) Economic Competition

a) We discussed earlier in the chapter on 'Economic Aspirations' the factors of middle class job competition and differential characteristics of long-distance migrants. The accelerated migration stream from Tamil Nadu and Kerala, tended to consist of upper caste (Brahmin, Nair, Menon) urban educated persons (See Mythili, 1959, K.S. Nair, 1975) who had better chances of being absorbed in the fast-growing tertiary sector and the new industries with their increasing emphasis on educational equipment. These migrants from the South thus posed a competition to the educated, lower-middle and middle class of the Marathi community in Mumbai. This class was urban, vocal and conscious of its linguistic identity due to the recent Samyukta Maharashtra Movement and the formation of Maharashtra.

b) The Kannadigas and especially the Telugus did not pose such a great threat because these groups entered chiefly into their own traditional occupations - different from those aspired to by the Marathi community. The majority of Telugu migrants provided the labour force for Mumbai's 'construction' industry, while a smaller percentage of them traditionally worked as craftsmen in the textile industry. Kannadigas were concentrated in the catering service - a preserve of those from Udupi in Karnataka - and also in the railways. The catering service was not considered prestigious enough among the Marathi community.

c) In the newer chemical and engineering industries of the city, however, both Zachariah (1968) and Joshi (1976) observed a high proportion of migrants from Kerala, Tamil Nadu, West Bengal and Maharashtra. They also observed concentration of the Kerala-born in clerical positions. (Zachariah K.C. 1968, Pp. 318; Joshi H & V, 1976, Pp. 138-146)

These details, to an extent, help to explain the differential attitudes of the native community to different South Indian groups. However they do not answer the question as to why South Indians were labelled as outsiders, while similar resentment was largely absent in the case of the Hindi-speaking groups, inspite of their greater numerical strength.

d) The absence of a direct clash of economic interests due to occupational differences in the case of the Hindi speaking communities was perhaps an important factor. Hindi speakers from U.P. and Bihar were chiefly concentrated in the dairy business and allied activities. Some of them traditionally worked as textile labour. Those from Rajasthan and Madhya Pradesh were in the construction industry, sales, commerce and professional fields. Punjabis were chiefly in small business and industries. Competition with the native community from these groups for jobs was not altogether absent. Migrants from Punjab, Rajasthan and West Bengal, were found in administrative, managerial and executive positions. However their competition was not a marked one in respect of lower cadre tertiary jobs.

There were other equally relevant factors in the situation which cannot be ignored.

ii) An important factor was language, especially in the context of a nationwide new awareness of the linguistic identity.

a) The Hindi speaking group have always been a familiar part of the Mumbai scene. At the turn of the last century, Hindi-Urdu speakers had a share of about 15 per cent in the total population of Mumbai. (Lakdawala et al, 1963, Table II-17, p. 29) Hindi is spoken on the northern border of Maharashtra and therefore was not an unfamiliar language. Even in the pre-Independence days the Marathi community had willingly welcomed Hindi as the national language and India's lingua franca. The attitude of the acceptance of Hindi as the link-language is prevalent.

b) The Hindi and Marathi have a common script (Nagari) Outside the Hindi speaking provinces, Maharashtra is the leading State where Hindi is most understood and spoken. Communication with the Hindi groups, therefore posed no serious problems.

c) Even after the arousal of regional linguistic identity due to the Samyukta Maharashtra Movement and nationwide language debate, the attitude to Hindi speakers was therefore one of greater tolerance than that to speakers of Tamil and Malayalam, languages which sounded alien and unintelligible.

d) The general anti-Hindi stance of the South Indians, the anti-Hindi violent agitations encouraged by the DMK in the South, and preference to English by the South Indians, both by the educated upper class as well the non-Brahmin pro- DMK groups, seems to have caused a sharp reaction among the native Marathi community against the South Indian groups of Malayali and Tamils, as revealed in our content data (See Chapter VII)

e) The South Indian's preference for and reliance upon English, and especially his lack of interest in Marathi, thc rcgional language, also seems to have proved an irritant and provocation to the native group which consisted of a large proportion of rural migrants with lower levels of education and with heightened aspirations regarding its regional identity. (See Ch. V)

A few instances of vocal resistance to the use of Marathi by members of the South Indian communities were then sufficient to strengthen a negative reaction against these groups, as revealed in our content data.

Boundary Disputes

The boundary dispute is really speaking the problem of regional identity of the Marathi community. It is but natural that the resolution of this problem should be sought in the capital city, which ideally speaking represents or ought to represent the regional identity. In Mumbai, the Shiv Sena which claimed to champion the Maharashtrian cause, therefore, could not afford to ignore the boundary dispute. The struggle for the resolution of an issue like that of Belgaum-Karwar became both a responsibility and an opportunity for the Shiv Sena.

The Maharashtrian concept of Maharashtra, as evolved during the British period, included, apart from Konkan, western and southern Maharashtra districts, region of Vidarbha-Nagpur (then a part of C.P. and Berar), Marathwada (then a part of Nizam State) and Goa (a Portuguese colony) One of the early articulations of the concept of united Maharashtra was found in 1891 in Tilak's *Kesari*. The Samyukta Maharashtra Movement for the formation of such a province or State was a development of the 1940's when national independence became an immediate possibility. However eminent intellectuals and public personalities like Tilak, Vinoba Bhave, S.V. Ketkar, D.R. Gadgil, had earlier contributed to the development of the idea and image of Samyukta Maharashtra. (Phadke, 1973, p. 121-125)

In 1960, Samyukta Maharashtra became a reality. However, the goal was not fully realised. Several Marathi-speaking areas were still outside Maharashtra. Maharashtra had its boundary common with Andhra on the east, Madhya Pradesh and Gujarat in the north and Karnataka in the south. Maharashtra had no dispute with Andhra, Madhya Pradesh and Gujarat. The boundary problems between these States were amicably settled.

Northern Boundary

Occasionally some members of the community were vocal in the press about non-inclusion in Maharashtra of Marathi speaking areas in Palaghat district (Madhya Pradesh) More often people grieved at the loss of the tribal district of Dangs and several villages of Navapur (Dist. Dhulia) and Umbergaon (Dist. Thane) taluka, to Gujarat as seen in the content data. However, there was not sustained agitation or movement of the local people in these areas. The Marathi community therefore, on the whole had accepted the decision about northern boundaries, though occasionally members criticised the Government for betraying Maharashtra.

Goa

Maharashtrians eventually reconciled themselves even to Goa's decision to remain separate as expressed in the referendum held in January 1967, which favoured retaining independent status of Goa and rejected the alternative of merger with Maharashtra. Besides, the sting of the opinion poll was lost when the Maharashtrawadi Gomantak Party's government upon its return to power after the poll, gave recognition to Marathi as the official language of the State of Goa. (Mrt. 10.4.68) Even the Sahitya Academy's recognition of Konkani as an independent language in (19) did not seem to have posed a very serious problem. The Maharashtra Government's Language and Literature Board today gives annual prises to publications both in Marathi and Konkani. After all, the Konkani spoken in Goa is also spoken in South Konkan. Thus Maharashtra was more or less reconciled to Goa's verdict against merger with Maharashtra.

Maharashtra-Karnataka Border The Nature of the Dispute

However, Maharashtra's dispute about its boundary with Karnataka and especially the problem of Belgaum remained provocative.

Before 1956, the four districts of Belgaum, Bijapur, Dharwar and Karwar formed part of the former Mumbai State. In 1956, upon the recommendations of the States Reorganisation Commission, these districts of North Karnataka were merged in the new State of Mysore. In the process large Marathi speaking areas got included in Mysore and some Kannada speaking areas were left over in Maharashtra, i.e. bilingual Mumbai. The then Chief Minister of Mysore, Nijalingappa, on the floor of Mysore Legislative Assembly on 24.12.56 had conceded that large Marathi-speaking areas were included in Karnataka, which he would not hesitate to return (q.v. Antulay A.R., 1968, Pp. 13-15)

The representatives of Maharashtra had suggested the following principles for the division of the area and demarcation of the boundary (1) The village as a unit popularly known as Pataskar formula – accepted for settlement of boundary between Madras and Andhra (2) Geographical contiguity, (3) Relative majority of the two groups Marathi and Kannada according to 1951 Census (4) Wishes of the people (voiced through elections) The representatives of Mysore, however, did not agree with these principles except that of geographical contiguity.

In the meanwhile a popular front, Maharashtra Ekikarn Samiti emerged in the area which fought and won the parliamentary and assembly and local body elections since 1957 in almost all the disputed villages and towns, on the merger issue. The content data has references to these events. People's representations were being continuously made to the Governments at the Centre and at Mumbai. The Maharashtra legislature passed a resolution urging the Union Government to settle this dispute without further delay. (Mht. 6.4.66; Mrt. 6.4.66)

Finally the Parliament appointed a one-man Commission of Meherchand Mahajan, former Chief Justice of the Supreme Court for the resolution of the dispute. The Commission submitted its report to the Union Home Minister in August-September 1967, which reached the Maharashtra State Assembly in November 1967. Maharashtrians found the Commission's report extremely frustrating. The report was full of contradictions and had no consistent or stable yardstick for the division or the areas. The total lack of consistency on the part of the Commission in evolving or applying any definite principle for the solution of the border problems seemed appalling. (See Antulay A.R. 1968)

For example, the Commission did not dispute the Maharashtrian character of Belgaum city. It conceded 'social and cultural affinities with the Marathi speaking people of Maharashtra and the Maharashtrian character of the city', but did not let these facts influence its decision. (Mahajan Commission Report p. 90, q.v. Antulay 1968, p. 179) Similarly the Commission did not think it fair and just to throw over 90,000 non-Marathi persons (46,793 Kannada and 43,960 minority community persons) into Maharashtra, but the Commission found it just and equitable to throw over 1, 27,000 (83, 672, i.e. 46 per cent Marathi and 43, 960 minority persons, by the 1961 Census) to Mysore State. (Antulay, 1968, p.11, Mahajan Commission Report, p.87)

After a long wait of one decade for redressal of its grievances, the Marathi community was extremely frustrated and angry and rejected the Commission's report. The opposition parties in Maharashtra publicly burned the copies of the 'unjust' report. Even the State Government sponsored a resolution in the State Legislature which rejected the Commission's report. The opposition parties tried to shake the Congress rule in the State by exploiting people's frustration over the boundary issue.

The Centre's Responsibility

New Delhi's *ad hoc* approach to the boundary disputes, on the whole, was responsible for the situation. Its favourite method of appointing a commission of enquiry was only 'a desperate bid to buy time' by putting vital issues involving people's emotions into cold storage for a long time, rendering them intractable and politically explosive. Worse still, it made the people grow bitter and lose faith in the democratic processes of resolving claims and solving issues. Instead of evolving and adopting definite principles for solving issues the Congress High Command and the Central Government left the solutions to the good sense of the opposing parties. What ultimately mattered was a Party's bargaining power or its capacity to threaten the very existence of the ruling Party. The opposition parties in Maharashtra resorted to the last step to fight against the 'injustice perpetrated' on them by the Commission.

The Response of the Opposition

Both the CPI and SSP had seen the need for raising a common front of the opposition to intensify the border boundary struggle. (Resolutions passed in Second Conference of Maharashtra SSP, q.v. Kulkarni A.G., 1968, p. 449-50) The leaders of the PSP were actively associated with the MES. Even the Jan Sangh, which because of its national policy had been aloof from linguistic agitations, demanded an urgent solution to the problem. (Kulkarni, p. 550) The Peasants and Workers Party passed a resolution to intensify the agitation for the inclusion of Belgaum and other areas in Maharashtra.

The new coalition of these political parties of the left – the Sampoorna Maharashtra Samiti (SPMS) – organised a border conference at Kolhapur in December 1967, to block the way of Congress members to their annual conference at Sangli. The border conference had a limited success. However these national political parties like SSP, CPI and PSP had to work within the constraints of their national policy. Besides, the national leadership of the party or the leadership of other state branches did not always see eye-to-eye with the members of the Maharashtra branch especially with respect to linguistic-regional issues. Other Party programmes and intra-Party struggles of these national parties kept their members preoccupied. The leaders and workers of national parties could not give single-minded attention to the programmes of the SPMS. After the border conferences, the

SPMS therefore, slowly lapsed into silence. After all the Belgaum issue was not as important as that of the inclusion of Mumbai in Maharashtra. The content data reveals that the SPMS was disintegrating by 1968. It was badly mauled in the 1968 civic elections of the Mumbai Municipal Corporation. The Shiv Sena in alliance with the PSP had emerged victorious with 40 and 11 seats respectively to their credit in the total of 140 seats.

Boundary Dispute and the Shiv Sena

Where the national opposition parties failed, the regional parties could step in to assure a better performance. The Peasants and Workers Party and the Shiv Sena which were born to champion and protect Maharashtrians's rights, were free from the constraints of a national organisation and could take a lead and carry out a more sustained agitation on a regional level. The Shiv Sena thus lent support to the MES and carried out a *bandh* in Mumbai in support of the people of the boundary area.

However, while doing so, the Shiv Sena could not help giving its own colour to this agitation. The Samyukta Maharashtra Movement was successful in carrying out its agitations peacefully because the leadership had totally eschewed the use of violence. The Shiv Sena leadership's acquiescence to violence could not help influencing the character of its agitation. Apart from people's desperation and bitter frustration over a long-pending boundary issue, the youthfulness of the Shiv Sena's volunteer force was a relevant factor influencing the character of the agitation. (Most of the persons arrested by the police during the riots were very young boys, often below the age of twenty-one; also see Ram Joshi 1970) However, the Shiv Sena leadership's tacit acceptance of violence as an effective way of bringing pressure on the authorities seems to be a crucial factor in turning a peaceful, popular agitation into a mass riot in February 1969.

However, the day-to-day news reports from the Daily Maratha, which served as an organ of the SPMS, the opponent of the Shiv Sena, also throw light on how each opposition party in Mumbai, at the initial stages of the agitation tried to exploit the situation to its own advantage. Initially these parties supported the bandh. They almost justified the mass violence and even blamed the police for excesses and provocation. But they ultimately disowned their share of responsibility in the rampage, when they discovered the large-scale loss and destruction of property and when the press and the public started blaming the Shiv Sena for the events. New Delhi's responsibility in the whole affair, in driving people to desperation by its politics of expediency and its lack of determination and direction for a timely resolution of issues, also cannot be ignored.

The agitations for the border dispute provided a linguistic-regionalist issue which the Shiv Sena, as a champion of the Maharashtrian's rights, could legitimately take up. The Shiv Sena, in alliance with PSP, had by then emerged as the major opposition party in the Municipal Corporation. Its growing strength needed new programmes that would extend its appeal and influence into the wider region of Maharashtra, if it was to develop into a regional Party. The boundary agitation provided just such a programme.

The BPCC and Maharashtrians

The Mumbai Pradesh Congress Committee and Maharashtrians were poles apart. The BPCC had been the focus of power – political and also economic. It was represented by city's leading merchants and industrialists, chiefly from Gujarat. It had the status of a special Pradesh Congress committee exclusively for the city and carried much weight in the Congress organisation. Maharashtrians were separated from the BPCC by the 'overlapping' distance of class and language because the Marathi community, by and large, represented the industrial proletariat and the middle-class intelligentsia. Members of the economically weaker Maharashtrian community had little say in the BPCC

With the rise of the Samyukta Maharashtra Movement, the distance between the BPCC and the Maharashtrian community began to widen. The struggle for Samyukta Maharashtra was intense in Mumbai since the chief issue was the inclusion of Mumbai in Maharashtra. The struggle was led by the Samyukta Maharashtra Samiti – a coalition chiefly of leftist parties – the CPI, PSP, PWP and other smaller parties, while those who arrayed in opposition were the industrial and commercial bourgeoisie in Mumbai, represented by Mumbai Citizens Committee, Indian Merchants' Chamber, and the Mumbai Pradesh Congress Committee. Though the struggle assumed the character of a class-struggle, it simultaneously was a linguistic-regionalist struggle.

The movement had raised Maharashtrian expectations. In spite of being an economically weaker community, Maharashtrians aspired to lead the metropolitan city. The community was devoid of economic power but had the numerical strength of a majority community. After 1960, however, it found itself relatively shrinking in numbers and unable to balance itself against all the other communities put together, whom the BPCC claimed to represent. The content data amply substantiates the alienation of the Marathi community, the distance frustration, and its sense of apprehension and insecurity in relation to the BPCC

The existence of an independent Pradesh Congress committee for Mumbai dates back to 1920. The Congress accepted the linguistic principle for organisation of provinces in 1921 and implemented it in the organisation of its Pradesh Congress Committees. However, Maharashtra until 1960 was divided into four Pradesh Congress Committees Maharashtra Pradesh Congress Committee for Western Maharashtra; Vidarbha and Marathwada each had a Pradesh Congress committee. Mumbai had its own Pradesh Congress Committee which worked linguistically for both Gujarati and Marathi.

After the formation of Samyukta Maharashtra, there was a move within all the political parties for the unification of their various units spread over the Maharashtra region. The Congress unified its committees from Western Maharashtra, Vidarbha and Marathwada, but allowed the independent existence of the BPCC to continue. Y. B. Chavan, during discussions on the bifurcation of bilingual Mumbai, had assured the nine-man parliamentary committee that the opinion of the Congress workers from Mumbai would be taken on whether there should be an independent BPCC in Maharashtra. Even after the formation of Maharashtra State the BPCC members claimed a separate Pradesh Congress Committee. The BPCC, the only Pradesh Committee for a city in the entire country - thus continued its independent existence. (Kulkarni A.G., 1968, p. 316)

After the formation of the BPCC, the Maharashtrian intelligentsia gradually lost hold of Congress leadership in Mumbai. The close co-operation that existed between the political leaders and workers of Western Maharashtra and Mumbai, in the 19th century and early 20th century, slowly disappeared. The BPCC progressively became alienated from political events and personalities of Maharashtra, especially after Independence. Also the younger generation Maharashtrian leadership consisting of the urban educated middle class increasingly turned to leftist parties - the CPI and the Congress Socialist Party. On the whole, non-Maharashtrians increasingly led the Congress organisation and thereby controlled civic and state policies in Mumbai.

Prior to 1946, all the BPCC presidents were non-Maharashtrians. This was inspite of the fact that the Marathi community was the city's single largest community, considerably active in the Congress and in the struggle for national freedom. In 1946, S.K. Patil was the first Maharashtrian to become the President of the BPCC However, the Marathi community and S. K. Patil both, sort of disowned each other. It is clear from the content data that the Marathi community was not keen to own S. K. Patil as Maharashtrian. On the other hand, S. K. Patil did not consider himself a representative of the Marathi community but proudly declared himself a 'cosmopolitan'. (Kulkarni A. G., 1968, p. 148)

Paradoxically, the BPCC under the leadership of S.K. Patil continued to follow a policy which ultimately transformed it into a non-Maharashtrian and to some extent, even an anti-Maharashtrian organisation. It increasingly came under the influence of the Indian Merchants' Chamber and eventually assumed a pro-capitalist posture. (Kulkarni A.G., 1968. p. 153) When the demand for Samyukta Maharashtra was repeatedly voiced by the Samyukta Maharashtra Parishad, and was supported by the MPCC leaders, the BPCC vehemently opposed it. S.K. Patil refused to associate with the Samyukta Maharashtra Parishad from the very beginning.

BPCC leaders believed that Mumbai, being a 'cosmopolitan city', could not be made 'an appendage of Maharashtra'. (See Phadke, p. 189-90) They increasingly projected and used 'the cosmopolitan character of Mumbai' as a reason and justification for keeping Mumbai separate from Maharashtra and for retaining its independent status. Other influential bodies representing non-Maharashtrian communities in the city also took a stand against Samyukta Maharashtra. The Indian Merchants' Chamber, at its meeting (26.8.48), declared Maharashtra's claim to the city to be unreasonable. The Mumbai Citizens Committee (with hardly any Maharashtrian members) representing the interests of a small but vocal and influential minority, also opposed the formation of linguistic provinces and demanded a separate city-state status for Mumbai. (Phadke, Pp. 237-238 & p. 293)

The States Reorganisation Commission in its report in September 1955 rejected the demand for Samyukta Maharashtra and instead recommended a balanced bilingual State of Mumbai, excluding Nagpur-Vidarbha region. The BPCC at an emergency meeting passed a resolution urging acceptance of the balanced bilingual State, while many members had not even read the S.R.C. report. Following this, the BPCC sent a delegation to Delhi to meet the Congress High Command (CHC) and the Home Minister, to convey the BPCC's acceptance and to stress the need of urgent implementation of the S.R.C. report. It was led by K.K. Shah and included two Muslims and a South Indian. Strangely enough the delegation had no Maharashtrian member. The Mumbai Citizens Committee also sent a telegram to the Home Minister urging him to consider independent status for Mumbai in 'the national interest'. (Phadke, 1973, p. 225-226)

In 1949, G B. Mahashabde, a Maharashtrian, became the General Secretary of the BPCC His pro-Maharashtra leanings, however, were not approved by S.K. Patil and Mahashabde consequently had to resign. Patil also opposed the inclusion of the rebel Maharashtrian, T.R. Naravane, in the Mumbai (State) Cabinet and instead wanted K.K. Shah to be included. According to Mahashabde, Patil made conscious efforts to keep Maharashtrian leaders of the BPCC away from power. (Mahashabde, q.v. Kulkarni A.G., 1968, Pp. 153-154. Also see Phadke, 1973, p. 204-

205, p. 268-272) Ultimately, Narvane and Mahashbde revolted against the so-called 'cosmopolitan' leadership of the BPCC They alleged that the BPCC functioned under the domination of Gujarati capitalists, who were opposed to Samyukta Maharashtra. These rebels later founded Congress Jan Parishad which joined the front of the Samyukta Maharashtra Samiti. (Kulkarni, ibid, phadke, ibid)

BPCC and the Alienation of the Marathi Community

The BPCC's progressively anti-Maharashtrian stance was bound to provoke a reaction from the Marathi community. The Samyukta Maharashtra Movement eventually acquired class overtones since the leftist opposition parties rallied around the demand of Samyukta Maharashtra. The movement, however, also contained within it reactions of an economically weaker linguistic community to the so-called cosmopolitanism of the BPCC and MCC In the 1950's the Marathi community thus was totally alienated from the BPCC

This alienation of the Marathi community found expression in the community's distrust of the Gujarati elite representing those organisations. Even in the business of Government of the bilingual State, suspicion of discrimination against the Marathi community was voiced by eminent men like B.R. Ambedkar and C.D. Deshmukh. (Ambedkar, B.R., 1955, - p. 22; Deshmukh C.D., 1972, p. 158-159) This discrimination was often the theme of the speeches of many opposition leaders from Maharashtra in the Mumbai State Legislative Assembly. Congressmen from Maharashtra, though they rarely aired these grievances publicly, repeatedly made attempts to draw attention to their grievances within the Party. (See Phadke, p.66-68)

The Mumbai Government accepted the Greater Mumbai Plan in the late 'forties. Maharashtrians felt suspicious of the plan because they saw in it a step preparatory to the formation of an independent city State. Ambedkar commented that the object of including large surrounding areas in Mumbai, could not but be 'to make Mumbai viable' – as a city state. (Ambedkar, B.R., 1948, p. 39)

Fear of Non-Marathi Collusion

The Maharashtrians also felt apprehensive of the collusion of various communities which often aligned themselves in a common front against the Marathi community, especially against the community's demand for inclusion of Mumbai in Samyukta Maharashtra.

During the days of the Kher Ministry, a non-official resolution demanding formation of Maharashtra State with Mumbai was tabled by a Maharashtrian member of the Mumbai Legislative Assembly. However, at the time of discussion the resolution was split in two parties; the first recommending the creation of linguistic States and the second regarding the inclusion of Mumbai in Maharashtra. It was found that the members from Karnataka, though they supported the first part of the resolution (regarding the formation of linguistic States), they, along with several Gujarati members from the Cabinet and the BPCC, abstained from voting over the issue of the inclusion of Mumbai in Maharashtra. (24.10.48) The widespread impression in Maharashtra was that the Karnataka M.L.A.s acted in collusion with Gujarati legislators to prevent Maharashtra from getting Mumbai. (Phadke, p. 199)

At the time some Maharashtrian Congressmen believed that the middle class South Indian population of the city, feeling apprehensive that its chances of employment in Mumbai may get jeopardised if Mumbai formed part of Maharashtra, might vote against Maharashtra in the event of a plebiscite over the Mumbai issue. (Stern R., 1970, p. 48)

The fear of collusion by the non-Marathi communities came to the fore during the Samyukta Maharashtra Movement and was occasionally articulated. In the context of Gujarati opposition to the inclusion of Mumbai in Maharashtra, people felt that the Government of composite or bilingual Mumbai State dominated by the Gujaratis would not care to safeguard the legitimate interests of the local people. It was also believed that the non-Marathi entrepreneurs preferred to recruit people from their own regions rather than from Maharashtra. (Phadke p. 74-75) A fear of discriminatory hiring practices against the Marathi speaking people was expressed by some Congressmen. Naravane claimed that there was a letter in circulation advising the city's industrialists to reduce the recruitment of Marathi speaking labour. (Stern, R. 1970, p. 48)

Cosmopolitanism of B.P.C.C

By excluding the members of Mumbai's largest single community from consideration and by overplaying its 'cosmopolitanism', the BPCC leadership contributed much to alienate the Marathi community and to vitiate the relationship between the Marathi and Gujarati communities of the city. During the fifties, the economically and politically powerful groups tried their strength through the BPCC to bring pressure on the Central authorities to sever Mumbai's ties with Maharashtra and turn it into a city-State under the name of safeguarding minority communities and of cosmopolitanism. This cosmopolitanism, therefore, became suspect in Maharashtrian eyes.

Maharashtrians a Minority against the City's Other Communities

It is not surprising in the context that the Marathi community with its weaker economic position and its relatively dwindling numerical strength, felt increasingly insecure about its position in metropolitan life. It felt that the city's other minority communities, under the influence of BPCC and its allies were likely to align themselves against Maharashtrians, in support of a city-State. This meant virtually reducing the Marathi community to the position of a minority community - inspite of it being the city's single largest group.

Even after the formation of Maharashtra State, the BPCC continued to play the role of guardian to the non-Marathi minorities and of champion of 'cosmopolitanism'. The content-data pointed out that the demand for an independent or centrally administered city-State for Mumbai was revived in 1966 at the initiative of a South Indian member of the BPCC perhaps at the instigation of the old guard in the Party. The apprehension of an alignment between other communities and the recurrence of similar demands seemed to have made the Marathi community acquire the characteristics of an aggressive minority. It increasingly took an aggressive stance towards the BPCC, B.C.C. and such other organisations that assumed the role of champion to the cause of minorities and of cosmopolitanism.

Apart from the organisations of the B.C.C., the Merchants' Chambers and similar associations, there also was the English press, the so-called national press because of its nation-wide circulation, which supported the BPCC's 'cosmopolitanism' and by and large had opposed the formation of the linguistic State of Maharashtra and Mumbai's inclusion in it. The Maharashtrian community's attitude of suspicion and criticism of the English press in the sixties was an outcome of these foregoing events.

The last one to join this group of 'cosmopolitanists' was the South Indian migrant, particularly the urban educated, vocal and mostly upper-caste South Indians in search of white-collar jobs and executive positions. Consistent with his cosmopolitanism the South Indian migrant championed his right of freedom of movement in the country and relied upon the English language for communication in social intercourse.

The championing of 'cosmopolitanism' by various groups in Mumbai appeared to be a garb for their vested interests, a subtle means of holding themselves indifferent to the aspirations of the majority community of the city, to save themselves the trouble or efforts of identifying themselves intimately with the surrounding region, its language and people and, in the process, offending them.

Consequently it provoked an explosive reaction manifesting itself in the form of an aggressive regionalist movement of the native regional community.

CHAPTER VII

SELF-VIEW AND THE PROTEST MOVEMENT

It should be clear from the discussion in the foregoing chapters that the Maharashtrian community's grievances and frustrations which led it to express itself in the language of protest, are closely related to the community's expectations about itself and its place in the metropolis, besides being linked with its situation in the metropolis.

People's Perception of Themselves and their Situation

In the first chapter, it was observed that problem situations originate discontent and liberate needs, but they do not always produce social movements. People agitate for change only when they feel they can legitimately aspire for improvement in their condition. 'People become most intensely discontented when they cannot get what they think they deserve, not just what they want in an ideal sense.' (Gurr and Graham, 1969) What people think they deserve depends on their past experience, present context and their generalised beliefs about themselves and their situation. In other words, the situation the Maharashtrian community in Mumbai perceived itself to be in and the self-view held by the community is significant in the rise of the Shiv Sena movement. Overcrowding, unemployment, job competition and such other sources of strain in themselves did not trigger collective action; these became a cause of intolerable discontent because of the community's perceptive self-appraisal.

Apart from the strains of the worsening objective situation, the Marathi community's frustrations arose from the community's expectations related to its placement in the metropolis as the host community of the State and its special relationship to the metropolis as its State capital.

The Maharashtrian frustrations thus stem from the community's perception of its own situation in comparison with that of some significant others in the metropolis. They emanate from the community's expectations regarding itself, its due place or status in the city and again from what the city should prospectively hold for them in contrast to what it preferred to other communities of the metropolis. These attitudes determined by the community's expectation-level regarding its relationship with the metropolis, when juxtaposed with the strains of worsening objective conditions led to mounting frustrations and to a point of explosion.

In this chapter an attempt is made to explore more closely this world of expectations and aspirations, of the community's self-view, and its perspective self-appraisal and how this was related to the community's frustrations and, sequentially, to a protest movement. The number of entries taken into consideration in this chapter, is relatively small – two hundred in all. These entries dealing with the theme of 'Self-View' of the community are divided into the following sub-themes (1) Aspirations and ideals of the community (2) Introspective evaluation of the self-community (3) The self-community and others (also described as 'Self and others') (4) The community and the arbiter.

The distribution of the entries is as follows

Self-View of the Community	Letters	Editorials	Reports and Articles
1. Aspirations and Ideals	4	8	31
2. Introspective Evaluation (Of the self-community)	29	2	31
3. Self and others	16	12(9+3)	46
4. The Community and the Arbiter (the Central Government and CHC)	-	6	3
	59	28	117
	Total No. of Entries		204

1) Some of the entries included here overlap with those considered in the sixth chapter. For quantitative analysis, i.e. for counting their intensity value on the affective scale, all such entries were taken into consideration in the preceding chapter and therefore they are not again put on the affective scale.

2) It may be noted that a large number of entries explored here, do not fall on the scale previously used for assessing the ntensity of grievance and its transformation into the articulation of collective protest. These entries articulate the community's aspirations, ideals, expectations, etc., express its views about itself, its own drawbacks and strengths, how it appeared to others; as also the community's views about 'others', how these 'others' behaved, their placement, or where or how they stood, etc. Though some of these entries occasionally voice a grievance or a protest, they are preoccupied more with the community's assessment of itself in the light of its aspirations and ideals.

3) There exists a large number of letters in the category of 'Introspective Assessment of Self'. These put forward the common people's own views about the community's behaviour in certain respects and as such, are important for this study. However, the aspirations and ideals of the community do not find articulation in the common man's letters but through the agency of community leaders hailing from different walks of life, on various public occasions. That a relatively large number of entries in this category are included under reports and articles reflects this situation.

4) People's aspirations expressed in the context of specific themes were taken into consideration and discussed in the earlier chapters. Here, aspirations of a more general nature are explored. Many of these aspirations found expression at the time of the birth of the new State since the formation of Maharashtra was a landmark in the fulfilment of the Maharashtrian community's desire for a unilingual Maharashtra State. To all purposes, therefore, the formation of Maharashtra State was a fitting occasion to reiterate the ideals and long cherished aspirations of the people.

Though a large majority of entries are from the *Daily Maratha*, parallel thoughts and attitudes were also found in the content data derived from other journals. As stated in Chapter II, we have drawn upon two newspapers from Pune, *Sakal* and *Kesari*, besides the six journals from Mumbai, for entries on the theme of 'Aspirations and Ideals'.

The majority of the entries contain voices and opinions expressed by community leaders of various strata and colours, and therefore may be taken to represent the prevailing public opinion and attitudes.

I

Content Data

1. Aspirations and Ideals

It is natural that collective aspirations are expressed by community leaders on public occasions rather than by individuals in the context of personal life.

Some of these entries articulate aspirations hinged to the status of the Marathi community in Mumbai and express optimism at the prospects of commanding high status in the metropolis. The emerging picture in these projected aspirations is that of a community which often saw itself in the role of leader and defender of the nation's freedom. Another vocalised aspiration (one even by the *Marmik*) was that Maharashtra was to serve as the link between the north and the south and was to be the confluence of India's variegated culture.

Thus the projected image is a far cry from that of an isolationist, parochial community, but one entertaining hopes of playing a leadership role.

a) Maharashtra and Mumbai (Aspiration and Reality) Letters

Of the small number of letters voicing the community's ideals and aspirations, one from early 1960's articulates Maharashtrian aspirations and expectations about the city of Mumbai and its place in the life of Maharashtra.

Early in 1960, as the prospects of formation of Maharashtra State with Mumbai as the capital appeared certain, there was considerable discussion as to what should be appropriately the name of the new State. This was the context of the letters

The letter asserts that the city of Mumbai, spread between the Thane and Colaba districts of the Konkan coast, had always been recognised as part of Maharashtra region till 1920. It was then (1920), that an independent Pradesh Congress was set up for the city. During the days of Ranade and Tilak, Mumbai city was not only the centre of national life but was also the political and cultural centre of Maharashtra region. Important political events in the life of Maharashtra, like the Home-Rule League Conference and the Mulshi Satyagraha were launched here in this city. The prospective State including Mumbai, therefore, can be named appropriately only as Maharashtra State. (*Kesari* 29.1.60)

Editorials

The editorials written on the eve of the formation of the State of Maharashtra (with Mumbai as the capital city) voice a sense of fulfilment, that the State of Maharashtra like Marathwada and Vidarbha which, until then, were parts of different States, was being united for the first time. These editorials express sorrow, however, that Goa still was under Portuguese regime and look forward to its liberation and union with Maharashtra. They also looked forward to greater emotional integration of various sub-regions of Maharashtra including Mumbai's metropolitan region. The editorials enumerate several economic problems facing the State and express the hope that the united Maharashtra would be able to face them with greater strength. Forming of the new State of Maharashtra was also an occasion for introspection and renewed self-assessment.

An editorial written on the eve of the foundation of the new State refers to the long-drawn struggle of the Marathi community for obtaining the State of Maharashtra with Mumbai as the capital, inspite of the demand for the State being a natural and normal one. The editorial observed that the Marathi community in Mumbai in the past few years had remained ignored and felt slighted by other communities who managed to climb up to high positions in the city. The editorial articulated the Marathi community's aspiration when it stated that the birth of the new State was the high time to bring about a change in the situation and the Maharashtrian who lay low at the bottom must come up and achieve status, by entering the professions, business and industry through co-operative effort. They would have to earn an identity which would be respected by other communities in the city. (Nvk. Ed. 30.4.60)

b) Maharashtra 'The Leader of the Nation'

1) The editorials observe that Maharashtra in recent years had failed to play major role in Indian politics because of an absence of the Maharashtrian leader of national stature. However formation of Maharashtra State was not an occasion to be pessimistic. (Sakal 26.4.60; Nvk. 22.8.66)

2) With Shivaji as the revered hero of Maharashtra, the aspiration for national service and leadership was an inevitable aspect of Maharashtrian self-image.

The *Maratha* expressed this national sentiment (in rather dramatic language) and the aspiration for leadership when it wrote in its editorial 'The sods of Maharashtra's earth are more valuable to us than 22 carat gold'; and when it pronounced 'It is our aspiration and ambition that Maharashtra should lead India on the path of her progress.' (Mrt. Ed. 27.6.63)

3) The *Maratha* missed no opportunity to write editorials on the life and mission of eminent Maharashtrians like Jagannath Sankarsett, Bhau Daji and Dadoba Pandurang who made outstanding contribution to the building up of modern Mumbai during the nineteenth and early twentieth century. (Mrt. Eds. 4.4.65, 30.7.65)

The gap between this self-image, the collective aspiration, and the reality of the situation in Mumbai as felt by the Maharashtrian community is well articulated in a *Navakal* editorial

4) 'It is but natural that the Maharashtrians feel that they should be playing the role of leadership in Mumbai and Maharashtra. That it is their privilege and right to play the role of the host-community in Mumbai and Maharashtra and to assume the leader's role. But in the very State capital, the Maharashtrian lags behind in every walk of life and is deprived of opportunity and leadership in every respect. This gap between the aspired, the aimed and the existing reality is far too deep and wide not to cause hurt. However, the Maharashtrian must learn to accept his own shortcomings and try to adjust himself to reality. The State

Government also must know how to protect Maharashtrian interests and help to remove his insecurity and shortcomings for them to go forward. (Nvk. Ed. 22.8.66)

Editorials: Sakal 26.4.60; Nvk. 30.4.60, 22.8.66; Mrt. 22.6.63, 4.4.65, 30.7.65.)

c) Maharashtra, the Sword-arm and Defender of the Nation's Freedom

More than a dozen entries in the categories of reports, articles and editorials, vocalise the community's desire and belief in its role as the defender of the nation's honour.

This disposition seemed to be almost an obsession with the community. Emulating Shivaji, the venerated symbol of the community's identity and honour, the community looked upon itself as being entrusted with the mission of serving India and defending her freedom and honour. Taking great pride particularly in this role of the warrior defending his nation's honour when at stake was for the community but a reinforcement of its traditional role epitomised by Shivaji and his mission.

'Maharashtra is India's sword-arm, arm of defense and it must remain so', so goes a famous quote by Savarkar, the early revolutionary. He made this statement in 1961 in a speech on his birthday. 'The Marathas went to rescue and defend their fellow-nationals right upto attack in the north-west. Did a Rajput bring succour to Maharashtrians in Pune?' Savarkar further added, 'One is not finding fault with others but pointing out that it did not happen. Long before anybody in India did it, the Marathas crossed the Narmada to fight the encroachapter at Panipat and to defend the sovereign at Delhi.' He added, 'This is what is expected of Maharashtra and it shall carry on this tradition.' (Mrt. 28.5.65)

The speech articulates the collective aspiration and self-image of the Marathi community very well.

Independence Day and Republic Day were occasions to revive these aspirations and images. On Independence Day 1962, the *Maratha* published an article 'Maharashtra India's Sword-arm'.

The article traced the various revolutionary efforts in Maharashtra to overthrow British rule, beginning with the Umaji

Naik rebellion in early nineteenth century, the armed insurgence by the Bhangre brothers in 1844, and the more ambitious effort by Vasudeo Balwant Phadke in 1875, which inspired later revolutionaries like Savarkar. (Mrt. 15.8.62)

Another article in the same issue gave information about those who had participated in the struggle for independence in Maharashtra and ends with salutations to Maharashtra's tradition of fighting for freedom. (Mrt. 15.8.62)

In 1962, the clashes with the Chinese developed into a serious threat of a China-India war. Y. B. Chavan, Chief Minister of Maharashtra, in his radio broadcast, referred to the critical situation as a time of trial and test of people's patriotism and declared that Maharashtra could not afford to rest unless the Himalayas was free of the threat. (Mrt. 2.11.62)

In the critical situation that followed, Krishna Menon was relieved of the defence portfolio in the Nehru cabinet and Y.B. Chavan, then the Chief Minister of the two-year-old Maharashtra State, was appointed to the office. The *Maratha* reported.

At a large all-Party public meeting called to declare solidarity with the Government of India and to felicitate Chavan on his appointment as the Defence Minister, S.M. Joshi reminded the people of Chavan's public promise as a Chief Minister, to Nehru, at a similar meeting at Shivaji Park at the time of the formation of Maharashtra State. At this meeting, Chavan had declared that the Sahyadris would not spare itself to defend and save the Himalayas. S.M. Joshi averred that the time had come to fulfil the symbolic promise given on behalf of Maharashtra to the Prime Minister. (Mrt. 12.11.62)

Chavan's appointment was seen as a great honour, not only to Chavan, personally but also for Maharashtra and its people.

According to the *Maratha*, Chavan's appointment was a public recognition of Maharashtra's valour and willingness to sacrifice for the nation. It was a welcome event especially after the severe criticism to which Maharashtra and Maharashtrians were subjected to during the Samyukta Maharashtra Movement by some people as being parochial and quarrelsome. In keeping with Maharashtra's tradition, Chavan must carry out the responsibility placed in him by the destiny, the editorial advised. (Mrt. Ed. 13.11.62)

Editorial Mrt. 13.11.62
Reports and Articles Mrt. 15.8.62 (two articles); 28.10.62, 2.11.62, 3.11.62, 12.11.62, 6.2.63, 28.5.65, 5.5.68.

d) The Shivaji Symbol

Shivaji, the 17th-century hero of Maharashtra, played an important role in shaping the Marathi community's self-image. Shivaji was the foremost among those who welded a nation out of the simple peasant-folk of Maharashtra. As the founder-builder of the 'Maratha' (Maharashtrian) nation and as the defender of the Deccan and the South against the Mughal emperor from Delhi, Shivaji has been the supreme hero of Maharashtra. Shivaji became for Maharashtrians, a symbol of the nation's aspiration for freedom and honour.

Shivaji was the inspiration of one of the earliest Maharashtrian nationalist groups of the Indian sub-continent to have challenged the powerful British. The Maharashtrian aspiration for national service and leadership has been shaped by the Shivaji legend.

This symbol of Shivaji has been exploited by vastly different groups and political parties to propagate their ideas and programmes. Thus, if Shivaji was the national hero for those who participated in the freedom movement, he also was the source of inspiration for those involved in the Samyukta Maharashtra Movement. The Shiv Sena took its name after Shivaji and his saffron flag became its standard. Earlier in August 1966, the Sampoorna Maharashtra Samiti's protest-marchers who gheraoed the Sachivalaya, also carried the same saffron flag (See Chapter III)

Strangely enough, though the Shiv Sena was named after Shivaji, who is invoked in all important Shiv Sena functions, there was little about the great hero in the pages of the *Marmik.* On the other hand the *Daily Maratha* published four editorials on Shivaji during the span of three years from 1963 to 1965.

Editorials

Shivaji in the editorial writings of the *Maratha* emerges as the hero who was broadminded, tolerant of other faiths and free of fanaticism. He was not only the prophet of freedom and the hero who welded a nation out of Maratha peasantry, but he was also a visionary ruler who foresaw the threat of European naval powers and recognised the importance of maritime strength for a country with long coastal stretches. One of the editorials remarks that if there was no Shivaji, there would have been no Maharashtra. (Mrt. Ed. 13.6.64) (Mrt. Eds. 25.4.63, 3.5.63, 13.5.65, 13.6.65)

Reports and Articles

The *Daily Maratha* reproduced a forty-year-old article on Shivaji by a well-known writer-journalist, on the birth anniversary of Shivaji in 1964, and observed that Shivaji's greatness did not lie in his being a great warrier or a general, or as an empire-builder. According to the article, Shivaji was great because he built a nation out of poor, illiterate peasants and inculcated in them national spirit and pride. According to the *Daily Maratha*, the best way to pay one's homage to the great hero was to involve oneself in the efforts of nation-building. (Mrt. 13.5.64)

In 1966, there was a move to instal an equestrian statue of Shivaji at the Park already named after him in Central Mumbai.

At the meeting held on the occasion of the ritual worship *(Bhoomi Pooja)* of the spot selected for installation of the statue, the Home Minister of the State appealed to the industrial workers of Mumbai to donate one rupee each towards the installation in commemoration of the great hero who was a continual source of inspiration for patriots and freedom fighters. (Mrt. 18.2.66)

The textile workers of Mumbai donated a sum of Rs. 2 lakh. Y. B. Chavan, Defence Minister of India, presided at the installation.

The *Maratha* commented that the occasion was a major event which fulfiled a long-standing Maharashtrian aspiration to raise Shivaji's statue as a vital symbol of inspiration and strength in Maharashtra'a capital city. (Mrt. 6.11.66, 7.11.66)

An article in the Maratha in the early sixties, however, noted the vast gap between the Maharashtrian image of Shivaji and that of others of the Maratha hero.

While Maharashtrians always felt very proud of Shivaji and often even of the Peshwa rule, because these rulers fought with the Mughals and with the Europeans, the people of the other linguistic regions, however, seemed to have wrong notions of Shivaji and the Maratha warriors, as robbers and plunderers. On the other hand, Maharashtrians looked upon Rana Pratap also as a national hero. That the people of other linguistic regions should have misgivings about Shivaji and should feel closer to the British and the Mughals rather than the Marathas was a puzzling phenomenon. It necessitated further research and an objective re-assessment of the Maratha heroes by Maharashtrians. (Mrt. 1.5.62)

The article is symbolic of the doubts regarding the self-image that occasionally disturbed the members of the community. However, by and large, the image of Shivaji as the ideal hero and the 'Marathas' (Maharashtrians) as a community with a mission to fight for justice and to defend the nation's honour always remained, in spite of occasional criticism by 'insiders' and 'outsiders'.

e) Nationalist and Egalitarian Ideals

Other frequently expressed objectives were those of national service and the establishment of social justice. It was believed that the Maharashtrian community with a relatively small economic disparity within itself would be able to achieve an egalitarian and socialist society, earlier than other regional communities if it persevered with its efforts ('Socialist Maharashtra in Socialist India', was a popular slogan during the Samyukta Maharashtra Movement)

Reports and Articles

i) In 1960 during the celebration of the forthcoming formation of the Maharashtra State, the Chief Minister of the proposed State, Y.B. Chavan, declared that whatever was best in Maharashtra would be offered in the service of India. (*Sakal* 28.4.60)

ii) At the celebration of the Shivaji birth anniversary which overlapped with the birth of Maharashtra State, the Chief Guest, a minister in Maharashtra cabinet, expressed his hope that Maharashtra would follow the path laid by its great hero, Shivaji and earn a name by fighting against injustice and through service to India. (Sakal 28.4.60)

iii) The Chief Minister of Maharashtra (V.P. Naik) speaking at the centenary celebration of Mumbai's oldest and largest market (formerly Crawford Market, renamed as Mahatma Phule Market) observed

Some people like to offer advice to Maharashtra urging it to cultivate a national outlook. However, these people should know that even without their advice, Maharashtra knew how to think in patriotic and national terms. In fact, it has been a tradition with Maharashtra to think in national and non-parochial terms. (Mrt. 16.3.69)

Early in 1960, discussing the future of the proposed new state of Maharashtra, the Chief Minister of bilingual Mumbai, Y. B. Chavan, pointed out that the rightist Swatnatra Party had no following in Maharashtra. He further expressed his belief that the objective conditions of society in Maharashtra combined with a high degree of political consciousness among the people of the region provided congenial environs for an early development of a socialist society in this State. The presence of a large number of Maharashtrians among the leaders of major leftist groups and parties in India was also symbolic of this possibility according to Chavan. (*Kesari* 26.1.60)

Similar belief was reiterated by another Chief Minister V. P. Naik at a public meeting of the textile workers in Mumbai, who had gathered to felicitate him on his appointment as the Chief Minister of the State. He expressed his belief that the dream of a socialist society would be realised sooner in Maharashtra than perhaps elsewhere in India (Mrt. 17.2.64)

f) The Integrationist Role
(Link between the North and the South)

The ideals and aspirations vocalised by non-political leaders, by leading literary and cultural personalities, emphasised Maharashtra's role as the link between the North and the South of India, and as an integrative force.

i) In January 1960 when the formation of a unilingual Maharashtra was almost a settled matter, the President of the Mumbai Marathi Literary Conference, Mahadeoshastri Joshi, stated in his presidential speech

Even if Mumbai in the new proposed set up, comes to receive recognition as part of Maharashtra, the city, we must remember, belongs to all those who love it and work for making it a better place to live in.'

Mahadeoshastri Joshi expressed his belief that Mumbai was the confluence of the cultures of Maharashtra and Gujarat and should continue to be so. (*Kesari* 28.1.60)

ii) Five years later, speaking at the session of the Maharashtra Sahitya Sammelan at Pusad (Vidarbha), Y. B. Chavan said that Marathi, the language of Maharashtra, had been a bridge between the North and South India. It developed through the contribution of many who came from outside Maharashtra and its vocabulary was enriched by warriors and wanderers of distant lands, travellers and monks. This has given Marathi adaptability, an ability to absorb influences and an inclusive quality. (Mrt. Ed. 3.1.65)

iii) Among the non-Hindi States, Maharashtra stood foremost in the matter of the propagation of the Hindi language according to the special report of the Central Education Department.

While only 3.48 per cent of people in Gujarat and 5 per cent in Bengal knew Hindi, 9 per cent of people of Maharashtra were conversant with the language; thus Maharashtra seemed the most willing among the non-Hindi States to learn Hindi. (Mrt. 5.7.65)

An occasional article tracing the history and development of Marathi emphasised the central position of Maharashtra on the map of Indian sub-continent and its inevitable role as a link between the North and the South. (Mrt. 1.5.67)

iv) Surprisingly even the *Marmik* evinced this integrationist spirit when it published introductory articles on two non-Marathi artists who identified themselves as Maharashtrians.

In one of its issues the *Marmik* introduced Sachin Shankar, the well-known dancer from the North, who had staged a ballet on Shivaji. In his interview with the *Marmik*, Sachin Shankar observed that he was proud to identify himself with Maharashtrians and Maharashtra, where his art received appreciation. (Mrm. 15.8.65)

Bhimsen Joshi, the well known classical singer, though Kannada-speaking by birth, had adopted Maharashtra as his land of mission (Karmabhoomi) where his art was received with appreciation. He refused to be felicitated as a Kannadiga and told the Kannada Association in Nasik that he was happy to call himself a Maharashtrian. (Mrm. 26.6.66)

On the eve of the civic elections of 1968, which the Shiv Sena contested, Thackeray advised the non-Maharashtrians in Mumbai that it was time that the non-Marathi of Mumbai called themselves Maharashtrians or 'Marathi' (rather than non-Maharashtrians or 'non-Marathi') as it would be an index of their genuine identification with Maharashtra. (Mht. 27.2.68)

The Chief Minister of Maharashtra, (V. P. Naik), exhorted the businessmen and industrialists of Mumbai at the Indian Merchants' Chamber function that they should give up their feeling of being 'outsiders'. He further stated that if they genuinely identified themselves with Maharashtra and its community, there was little reason for them to feel insecure in Mumbai or in Maharashtra. All those who were domiciled in Maharashtra, were Maharashtrians. (Nvs. 9.3.69)

2. Introspective Evaluation

About fifty entries in the content data are found to reflect an introspective mood, and given to analysis and assessment of the Maharashtrian community's performance in the socio-economic, political and cultural life of Mumbai, in an affort to discover the factors responsible for the community's failure and to come to grips with its shortcomings. Among these entries, twenty-five are readers' letters; the rest consist of reports, articles and occasional editorials. These entries also, like the earlier ones on other themes, are mainly from between 1964 and 1968. Presumably, this suggests that there was an attempt by the community at self-evaluation while simultaneously voicing grievances.

a) Failure in Communication (Importance of English and Hindi) Letters

About half-a-dozen letters express the opinion that the Marathi man's failure to recognise the significance of the English language and to be well conversant with it has been responsible for the Maharashtrian community's inability to make a mark in the industrial and commercial world of Mumbai.

According to these letters, failure to have a command over the English and Hindi languages was a definite handicap for the Maharashtrian youth aspiring to be successful in Mumbai where the regional language – Marathi – had little status or currency in the important areas of administration, commerce, industry and even the cultural life of the metropolis. Here English still held court, and Hindi was slowly displacing the regional languages, Marathi and Gujarati, as the language of communication, in Mumbai city's increasingly mixed population. Failure to use these languages in circulation among the elite and those who commanded power and wealth, curtailed the Maharashtrian's opportunities in various careers, besides depriving him of effective communication.

The Marathi community's preoccupation with the development of its regional language, Marathi, the earlier Mumbai Government's policy of giving emphasis to regional languages and gradual discouragement to English language were additional factors responsible for the Marathi youth's small percentage in institutions of higher training and his poor performance in the job competition among the educated. According to some of the letters, lack of fluency in English further accentuated the Maharashtrian's traditional or natural reserve, to his further disadvantage.

(Letters Nvk. 30.7.62, 7.8.65; Nvs. 1.1.64, 7.8.65; Mht. 23.11.65; Mrm. 22.5.66)

Reports and Articles

The points made by these letters are supported by reports and articles in the press. The State Government's educational policy and various shifts in it also became a target of criticism. The reports and articles maintained that the Marathi youth lagged behind others in employment, higher studies and technical and scientific education, chiefly because of his lack of good English and insistence on using the regional language.

An article in a daily commented that as long as English continued to be used as the medium in All India Competitive Examinations, in Central Government and the Defence Services or for executive positions in private firms as well, there was no use in the Maharashtra Government or the Maharashtrian youth adhering to the regional language. (Lks. 1.7.63; Mrm. 19.6.66, 2.1.66)

According to another article, the Marathi community's preoccupation with Marathi language was an indication of its members' self-centered complacency. Maharashtrians were advised to learn and use English and Hindi effectively to enable themselves to get their viewpoints across, to establish a rapport with others and to win them over. (Nvs. 26.4.60; Nvk. 20.5.70; Lks. 1.2.70)

b) Maharashtrian Personality Traits

Some other letters see the fault in Maharashtrian personality traits.

The absence of extrovert qualities, lack of sociability bordering on insularity, put the Maharashtrian at a disadvantage in matters of his communication and relationships, with others, i.e. the non-Marathi people, according to these letters. (Nvs. 4.8.65, 7.8.65, 11.8.65, 14.8.65; Mrm. 22.5.66)

A tendency to arguments and wordy discussions combined with an absence of practical outlook supported by hard work, were some other traits that hampered the Marathi community's progress, said some letters. (Mrm. 3.7.65; Nvk. 12.5.66 – two letters)

Some of the letters maintain that unless Maharashtrians replaced their over-critical, negative attitude to members of their own community with a positive attitude of co-operation, there was little hope for change in the community's situation. (Mrm. 29.8.65, 3.7.66, 11.9.66; Nvk. 22.9.66)

Response to some of the reported speeches and articles supporting this perspective is articulated by a few letters (Nvk. 14.8.66; Mrm. 31.7.66; Nvk. 22.9.66)

c) Failure on the Economic Front

It is surprising that so many letters in the mid-sixties discuss the question of Maharashtrians being overtaken by others. It was an index and a measure of the community's frustration on several fronts.

A few letters highly critical of the Maharashtrian character contend that Maharashtrians often start business on scant capital and are oblivious to using financial potential for the furtherance of their ventures. Being law-abiding and stricture-prone, they hardly know how to make compromises for the advancement of their business prospects. Although intelligent and hard-working, they are not sufficiently flexible or shrewd and hesitate to take financial risks.

Some of the letters also complain that Maharashtrians are not sufficiently hard-working. Consequently, they turn out poor businessmen or entrepreneurs, and hardly achieve major material success.

Letters: Nvs. 27.1.61, 26.1.64; 11.8.65, 14.8.65; Nvk. 12.7.64, 22.9.66; Mrt. 8.7.66; Mht. 22.6.66, 19.4.67, 11.4.68)

Around 1966-67, several journals published articles and reports discussing the factors responsible for the Maharashtrian's ineffectiveness to make a mark in Mumbai's business or industry. The *Maharashtra Times* conducted a press survey to assess the place of the Maharashtrian in several areas of economic activity in the metropolis. Such a trend was symbolic of the rising expectations hinged upon the recent formation of the new State of Maharashtra, and also signified the widespread sense of frustration among the community.

An article in 1967 speaks about the activity in the Phule market (Crawford Market), Mumbai's biggest vegetable and fruit and fish market.

The business in Crawford Market was largely in the hands of Maratha vegetable, fruit and fish merchants. After Partition, the situation changed with the coming of the Sindhis whose business expertise led them first to make an entry in to retail sale of fruits and then eventually to capture wholesale trade in fruit and vegetable markets in Mumbai by dint of hard work, good salesmanship and sheer business acumen. 'The Maharashtrian attitude,'the article observes, 'was that of an employee in a service, who was willing to work only for a limited amount of time and therefore obtained only limited success.' (Mht. 1.10.67)

Reports tell stories of the Maharashtrian's lack of success in the fields of advertising, medical salesmanship and other occupations, open to enterprising, hard-working educated young men in Mumbai.

According to the *Maharashtra Times* survey, of five thousand sales representatives only two hundred were Maharashtrian. In the advertising business, with an exception of one or two, there were hardly any well-known Maharashtrian firms. The Maharashtrian's unwillingness to take up challenges and risks, his concerns about job security, an absence of business tradition and the consequent lack of business expertise and commercial acumen and his indifference to acquiring command over English language were enunciated as reasons for the Marathi community's backwardness in these fields.(Mht. 1.10.67, 8.10.67, 10.12.67, 22.1.70)

Letters complain that Marathi speaking workers and employees, though intelligent, are reluctant to do hard work and therefore fail to make use of opportunities. (Nvs. 27.1.61; Mrm. 1.5.66; Mht. 22.6.66, 19.4.67, 11.4.69)

A letter published in the *Maratha* articulates a totally different viewpoint regarding Maharashtrian performance. It strongly asserted that it was wrong to believe that Maharashtrian shortcomings were chiefly responsible for the community's backwardness in Mumbai. The self-disparagement was therefore highly misleading.

The Maharashtrian's poverty and lack of material success were due to the values he had come to respect and cultivate and not for any other reason. Politically conscious since the early days of British rule, the Maharashtrian had participated in the struggle for independence on a large scale; also he was in the forefront in the trade union movement. The Maharashtrian, therefore, could not be branded as 'narrow-minded and begrudging', only because he demanded his rights. Certain sections of the Marathi press which were thus belittling the Maharashtrian were spreading false impressions about him.

The severity of self-criticism evinced in many of these letters and reports in the press was thus tempered by the tone of self-respect and assurance in an occasional letter. Also, some of the letters alluded to eminent Maharashtrian achievements in various fields other than trade and commerce.

Letters Mrm. 24.4.66, 17.7.66; Mrt. 27.8.66

The *Marmik* published 'success stories' of a few well-known Marathi persons in the field of business and industry. (Mrm. 10.4.66, 10.9.67, 17.9.67 and several others)

d) The Maharashtrian Situation in Mumbai

Reports and Articles

A long article published in early 1965, in *Marmik*, strangely enough, was devoid of the aggressive stance against 'outsiders' which became more prominent in its later issues.

The article puts the blame for Maharashtrian backwardness on his backward-looking gaze, on his tendency to eulogise past achievements and in the process, let present opportunities slip by. This obsession with the past made the Marathi person self-complacent, until he suddenly realised that he was overtaken by others, the article observed.

The article claimed that by and large, the Maharashtrian is a man of integrity - a quality useful for success in business; but he lacked the necessary spirit of enterprise. As a result, 'outsiders' had come to control business and industry.

The article further observed The South Indian migration to Mumbai began as a trickle in the early 1930's and 1940's slowly growing into a large stream. On the basis of three qualities (never cultivated by Maharashtrian) – perseverance, industriousness and knowledge of English – the South Indians captured the employment market of government services, private business and industrial firms in Mumbai.

Lack of concern for the community, and lack of unity within its fold were additional drawbacks of the Maharashtrian community. The South Indian community knew how to be united and help their own people. It was no wonder, therefore, that they soon dominated the offices in Mumbai, the article observed. (Mrm. 10.1.65)

An article on the same theme published in the *Maratha*, presented a totally different point of view. The mood of the article was not so much of self-criticism but of injured self-respect and grievance demanding redressal of injustice meted out to one's community.

Maharashtrian complacency, the parochial practices of others and the State Government's lack of concern for protecting Maharashtrian interests, were together responsible for the precarious situation of Maharashtrians, according to the article. (Mrt. 31.1.65)

A number of articles discuss the problems of Maharashtrians in Mumbai and their attempts to come to grip with them. A popular farce on the Marathi stage in 1966 was a satire on the Maharashtrian situation in Mumbai. ('The blind man mills the flour, while the dog laps it up!')

Even a book on this subject appeared in the mid-sixties. This small publication called 'Why Maharashtrians lag behind others?' received considerable publicity since the topic was close to people's hearts at that time.

According to the book, Maharashtra's success and lead in family planning and population control combined with the high wages available in Mumbai, caused a flow of migration from regions with higher population density, like Kerala, Karnataka, Uttar Pradesh. Consequently, the proportion of Maharashtrian population in Mumbai was fast dwindling while the Maharashtrian adult earner faced increasingly keener competition from 'outsiders'.

The reviews seemed to agree with these points made in the book. (Nvs. 11.7.65; Mrm. 27.6.65; Lks. 27.2.66)

Articles analysing causes of Maharashtrian failure on the economic and political front continued to be published until the late sixties and the theme held popular attention as late as 1970. (Mht. 26.6.66, 24.3.68, 31.3.68, 7.1.68) It is obvious that the problem of his failure 'to make a mark in the metropolis', weighed heavily on the Maharashtrian's mind. The trend of self-analysis and self-evaluation continued almost through the sixties.

A columnist writing in the *Navashakti* in 1961 had observed

The variegated culture and life of Mumbai hardly carried an impress of Maharashtrian influence as it should, inspite of the Maharashtrian being the largest single majority community of the city. This was not the case with Kolkata where the Bengalis have left an indelible mark of their culture on the city's life. What was the reason for this difference? Presumably, the absence of Maharashtrian impress on Mumbai was an index of Maharashtrians' own feeling of inferiority and reticence. (Nvs. 19.11.61)

Seven years later the Maharashtra Congress Chief, Vasantdada Patil, in his speech, still referred to the same problem Mumbai was in Maharashtra, but Maharashtra was not in Mumbai. Why? The reason for this phenomenon was the Maharashtrian's alienation from Mumbai. According to the Congress Chief

The Maharashtrians, who came to Mumbai for livelihood from the interior of Maharashtra, looked upon the city as an interim abode, and therefore never really took up the challenges presented to them in Mumbai. Should the Maharashtrian endeavour to diligently root himself in this city, his sense of alienation would pass away and he would not feel threatened by outsiders. (Mht. 1.4.68)

On yet another occasion, the Maharashtra Congress Chief asked the Maharashtrian community to solemnly consider the place of Maharashtrian in the extraordinarily wealthy city like Mumbai.

The Maharashtrian had hardly any share in the ownership of the city's great wealth land, buildings, banks, factories, business-firm, etc. Mumbai's affluence belonged to those who controlled its commercial activity. On the other hand, the Maharashtrian had always felt shy of business and had sought the security of an employment. And now, the Maharashtrian raised a movement to demand a percentage of jobs held out by these commercial and industrial magnates of Mumbai.

The Congress Chief commented 'It was high time that the Maharashtrian youth oriented himself to new paths of achievement, of business, of industrial entrepreneurship and this through co-operative means and methods, rather than go a begging for jobs.' For the industry could hardly keep pace with the accelerated number of job-seekers. (Nvk. 4.5.70)

The *Maharashtra Times*, in 1968, reported a mock trial at Thane, in which 'Bal Thackeray' was put in the dock under the article 153-A of the Indian Penal Code for endangering peace and threatening the law and order situation by founding the Shiv Sena which encouraged fissiparous tendencies in the country. After a hearing from Thackeray (who denied the charges against him), the mock court declared Thackeray guilty of the charges and gave him the punishment of residing in 'Matunga' (little Madras of Mumbai), wearing a white lungi and being on a diet of idlis for the day and dosas for the night. (Mht. 5.2.68)

(Reports & Articles Mrm. 6.11.60, 16.8.64, 15.8.65, 6.2.67, Mht. 5.2.65)

Editorials

Very few editorials display introspection or self-assessment.

One of these few editorials asked the Maharashtrian community to make a stark assessment of their situation and with diligence try to remove the community's shortcomings without which there was no hope for it to succeed in competition against others or to make onward progress. The editorial warned the Marathi community against putting the blame entirely on other communities. (Nvs. Ed. 18.5.65)

Another editorial invited the community to make a firm resolve of indefatigable efforts to earn for the Maharashtrian a high status in Mumbai. (Nvk. Ed. 1.5.66)

Most of the editorials which articulate frustration, however, also voice a protest against the existing conditions and suggest or support action for the redressal of these grievances.

3. Self and Others

The attitudes and behaviour of 'others' were relevant and significant factors in shaping the complex Maharashtrian response to events in the interactional setting of Mumbai. This response at the formal level consisted of an appeal by the community leaders of Maharashtra, to the non-Marathi communities, to identify themselves with Maharashtra and Maharashtrians. A reference to such appeals, has been made earlier in the chapter. (See Integrationist Role – Mht. 27.2.68; Nvs. 9.3.69)

However at another, deeper level, the Maharashtrian response to 'others' in the context of Mumbai, was an emotional reaction against 'others' or 'outsiders', chiefly the South Indian community. Apart from the clash of economic interests, other factors too contributed to the distance and tension between the Maharashtrian and South Indian communities.

The South Indian's indifference to learning Marathi, when this language had become the symbol of the new State's identity, his regard for, and adherence to the English language for communication at a time when the Marathi community was newly aspiring to replace English by Marathi in the State's administration, general anti-Hindi attitude as against the Maharashtrian's acceptance of Hindi as the national link-language, and the South Indian's apparently rigid regional dietary habits and lifestyle, even in changed circumstances – all these counted as irritants for drawing out Maharashtrian reaction. Also, the accelerated inmigration from the South in late fifties and in the sixties encouraged the tendency among the South Indians to live in homogeneous pockets of their own people, which minimised the chances of bridging linguistic barriers through integrated living.

All these, severally, drew a negative Maharashtrian response which was further fed by the events in Tamil Nadu. For the Maharashtrian the DMK was seen as the representative of the South Indian community. The DMK's separatist politics and recurrent violent anti-Hindi agitation in the party's homeland was perceived by the Maharashtrian as insular and aggressively parochial. It seemed to have contributed to fortify, or justify the Maharashtrian's negative reaction to the DMK in particular and the South Indian in general in Mumbai.

This negative reaction found expression initially in voicing grievances and protest through the press, later through popular activities and action groups which professed to offer remedial action. Eventually, this reaction got transformed into support for the Shiv Sena, which claimed to regain for the Maharashtrian his self respect, in programmes, for instance like that of boycotting films made in Madras Studios. A stronger reaction of antipathy was the manifestation of the anti-hawker outburst mentioned in one of the earlier chapters.

Support to the Shiv Sena seems to have stemmed, as maintained all along, chiefly from the Marathi community's major grievances and frustrations which needed an articulation and a voice. A chain reaction of the parochial concerns of major groups of 'significant' communities in the metropolitan and national setting also seems to have contributed to, or encouraged the perceptions and attitudes that lent support to the Sena. When, therefore, the Shiv Sena emerged to single-mindedly champion the Maharashtrian 'cause', the organisation was received with enthusiasm, irrespective of its political ideology.

a) Maharashtra and DMK's Language Politics

While the Shiv Sena emerged in Mumbai in the mid sixties, the DMK was going strong in the South. In the 1967 general elections, the DMK emerged triumphant to become the ruling party in Tamil Nadu. The DMK's separatist stand and its anti-Hindi protest, active throughout the decade beginning from the early sixties, had repercussions in Maharashtra. Maharashtra and Gujarat have been the two non-Hindi States which accepted Hindi without any reservation, as the link-language of the sub-continent and as the official language of administration in the Indian Union.

The DMK during its anti-Hindi agitation in 1963, had threatened to burn the Constitution. (Mrt. 4.11.63, 17.11.63) In 1967, when the DMK came to power it introduced Tamil as the State language and accepted English as the official second language to displace the Hindi language and its Nagari script. (Mrt. 15.4.67) At that time, the Official Languages (Amendment) Bill was under discussion in the Lok Sabha. (Mrt. 11.9.67, 5.11.67) On 16 December 1967, the Parliament passed the Languages bill under protest from the DMK and some other quarters. (Mrt. 17.12.67) No sooner than this Official Language (Amendment) Bill was passed, a move was set afoot for further amendments to obtain parity for non-Hindi speakers with the Hindi-speaking people. The grievance of the southern people, especially of the Tamil students, was that the burden of language learning for the non-Hindi people was greater than that of the Hindi-speaking people. They wanted more radical amendment which would obtain parity of the burden. (Sakal 14.1.68)

The DMK's strong reaction to the three-language formula developed into a statewide anti-Hindi and anti-North agitation in Tamil Nadu. The protest movement became intense and occasionally took a violent turn. (Mrt. 22.12.67) News of forced closure of cinema-houses showing Hindi films in Tamil Nadu, occasional incidents of destruction of property and victimisation of citizens from other states, kept coming from the South. (Mrt. 11.9.67, 22.12.67, 23.12.67; Sakal 19.1.68, 20.1.68)

In January 1968, the Madras State Assembly passed a resolution favouring the two language formula - Tamil and the English as official languages of the state, in place of the three language formula recommended earlier by the Central Government (Sakal. 24.1.68) This drew a reaction from the people of the North. Seth Govind Das demanded resignation of the Tamil Nadu State Government for passing a language bill against the Constitution. On the other hand, Kamaraj pressed for changes in the language bill passed by the Lok Sabha in December 1967. (Mrt. 16.2.68)

The situation in Tamil Nadu was still restive. Madurai students continued with their anti-Hindi agitation in favour of Tamil autonomy. (Mrt. 19.2.68) This was followed by the news of burning of the 17th section of the Indian Constitution and the hoisting of a separate flag of independent Tamil Nadu during the student anti-Hindi agitation. Madhu Limaye accused Tamil Nadu leaders, Kamaraj and Rajagopalachari, for encouraging student agitation. (Mrt. 22.2.68, 23.2.68) There was an attempt at burning the Indian national flag and the Constitution by the student leaders in Madurai and the schools and colleges closed down in Tamil Nadu. This led to clashes between students and the police. (Mrt. 27.3.68, 31.3.68) On the heels of its anti-Hindi policy, the State Government of Tamil Nadu threatened the closure of the National Cadet Corps in schools if the Central Government insisted on the use of Hindi. (Mrt. 31.3.68)

The reactions in Maharashtra to these events found expression in the press. The Tamil people's insistence on Tamil as the State language was found acceptable; their stand against Hindi – language that had the widest use in India, and their insistence on the use of English – a foreign language, for central administration, drew a negative response. Moreover, members of the Marathi community wanted to know why their demand for the use of Marathi in the administration and public life in Maharashtra was considered parochial. Maharashtrians believed this was an instance of the pot calling the kettle black.

These reactions were noted in the press through letters, reports, articles and editorials. Every genre of writing and all the papers this study covered, unanimously voice this grievance. The *Marmik's* perhaps was an extreme reaction, but the Maratha was no less vehement. In fact, the *Maratha*, known for its outspoken, hard-hitting editorials did not hesitate to criticise the Tamil stand over the language issue.

Letters

Here is a sampling of few letters that articulate this complaint

The Chief Priest of Rameshwaram Temple narrated the story of how, when the tidal wave disrupted life in Rameshwaram island, the community of Maharashtrian priestly families (who happened to have migrated from Maharashtra a few generations earlier) in charge of the ritual worship of the temple, received no local help and suffered because of the local Tamilian's anti-Brahmin and anti-Northerner attitudes. The priest therefore appealed to the people in Maharashtra for assistance and help. (Lks. 5.1.65)

Two letters written in the context of some rioting and disturbances following the 1967 General Elections complain that small disturbances in Mumbai received publicity and brought about immediate demands for an inquiry by the South Indian MPs as well as by the Tamil Nadu Government. This, however, led to Maharashtrians being unfairly labelled as parochial.

The Tamils in Madras had carried on a prolonged agitation against the Hindi language and had boycotted Hindi films, but nobody had interfered with the exhibition of Tamil films in Maharashtra. Though the DMK Government had continued for long with its extremist and separatist demands, the Central Government did not set up an inquiry into the violent anti-Hindi agitations in the South.

Letters Nvt. 9.4.60; Nvs. 20.7.65; Lks. 5.1.65; Mrt. 25.3.66; Mrm. 19.6.66, 10.7.66, 12.3.67

Reports & Articles

The anti-Hindi stir in the South, chiefly in Tamil Nadu, provoked a strong reaction against DMK policies and programmes and had some repercussions in Mumbai. When the anti-Hindi protest in Tamil Nadu led to an agitation against Hindi films in the South, it sparked off a similar reaction in Mumbai against films produced in Madras studios. The Shiv Sena declared a boycott of films from Southern studios. (These events have been recorded in Ch. III)

Though the *Daily Maratha* interpreted the Sena boycott as an anti-national, anti-Hindi act, by and large it received people's support or approval as is evinced by the letters from *Marmik* mentioned earlier.

Reports & Articles Mrt. 11.9.67, 22.12.67, 23.12.67, 9.3.68, 11.3.68; Mrt. 12.3.68, 24.3.68, 24.4.68; Mrm. 10.3.68; Lks. 8.3.68;

Nvs. Ed. 4.5.68; Sakal 14.1.68, 16.1.68, 19.1.68, 20.1.68, 29.1.68; Kesari 29.1.68, 31.1.68.

Editorials

A majority of editorials reflecting Maharashtrian reactions to South Indian attitudes are from the *Maratha*. Even prior to the establishment of *Marmik*, the *Maratha* had sharply criticised the DMK and its policies.

However, the most stringent criticism leveled by the *Maratha* against South Indian attitudes was with regard to the language issue.

In 1965, the language issue had become quite provocative and riots over the issue had already engulfed Tamil Nadu. Writing in February 1965, the Maratha very sharply criticised the anti-Hindi attitudes of the southern communities.

These attitudes unfortunately were being encouraged, the editorial said, by a senior statesman like Rajagopalachari. The *Maratha* thoroughly disapproved Rajagopalachari's suggestion to continue with English as the official language of Central administration. Spoken only by a very tiny percentage of people, English, even in Tamil Nadu, was not the language of the people. To continue with the English language in spite of this, therefore, meant, according to the *Maratha*, to retain domination of a large majority of Indians by a handful of the English knowing.

The topic recurrently drew the *Maratha's* attention and it published four more editorials on the subject in the month of February. (Mrt. Ed. 13.2.65, 22.2.65, 27.2.65, 28.2.65)

The *Maratha* made the following points in these editorials

i) The demand to continue with English instead of Hindi was an expression of a total lack of self-respect as Indians, indisputably an anti-national and separatist attitude, encouraged by the DMK and senior leaders like Rajaji.

ii) The *Maratha* conceded that in all likelihood, the resistance to Hindi was a reaction to the overzealous and aggressive stance of the pro-Hindi faction from north India; however this did not make such a resistance rational or justifiable; nor was the retention of English as a language of administration in India, a proper solution to the problem.

iii) An apprehension lurked in the minds of the Tamil people that the use of Hindi would deprive them of jobs in the Central Government services. Firstly however, this situation could be a threat only to a minuscule proportion of the Tamil people and not the large majority, the *Maratha* argued. And even in case of that small number of persons, this apprehension was false. If people could learn a foreign language and master it, they certainly could learn and use Hindi efficiently if they wanted to.

iv) The resistance to Hindi was chiefly in Tamil Nadu, not in Andhra where people knew Hindi/Urdu, or even in Kerala or Karnataka. This resistance, in the *Maratha's* opinion, was the result of a lack of firm conviction and decision on the part of the Congress leadership. The answer therefore lay not in the continuity of English as a second language in Indian administration, but in the firm implementation of the use of Hindi.

v) The *Maratha* compared India with other nations with many languages. China too had seven vastly different dialect-languages with a difficult script consisting of 2000 cuneiform characters yet managed to work out a simple common language and script. Indonesia chose one of the many languages in their country. Burma accepted Burmese from the three languages in that country. India also could solve the problem, the *Maratha* advised, if a reasonable attitude was adopted towards Hindi.

vi) The imposition of Hindi on non-Hindi speakers was considered a great wrong, and was used as a justification for continuing with English. However, this argument was hollow because English also had been imposed. In fact, the real clash was not between the Hindi-speaking and non non-Hindi-speaking but between the common people and the adherents of English, i.e., the English educated (Mrt. 7.6.65)

(Mrt. Ed.s 10.2.65, 13.2.65, 27.2.65, 28.2.65, 7.6.65)

In 1938, the *Sakal* from Pune writing in the context of the anti-Hindi stir in Tamil Nadu, strongly criticised, in its editorial, Annadorai and his party for encouraging the language agitation and related violence by students in Tamil Nadu, by closing down schools, colleges and other institutions indefinitely. (Sk. 16.1.68)

b) Being Labelled Parochial
Cosmopolitanism and Parochialism

We have earlier seen that the regionalist demands stemmed chiefly from Maharashtrian frustrations and grievances. These demands also seem to be reactions born of the interaction between communities in the metropolitan and wider national setting. Maharashtrians resented their 'parochial' label. The non-Marathi press in Mumbai, particularly the English press with its nationwide circulation, was viewed as being responsible for projecting the 'parochial image' of the Maharashtrian community.

During the Samyukta Maharashtra Movement, the Maharashtrian community's demand for their linguistic state including Mumbai city, was often criticised as narrow, parochial and against the national interests, by the Centre, city's non-Marathi civic and political leadership, Mumbai Citizens Committee representing Mumbai's industrialists and businessmen, and by Mumbai's Indo-English press which upheld 'cosmopolitanism' as a value against the regional 'parochialism'. (See Phadke 1973, Kunte, Prabhakar 1956)

The memories of this widespread censure of the Marathi community's struggle in the late fifties for a linguistic State were still fresh in the minds of the people in the mid-sixties. In the wake of the clamour from various quarters of Maharashtrian society for priority for the local/the native/the Marathi speaking people, in jobs, housing and economic opportunities, the Marathi community found the former criticism and censure being revived. The national (English) press and the 'cosmopolitan' non-Marathi communities of Mumbai saw in these demands of the native community, parochialism at worst – a threat to the unity of the nation.

The criticism from the English press drew a pretty vehement reaction from the Maharashtrians partly because of the role the English press had earlier played during the Samyukta Maharashtra Movement, in siding with those who demanded a centrally- administered Mumbai city. (Kunte, P. 1956, p. 9; Ranadive V., 1956, p.24) Another reason for a strong reaction against the English press perhaps, was the belief that being manned predominantly by South Indian journalists, it allegedly supported and furthered South Indian interests and ignored the voice of the native Maharashtrian community.

(Mrm. 15.1.67; Nvk. 3.3.67, 23.7.67; Nvs. 5.3.67; Kes. 1.9.67)

Maharashtrian Reaction

A number of articles, comments and a few editorials in the press document the Maharashtrian reaction to the charges of parochialism and stoking inter-community tensions due to their insular and narrow behaviour. Earlier (in Ch. 3 & 6) there was a reference to the voicing of similar grievances. This kind of criticism levelled at the Marathi community was seen as misinformed or mischievous and it evoked strong resentment.

When the atmosphere was still fraught with the tension of the 1967 General Election campaign, a *Navashakti* commentator referred to allegations in circulation in the national press that the Shiv Sena and the Marathi community whose cause it championed were making life difficult for members of the city's South Indian communities.

The commentator was sad that the Marathi community often found itself being slandered or censured in its own State capital on flimsy grounds; this was because it lacked control over the economy, and consequently over the civic, cultural and political life of the city. (Nvs. 5.3.67, 12.3.67)

The *Navakal* editorial considered that the allegation was a calculated effort to raise a hornet's nest in the English press and thereby throttle the voice of Marathi people. The editorial agreed that the Shiv Sena exhibited extremist tendencies and disapproved its anti-South Indian tirade. But it gave the Sena the credit for boldly voicing the Marathi community's long pent-up grievances and frustration. The fact that even the SPMS had to include in its election manifesto, the demand for 80 per cent of jobs and houses for the Maharashtrians, was an indicator of the gravity of these grievances and demands. (Nvk. 3.3.67)

In yet another editorial written in July 1967, the Navakal observed that the Maharashtrian grievances in Mumbai and the rise of the Shiv Sena to voice these were in a sense a reflection of the unfair attitudes and policies of the powerful non-Marathi communities of Mumbai. If the non-Maharashtrians changed themselves and if the State Government took certain steps to safeguard Maharashtrian interests, the bogey of the Shiv Sena would vanish. (Nvk. 23.7.67)

There have been references earlier to the news of violent clashes in mid-1967, allegedly between the Shiv Sena followers and the residents of a large South Indian hutment colony in a north-eastern suburb of Mumbai and to the reports of a proposal for an inquiry into the incidents by the DMK and CPI members of Parliament from Tamil Nadu.

Members of the Marathi community voiced strong criticism of the proposed enquiry through reader's letters to the press, which we have noted in an earlier section.

Editorials

A *Maharashtra Times* editorial criticised the DMK for its unfortunate decision to send the M.Ps from Tamil Nadu to enquire into the alleged incidents of violent clashes between the Shiv Sena and members of South Indian communities in Mumbai.

The editorial observed that the charge that the lives of the South Indians in Mumbai were in danger, was an extremely unfair exaggeration and that the representatives of separatist DMK and of the CPI (M), who supported Naxalite violence, had little moral right to sit on judgment on others' alleged violent behaviour.

The news of violence which was relatively minor was blown out of proportion. The editorial further opined that had the Maharashtra Government implemented the policy of priority to the natives of the State which many other States had silently carried out, there would have been neither the predominance of South Indians in Maharashtra's capital nor there would have been a Shiv Sena. (Mht. 25.9.67)

It was no wonder therefore, that *Marmik* editorials voiced strong reactions against opinions, actions and behaviour of South Indians.

In response to a remark by Kamaraj, the Congress chief, at a public speech in the city, that he would like to live in 'cosmopolitan' Mumbai, the *Marmik* observed in its editorial that people from all provinces found it advantageous to live in Mumbai for various reasons and therefore liked this city which was known to be 'cosmopolitan'. Maharashtrians alone, who provided the city with its blue and white-collar work-force, found life in Mumbai rather difficult.

Critical of South Indians, especially of Tamilians and Malayalis (Keralites), for their parochial attitude at home and cosmopolitan outlook outside the home-state, the editorial rhetorically asks

'Would the people of Tamil Nadu welcome people from other provinces to compete on a large scale for jobs and housing in Tamil Nadu? Is it not true that Maharashtrians have accepted Hindi as the national language which is hated in Tamil Nadu? Did not the DMK try to oust Brahmins and non-Tamils from Tamil Nadu? And did not the DMK speak the language of autonomy and separatism? Have they not disrespected the national flag by burning it?'

Yet the Tamils are not labelled 'parochial'. On the other hand, when they come to Mumbai, they try to teach us 'nationalism'. (Mrm. 5.6.66)

'Cosmopolitanism' of Mumbai

Criticising Mumbai being termed as a 'cosmopolitan' city, the *Marmik* in one of its editorials comments remarked:

'Who are these, who profess Mumbai's cosmopolitanism? They are outsiders, the migrants chiefly; those who came to own or occupy land and property in Mumbai, in the name of 'cosmopolitanism'.'

Since the migrants serve as vote banks to candidates in elections, political parties and candidates speak of 'cosmopolitanism' in Mumbai.

The *Marmik* further maintained that in Maharashtra alone everyone has been welcome. Nowhere else, but to Mumbai did people from all over the country migrate, were welcomed and lived happily. But the time had arrived to put an end to this state of affairs. This was the only reason, claimed the *Marmik*, why it went into publishing a list of employees in various city establishments. (Mrm. 14.8.66)

Indian Express (13.3.66) in the context of Maharashtra's demand for the merger of Goa into Maharashtra had published an article which expressed an opinion that Maharashtra was getting self-centred, parochial and anti-cosmopolitan.

In reply, the *Marmik* vehemently observed that nowhere else in India, was life as plural as in Mumbai, the capital city of Maharashtra and yet the English press never stopped advising Maharashtrians to be 'cosmopolitan'. The *Marmik* asked whether it was not an expression of the anti-Maharashtrian attitude of South Indians who dominated the Indo-English press and Central Government service. (Mrm. 22.5.66)

Another article in the *Marmik* on 'cosmopolitanism' in Mumbai observed that this 'cosmopolitanism', often extolled by social, political and cultural V.I.P.s, had chiefly a negative connotation. The English language and English-oriented culture was often considered the 'cosmopolitan culture' of Mumbai which has displaced vital Indian regional cultures. (Mrm. 2.7.67)

4. Community as Arbiter

Centre's Injustice

The Maharashtrian community had a feeling of being subjected to injustice by authority, by the Central Government and the Congress High Command. This was a fairly widespread feeling and stemmed especially from the fact that for a long time the demand for unilingual Maharashtra with Mumbai as the capital had remained unacceptable to the Central leaders. It was also rooted in the fact that Maharashtra's grievances regarding its claim for the border areas in Karnataka and the distribution of river waters had remained unresolved for long.

The Maharashtra community's alienation with the Central leadership and suspicion about the Centre's attitude or indifference to Maharashtra, often found expression in statements by community leaders of various levels.

The local Congress leaders from Pune in 1964, at a meeting of Pune Municipal Corporation protested against the news that the Maharashtra Congress Chief (Vinayakrao Patil) was forbidden to hold a public meeting at Nagar Haveli, the former Portuguese colony on the Gujarat-Maharashtra border on the west-coast, which had been under Central administration since its liberation along with Goa.

Another Congress leader, a Member of Parliament, Shankarrao Moray, speaking as a Chairman at a conference on the irrigation and Water Supply Problems of the Pune District, observed that Maharashtra had no status in the eyes of the Central Government.

Referring to Maharashtra's water disputes with Andhra and Mysore now Karnataka, Shankarrao Moray maintained that Maharashtra's problems were often shelved by the Centre. If Maharashtra asked for more water, it was dubbed as narrow, regionalist and quarrelsome. Neither the MPs nor even the Maharashtrian ministers could move the Centre in the matter. The thirst of Andhra and Mysore for more water was not quenched in spite of their being well-irrigated States. Maharashtra, on the other hand, was known for its eternal scarcity and shortage of water. River waters, being nature's resources, ought to be distributed on the principle of equity. (Mrt. 12.6.65)

These perspectives found vocal expression chiefly in the three independent papers; in a pronounced manner in the *Maratha* and the *Marmik* and in a temperate language in the *Navakal.* These, however, seemed to be widespread among the politically-conscious urban members of the Marathi community.

In 1966, commenting on the reshuffle of Indira Gandhi's cabinet, the *Maratha* commentator observed that the reshuffle did not give better representation to Maharashtra. Promotion of one Maharashtrian member from the post of Parliamentary Secretary to that of Deputy Minister in the same Irrigation Department was balanced by elimination from the Central Cabinet of another Marathi-speaking Minister (Mr. Hazarnavis) from Madhya Pradesh. Maharashtra thus was not allowed to gain in importance, the commentator observed (Mrt. 10.2.66)

Reports & Articles: Mrt. 10.6.63, 8.9.63, 15.2.64, 12.6.65, 10.2.66; Mrm. 27.8.67.

Editorials

The concern about representation to Maharashtra in the Central Cabinet formed the theme of two of the *Maratha* editorials.

In May 1962, the *Maratha* grieved that there was not a single Maharashtrian minister in the Nehru cabinet. This statement was somewhat misleading since S.K. Patil from Mumbai was in the Cabinet, but presumably discounted by the *Maratha* as he was held in disfavour by the Marathi community.

The editorial maintained that Maharashtra, being in the bad books of Nehru and the Central leadership because of the Samyukta Maharashtra Movement, did not receive proper representation in his cabinet (Mrt. 10.5.62)

Another editorial complaining against unfair treatment to Maharashtrians and Maharashtra, observed that the absence of a strong man from Maharashtra who could effectively represent and protect Maharashtra's interests in the Central Cabinet was one of the reasons for this indifference and neglect. The editorial directed its criticism at the leaders of the Maharashtra Congress for their inability to carry weight with the Central leadership or the Central Government. Even Y.B.Chavan, considered to be a diplomatic politician, had an uncertain position in the Central Cabinet. It pointed out that able Maharashtrians like B.R. Ambedkar, C.D. Deshmukh and N.V. Gadgil had to leave the Cabinet because of their differences with Nehru on matters of principle.

The editorial also observed that there were no high-level Maharashtrian officials of the I.C.S. cadre in the Central Secretariat. The *Maratha* blames the dominant Gujarati Ministers of the older Mumbai and bilingual Mumbai States, who impeded the promotion of the Maharashtrian officials to the Central Secretariat. Consequently, there was no one to represent Maharashtra in the Central administration, when interests between States clashed. (Mrt. Ed. 1.4.63)

The *Maratha* complained that national honours and decorations often were not fairly conferred, for a good number of Maharashtrians, eminent in various fields of art and culture, were least taken cognizance of. (Mrt. 28.1.62)

II

Having peeped into the Maharashtrian community's world of expectations and aspirations regarding Mumbai the capital of their state, and having acquainted ourselves with the community's self-view, the question arises; how far are these aspirations legitimate, in the sense of being consistent with facts? Is the Maharashtrian self-image as seen in the role of leadership in the metropolis consistent with its capabilities and achievements? What role has the Maharashtrian community played in the city of Mumbai? What was the 'status' of the community in the past in this metropolis, often described as the most 'cosmopolitan' of Indian cities?

After Independence, in the context of reorganisation of Mumbai state, the issue of who had developed the city had figured prominently. At that time it was claimed that 'the city owes its growth and development to various communities, but particularly to the Parsis, Kutchis, Bhatias and Gujaratis'. It was believed that 'the civic and cultural life of Mumbai is essentially cosmopolitan' and therefore 'Maharashtra can claim no particular affinity with it'. (The Mumbai Committee, n.d., Pp. 9, 19) Even after the inclusion of Mumbai in Maharashtra, the image of Mumbai as a 'cosmopolitan' city has not faded. In fact with the increasing heterogeneity of the city, the image seems to have grown stronger, especially among the non-Marathi communities of the city.

There is no doubt that various communities from Gujarat led by the Parsis, with their financial capital, enterprise and business acumen vastly contributed to the commercial and industrial development of Mumbai. In fact, trade and commerce in the whole of Maharashtra has always been in the hands of the Gujarati and Marwari trading communities. Even industrial enterprises were the preserve of these communities. Unlike most regional communities the absence of a trading community has been a peculiar characteristic of Maharashtra's economy and social structure. (Singh G.S. 1966, Pp. 58-59, Kulkarni A.G., 1968, Pp. 60-61; Phadke, 1973, Pp. 69-70)

But if the enterprise and capital for Mumbai's industries came from communities of Gujarat, the labour was primarily from Maharashtra. Mumbai's trade and industry depended to a large measure, on the raw materials and markets of the Maharashtra hinterland. Water and power feeding the industries, also came from Maharashtra. Moreover, Mumbai had been the very hub of Marathi culture and life, after the coming of the British.

It would be useful therefore, to explore briefly the relationship of the Maharashtrian community with Mumbai, as the city developed following the establishment of the British rule. In the process, we would also be able to assess the relevance of the community's aspirations regarding its role and relationship with the city.

Mumbai and Maharashtra
A Historical Perspective

Mumbai always has been a composite city with a mixed population of communities speaking various languages and following different religions. Yet, it always has been a city with a large majority of its population made up of the Marathi-speaking people - migrants from its immediate hinterland in the north, south and east. Even in the earlier days, 'the greater part of the city's population was made up of the *Maratha* labourers from the Deccan'. Until about the 1920's the leading Marathi speaking castes were present in the city's bureaucracy. The Pathare Prabhu (Kayastha) who belonged to the island and the surrounding area, had served both the Portuguese in Mumbai and the Peshwas in Pune, '...their monopoly of clerkship was so great that their caste name became a synonym for an English writer'. (Dobbin Christine, 1972, p. 6-7)

Mumbai began to grow very rapidly due to increasing industrialisation and migration, only after the Second World-War and especially after Independence. Until then the Marathi community had a clear majority in the city. More importantly, Mumbai has been the principal centre of Maharashtrian life and culture as of no other community. Pune, though it was the capital of the Peshwas and reputed as an intellectual centre, could never displace Mumbai from its unique place in Maharashtra's life, as the chief nourishing mother-city of the province.

Before the turn of the nineteenth century between 1881 and 1900 the city's Marathi population varied between 53.7% and 50.2%. In 1921 the Marathi-Konkani population made up 56 per cent of the city's total population (Marathi 53 per cent, Konkani 2.6 per cent, see Table vi-10, Ch. VI) Even in 1941 the Maharashtrian population (51 per cent) was large enough to balance all the city's other communities put together. However, from 1951 onwards the heavy influx of long distance migrants gradually deprived the Maharashtrians of their clear majority. But the community continued to be the single biggest majority group of the city.

Maharashtrians and 19th-century Mumbai

The island city of Mumbai had an exciting and eventful life in the 19th century, especially during the later half. Mumbai, the capital city of Western India, was a gateway to India for foreign powers from Europe. Here a stabilizing British rule had set in motion the processes of modernisation.

Contact at close quarters with the ruling British community on account of the collaboration of business interests by the local communities (chiefly Parsis and Banias from Gujarat) led to changes of far-reaching impact on the indigenous population of Mumbai and of Western India. The introduction of Western education and associated values, the emergence of the native press and the consequent social and political ferment leading to reform and freedom movement and the rise of modern industry were the major changes resulting from this contact.

Nana Shankershet (1802-1865) and his junior contemporaries like Dadabhai Naoroji, Bhau Daji Laud and others were the chief architects of modern Mumbai, emerging under colonial rule. Himself a businessman and a banker and closely associated with Parsi merchant-princes like Jamshetji Jeejibhoy, Shankershet combined in himself the roles of a donor, a pioneer and reformer. He not only represented Mumbai's 'Hindu' society but also, easily became the leader of 19th- century Mumbai. (Rev. Dr. Wilson,

1864, in Balkrishna Nilaji, 1867, p. 17) Demanding the right of representation for Indians in the Governor's Council and in the Jury, he became one of the first five Indian members of the provincial council of the governor (1862-1865). (Dobbin, 1972, Pp. 24-25)

It is often believed that Marathi community had no share in ushering modern industry or banking in Western India. (See Mumbai Committee's Memorandum submitted to L.P.Commission N.D.) It is a fact that Parsi and Hindu Communities from Gujrat were in the forefront in these fields. However, Marathas were not totally absent. In Shankershet, the community had an outstanding exception. One of the first Indian directors of some of the city's first major banks, he was also closely associated with the city's first major banks, he was also closely associated with the city's early cotton spinning and weaving mills. On 16 April 1853, the first train in Asia ran between Mumbai and Thane. Shankershet's active involvement and lion's share in the effort is recorded. (Dadabhoy Naoroji, 1864, in Balkrishna Nilaji, 1867, p.8) The office of the G.I.P. railway operated for some time from Shankershet House in Girgaum. Shankershet was also one of the founding fathers of the Mumbai Steam Navigation Company in 1845. (Telegraph and Courier 1.11.1850, Times of India 19.1.1864, 9.3.1864, 18.4.1864, q.v. Kulkarni P.B. 1959, Pp. 247-277) Earlier some important Muslim families from Konkan like the Rogay, Makba and Ghattay were connected with ship-building activity and trade in Mumbai. (Dobbin, 1972, pp. 11, 15, 159, 230-240)

Shankershet's initiative in and contribution to the field of education and reform is better known. Several of the city's prestigious institutions of education (The Native Education Society, The Elphinstone College, the Government Law College, the Grant Medical College, Sir J.J. School of Art, and above all the University of Mumbai) saw the light of the day because of the tireless pioneering effort and enthusiasm of persons like Shankershet, Dadabhai Naoroji, Bhau Daji Laud, Naoroji Furdunji, and the munificent donations of the merchant-princes of Mumbai and the encouragement by the enlightened rulers.

In the 19th century, the Marathi community led other communities including the Parsi, in the field of education. All the first four graduates of the University of Mumbai were Maharashtrians. The board of education and heads of educational institutions in the Mumbai Presidency repeatedly regretted that Mumbai's leading commercial communities showed little interest in education. As a result, high schools in Gujarat were not successful in producing Gujarati graduates and a few prominent Maharashtrians (G.H. Deshmukh, A.P. Turkhadkar) played a major role in laying down foundations of new education in Gujarat. (C. Dobbin, 1972, Pp. 32-33, 228, 257)

The newly-established institutions of Western education produced a startling crop of talent during the succeeding four or five decades. Those who studied and worked in these institutions were outstanding men who made a marked contribution to the public life of Mumbai and that of the nation. Among these were Dadabhai Naoroji, Naoroni Furdunji (the scholar-teacher) the Zoroastrian scholar Kharshetji R. Kama, the revolutionary Sorabjee Shapurjee Bengali, political activists like Pherozeshah Mehta and Dinshaw Wachha, public men and reformers like Badruddin Tayyabji, Karsandas Mulji and a poet like Narmada Shanker. And also there were several Maharashtrian leaders and scholars, like Justice M.G. Ranade, orientalist R.G. Bhandarkar, Bhau Daji Laud and the Turkhadkar brothers, pioneer journalists like Jambhekar and Mandlik, and several others.

Press Politics and Social Reform in 19th Century

The Press

Another significant pioneering activity of the times was the rise of the native press which served as an instrument of social and political awakening in Western India. The earliest native paper in Mumbai was the Parsi-Gujarati *Mumbai Samachar* (1822), run by Parsis with the assistance of Parsi business houses. The *Samachar* dealt chiefly with commercial matters of interest to the business community. (S. Natarajan, 1969, p. 74, Dobbin, 1972 p. 54) Dadabhai's *Rast Gofter* and the Gujarati-Hindu paper *Satya-Prakash*, were established only in 1852.

The early Marathi press on the other hand, was a product of the intellectual ferment aroused at the newly established institutions of higher education (the Students' Literary and Scientific Society under the chairmanship of Dadabhai, in the Elphinstone College). It soon became a vehicle of political and social awakening and of the cross fertilisation of ideas between Mumbai and Pune, the second urban centre of Western Maharashtra. The first Marathi newspaper *Mumbapur Vartman* was started in 1828. (Priyolkar, 1974, p. 110) However, the first important Marathi journal to make a mark on Mumbay's elite was the *Mumbai Durpan* established in 1832 by Jambhekar with the specific intention of instructing the public and encouraging discussion. A majority of Marathi journals evinced this sense of mission. (C. Dobbin, 1972, Pp. 54-55) Throughout the 19th century, a number of pioneer Marathi journals, unlike their Gujarati contemporaries, were Anglo-Marathi journals carrying an English column. (Dobbin, 1972, p. 196)

The need for internal reform of Indian society, female education and inability of Mumbai's aristocracy to lead any political or social reform were themes often discussed in the Marathi press. 'Criticism of the existing order of society was therefore a commonplace in Marathi press long before the first generation of Parsis took to new education'. (Dobbin, p. 54-55) These journals were unhesitant in their criticism of either Brahmin conservatives or British economic policy. Among the political questions that received attention repeatedly were demand for direct representation for Indians in the provincial and higher Councils, and the criticism of the large number of appointments of the British in the un-covenanted Civil Service. Criticism of the Government administration was thus more widespread in the Marathi press, compared to that in the Gujarati press. The Marathi Press increasingly placed great stress on its role as guardian of popular liberties and therefore Lytton's Vernacular Press Act of March 1878 was viewed as the confirmation of the inherent despotism of the regime. (Dobbin, 1972, p. 199-201)

The Marathi intellectuals also took recourse to the English press in Mumbai to criticise the government. A 'Hindoo's' (Bhaskar Turkhandkar, brother of A.P. Turkhadkar, the founder of the Prarthana Samaj) eight letters published in the Mumbai Gazette as early as 1841 consisting of logically reasoned, severe criticism of the British Government's economic policy for draining India of its wealth long before Dadabhai published his comprehensive study of Indian poverty – *Poverty and Un-British Rule in India* (1901). (Naik J.V. 1975-76, Journal of Univ. of Mumbai, Art, Vol. XLIV & XLV Pp. 80-81)

Again, Mumbai saw its first working-class journal with the emergence of two Marathi papers in the 1880's *Deen-Bandhu* (1877) and *Shetkaryancha Kaivari* (1885) With the cotton textile mills going into production in mid-19th century, the city saw its new class of industrial workers, - millhands, mostly of peasant stock from coastal Ratnagiri and Satara and Ahmednagar districts. The Anglo-Marathi press mentioned earlier, represented upper-caste, middle-class all-India concerns; but the new section of the press however, focused on the grievances and concerns of the new class of industrial labour. Of this, the *Deen-Bandhu* was the organ of Jyotiba Phule's Satya Shodhak Samaj, while the *Shetkaryancha Kaivari* represented the agricultural communities of the Kunbi, Bhandari, Agri, etc. (Dobbin, 1972, Pp. 209-210)

The Reform Movement

The Brahmo Samaj was the source of inspiration for the rise of a parallel movement in Mumbai, the Prarthana Samaj, founded by Atmaram P. Turkhadkar in 1867. The Samaj successfully continued to publish its message through its journal *Subodha Patrika* (1877)

In 1873, the Samaj began its first night school for mill-workers and domestic servants. The activity eventually grew into a movement in Mumbai. With the co-operation of the members of the Samaj, Ranade started Indian Social Conference (1887), an all-India platform for furthering social reform activities along with political reform activities of the Indian National Congress. (Dobbin, C. 1972, Pp. 253-254)

Depressed Class Mission

However most important was the emergence and the growth of the Depressed Class Mission in Mumbai (1906) by an erstwhile

Prarthana Samajist, Vithal Ramaji Shinde (1873-1944) Shinde, through his dedication and untiring efforts spread the message of the mission to centres all over India. The Depressed Class mission was the first all-India organisation in the service of the 'untouchables', active long before Gandhiji came to include eradication of untouchability in his social and political programme or even before Ambedkar appeared on the Indian scene. (Shinde V.R., 1958)

The First Mill-Workers' Organisation (1884)

Equally important was the development of leadership and organisation of the mill-hands of Mumbai, prior to the turn of the century.

N.N. Lokhande, the editor of the *Deen-Bandhu*, in 1880, used his paper to air workers' grievances and suggesting steps to ameliorate workers' conditions. With the appointment of the Factory Commission (1884), Lokhande, determined to push forth workers' representatives into the Commission's hearing, formed the Millhands' Association (1884) The Association arranged large meetings in Parel and Byculla to obtain worker's sanctions for what was perhaps the first memorandum of the Indian workers' demands, for fair wages and working hours and for representation on the Factory commission. This was the city's first mill-workers organisation. This organisation was successfully used by mill-hands to protest against wage arrears and reduction in wages when workers in two of Mumbai's mills went on strike in 1885. (Dobbin, 1972, Pp. 209-210) These were the first workers' strikes in Mumbai.

Politics

The Mumbai Association (1852)

The establishment of the Mumbai Association (1852), the precursor of the Indian National Congress, was the first major political event of the nineteenth century, symbolic of the political awakening of the citizens of Mumbai. Established at the initiative of leaders like Shankershet, Dadabhai and others, the Mumbai Association pleaded for larger representation for

Indians in the Governor's Council, for greater share for them in the administration and in the uncovenanted Civil Service. Jagannath Shankershet was the president of the Association; Naoroji Furdunji and Bhau Daji Laud were the first joint secretaries who drafted the petition. (J. Massellos, 1968, p. 50; C. Dobbin, 1972, Pp. 82-83)

The Indian National Congress (1885)

The founding of the Indian National Congress took place against the background of the social and political awakening in Maharashtra, during the last quarter of the 19th century. The first session of the Congress could not be held in Pune, as planned earlier, because of the outbreak of cholera in that city and therefore the venue was shifted to Mumbai. (See Annie Besant, 1915, 4-5)

However, the Sarvajanik Sabha of Pune and its Secretary, C.D. Joshi were greatly instrumental in organizing the first session. 'But for the indefatigable labours of its (Sarvajanik Sabha's) Secretary, Mr. Ganesh Dutt Joshi, the Indian national Congress would not have been started so easily'. (Dasgupta H. N. 1946, p. 130) The credit for drafting the rules in regard to the constitution and working of the Indian National Congress goes to the Pune Congress Committee". (John Murdoch, 1898, p. 65, q.v. Kulkarni A.G., 1968, p.77) The Marathi community thus played a major role in the organisation of the opening session of the Indian National Congress in Mumbai in 1885.

At the Turn of the Century

During Tilak's leadership, the centre of political activity and the focus of the nation's attention shifted for a while to Pune from Mumbai. Tilak was then such a popular and respected leader that the Gujarati masses of Mumbai referred to him as 'Bhagwan Tilak'. Radical thought and activity in the reform movement belonged to Agarkar and Jyotiba Phule. They enhanced the Maharashtrian's status and added to the community's stature in Mumbai. G.K.Gokhale, an able parliamentarian and a close colleague of Pherozeshah Mehta was then in the forefront of the constitutional politics of India. The fact that the Marathi community's leaders led the nation, lent the Marathi community a national stature and kept its 'status' high in the country and in 'cosmopolitan' Mumbai irrespective of community's economic position in the city. Besides, the community still held a numerical majority in the city till 1921.

The Socio-political Scene in the Hinterland

The 20th century and rise of new forces

Here I may point out that the territorial and linguistic identity of a community was not a habitual and accepted mode of categorising people in 19th century Mumbai or in India. The early 20th century seems to be the beginning of social consciousness of such an identity. People in 19th century India perceived and thought of communities more often in terms of their religion (Hindu, Muslim, Christian, etc.) and essentially in terms of ritual-caste as an integral part of religion in the case of Hindus.

With the growth and spread of knowledge and the increasing secularisation of life, religious categories of social identity slowly began to fade into the background in the twentieth century India. However, with the introduction of the process of democratisation, caste in its social aspects eventually gained in prominence as a focal point for social identity during the early 20th-century Maharashtra. The evolution of a nascent social consciousness of a broader territorial-linguistic identity which accommodated and bound together caste and religious difference into a larger community sharing a common territorial culture was a later development in the 1940's and 1950's.

The introduction of the democratic principle with the implementation of Montague-Chelmsford Reforms in 1919 and democratisation of the socio-political structure inevitably led to the politicisation of masses and to increased caste and group rivalries in Maharashtra. The end of Brahmin hegemony opened up two foci of caste-conflict (1) Brahmin versus non-Brahmin and (2) the scheduled castes v. caste-Hindus. Society in Maharashtra from 1920 onwards became an intensely divided house.

Fraught with these new internal dissensions and preoccupied with caste-conflicts, the Maharashtrians failed to provide a leadership which could attend to primarily to all-India concerns with sustained interest or one which could lead a composite metropolitan city along with it. The urban elite, the Brahmin and other upper castes, which earlier provided such leadership, were internally losing their hold over the society-at-home, with the rise of the non-Brahmin. The interests, predispositions and experience of the non-Brahmin leadership, on the other hand, were not particularly oriented to handling concerns of a composite metropolitan city or that of a larger national society. These are important factors related to the Marathi community's loss of leadership in metropolitan Mumbai as well as in national political life.

Non-Brahmin Movement & Congress Politics

With the rise of Gandhiji in India after 1920 the political scene in India underwent radical change. Gandhiji, through his various programmes had for the first time involved the rural masses and ensured their participation in the freedom struggle. The Indian National Congress thus became a mass movement and a mass organisation. The leaders and workers of non-Brahmin movement in Maharashtra entered the Congress around 1929. (Kulkarni A.G., Pp. 90-92)

With the mass-entry of non-Brahmins in Congress, the Brahmin and upper-caste leadership slowly lost control of the Congress in Maharashtra. While the Congress expanded in Maharashtra, spread its roots in the rural areas and became a popular movement, the Maharashtra Pradesh Congress Committee increasingly came under the domination of the Maratha caste-cluster. (Kulkarni Pp. 92-97; 146-147; Phadke, 1973, Pp. 80-82)

The estrangement between these two major groups of the society in Maharashtra affected the Marathi community's position in the Congress.

Consequently the MPCC carried little weight over the Mumbai Pradesh Congress Committee. And as we have noted earlier the Marathi group was ineffective in the BPCC which was one of the most powerful of Pradesh Congress organisations.

The Intelligentsia and the Congress

Simultaneously, the Brahmin and upper caste intelligentsia which dominated Congress leadership in Mumbai and Maharashtra in the 1920s and 1930s slowly got alienated from the Congress. The old guard of the upper caste Maharashtrian leadership in Maharashtra and Mumbai (Kelkar, Munje, Jayakar and Aney) joined the Swarajya Party. In the process, they cut themselves off from the masses. The younger generation of the Marathi upper-caste intelligentsia increasingly turned to the political philosophy of the left. These young men were attracted to the communist and socialist movements inside and outside the Congress.

As a cumulative result of these events, the leadership of the Mumbai Pradesh Congress Committee, after the 1920's went into the hands of Gujarati and Parsi communities in Mumbai.

Trade Union Activity

With the establishment of the communist and socialist groups in the 1920's and 1930's, the industrial city of Mumbai became a major centre of trade union activity. However, the leadership of trade unions in Mumbai was for long in the hands of a liberal leader like N.M. Joshi, before the communists arrived on the scene.

We have earlier mentioned Lokhande's efforts in the 1880's of building up the city's first labour organisation and carrying out the city's first strikes. In 1908, the textile workers of Mumbai went on a general strike to protest against Tilak's arrest. The strike was hailed by Lenin as symbolic of the political awakening of Indian workers. (Desai A.R. 1976, p.210)

In 1920, as a result of the efforts of N.M. Joshi and Joseph Baptista (both Marathi-speakers), the All India Trade Union Congress was established in Mumbai. It was the first national-level effort to organise industrial workers of India. (Desai, 1976, p.211) For a decade after this, the leadership of AITUC remained with Joshi. By the end of 1920's communists had built up a strong Girni Kamgar Union with a membership of over 50, 000 workers from among the textile workers of Mumbai. (1928) The very same year it successfully conducted a three-month strike which considerably influenced Indian trade union movements. (Karnik V.B. 1967, q.v. Kulkarni p.103)

After Independence, the Congress, the Communists and the Socialists controlled most of the trade union activity in Mumbai. Only after 1970, did the CPI (M) and the Shiv Sena's Kamgar Sena become active in the field. The majority of workers in the leftist movements and trade union activity in Mumbai have been Marathi speakers. The fact that the members of the party cadre spoke Marathi and shared regional and cultural affinity with the industrial worker facilitated their organisational activities. (Kulkarni A.G. 1968, p.103)

Mumbai & Marathi Language

In the early phase of British administration, as a matter of political expediency and of social necessity, the knowledge of 'vernacular' was made compulsory for its employees by the British East India Company. Marathi was taught to the British officers in the employ of the East India Company at the colleges of Fort William in Calcutta and Fort St. George in Madras. (Pinge S.M., 1960, p. 90-91) Mountstuart Elphinstone, the most enlightened of Governors of Mumbai, had made it obligatory for European civil servants in the Mumbai Government 'to pass an examination in Marathi (or in Gujarati, as well as in Hindustani)". (George W. Forrest, 1884, p. 115, q.v. Pinge, 1960, p. 102)

Since Elphinstone believed that the aim of English education in India was to create a class which would diffuse knowledge among the people and raise India to her rightful position among the nations of the West (Dobbin, 1972, p.28), he laid vital stress on the use of 'vernacular' as the medium of instruction. With his initiative and under his guidance was established 'the Native School Book and School Society' (1822), for dissemination of English education. Elphinstone, keen on involving Indians in the effort, sought the advice of J. Shankershet in educational matters. When the Board of Education was set up in 1840 it included three Indians, J. Shankershet, M.I. Makba, a Konkani Muslim, and Jamshetji Jeejibhoy. (Dobbin, 1972, p.32) (Selections from Educational Records, Vol. II, Pp. 16-17, q.v. Desai A.B., 1976, p. 147)

It was no wonder therefore, that Mumbai along with Pune became the chief centre of the development of Marathi language in modern times. Mumbai in the 19th Century became the major centre of Marathi press and literary and dramatic activities. The highest number of journals in Marathi is now published from Mumbai. The city happens to be one of the centres of publication of Marathi books. It is also a centre of several literary activities and movements.

The Marathi theatre, growing in the cultural environs of a composite city like Mumbai, enriched itself by absorbing influences from the contemporary theatre of the sister languages of Urdu and Parsi-Gujarati. Throughout the history of the contemporary (post-British) Marathi theatre, Mumbai remained its chief centre. Playwrights, actors, singers, technicians and craftsmen converged here to seek recognition. During the 1920's, the golden age of the Marathi theatre, the great Marathi actor-singer Bal Gandharva, was the idol of the theatre connoisseur of Mumbai, including Parsi and Gujarati patrons. The sheer vitality of the Marathi theatre and the constant traffic of thought and talent between its experimental and professional wings have influenced and led the theatre activities of other language groups in Mumbai. (Marathi Natya Parishad, 1961)

The Coming of the Indian Cinema

India entered the world scene of film-making as early as 1912, when D.G. Phalke, versatile but unassuming Maharashtrian, inspired by a street-show of the 'Life of Christ' (1910), produced the first Indian feature film ('Raja Harishchandra') in Mumbai and Nasik. (Barnouw E. & Krishnaswamy S., 1963, Pp.10-23) Through his early feature films, Phalke also created the genre of the mythological film which even to this day has great attraction for the Indian masses.

Thereafter, during the 1930's and 1940's the Marathi film-companies (the Prabhat from Pune, Atre Pictures and Rajkamal Kalamandir from Mumbai) produced feature films on social themes in Marathi and Hindi. These film companies (along with the non-Marathi New Theatres from Calcutta and Mumbai Talkies from Mumbai), led Indian cinema for about two decades.

Film-making then was more of an art and a product of the team-spirit of its participants rather than an industry. However, after the World War II, the Marathi film companies disintegrated.

Apart from the internal disruptive forces, the shortage of raw materials, the flow of 'black money' into film-making during and after the War, the drastic changes in the economy of film production, the new system of star-billing, the expansion and heterogeneity of the audience adversely affected Maharashtrian film companies. The increasing competition from capital intensive 'spectacular' Hindi films from Mumbai and Madras studios, eventually wiped out the Marathi film companies from Mumbai around the mid-fifties. Organised efforts for the revival of the Marathi film industry began only in the late sixties and the early seventies.

The Social and Cultural Scene

This account of the relationship of the Marathi community with Mumbai city and of the community's role in metropolitan life provides a perspective for the evaluation of the community's aspirations and self-image, voiced in the content-data presented in the first section of this chapter.

The facts presented seem to point out that the aspirations and the self-images entertained by the members of the community are fairly consistent with the community's abilities and performance, with the pioneering role that it shared with some other communities of the city, in the development of modern Mumbai. Since these aspirations seem to emerge from the community's performance level in the past they cannot be described as fantasies.

However, a combination of factors seems to have hampered the community's performance of its desired role of leadership of the metropolis, in the past few decades. The increasing caste-group rivalries and the consequent disorganisation of society in Maharashtra, coupled with the community's weaker economic position inevitably affected the community's performance in its encounter with other regional communities. However, caste-rivalry was an unavoidable function of the new egalitarian values adopted by the society.

The Marathi press, though it was alive to socio-political issues and continued to play the role of watchdog and social educator, relinquished the bilingualism of the 19th-century Anglo-Marathi press; it thus lost the wider circle of recognition and ability to influence public opinion beyond the confines of the regional society. Its voice was increasingly isolated and was heard less and less in the composite metropolis of Mumbai.

The growing aspiration to assert the community's status and role of leadership encountered the growing de-recognition of the community's voice. This could only intensify the relative deprivation caused by socio-economic factors discussed in the earlier chapters.

CHAPTER VIII

CONCLUSION

In the opening chapter, it was pointed out that there was no inevitable connection between structural strains and collective mobilisation. The group's 'perception of what is just, expected and possible' is likely to generate and mobilise discontent rather than a group's absolute situation. And what the group considers 'just, expected and possible' depends on its past experience and present context.

In other words, the origin of people's discontent lay in their sense of relative deprivation. We believe that it is the perception of its situation by the Marathi community, and not job competition or demographic concentration in itself, which triggered the birth of the Shiv Sena.

The discrepancy between the Maharashtrian's self-image, what he thought he deserved and could justifiably expect in his capital city on the one hand and what he got or encountered on the other, seems to be the significant factor in the mobilisation of regionalist discontent and the SS movement.

In this context, three kinds of relative deprivation were seen: (i) Aspirational deprivation, when the people's capabilities fail to keep pace with people's heightened expectations; (ii) Decremental deprivation, when people's capabilities decline in the presence of relatively steady expectations; (iii) Progressive deprivation, when a period of relatively speedy improvement in people's social and material conditions raise people's expectations about their future but capabilities stabilise or decline leading to an increasing gap between the expectations and capabilities.

If people's discontent and relative deprivation are unduely prolonged in an environment where people have learnt to use collective action or protest agitation as a legitimate means for the redressal of their grievances, and where history, tradition, norms or previous experience encourage or support such an action, people are likely to resort to these means.

The leadership and the ideology of the organisation also play an important part in encouraging or delimiting recourse to collective strife. Similarly, the legitimacy of the political system and measures used by it for suppression, channelisation or alleviation of collective discontent, also serve as vital mechanisms of institutional support or control to the collective action.

If our contention that the Marathi community's severe discontent about its situation was responsible for the rise of the Shiv Sena in mid-1966, it would be reflected in the content data for 1960-1970.

(A) With each passing year, the number of entries expressing grievances increased before the emergence of the Shiv Sena. With the progression of time, there were an increasing number of entries under the higher index points of the ascending affective-scale by the mid sixties, which support my contention. The formation of Maharashtra with Mumbai as the capital in 1960 was the happy culmination to the long-drawn struggle of the community and therefore early in the decade we are not likely to come across much expression of the community's discontent.

(B) While analysing and assessing the factors responsible for Maharashtrian discontent (which were found to be considerable and widespread), it was felt that besides the facts of economic competition and demographic concentration, the community's concerns about its language and its status or position in the socio-political life of the metropolis were of vital significance. If this line of analysis was correct, one should expect to find a good number of entries of the content-data under themes other than and besides the theme of economic grievances. If economic grievances were most crucial, we could expect the majority of entries to collect under this category, with a relatively negligible percentage of entries in other categories. A large number of entries under other categories however, would mean a broad confirmation of my contention.

(C) Further, if people's perspective about their situation is a significant factor in transforming the economic, demographic or other strains into stress and discontent, as we hypothesised, I expected to have a large number of entries under the category of 'self-view'. Not that I underestimated the significance of economic concerns and material conditions like job competition and/or the phenomenon of overcrowding. However, I believed that these sources of strain gain in significance because of the community's perspective for self-appraisal, in its comparison with other groups in the city of Mumbai. The community's image of itself in the interactional setting of Mumbai thus becomes a relevant factor in the context.

The following two tables present a consolidated picture of the distribution of the content data according to the themes as well as under the various index points of the affective scale.

Table – VIII – 1
Consolidated Distribution of Entries
By the Theme of Grievances

Sr. No.	Theme	Letters	Editorials	Reports & Articles	Total No. of Entries
1.	Civic Grievances (IV)*	44	27	133	204
2.	Economic Grievances (V)	102	50	247	399
3.	Marathi Language (VI)	134	6	64	204
4.	Identity & Status (VI)	85	41	162	288
	a) Identity & Culture on the Retreat	61	24	105	190
	b) Status of the community in Socio-Political Interaction	24	17	57	98
5.	Boundary Disputes (VI) (Letters only)	53	-	-	53
6.	Call for Organised Action For Redressal of Grievance (VI)	50	10	40	100
	Total	468	134	646	1248

7. Boundary Disputes (Editorials, Reports & Articles Entries entered on the Affective Scale but not included for qualitative Analysis	-	82	471	553
8. Self View (VII)	59	28	117	204
9. The Shiv Sena (III)	133	51	288	472
Total No. of Entries	660	295	1522	2477

* The Roman figure in the bracket indicates the number of the Cher that discuses the theme

Table VIII – 2

Distribution of Entries on the Affective Scale
Exploding Metropolis, Economic Aspirations, Social Interaction
Affective Scale

Index Point Index Value	AS 1	GE 2	FR/IN 3	PR 4	DE 5	CA 6	Total Intensity Value	No. of Entries*
1960	11	8	2	2	-	-	41	22E
1961	9	5	5	-	1	-	39	17E
1962	8	22	7	15	14	-	203	56E
1963	11	36	19	18	8	1	258	76E
1964	21	62	58	52	13	9	646	169E
1965	18	53	82	70	27	11	851	241E
1966	13	59	71	116	41	35	1223	279E
1967	11	53	62	86	36	26	983	231E
1968	4	8	17	37	25	6	380	89E
1969	3	16	1	9	5	-	99	34E
1970	4	7	4	10	10	1	126	34E
							Total No. of Entries	1248E

Exploding Metropolis (Chap. IV)	204
Economic Aspirations (Chap. V)	309
Social Interaction (Chap. VI)	645

* Entries regarding the boundary disputes, the Shiv Sena and those on 'Self-view' are not included in this table.

A glance at these tables, and also at the ones in the previous chapters, bears out the point that with the progression of time, the number of entries articulating grievances had increased. Also, the volume of entries under ascending scale-points had increased with time. The peak period for each major theme differed slightly; however, the peak period for all the themes reached a climax between 1965 and 1967. There is no mystique about this climax period. Half a decade after the formation of the new State, it was a good time for an assessment of its achievements. The concurrence of frustration of the Marathi community on many fronts during this period has great relevance to the mobilisation of the regionalist movement.

Significantly there was a noticeable drop in the number of entries on various themes of grievance after 1967. This was a recurring pattern in respect of almost all major themes of grievances (economic, civic and socio-cultural aspirations) which was not anticipated or visualised earlier.

The entries voicing grievances begin to surface around 1963, gain in quantity as well as in intensity by 1965 and reach a peak sometime between 1965 and 1967. Thereafter the entries drop almost suddenly in numbers, though they do not completely disappear during the decade. What can be the reason for this drop of entries after 1967? Are we to understand that the grievances were, by then redressed? Were these grievances of a temporary nature - a product of an artificially whipped-up propaganda?

The content-data suggests that the grievances were widespread. The articulation of these grievances, pans across all the six journals selected for this study and permeates the whole decade, as we have noted elsewhere; a large number of entries come from the *Daily Maratha*, which in fact, opposed Thackeray's Shiv Sena and the *Marmik*. Besides, many of these grievances appeared in print before the *Marmik* launched its aggressive propaganda for the Shiv Sena in 1966.

The pattern, therefore, seems to vindicate the point that the Shiv Sena, born of the Marathi community's deeply-felt and widespread grievances, played the role of a protest movement that gave a vent to collective discontent. Once the Shiv Sena came into existence and started championing the Maharashtrian cause to redress the community's grievances, these grievances needed and found little expression in the news-journals, perhaps because an alternative mechanism (the Shiv Sena) was available to them for expression, articulation and potential redressal. The community's grievances thus, presumably got channelised into an organised effort of a protest-movement. There was no need now to voice their grievances individually.

With the fall in the number of entries relating to Maharashtrian grievances after 1967, simultaneously there emerges a large number of entries on the Shiv Sena. This is in keeping with the above explanation.

The number of entries under different themes would give some indication of the relative strength of various popular grievances. The Table VIII-1, giving the distribution of entries by the themes, could be taken to broadly reveal the relative importance of the various themes as experienced by the community.

The various themes of grievances listed therein, namely 'Economic Grievance', 'Language' and 'Identity and Status' are the three themes which have drawn the highest number of letters. (102, 134 and 85 respectively) These themes have also commanded the highest number of total entries barring the theme of disputed border areas. However the theme of border disputes relevance may be discounted here, as on this theme letters are fewer. (See Chapter II)

The distribution of the large collection of entries from press-data thus suggests that 'Economic Grievance', the grievances related to 'Identity and Status' and 'Language' were crucial for the mobilisation of the discontent of the Marathi community. The 'civic conditions' in Mumbai as well as 'the boundary disputes' served as contributory sources of frustration. The Marathi community's self-view regarding its status and the role in the metropolis and its rights and privileges in its State-capital, provided a 'cause' and justification for mobilisation of collective action.

Given the community's expectations about its place in the State-metropolis, the demographic and economic factors appear most basic to the community's sense of relative deprivation.

i) Demography

The low and falling percentage (42 per cent) of the Maharashtrian population in expanding Mumbai in itself was a fact irksome to the community. In the context of the community's raised expectations regarding its status and role in the State-capital after 1960, the fact of falling percentage became a source of frustration and serious concern. Continuous migration to Mumbai from other States was thus seen with apprehension and alarm, with regard to maintaining the community's position or the majority status in the city. In all 227 entries under various themes: 'Inmigration and Displacement' (Chapter IV), 'Encroachment' and 'Identity and Culture on the Retreat' (Ch VI) deal with this matter. The qualitative analysis of these entries confirms this point.

ii) Economy

The 'means of wealth' of the metropolis were increasing with the growth of new industries and the expansion of the tertiary sector in the city. In the midst of this growth of employment opportunities, however, the Maharashtrian seemed to fare no better than before. The Marathi youth's position in white-collar jobs appeared stagnant, while the community's share in higher cadres of managerial, administrative and professional jobs had become disproportionately small compared to its share of population of the city – especially in the midst of the city's growing economic opportunities. The increasing marginalisation of the textile industry deprived the Marathi worker of his traditional area of work; while the increasing emphasis on skill and training in the newer industries simultaneously appeared to shut him off from alternative avenues of employment. In the midst of the growing economy of an expanding city, Maharashtrians faced aspirational, decremental and progressive deprivation. The demonstration effect of the new migrant groups to whom the benefits seemed to accrue, gave an edge to the community's frustration. Rather than job competition in any particular sphere, the lower socio-economic status of the community, in contrast to the better positions held by members of other communities, was a cause for a strong sense of disparity and frustration, especially in the context of heightened economic aspirations following the formation of Maharashtra State. (See Ch V)

A deeper cause for this malady seemed to be the excessive, intra-state regional imbalance arising out of heavy concentration of capital economy in the small geographical pocket of metropolitan Mumbai. It deprived the majority of the regional community of a legitimate share in the economic and educational opportunities available in the State. (See Ch V) The deteriorating civic and material conditions due to overcrowding following the concentration of the State's economy in and around the island city, added to the native community's frustrations and sense of relative deprivation.

iii) Language, Identity and Status

However 'Economic Grievance' alone was not the crucial factor in mass discontent. Grievances regarding their community's 'Identity and Status' and 'Language' were also predominant. These grievances in combination with 'Economic Grievance' became the crucial factors in the people's discontent.

The volume of letters on the theme of 'Language' is similar to those on 'Economic Grievance'. This means that the language issue contributed prominently to the discontent that mobilised the regionalist movement. This fact has not been sufficiently recognised by political observers of the regionalist movement of the Shiv Sena. However, the Shiv Sena's memorandum of demands included those regarding the Marathi language.

Here it may be pointed out that language is an issue which engulfs all the members of a society speaking that language, irrespective of their class or employment-status, whereas economic grievances are likely to be articulated only by those who directly or indirectly suffer economic deprivation of some sort.

It is not surprising that a large number of letters, larger than those on 'Economic Grievance', are found under the theme of 'Language'. Language, not only symbolises the territorial regional identity of a community, but serves as the community's most vital and intimate means of asserting this. Language, symbolising a people's identity, gets inextricably interwoven with the community's economic concerns. The language issue, therefore, often tends to be explosive.

The Samyukta Maharashtra Movement which was fought for the formation of the linguistic state of the Marathi-speaking people had roused the Maharashtrian community's expectations. It was generally expected that after the formation of the linguistic state, the official language of the civic and State Government in the capital city would naturally be the regional language, as in most other State capitals, and that this would bring about a greater use of the regional language in various areas of social life.

Though this was not an articulated objective of the Samyukta Maharashtra Samiti (the organisational arm of the Samyukta Maharashtra Movement), it was implied in the objective of the formation of the linguistic state. The Samyukta Maharashtra Parishad in its memorandum to the States Reorganisation Commission had visualised the possibility of the introduction of the regional language (Marathi), in administration, education and various other areas of the metropolitan life.

The question of the introduction of Marathi language in Civic and State administration in the city and of social recognition to it from the non-Marathi population of Mumbai, was more closely linked to the question of 'Identity and Status' rather than to economic concerns of the Marathi community. The Marathi speaking native citizens of the State were forced to recognise and respect English and Hindi, in the economic and social world of 'cosmopolitan' Mumbai. However, the native regional language of the State had little place in the metropolis. It was like the non-recognition of Bengali in Kolkata or of Tamil in Chennai. The migrants to Mumbai from other States could do without the slightest knowledge of the regional language, in the very State capital. In the context of the formation of the new linguistic State, the situation was seen as a slight to the State's language, which, according to the Marathi community, deserved better recognition in the State capital. This then was a source of deep frustration.

Self-view

We have maintained that a community's self-view and perspective for self-appraisal is significant for the transformation of strains in the social system into social grievances and popular discontent.

Analysis of a large number of entries (204) confirms that the Maharashtrian discontent of the sixties and mobilisation of the Shiv Sena movement can be understood better in the context of the community's expectations regarding itself, its status and role in the capital city of Mumbai (See Ch. VII, Part 1) These expectations were rooted in the community's historical role in the city as well as in its recent struggle – the Samyukta Maharashtra Movement – for the inclusion of Mumbai in the proposed Maharashtra State. The culmination of this struggle in 1960 in the formation – for the first time in history – of the unilingual State of Maharashtra, raised Maharashtrian expectations about the community's place in the city. Maharashtra being the home State for the Marathi speaking, it was believed that here, the Marathi community and its language had a natural claim on the State Government's attention for priority.

The Samyukta Maharashtra struggle had led people to believe that after the formation of Maharashtra, their situation in general and their economic condition and social status would improve in their capital city. It was presumed that Marathi as the official language of the State would regain its 'status' in Mumbai. It was generally expected that the Civic and the State Government administration in Mumbai would be conducted in the regional language (as in all other State capitals) These expectations were not always clearly expressed but generally taken for granted.

However, the actual developments in Mumbai in the sixties brought a rude shock to these popular expectations. The social reality and the economic structure of the metropolis were already tilted in an opposite direction of change. The industrial growth of Mumbai, begun in the fifties, was further accelerated within a decade and the tertiary sector expanded enormously (See Ch.V-II) These changes encouraged large-scale long-distance migration to the city. (See Ch. VI) The changing structure of the economy in Mumbai increasingly lent room for the more educated and thus facilitated absorption of the (long-distance) educated migrants in preference to the uneducated (short-distance) migrants.

With the slow fall in the percentage of the Marathi community and the increasing heterogeneity of the population, the city was poised for greater emphasis on English and Hindi as media of instruction and as languages of social intercourse. Consequently, the number of Marathi-medium schools, as well the use of Marathi in education and social intercourse, was relatively declining in the new capital city of Maharashtra during 1960-70. (See Ch.VI-I) These pointers from our content data are supported by data from other sources.

The expectation that the formation of Maharashtra and the inclusion of Mumbai as the State capital would boost the use of Marathi was not realised. It seems to be a clear case of 'aspirational deprivation'. In the economic and social position of the community, it was a case of mixed deprivation – aspirational, decremental and progressive.

These frustrations were further sharpened by impossible civic problems arising out of overcrowding of the metropolis and the long-drawn disputes over the boundary of the State. This simmering discontent was bound to seek voice. The Shiv Sena became that voice.

Regionalist Antagonism against South Indians

Among the questions asked while undertaking this project, was the one of how and why the South Indian community became the target of the Shiv Sena's antagonism. The data and analysis in the previous chapters seem to provide a plausible answer.

Several factors combine together to make the 'South Indians', especially the Tamil and Malayali groups, appear as a source for Maharashtrian frustration. For the Maharashtrian, the 'South Indians' became the major reference group with competing economic interests in the employment market of Mumbai in the sixties. The Gujarati community – the biggest minority group of

Mumbai – with its image as an enterprising business community, escaped being seen as a serious competitor for jobs in Mumbai, in spite of the fact that this community's share in tertiary sector jobs was higher than their proportion in the population of the city. (See Ch.V, Table V-7) Gujaratis were seen as a 'native' community of Mumbai. During the Samyukta Maharashtra Movement, Maharashtrian resentment was no doubt strong against a rich and powerful section of Gujarati businessmen and industrialists, which had staunchly opposed inclusion of Mumbai in Maharashtra; however, it subsided after the formation of Maharashtra.

Economic Competition

The rising stream of migrants from the South became a cause for provocation since these South Indian groups were potential competitors and a threat to the economic opportunities of the native community. In spite of the expansion of the tertiary sector during 1960-70, and consequent lowering of the rate of educated unemployment in Mumbai, there was increased competition for the Marathi youth from the job-seekers from the South. The percentage of South Indians among the job-seekers with higher levels of education, as well as among those employed in high-level posts of managerial, administrative and professional cadres was disproportionately high (19 to 20 per cent) to their percentage (9 per cent) in Mumbai's population (See Ch V, Sec. II, Table V-7)

Thus, all the valued status-jobs of the growing economy seemed to escape the grasp of the native community and had accrued to the relatively new group of South Indian migrants.

The sense of deprivation from the high-status jobs appears to be a crucial factor for the disaffection of the Maharashtrian community with the South Indian. South Indian presence in the higher cadres of jobs meant a potential threat of increase in South Indian percentage in lower cadres of jobs too. After all, informal networks of clan and contact in recruitment were never absent in the job market. (See Ch.V, Sec II) The presence of the 'outside' group in high positions made the Maharashtrian more keenly aware of his lower economic status in his own capital.

There already was growing unemployment among the industrial workers from Maharashtra, due to the rationalisation of the textile industry and recession in manufacturing divisions in the sixties. In the midst of a growing and expanding economy the Maharashtrian worker was faced with hardships and unemployment; while jobs in industries were often getting filled by new groups of migrants among whom South Indians especially those from Kerala, predominated. A comparison by the Marathi worker with these new groups and his consequent feeling of deprivation seemed inevitable (See Ch V)

Demography

The migrants from southern States together made a relatively small percentage (8 per cent) of the city's migrant population until 1951. However, this migrant population almost doubled (15.7 per cent) by 1961.

The Malayalis – the most recent group of Southern migrants competing with the natives of the State for tertiary and high cadre jobs - almost doubled in population during 1961-71. Tamil speakers increased in number by 52 per cent. On the other hand, Kannadigas and Telugus, the older familiar groups following economic pursuits different from those of the Marathi speaking showed relatively little increase in their population during the sixties (See Ch VI, Sec. II)

Social Characteristics

i) The language distance between Marathi (of the North Indian languages group) and Tamil and Malayalam (of the Southern languages group), made Tamils and Malayalis conspicuously 'alien'. Their tendency (common to all migrants) to live an insular life within the precincts of their own group, accentuated their linguistic-cultural distance from the native communities of Mumbai.

The South Indian's especially the Tamilian's adherence to English combined with his anti-Hindi attitude and sheer indifference, even resistance to the regional language Marathi, seem in no small measure responsible for incurring Maharashtrian resentment.

The managerial and administrative posts were held by upper-class, upper-caste South Indians. They relied more exclusively on English for communication across the boundaries of the linguistic community and were generally indifferent to the use of the regional language. In the context of Marathi consciousness sharpened by the Samyukta Maharashtra Movement, this attitude seemed to become a cause for provocation. Since a people's language symbolises their identity, these facts assumed an extraordinary explosive significance which was not sufficiently realised especially by the highly educated.

The hardships that the native or host community had to face due to overcrowding and scarcity of basic civic amenities, especially the extreme shortage of housing for the middle and lower classes, in the wake of increasing migration, became focused on South Indians, the most recent and linguistically most conspicuous group of migrants.

Thus several factors combined together to make the South Indian group – the latest to arrive in an overcrowded metropolis - a target of Maharashtrian frustration and discontent; a situation that may have emerged even if Thackeray had not appeared on the scene. Thackeray's role, for all practical purposes, perhaps accentuated and sharpened people's incipient perception and led them to more vehement expression and action.

Social Variables Shaping Collective Action

Under Thackeray's leadership, this popular discontent and frustration of the Marathi community got channelised into the protest movement of the Shiv Sena, in the mid sixties. In the early seventies, the Shiv Sena emerged as an aggressive, volunteer force of Marathi youth. Aggressive language, intimidation and mob violence came to be associated with the organisation of the Shiv Sena.

Youthful Organisation

The intense frustration and ebullient enthusiasm of Thackeray's youthful followers, who were easily swayed by emotions, could be factors responsible for the Sena's aggressive stance and rowdy behaviour. (Ram Joshi, 1970) It also may be conceded that the anti-Shiv Sena propaganda emanating from the established contending parties and the 'national' English press, perhaps exaggeratedthe Shiv Sena's mob violence in the early days of the movement. (Nvs. 12.3.67; Kesari 1.9.67; Sadhana 21.10.67)

Leadership

However, the role of leadership in directing Shiv Sena's followers to aggressive behaviour and strong-arm tactics is unmistakable. The belief of the Shiv Sena leadership in the efficacy of intimidation and mob violence, for achieving social ends is responsible for the Sena's aggressive style and politics. In an interview given in 1978, Thackeray stated, 'It is my belief that no demand, howsoever just and reasonable and clearly expressed through the normal constitutional channel, would be conceded by our Government unless faced by mob violence.' (*Caravan*, Jan, 2, 1978) Similar faith in the efficacy of mob violence in the event of the failure of other means was expressed by a Shiv Sena Mayor in a personal interview. (December 1973)

The Sena leader's statement presents the Shiv Sena philosophy in a nutshell and explains its aggressive actions. It also is a commentary on the Indian political situation. The Central and State authorities cannot escape a share of responsibility in the matter.

* * *

The generation of Indians that grew up before Independence and found their vision of undivided India shattered by the Partition often reacts with strong misgivings regarding any claim of local or regional demands. Loyalty to regional objectives is labelled as separatist and anti-national. However, regional and national interests are not necessarily mutually exclusive. To say that the regionalist movement is against the national interest is to fail to grasp its importance as the voice of a regional community's grievances.

In theoretical analysis, it should be possible to separate the Shiv Sena's regionalism from its politics of intimidation and its anti-communist stance. It can be seen from the content-data that the popular support to the Shiv Sena is neither for its style of politics nor for its dislike of communism. As is borne out by the content data, the Shiv Sena was born out of widespread discontent and a sense of relative deprivation of the Marathi community in the metropolis following the formation of Maharashtra State.

The Shiv Sena thus served as a protest-movement that voiced the Marathi community's simmering discontent regarding its position in metropolitan Mumbai, diminishing economic opportunities and the loss of identity and status in the state capital in the 1960s.

The national political parties, under the constraints of unitary party system often find it difficult to register and reflect conflicts of regional interests. In Maharashtra, they failed to respond adequately to the conflict of interests generated by the excessive concentration of industry and commerce in a small metropolitan area and of the growing regional imbalance. Failure of the parties to respond to the conflicts and to the new aspirations of regional forces seems to have thrown up the regionalist movement. The Shiv Sena responded to these new needs and therefore received wide popular support.

As seen from the content data, the support to the Shiv Sena was drawn from the discontent chiefly related to (i) economic grievances (ii) lack of importance given to Marathi language.

The Shiv Sena brought up the question of priority to local persons in jobs and other economic and educational opportunities. The demand for priority in jobs to 'locals' could not be met because migration from other parts of India had made Mumbai's population heterogeneous in character.

Minority rights are rightly safeguarded by the Indian Constitution. However, as Ambedkar once remarked (quoting Lord Birkenhead), 'there are cases when a minority is a majority'. (Ambedkar B.R., 1948, p. 15) This happens when the majority community is economically weaker and numerically not sufficiently strong to influence the minorities, who jointly more than balance against and/or resist the influence of the majority community. In such situations rights and privileges normally taken for granted and enjoyed by the majority get suspended or unimplemented and need re-stating and under pinning.

With the continuous influx of migrants, the growing linguistic heterogeneity of population and the falling percentage of the State's native community, Mumbai faced such a situation. The regional community being economically weaker, though it constituted the single largest group of the city, carried little weight and lost the normal privileges and rights that accrue with that weight. After the formation of Maharashtra, the native regional community was reluctant to accept this secondary position in its own state. This bid for a prime position for the regional community in its state capital was voiced in overt terms by the Shiv Sena.

The Shiv Sena's cry attracted national attention to the problem. The rise of the Shiv Sena forced the National Integration Council to look into the question of priority to the local people. At its meeting in June 1968, the Council recommended that where qualified local persons were available, they should be given major share of employment. The National Labour Commission (NLC) also dealt with this matter; the trade unions represented in favour of preference to local persons, particularly in the public sector and in technical and clerical posts in reputed private sector concerns.

Normally migrants to a metropolitan area, during their period of domicile, acquaint themselves with the language of the region and adopt it for social intercourse outside their homes. This happens in natural course in most places. In Mumbai, a city with a composite population, with its increasing heterogenity (See Ch. VI), recognition to the regional language and general replacement of English by the regional language in the public life of Mumbai, became a struggle. The strongest resistance to the regional language occurred in the name of English, 'the most understood' and 'the international' language. The linguistic minorities who had little chance of their language being recognised as a major language in the city tended to support English.

People's enlightened participation in the government, necessary for nation-building and success of the democratic system, makes it necessary for the processes of government and administration at all levels to be conducted through the people's language. The demand for greater use of Marathi and the expectation that the domiciled citizen acquaint himself with the regional language are consistent with this condition and with the new regional aspiration and cannot be described as unjust or undemocratic.

The Shiv Sena was neither the first, nor the only one to demand recognition to the regional language or its greater use. Earlier the Samyukta Maharashtra Samiti and later the Sampoorna Maharashtra Samiti and their unit parties, the PSP, CPI, the SSP, the C.P.M., etc. preceded the Shiv Sena in this struggle for gaining recognition to the regional-national language in the administrative and procedural machinery of the Mumbai Municipal Corporation. The content data records the tussle between opposing groups in the civic government over the issue of the introduction of Marathi in the procedures of the Civic council and civic administration.

In the general atmosphere of resistance to the regional language, however, it cannot be denied that the Shiv Sena's presence has forced some new awareness about the regional language and its due place in Mumbai. In mid-1974, when Thackeray threatened to demolish the signboards of establishments which failed to display their names in Nagari (Marathi) character, several establishments painted their signs in Marathi, alongside those in Roman characters. (Until then these establishments rarely cared to do so inspite of being so required under Sec. 147 (a) of the Indian Companies Act. (See readers' views, Times of India, 27.9.74, 5.10.74, 8.10.74) Even this symbolic change meant an achievement in an atmosphere of indifference and resistance to the regional language, in Mumbai. However non-Marathi communities' attitude including that of South Indians seemed to be slowly changing.

Though the immediate provocation for the rise of the regionalist movement was provided by popular discontent over economic opportunities for the 'locals' and the status of the Marathi language in Mumbai, this frustration has its roots in a much larger problem of the regional economic imbalance. Excessive concentration of capitalist economy in the small area of metropolitan Mumbai has led to large economically depressed backward areas devoid of opportunities in the rest of Maharashtra and especially in the adjacent districts of Konkan the source of the majority of intra-state migrants to Mumbai. It is perhaps no mere coincidence that a large number of leaders, active workers and supporters of the Shiv Sena, hail from the Konkan districts.

The widening of the social distance and the communication gap between the 'cosmopolitan' city and the excessively under-developed areas of Maharashtra region seems to be an inevitable concomitant of the extreme spatial economic imbalance. Such an imbalance if left to grow inevitably has huge social repercussions.

The rise of the regionalist movement of the Shiv Sena was a symbolic cry against this growing concentration of job opportunities in Mumbai and the consequent deprivation of the community.

* * *

A protest-movement seeking redressal of its grievances in a democratic set-up is likely to enter into the democratic competition for power through elections and a bid for popular support since political power is the means for solving problems. In the process, the movement often gets transformed into a political organisation and a party. Concern for power eventually forces the movement or the organisation into acceptance of some compromises as well as a political-economic programme that would command wide support.

Realising that capturing political power was essential for implementing its demands, the Shiv Sena made a bid in a big way, for entry into the Mumbai Municipal Council. It won Municipal elections in 1968 and has ever since been a force in civic politics, where it contributed to an extent, to efforts for redressal of civic grievances regarding displacement of old residents, housing difficulties, etc. It also consistently has pressed for the Marathi language in civic administration.

However, the Shiv Sena has shown little inclination or capacity to understand the complex economic problems underlying Maharashtrian grievances and therefore has failed to develop any consistent programme related to those issues. Apart from the Shiv Sena's politics of intimidation and alleged corruption in its ranks, this has been the main reason why the Marathi community seems to have lost interest in the Shiv Sena and has been disaffected with it since the mid-seventies. In the general elections in February 1978 and even in the elections to the State Assembly the Shiv Sena failed to obtain a single seat out of the thirty-four it contested in Greater Mumbai. Its presence in the Civic Council, however, is an indication that Maharashtrian grievances are still not redressed.

Appendix – A-I

The official sales figures* of the six journals selected immediately before and after the rise of the Shiv Sena are presented below. In the brackets are given their founding years and the abbreviations of their names as used in the content-data. The figures are as given in the annual reports of the Registrar of Newspapers for India. Unofficial estimates tend to be higher than presented here. However, it is obvious that actual readership or the circulation figures are likely to be at least two or three times the figures of copies sold.

Name of the Journal	1965	1966	1969
1. The Loksatta (Lks), (1948)	1,29,142	1,42, 330	1,33,568
2. The Maharashtra Times (Mht), (1962)	60,979	65,056	79,936
3. The Nav Shakti (Nvs), (1932)	31,834	34,442	33,651
4. The Daily Marstha (Mrt), (1956)	62,371	67,093	77,312
The Sanj Maratha (Sanj Mrt), (1956)	13,152	N.A.	2,769
5. The Navakal (Nvk), (1923)	5,096	5,693	17,368
6. The Marmik Cartoon Weekly (Mrm), (1960)	18,532	25,475	37,638

The *Sakal* and the *Kesari* from Pune had a sale of about 78,000 and 32,000 in 1966-67. For comparison we give below the figures of three English dailies from Mumbai for 1966

The Times of India (1838)	1, 49, 202
The Indian Express (1951)	1, 01, 855
The Free Press Journal (1932)	81, 020

* Source: Press in India, Part II Annual Report of the Registrar of the Newspapers for India, (1965), 1966, 1969), Ministry of Information & Broadcasting, Government of India, New Delhi

Appendix A-II

Entries

	Name of the Journal		
1	Jobs & Employment		Themes
2	Educational & Training Opportunities		
3	Opportunities in Business & Industry		
4	Food & Related Problems		
5	Housing & civic Amenities		
6	Law & Order Problems Anti-Social Activities		
7	Marathi Language		
8	Identity & Culture		
9	Status in Socio-Political Interaction		
10	Border Disputes		
11	Centre-State Grievances		
12	Self and 'Others'		
13	Shiv Sena		
AS	ASPIRATION	1	Affective Scale
GR	GRIEVANCE	2	
FR	FRUSTRATION	3	
IN	INSECURITY	4	
P.	PROTEST	5	
D.	DEMAND	6	
C.	CALL FOR ACTION	7	

Appendix A-II .... Contd

1. Themes

List of Themes used for Classification of Content-data

1. Jobs and Employment
2. Educational & Training Opportunity
3. Opportunities of Business & Industry (Other Economic Opportunities)
4. Food and Related Problems
5. Housing and Civic Amenities
6. Law and Order Problems Anti-Social Activities
7. Marathi Language
8. Identity & Culture
9. Socio-Political Interaction
10. Boundary Disputes
11. Grievances against rbiter (Centre-State Grievances)
12. Self and 'Others'
13. The Shiv Sena

2. Affective Scale

Distribution of Entries on the Scal

Index Point	AS	GR	FR/IN	PR	DE	CA	Total	No. of
Index Value	1	2	3	4	5	6	Intensity Value	Entries
Units Classified	-	2	2	1	-	-	-	5
Intensity Value of Units Classified	-	4	6	4	-	-	14	5

Appendix A-III

The Riot Reports

8.2.69: Covering the events of the 8th February, the *Maratha* of 9.2.69, reported of attempts by crowds to take out processions in North Mumbai, in defiance of prohibitory orders by the police. The report added

Following this, the police made lathi-charge and used tear gas, which enraged the people. Angry mobs in the working class areas of Naigaum, Parel Sewri, Chinchpokli, Byculla and Bhoiwada, resorted to stone-throwing. In the skirmishes, ten B.E.S.T. buses and several milk booths were set on fire. The police arrested the municipal councilor and Shiv Sena leader, Dattaji Salvi, along with ten others. Near the Chitra Cinema, Dadar, the police resorted to ten rounds of firing to disperse irate mobs, in which two persons died.

9.2.69: The riots continued on the 9th, a Sunday. The *Maratha* of the 10th, rounding up the previous day's incidents, announces in its headlines

'Mumbai burning! Riots everywhere! Twenty-four buses, several milk booths and police chowkies burned! Five railway stations set on fire!'

Headlines also declaim 'Several shops looted! Public Property destroyed!' (Mrt. 10.2.69)

On Sunday, the police commissioner declared a curfew for three days, beginning from that very day, the 9th, from 8 p.m. to 5 a.m. The review of the day's news states, that the police had to open fire during the day, at several times in different parts of the city. Ten persons died as a result of police firing, several others being injured besides. The report mentions that a thousand persons were arrested on Sunday, including the Shiv Sena leaders, Bal Thackeray, Manohar Joshi and Datta Salvi, under the Defence of India Act. (Mrt. 10.2.69)

The Beginning

Detailed reports of the riots of the 9th, state that the trouble broke out on Sunday in Dadar, near the Plaza Cinema, when an angry mob burnt down a bus and began to throw stones at cinema posters and banners. Shortly after, the shops in the surrounding market area closed in panic. The police confronted the crowds with tear gas and lathi charge. The news spread, inciting crowds in Mahim to burn a milk booth, break open a hotel near the Paradise cinema, to burn its goods and furniture, and then to set a fire the ticket office of the Mahim Road railway station. The crowds even attempted to throw railway sleepers across the tracks to obstruct train traffic. (Mrt. 10.2.69)

The police opened fire on a mob engaged in stone-throwing at a police-van in Mahim, the news of which reached Dadar to provoke crowds assembled there to set fire to the Kirtikar Market. Forty milk booths were burnt down in Dadar, five at Santa Cruz. (Mrt. 10.2.69)

Road Barricaded

Several streets in the areas from Dadar to Lalbaug were barricaded by the infuriated mob to obstruct vehicular traffic and police vans. (Mrt. 10.2.69)

Shops broken open in Lalbaug

Rioters in Lalbaug were on the rampage, destroying and burning whatever caught their fancy. The crowds stoned sign-boards of shops. They attempted to break open shops and damage them. At Sewri, the crowds attacked the car of the Deputy Commissioner of Police. (Mrt. 10.2.69) The police arrived in time to stall the looting of the Century Bazaar, Prabhadevi; they opened fire to disperse the mob. (Mrt. 10.2.69)

Destruction of Rail and Road Transport

The B.E.S.T. withdrew its fleet of buses from the roads in the afternoon following the incidents - 20 buses being gutted in fires and 116 being put out of order. The State Transport buses leaving Mumbai were suspended.

There was stone-throwing at almost all the suburban railway stations, between Dadar and Victoria Terminus, and attempts were made to set a railway bogey on fire, on the Harbour branch and at the Currey Road railway station. (Mrt. 10.2.69)

Post Office and Congress Office Burnt

A post office was set on fire at Prabhadevi. The R.P.C.C. branch office in Khedgalli Lane was set on fire. The riot spread to the Portuguese Church area in Dadar where the police opened fire. (Mrt. 10.2.69)

Riots in Girgaum

The police made a lathi-charge on a crowd of people gathered to defy the curfew order, at 7 p.m. at the Portuguese Church in the Girgaum area. Milk booths and police chowkeys in the Mangalwadi, Zaobawadi, Chirabazar, Round Temple and the Thakurdwar areas of the Girgaum district, were set on fire by mobs. (Mrt. 10.2.69) The riots were spreading to the far-off northern suburbs of Malad, Borivali, Santa Cruz, etc., (Mrt. 10.2.69)

10.2.69 Even on Monday, the 10th, the riots were not under control. In fact, they appeared to be getting worse. Reporting upon the previous day's incidents, the *Maratha* of the 11th gives, for the first time, the news in headlines of shops being subject to vandalism

'Shops in Mumbai broken open looted and destroyed! Shops of all linguistic and ethnic communities looted without any discrimination! Cars set on fire! The situation worsening after midnight! Army men likely to be called!' (Mrt. 11.2.69)

At a press conference on the 10th, the Police Commissioner expressed his opinion that the riots, in all likelihood, were pre-planned. He informed newspaper reporters that even after the clamping of the curfew the police had to resort to firing several times at irate crowds on the rampage on Monday. (Mrt. 11.2.69)

Appendix – A. IV

Excerpts from Content Data

1. People's Grievances

Jobs and Employment

1. As early as 1961, a letter complained that business firms and foreign concerns in Mumbai were becoming South Indian preserves due to neopotism and clan-favouritism. To obtain a fair deal for the Maharashtrians who, (according to the letter) were equally capable and industrious, the letter suggested measures like (1) A rigorous implementation of the rule of notification of vacancies by the companies to the Government Employment Exchange; (ii) a proportionate recruitment of candidates from each state; and (iii) maintaining a certain proportion of the native candidates of the state in employment within the state. (Nvs. 24.1.61)

2. A letter published in 1964 refers to the prospect of 15-20, 000 new jobs in the four factories then being set up in Maharashtra in the public sector under the auspices of the Defence Ministry. It further quotes the assurance given by the Minister for Industries of the Maharashtra State Government, regarding recruitment of local people to unskilled jobs in these factories. However, in spite of the Ministers' assurance, the letter complains, Marathi-speaking persons continued to be denied these and similar other jobs in Maharashtra. (Mht. 17.12.64)

3. A readers' letter in 1965 comments on the almost total absence of Maharashtrian personnel in the officers' cadre, in all departments, of the MIG factory at Nasik. All posts, the letter complains, even those at the technical training centre specially opened to train new candidates, were filled up by South Indians – right from the post of the Principal to those of the teachers, from the senior technical officer even down to the foreman. This was also true of the recruitment of student trainees. Even among the two batches of students selected for training in the Russian language there was not a single Maharashtrian. The centre was

run by the State Government itself at great expense. (Mrm. 5.9.65)

Another letter reproduces an advertisement of the Hindustan Aeronautics Ltd., Bangalore Division, published on 16.8.67, for the post of a Medical Officer which in addition to the other necessary qualifications called for knowledge of Kannada/Tamil as well.

The letter writer remonstrated that a like requirement of the knowledge of Marathi/Hindi was not stipulated for the similar post of a Medical Officer at the Hindustan Aeronautics in its Nasik Division; and that a South Indian doctor, appointed over a year earlier, was later promoted to the Senior Medical Superintendent's post. The letter sarcastically adds that the appointment of a South Indian doctor was perhaps the right thing to do in the Hindustan Aeronautics at its Nasik Division in Maharashtra where every single officer and even the subordinate staff, was imported from the South! Long live the Constitution of India! (Mrm. 17.9.67)

Lists of names of persons in the Officer's cadre at the Hindustan Aeronautics at Nasik and reports about the MIG (HAL) factories at Nasik regularly appeared in the *Marmik* as an exposure of the large-scale appointments of South Indians. (Mrm. 12.6.66, 15.3.70, 13.6.71)

In 1968, Atre's *Daily Maratha* published a report of the impending resignation of a Maharashtrian I.A.S. officer, - the Chief Administrative Officer – at the MIG factory at Ozar over some serious differences of opinion with the General Manager of the factory, regarding the recruitment of personnel in the technical categories. (Mrt. 4.5.68)

The report also carried the complaint of a disproportionately large number of appointments of South Indians by the South Indian General Manager of the factory, not only to the mechanical and technical divisions or cadres but also to the subordinate posts of class III & IV, like drivers of staff vehicles. The report further stated that the 200 farmers who were deprived at their land for the sake of the factory site had received their monetary compensation only in small instalments and that inspite of the assurance given in the Central Government Directive about technical training and jobs for the children of those deprived of their land, such a prospect seemed a far cry from reality. Presently these children were working as domestic servants in the officials' households. (Mrt. 4.5.68)

A letter from the General Manager of the Hindustan Aeronautics, Nasik, appeared in the *Maratha*, the following month.

The letter described the allegations of injustice to the farmers regarding purchase of their land and to Maharashtrians regarding their salary grades as 'baseless'. (Mrt. 28.6.68)

The letter however offered no explanation about the news of the Chief Administrative Officer's resignation or regarding training facilities to the farmers' children.

A similar tale is unfolded through other letters and reports from journals.

A reader's letter in 1967 states that more than 11 acres of fertile land under paddy cultivation in Waveghar Village in Panvel Taluka (across the Mumbai Harbour), was acquired for Hindustan Organic Chemicals. The Maharashtra State Government provided water and electricity facilities for this vast industrial complex. The benefits of these sacrifices, the letter complains, were being reaped by a large number of officials recruited from Tamil Nadu and Kerala. The letter requested the *Marmik* to raise its voice to warn the State Government against this unfair act. (Mrm. 26.2.67)

A reader of the *Maratha*, resident of Turade, another village in Panvel (Dist. Kolaba), writes

The Government has failed to keep its word to several of the families who were deprived of their precious land under paddy cultivation that they would be given jobs in the factory. The letter-writer complained that inspite of daily treks to the factory not a single person of the village got a job at the factory, while the Managing Director recruited his own men into various big and small posts. The Central (Government) Secretary's visit to the location of the project, especially to look into the problem of jobs for the displaced people of the village, was ineffective.

The letter remonstrated that neither the Central nor the State Government seemed to move in the matter unless the people were united in a protest-agitation; and warned that the responsibility for the consequences of such action would lie upon the authorities. (Mrt. 22.4.67)

Earlier, a resident of the Kolaba District on the mainland across the Mumbai Harbour had complained that the local educated youth found no place in the new industries coming up in the fast-developing towns of Roha and Khopoli in the Kolaba District. The letter further sounded a note of warning that unless the local people united speedily to safeguard their interests, they would be displaced by the immigrants not only in the matter of jobs but also in that of the local self-government and the Panchayat. (Mrm. 17.7.66)

Two years earlier, at the Bhoomi Pooja (land invocation ceremony) for the inauguration of the industrial estate at Roha, (Mrs.) Durgabai Deshmukh warned the people of Roha and Kolaba, documents a *Daily Maratha* Report, that the industrialists who came to develop industries in their district would reap the fruit of their invested monies two-fold, while the peasants deprived of their land with sweet promises of prosperity, would be left high and dry without any means of survival. The peasant likely to be deprived of his land, she maintained, must receive a guarantee of training and of a skilled job for himself and for his children, and that even the womenfolk must be assured of a wage. The benefits of the development of the area must first reach the deprived peasants, she declared. (Mrt. 15.2.64)

2. People's Responses

Jobs & Employment

A reader of the *Daily Maratha*, in his letter, appeals to P. K. Atre the founder-editor of this newspaper and, the erstwhile leader of the Samyukta Maharashtra Movement to lead an all-party movement to fight against the injustice perpetrated on Maharashtrians in employment and other walks of life in the very state capital. (Mrt. 15.7.66)

A letter demands an enquiry into the state of affairs at the Government Employment Exchange. Of the unemployed registered there, only those with connections and influence could get jobs, the letter complains. It declares a need for a struggle by the Marathi people, another following the earlier Samyukta Maharashtra Movement, to assert and obtain recognition to the Maharashtrian's fair claim to jobs in Mumbai. (Mrt. 10.9.66)

Four other letters express similar views in less intense terms. They speak of establishing organisations (Maharashtra Pragati Samiti, Bekari Nivaran Yojana, Unemployed Persons' Association and Maharashtra Hitvardhini) to protect and further Maharashtrian interests in employment and professions, 'to fight the menace of unemployment of the youth' and to 'raise the status of Maharashtrians in Mumbai.' (Mrt. 17.2.66, 7.9.66, 29.5.67, 8.6.67)

The political parties had to take note of the growing pressure of people's grievance and response. The SMS, which during the 1967 General Elections, supported Krishna Menon for the parliamentary seat had put up its own candidates for the State Legislature. Atre's *'Daily Maratha'* was a staunch supporter of the SMS. The following excerpts are from the Election Manifesto of the Sampoorna Maharashtra Samiti.

'The Congress Government in Maharashtra has been thoroughly unsuccessful in protecting Maharashtrians and their interests in Mumbai. The Maharashtrian is getting driven out of Mumbai – his own capital city. The State Government has been unable to give him protection in jobs or provide him inexpensive housing. The new factories started in Maharashtra at Varangaon or Ozar, under (Yeshwantrao's) Defence Ministry, have recruited 70% of persons from outside Maharashtra, for even unskilled jobs .... The responsibility for these sins lies with the Congress Government.'

'The sixteen-point programme of the SMS presented in the Manifesto, included the following major demands

(1) The integration of Goa with Maharashtra

(2) A larger share for Maharashtra in the nation's revenue resources.

(3) Seventy to eighty per cent of jobs in Mumbai's industries and offices, to be reserved for the Marathi people.

(4) Urgent installation of the Konkan Railway.'

Reports (Mrt. 11.2.67, 20.2.67)

About a year later, the *Daily Maratha* carried the following news item

"Peasants and Workers Party's Organisation for Maharashtra Youth"

'The PWP has begun its efforts at organising the Maharashtrian youth of Mumbai. With this goal in mind, the Party has launched a 'Maharashtra Yuvak Sangh'. It wants to ensure

(i) That unskilled labour in industries in Maharashtra be Maharashtrian

(ii) That Maharashtrians receive priority in skilled labour

(iii) That the administration of the State be urgently switch over to use the people's language i.e. Marathi

(iv) That knowledge of Marathi be obligatory for employment in Government and semi-Government establishments, in Mumbai

(v) That the expanding jurisdiction of Marathi is no threat to the commercial and industrial significance of Mumbai.' (Mrt. 12.4.68)

Entry to Business & Industry

From the reported speech of a leader of the Samyukta Maharashtra Movement and well-known economist (D.R. Gadgil), on the eve of the foundation of Maharashtra State

'It is a great day of fulfilment of the people's sacrifices and struggle. It is also a time for social stock taking. It is high time that Maharashtrians learn to look into the future and stop looking back into the past history of the community. If the Marathi people want to create a Maharashtra without want, they must cultivate practical thinking and a pragmatic approach. They can no longer afford to look down upon or keep away from the field of trade and commerce. Accumulation of capital is the first step towards building a rich Maharashtra. Maharashtrians will have to learn many things from other communities. And they must realise that building a good business or industry is also a service to the nation. However, Maharashtrians will have to remember that they have no other alternative to co-operative effort'. Report (Nvk. 28.4.1960)

From an editorial felicitating one of the founders of the Bank of Maharashtra, Shri Varde

'A Maharashtrian is normally expected to go in for a salaried job; he might go in for cultivating land. He may dabble in social work or even in politics; he may preach from the pedestal, or even write plays and get involved with dramatic activities. However, he is never supposed to touch business, commerce or industry! These were fields, according to Maharashtrian belief, only for the Gujaratis, the Marwaris, the Sindhis or the Punjabis. It is no wonder that Mumbai's trade, commerce and industry were controlled by these communities, while the Maharashtrian and (the rest of) Maharashtra, remained backward in these fields of human achievements. Credit goes to the founder of the Bank (Mr. Varde) for being one of those few who tried to remove the misconceptions of Maharashtrians and assisted them to settle into and make achievements, in these new fields. Ed. (Mrt. 2.12.65)

From editorial comments on advice by a leader of the co-operative movement and the-then Chairman of the Maharashtra State Congress Committee

'The non-Marathi communities of Mumbai have built many great edifices and public institutions and contributed to the city's wealth and well-being. There are hardly any great buildings or institutions associated with the name of Maharashtrians. It is a sad commentary on the economic achievement of the community.

Mere demands and agitations for 80% of jobs, might obtain for the Maharashtrian some employment, but will not earn him the status he aspires. A venture into the world of business and industry alone can earn him that position. However, he can make a small beginning only by building credit co-operative societies consisting of persons from middle and low-income groups, which would offer him loans and obtain Government assistance. Slow and steady pursuit of industry through co-operative effort alone is the key to a better future for the people.' Ed. (Nvk. 6.10.67)

The State Government's policy of prohibition had undergone a sea-change by 1968, and the Government decided to make open the sale of toddy all over Maharashtra including Mumbai. It planned to hold an auction for licenses for toddy-shops. (Mrt. 18.3.68)

The demand of the local toddy-tapper caste (Bhandari) of Mumbai was for priority consideration to the co-operative societies of the Bhandari community. The memorandum of the community made the following points

'The auction or the tender system for granting licences to toddy shops would earn money for the State Government. However, it would deprive the traditional community of toddy-tappers of their hereditary occupation. Also, it would put the toddy business into the hands of contractors and bootleggers who had become rich on illicit liquor during Prohibition. The licences for toddy shops, therefore, should be given without auction to those who were in this business during 1939-59, i.e. prior to the prohibition period. Twenty-five per cent of licences outside Mumbai as well should be reserved for the Bhandari community'. Report (Mrt. 8.8.68); Ed. (Mrt. 12.8.68)

A news report in 1969 stated that an auction of stalls for shopkeepers in the Worli market by the Municipal Corporation was postponed by the Shiv Sena demonstrations against it. The Shiv Sena demanded that 80% of the stalls be reserved for local retailers without an auction. A reader's letter in this connection observes

'It is a fact of common observation that the Maharashtrian retail trader is not economically strong enough to survive the cut-throat competition of the auction. The system of tenders and auctions find favour with those who already have made money and built up a capital. A Maharashtrian who has to depend on his hard labour alone, and has little capital for business, will never be able to make an entry in the business world where money alone seems to hold a key to open all doors. The local Maharashtrian, therefore, should be given priority in the case of municipal stalls.' Letter (Lks. 28.5.69)

The question of priority for the local people in respect of stalls in Municipal markets became a hotly-discussed, newsworthy subject. The question was referred to the Advocate-General of the State, who dismissed it as anti-Constitutional.

A *Navakal* editorial on the subject, severely criticised the unsympathetic attitude of the Advocate-General (Mr. Seervai) He had dismissed a bill regarding reservation of 80% of stalls for Maharashtrians, sponsored by the Shiv Sena in the Mumbai Municipal Corporation. The Advocate-General's dismissal was based on the following grounds (1) the lack of a precise criterion for the definition of Maharashtrian (both mother tongue and period of domicile were treated as criteria.) (ii) the mother tongue criterion, according to the Advocate-General, involved discrimination by language and went against Articles 14 and 15 of the Constitution.

The editorial observed that such a decision on the question of priority for locals, suggested that the Constitution favoured a kind of social Darwinism and protected the affluent and established interests. The editorial declared that if the Constitution could not protect the local poor and was going to be used in the service of established interests, it was high time that the nation applied itself to building up a new Constitution which would reflect the times' changing needs. Ed. (Nvk. 14.2.70)

Educational Opportunities

On 13.5.67, the following two news-items appeared in *Daily Maratha.*

i) Prabhu Seminary School in Danger

The century-old building of the Prabhu Seminary School (Marathi) stands in a dilapidated condition in Bhai Jivanji Lane at Girgaum. The impending monsoon is a great threat to the building and the lives of 500 pupils and their teachers normally accommodated in the building, would be in danger. (Mrt. 13.5.67)

ii) A Building for the Hindi Bhavan

A large edifice for the Hindi Bhavan is soon going to be built in Mumbai to accommodate a Hindi School run on the lines of convent-school system. Seth Govind Das, while giving this information to the press, suggested that the Hindi Bhavan would favour efforts for natural integration (through co-operation with the Gujarati and Marathi languages). (Mrt. 13.5.67)

Food and Related Issues

There are two entries, an article and a news report, dating from the sixties, relating to a proposed scheme of water supply for Mumbai from river Kalu near Kinhavali village in Thane district.

The article criticises the proposed scheme of utilising the waters of the Kalu for supplying the fast-growing metropolis of Mumbai was going to deprive several villages of their vital source of water. Further, the article complains, the scheme would uproot 39 villages and 15 thousand acres of land under paddy. It therefore, appeals to the citizens of Mumbai to look somewhere else for other sources of water for the city. Art. (Mrt. 23.2.63)

About a year later, the villagers of Kinhavali made a representation to the authorities and protested the proposed scheme. (Re. Mrt. 2.4.64)

Both these entries express apprehension and resentment at the prospect of being deprived of their water supply and land, to tend the needs of the metropolis.

A similar grievance found expression in an article written in 1968. It represents a case of a large number of farmers, ten thousand according to the article, who were being uprooted from their fertile paddy land in Igatpuri Taluka, by the proposed Upper Vaitarna dam for supplying water to Mumbai. (Art. Mrt. 11.4.65)

Editorials and reports also recorded criticism, however with little consequence. (Ed. Mrt. 16.4.68; Re.Mrt. 16.4.68; Art. Mrt. 2.5.68)

Two letters suggest that the situation in the metropolitan region outside Mumbai has not much improved. The two letters came from two villages in the adjacent districts of Kolaba and Thane.

One from the mainland across the harbour complains of the extreme scarcity of drinking water for the village with population of 1500. The other, from Thane district, tells the story of woes and difficulties of villagers in obtaining electricity for domestic use for a village community. (Letters, Mumbai Sakal 20.6.77, 20.6.77)

Appendix A. V

1. Electricity

Only 4.03% of villages in Maharashtra were electrified by 1964; comparable percentages for some other States during the period, were as follows

Kerala 64.17%, Tamil Nadu 49.7%, Andhra 12.6%, Gujarat 6.4%, Punjab 21.3%. However the States of West Bengal and Bihar were worse off than Maharashtra.

By 1970, Kerala had more than 75% of its villages electrified, while only 30% of Maharashtra's villages were electrified by this time. (See Table 13.3, Maharashtra At a Glance 1971-72, Mumbai, Government of Maharashtra)

2. Drinking Water

In 1964*, only 75% of villages in Maharashtra had drinking water supplied by tap, well or tubewell. As against this, 90% of Kerala villages, 89% of West Bengal villages and nearly 79% of Tamil Nadu (Madras) villages had these sources of drinking water supply. The percentage even of Rajasthan villages having these amenities was higher than that of Maharashtra villages.

At the end of the 4th five year plan, during 1973-74, 14000 of Maharashtra's 35851 villages, i.e. nearly 40% of the villages still had very inadequate or no water supply.

* See Table 7 (Percentage distribution of villages with electric supply and by States) and Table 8 (Percentage distribution of villages by source of drinking water and by States), in 'Tables with Notes on Indian Villages Some Important Results', 1970,

The National Sample Survey, Eighteenth Bound (Feb. 1963-January 1964) No. 172; New Delhi, Government of India

3. Road and Rail Mileage

Per 100 sq. miles area, Maharashtra had 28 miles of road-mileage while the national average was 37 miles per 100 sq. miles. Maharashtra's road-mileage per lakh of population was 83 miles compared to 103 (per lakh of population) for the country as a whole.

Maharashtra which boasts of the first train in Asia between Mumbai-Thane had only 2.69 rail mileage per 100 sq. miles which is less than the national average of 2.95 miles per 100 sq. miles. (Kulkarni M.P., 1973, *Transport Development in Economy of Maharashtra*, 1973, p. 346)

Appendix A-VI

An article appeared in the *Maratha* early in 1964 which discussed Maharashtrians' plight in detail. The article was a copy of a memorandum sent by its author (Govindrao Shirke) to the State's Chief Minister. Here is a resume of the main points of the article.

Suppression of Maharashtrians & Encroachment of Outsiders on the Capital

When in 1960, unlingual Maharashtra was formed with Mumbai as the capital, it brought about fresh expectations among the common people of Maharashtra.

However, the people discovered that their expectations had vanished into thin air, and that their aspirations had been smothered in their capital city. It could not be denied that the Maharashtrian still found it difficult to get employment in the city for, apparently, these in economic control did wish so. The percentage of Marathi people in various fields of employment, if taken into account, could perhaps prove this. Even in the case of textile mills, a field in which the Marathi labour predominated, Marathi persons faced difficulties in getting jobs.

With a daily influx of about 300 families, i.e. about 1500 out-of-State migrants, the native Maharashtrians were faced with increasingly keen competition.

Such an incessant flow of migrants also threatened to reduce the Maharashtrian percentage in Mumbai's population to a mere 40%. With the prospect of gram panchayat and rural development schemes succeeding as they seemed to in the districts of Maharashtra, this percentage had chances of further reduction. Maharashtrians could become a numerical minority in their own capital city.

While out-of-State migrants got a foothold in Mumbai the natives of the State turned back to the districts for want of housing and employment in Mumbai.

If the natives of the State were to get employment and housing on priority basis, this could hardly be called parochialism.

The influx of population into Mumbai had been so immense that even a large percentage of delinquents were to be found from among out-of-State migrants. This, of course, was no reflection on the general out-of-State population but merely that Maharashtrians living in their own society functioned under greater social control, and therefore, were not as prone to delinquency as people of other States, away from their own society and its social controls. Among beggars too, those from other States constituted a greater percentage.

Even among the slum-dwellers of Mumbai, there existed a large proportion of non-Marathi persons. Most slums had come up illegally on Municipal, State and Central Government lands, but eventually attained legality under Slum Improvement Schemes. In short, the municipality and State Government had eventually to spend from its own coffers to legalise the slums and provide them with a minimum of amenities at nominal cost. 'Outsiders' or out-of-State migrants, thus, in due course of time were well-provided for at the cost of the State exchequer.

In the State Housing Board's tenements, there existed a very large proportion of non-Maharashtrians. The 'local' man often had to wait for as much as five or six years before his turn came while it often happened that a new migrant found a residence within the short span of 2 to 6 months. The benefits of co-operative housing societies too, more often accrued to the non-Maharashtrian.

To remedy the situation the article made these suggestions:

(1) Regional and Mumbai Employment Exchanges to be placed under an efficient Maharashtrian officer to look after the interests of the natives of the State.

(2) Maharashtrians to be given priority even in the Housing Board tenements.

(3) Loans to co-operative housing societies to be granted only if they had a certain percentage of Maharashtrian members.

These measures, the writer believed, would aid in protecting in the interests of the native community as well as discouraging the influx of out-of-State migrants. Since it was the duty of the State Government to safeguard the interests of the native community, the measures suggested could not in truth be considered parochial. (Mrt. 5.6.64)

The 1st of May, 1964 being Maharashtra Day and May Day, the *Maratha* published an article. Along important introduction to this article observed.

Mumbai only nominally belonged to Maharashtra as its capital. The reasons often cited for the Maharashtrian's condition in Mumbai were his ineffective performance in business and industry, his lack at making adjustments and his apathy to work hard as an employee, etc. However, the writing asserted that the real reason lay in the historical situation and the political forces in Mumbai impeding Maharashtrians. Had not the Maharashtrian proved himself worthy in co-operative business and entrepreneurship? If so, given capital and opportunity, he could even be a success in Mumbai's business world. (Mrt. 1.5.64)

Another article published in the *Maratha* in mid-1964, discussed the problems caused to the Maharashtrian community by unforeseen migration of out-of-State population. It appeals to Atre, the founder-editor of the *Maratha*, to assume leadership and guide the Marathi community in the struggle for redressal of injustices and in its quest for security and status in Mumbai, the capital of their State.

Encroachment of Outsiders on Mumbai

The article observed that the very mention of 'encroachment on Mumbai by 'outsiders'' had been treated as sacrilege and often dubbed as parochial. To avoid the disparagement of being called parochial, 'the Maharashtrian' was often defined as 'one who lived in Maharashtra' rather than "one who spoke Marathi – the language of Maharashtra region'. However, such clever jugglery of words, a subterfuge to avoid criticism, only evaded the real issue, the article observed. The article therefore declares that it intended considering the problems of Maharashtrian i.e.

of speakers of Marathi language, who traditionally lived in the Maharashtra region.

The article then pointed out that the Maharashtrian community's preoccupation with itself, its concern for safeguarding its own interests could not be described as 'parochial' since the very survival of the community in the city was at stake. Only those with vested interests, the encroachers themselves, would use this appellation for Maharashtrians on this count.

For example, to take the issue of the hawkers; several hawkers had settled themselves on footpaths and sidewalks in the Fort area. Day and night they occupied these pavements. The article observed that their number increased manifold during the previous few years and if this number was not curbed, the pedestrian was in danger of being totally ousted from footpaths for good. A majority of these hawkers were Muslims from Kerala. They sold smuggled goods, often even without licence, the article complained.

After a hot debate in the Municipal Council, if and when rule of law was imposed on these hawkers, the hawkers approached friend George Fernandes and under his leadership took out protest-march demanding that hawkers be given licences or jobs and employment, to win public sympathy. However, was it a responsibility of the Mumbai Municipal Corporation or of the State Government to provide a hawker's licence or a job to these migrant-hawkers, just because they decided to migrate to Mumbai? Was it the Kerala Government's responsibility or Maharashtra Government's responsibility to provide them jobs, the article asks.

The issue was at vital as that of introducing Marathi in the State and civic administration, the article opined. It observed that it would be interesting to go into the question of proportion of Marathi and non-Marathi hawkers who obtained licences, just as it was interesting to find out the proportion of Marathi and the non-Marathi among the employees of the State Government Housing Board as well among the tenants of the Board's housing.

The article then went on to make another point. It narrates that a well known company of all-India repute with its head office at Mumbai received a letter of complaint from a Southern

State that the company gave very few appointments to citizens of that State. On the other hand, the Government of Maharashtra hesitated even to enquire about the proportion of Marathi/non-Marathi in various offices and establishments in Mumbai.

Y.B. Chavan once mentioned of feeling proud, the article narrates, that citizens from all over India looked upon Mumbai as their home. Theoretically speaking, it is a situation of which the Maharashtrian should feel proud of. But how could he, when he was feeling suffocated and smothered in his home - his State capital - by the overwhelming presence of outsiders, when he himself felt like an alien in his own home-State?

This outspoken satement was not a product of parochialism, the article asserts. It further asks: Would any other (linguistic) community have liked to be dominated by others, outsiders in every walk of life, in their own home State?

The article asks: How did we (Maharashtrians) allow this to happen? Because we accepted and abided by the current norms without complaining or questioning the propriety; we accepted that the management and/or the owners recruited persons of their own communities. For instance, once we believed that the Parsi would more easily get a job in LIC than a Maharashtrian we stopped rebelling against these practices. Later, however, we realised that this was an unfair practice in a democratic set-up. The norms of recruitment to public sector jobs ought to change and the native or the local ought to get better representation. If these norms and patterns of recruitment behaviour did not change, this clash of interests was likely to be blow up into a very serious conflict.

The article observes that it was therefore high time that the Government appointed a commission for objective inquiry into these grievances. However it always took a long time to move the Government in any matter. It was necessary that the opposition parties build pressure on the Government for solution of these problems. The article ends with an appeal to Atre, the editor of the *Maratha*, to bring together the opposition parties for raising a voice against unjust encroachment on the Maharashtrian's rights. (Mrt. 5.6.64)

Appendix A-VII

The Samyukta Maharashtra Movement and its Objectives

The major goal of the Samyukta Maharashtra Movement (SMM) was the integration of all the Marathi speaking areas into a single State. (Samyukta Maharashtra Publication, n.d.p.20) The major battle of the movement was fought for the inclusion of Mumbai City in the proposed linguistic State of Maharashtra.

The protagonists of Samyukta Maharashtra – the Samyukta Maharashtra Samiti (the movement's organisational arm) and its predecessor organisation, the Samyukta Maharashtra Parishad, had claimed that the city of Mumbai was an integral part of the geographical region of Maharashtrs, of its economy and culture.

The claim, however, was challenged and refused by various Commissions (the Dar Commission, the J.V.P. Committee, the States Reorganisation Commission) appointed by the Central Government and Central leadership, between 1948 and 1954. Prestigious persons, organisations and representatives of powerful economic interests, like the Congress Government elite, the Mumbai P.C.C., the Gujarat P.C.C., the Indian Merchants' Chamber and the Mumbai Citizen's Committee, (earlier the Mumbai Committee), had arrayed themselves in opposition to the demand for the inclusion of Mumbai in Maharashtra. (See Stern 1970, Phadke 1973) The English-language press also, by and large, was antipathetic to the demand. (Phadke 1973, Pp. 187-193; 290-292, Kunte Prabhakar, March 1956, Pp. 9-10)

The 'cosmopolitanism' of Mumbai, in other words, the heterogeneity or linguistic plurality of Mumbai was the lever which the opponents of 'Samyukta Maharashtra' used to press for a separate Mumbai City, independent of and outside the proposed State of Maharashtra.

However, inclusion of Mumbai City as the State capital of the new State of Maharashtra in 1960 was a formal acceptance and vindication of the Marathi community's claim over this metropolis. Implied in this claim, were other expectations brought to consciousness by the long-drawn movement, occasionally articulated by the Samyukta Maharashtra Samiti. The demands made by the Shiv Sena regarding priority for the Marathi speaking in jobs and housing in Mumbai and for priority to the Marathi language especially, seem remotely or indirectly, implicit in the objectives of the S.M.S (for the unilingual Maharashtra State).

The Communist-led Sampoorna Maharashtra Samiti (SPMS) – the rump of the erstwhile SMS – in its 1967 election manifesto had included similar demands for priority to Maharashtrians in Mumbai. In the context of the controversy over the issue, S.A. Dange and P.K. Atre, both of whom were well-known leaders of the SMM, had supported introduction of Marathi in Civic and State administration and also priority for the Marathi speaking in jobs and housing. (Mrt. 25.1.67, See Ch. III)

These facts are a pointer to the links between the popular demands for priority championed by the Shiv Sena and the objectives of the SMM. For a clearer evidence of such links, we present below various relevant points from the Memorandum of the Samyukta Maharashtra Parishad to the States Reorganisation Commission.

In the context of the question of introducing the regional language in civic and State administration, the S.M. Parishad, in its memorandum, made the following important observation

1. 'The reorganisation.....raises no constitutional or political problems of its own. There is one direction in which, no doubt, certain transitional difficulties will have to be faced by migrants in all States. This is due to a transformation which is due to take place throughout India in near future. With the reduction in the importance of English in Indian administration, one of the factors which made for ease of movement of the intellectual proletariat will vanish and migrants from one linguistic State to another will not, in future, be able to neglect the regional language as they used to formerly. The regional language will more and more predominate in State administration and knowledge of it will become essential to most who want to follow any employment within the region. This must be considered to be on the whole a beneficial movement. Hitherto, in spite of large

movements of intellectuals from one region to another, there has arisen no effective understanding between various parts because, with the prevalence of English, the migrants did not feel called upon to familiarise themselves with the language, habits and ideas of the people of the regions to which they had migrated. The new requirement, however, beneficial in the long run, may, no doubt, create some difficulties in the transitional period. It may also create hardship wherever large linguistic minorities are permanently settled, unless a liberal linguistic policy is followed by all the States'. (S.M. Parishad Publication, 1954, Pp. 34-35)

2. In reply to the argument that Mumbai was not only the economic centre of Maharashtra but also served the needs of a large area and of the country or that it was the nation's major port or a centre of concentrated business activity, the SMM stated that these points were no arguments for treating Mumbai in a special manner. The memorandum of the SMM pointed out that certain States had a city or cities which served as economic nuclei for areas beyond the concerned States.

If Mumbai is to be separated from its immediate neighbourhood the same must happen to Calcutta, Jamshedpur, Ahmedabad, and to Madras, Hyderabad or Kanpur'. (S.M. Parishad, 1954, Mumbai, p. 68, Pp.74-75)

The stress of the above statement was on adhering to the principle of like treatment to all economically important urban centres. If knowledge of the regional language was a condition for employment and priority was to be given to the residents of the States elsewhere, the same rules would apply in the case of Mumbai. There was no need for treating Mumbai 'in a special manner' or for a set of different rules for it. (In other words, the existing plurality of Mumbai need not be a ground for furthering that plurality).

The SMM's memorandum had also pointed out that not only were all trade and business interests of the Maharashtra area concentrated in Mumbai city but also it was the chief place of employment for vast numbers of peasants and labourers in many districts of Maharashtra - especially from the Konkan, and the districts of Satara and Ahmednagar. The memorandum further observed that the vast bulk of the labouring population in Mumbai being Marathi, fulfiling their social and material needs like housing, was of vital interest to healthy social life not only in Mumbai city itself, but also in a large number of rural areas all over Maharashtra. The memorandum maintained that Mumbai was not only 'the largest urban centre of Maratha cultural, intellectual, etc., life' but also 'the focus of the economic life of Maharashtra'. (S.M. Parishad, The Memorandum to the States Reorganisation Commission, 1954, p. 61)

The Shiv Sena demand for priority for the native of the State, the Marathi speaking, in jobs and housing seems consistent with these expectations articulated in the memorandum, and in fact, may be said to emanate from these expectations.

3. In reply to the contention that the non-Marathi (those speaking languages other than Marathi) outnumbered the Marathi population in Mumbai and therefore Mumbai city should be treated in a special manner and not as part of Maharashtra, the memorandum further commented that such an argument 'will strike at the very root of the peaceful formation and functioning of the federal union. The argument would imply that any people who allow the settlement of speakers of other languages within their territory run the danger of losing parts of their territories in course of time'. The contention thus had implications with 'grave political import', warned the memorandum.* (S.M. Parishad, 1954, Pp. 67-68)

Needless to say that this argument by the SMP, about the territory of a linguistic region, easily extends to and holds good in case of the regional language. If a people allow the speakers of languages other than their language to settle within their

---

* While being outspoken in its claim on Mumbai for the Marathi speaking, the SMP memorandum had room for safeguards for the legitimate interests of the linguistic minorities. 'In a federal union peacefully and amicably formed, liberty of intercourse and settlement for citizens of various States is a sine-qua-non. Wherever a large number of speakers of languages other than the regional language of the State reside and settle and form important linguistic minorities, such measures relating to their interests...can be provided for...' (S.M. Parishad Memorandum, Ip. 67-68)

linguistic State, they run the danger of reducing their language to a second-class position. Not only would they be reluctant to let others settle in their region but might oppose it tooth and nail. **

Thus, the Shiv Sena demand for priority for the Marathi language in civic and State administration because it was the regional language, was no different from the aspirations and apprehensions articulated in the SMM memorandum.

4. While discussing the undesirable effects of the proposed separation of Mumbai as an independent or centrally administered unit, the SMP had expressed the apprehension that such an arrangement would cause hindrance to the city's fuller integration with the surrounding region of the Maharashtra hinterland. Moreover, such an arrangement, feared the memorandum, would lead to suppression of the Marathi language in the city's civic and general administration, and the federal language (Hindi/ English) would predominate.

The SMP in its memorandum had warned that in the event of the independent existence of Mumbai city 'there emerges a possibility of Marathi not being recognised as the main regional language of the city'. This possibility, according to the memorandum of the SMP, underlined 'the vital importance...of the whole question of the status of Mumbai city' for Maharashtra.

It should be clear from this, that the struggle against the separation of Mumbai from Maharashtra and for its inclusion in Maharashtra was also as much a struggle for the maintenance of the Marathi language as the major regional language of the city and for saving it from being suppressed under predominance of English or Hindi. The SMP feared that a separation of Mumbai from Maharashtra would endanger the very 'cultural existence

** During the controversy over Mumbai, Ambedkar, with reference to the non-Marathi majority in Mumbai pointed out that Mumbai was the home of the Maharashtrian community as of no other linguistic community. He further observed: 'Again it is not realised that the increase in the non-Marathi speaking people in Mumbai city is due to the absence of a local law restricting citizenship. If Mumbai State had had such a law this influx into Mumbai from all parts of India could have been halted and the Maharashtrian majority retained'. (B.R. Ambedkar, 1955, Chpt. 7-III, p. 23) and development' of the Marathi community, by separating it from its source of sustenance. A centrally-administered Mumbai 'would orient the whole administrative and educational life of Mumbai city in such a manner' that the large urban concentration of Maharashtrians 'would be cut off from the living contact with its own language, literature and culture'. (S.M. Parishad, 1954, Pp. 70-71)

The fears of the SMP about 'the whole administrative and educational life becoming oriented' to suppressing Marathi, were earlier noted in our content data and also observed from the various factors responsible for it - like the changing economic structure with its expanding tertiary sector and emphasis on training for industrial jobs; increasing migration and enlarging heterogeneity and plurality of the city's population; and the consequent emphasis on English medium instruction. In this context, the warning given by the memorandum, that such a development 'would be violently opposed and deeply resented by the speakers of Marathi' seems to ring with prophetic truth in retrospect.

We have taken the liberty to elaborate on the case presented by the Samyukta Maharashtra Parishad only to point out the close relation between its objectives and the objectives of the Shiv Sena movement.

BIBLIOGRAPHY

Official Publications and Reports

Barve Committee, 1959,
(1) Report of Study Group on Greater Mumbai
(2) Reports of the Panels (Housing and Housing Finance panel), Appointed by the Study group for Greater Mumbai, Mumbai, Government of Mumbai

Mumbai Committee, n.d. Memorandum Submitted to Linguistic Provinces Commission (Re Regrouping of Provinces), Mumbai Mumbai committee, C/o. Indian Merchants' Chamber

Mumbai Municipal Corporation, 1957-58, Brief Report on the Survey of Old Buildings in City, Mumbai, S. M. Corporation

Municipal Corporation of Greater Mumbai, 1964, Report on the Development Plan for Greater Mumbai, Mumbai, B. M. Corporation

Directorate (formerly Bureau) of Economics and Statistics, 1965, 1967, 1974, 1976, Maharashtra An Economic Review (1964-65), (1966-67), (1973-74), (1975-76), Mumbai, Government of Maharashtra

Directorate of Education (Maharashtra State), 1962, 1969, 1974, 1975,
(1) Education in Maharashtra Statistical Abstract 1961-62,
(2) Education in Maharashtra Statistical Epitome as on 31st March 1966,
(3) Education in Maharashtra Statistical Abstract 1970-71,
(4) Education in Maharashtra Statistical Abstract 1971-72, Pune, Government of Maharashtra.

Directorate of Employment (Government of Maharashtra), 1966, Mumbai
Labour Market; Mumbai, Government of Maharashtra

Gadgil committee (Committee for Regional Plane), 1965, Report of The Committee Appointed for Regional Plans for Mumbai, Panvel And Pune Regions, Mumbai, Government of Maharashtra

Gazette of India Extraordinary, 31.8.1956, States Reorganisation Act, Part II-Section I, Sr. No. 45, 1956, New Delhi, Manager of Publications, Government of India, 1956.

Indian Council of social Welfare (Mumbai), Nov. 1974, Report of the Seminar on 'Prevention of Begging and Rehabilitation of beggars', Mumbai, Research and Documentation Centre, Social Welfare and Development, I.C.S.W., Mumbai

Indian Merchants' Chamber, IMC Diamond Jubilee Souvenir, 1967, Mumbai

Institute of Town Planners, December 1975, Twenty-fourth Annual Town and Country Planning Seminar-Souvenir, Mumbai, Seminar Organising Committee The Institute of Town Planners, India.

Maharashtra at a Glance 1971-72, Mumbai, Government of Maharashtra

Maharashtra Gazette Extraordinary, 31.3.73, The Mumbai Rents, Hotel and Lodging House Rates Control (Amendment) Act, 1973, Mumbai, Government of Maharashtra

The National Sample Survey, Eighteenth Round (Feb. 1963-Jan. 1964), No. 172, Tables with Notes on Indian Villages Some Important Results; 1970, New Delhi, Government of India

Programme Evaluation Organisation, 1968, Regional Variations in Social Development and Levels of Living A Study of the Impact of Plan Programmes, New Delhi, Planning Commission, Government of India.

Report of the Mathadi Labour Enquiry Committee, 1965, Mumbai, Government of Maharashtra

Samyukta Maharashtra Parishad, 1954, Reorganisation of States in India with particular reference to the Formation of Maharashtra Memorandum submitted to the States Reorganisation Commission, Mumbai, S. M. Parishad

Samyukta Maharashtra Publication, n.d., 'United Maharashtra' Mumbai,

Karanatak Publishing House

Tekchand Report Report of the Study Team on Prohibition, 1964 Vol. I and Vol. II, Delhi, Planning Commission, Government of India

Census of India Reports

Census of India, 1961

Vol.I-India, Part II-A General Population Tables

Vol.I-India, part Ii-B General Economic Tables

Vol.I-India, Part II-C Cultural and Migration Tables

Vol. X Maharashtra, Part X (1-C) Greater Mumbai Special Migration Tables

Vol. X Maharashtra, Part X (1-B) Greater Mumbai Census Tables (General)

Vol. XI Mysore, Part II-C (ii) Migration Tables

Census of India, 1971

Series I – Pt.II-C (i) Social and Cultural Tables

Maharashtra State Legislative Assembly Debates

1962	Vol.6	Pt.II	no. 9.
1964	Vol.12	Pt.I, Pt.II	nos. 8, 24.
	Vol.13	Pt.I	
1965	Vol.15	Pt. I, Pt.II	no.6.
	Vol.17	Pt.I.	
1966	Vol.18	Pt.II	nos. 16, 18, 19 and 26.
1967	Vol.20	Pt.II	no. 5.
	Vol.21	Pt.II	nos. 29, 30, 35 and 39.
1969	Vol.26	Pt.II	no. 2, 3.
	Vol.27	Pt.II	no. 44.
1970	Vol.29	Pt.II	no. 25
1972	Vol.35	Pt.II	no. 28.

Rajya Sabha Official Report

18.2.69, Vol. LXVII no. 2, C.147 and 176

Lok Sabha Debates

1969 Vol. XXIV nos. 2, 3, 4.

1972 Vol. XXII nos. 25 to 32.

Other Works

Ambedkar B.R., 1948, Maharashtra as a Linguistic province Statement Submitted to the Linguistic Provinces Commission. Mumbai, Thacker and Co., Ltd.

Ambedkar B.R., 1955, Thoughts on Linguistic States. Aurangabad

Anand Sudhir, May 1971, (Mimeo), Rural-Urban Migration An Economic Study. Harvard, Harvard University

Anderson Neis (Ed.), 1969, studies in Multilingualism (International Studies in sociology and Social-Anthropology – Vol.VIII) Leiden, E.J. Brill.

Antulay A.R., 1968, Mahajan Report Uncovered. Mumbai, Allied Publishers Private Limited.

Balkrishna Kulamarva, 1966, A Portrait of Mumbai's Underworld. Mumbai, Manaktalas

Barnouw Erik and Krishnaswamy S., 1963, Indian Film, Mumbai, Orient, Longman

Berelson Bernard, 1952, Content Analysis in Communication Research. Illinois, The Free Press Glencoe

Berkowitz Leonard, 1975, A Survey of Social Psychology. Hinsdale, Illinois, The Dryden Press.

Besant Annie, 1915, How India Wrought for Freedom The Story of Indian National Congress told from official Records. Adyar, Theosophical Society, Madras

Bhattacharya Ardhendu and Nalpat Madhav, 1972 (Mimeo), 'A Decade of Industrial Dispersal from Greater Mumbai

Bose Ashish, 1973, Studies in India's Urbanisation 1901-1971. Mumbai, Tata-McGraw Hill Publishing Co. Ltd.

Blaug Mark, Layard Richard, and Woodhall Maureen, 1969, The Causes of Graduate Unemployment in India, London, Allen Lane Penguin Press.

Blumer Harold, 1957, 'Collective Behaviour' In Gittler J.B. (Ed.), Review of Sociology. New York, Wiley and Sons, 1957

Board Christophar, Chroley Richard J. Haggett P. and Stoddard D.R. (Eds.), 1976, Progrcss in Gcography International Reviews of current Research (Vol.8)

London, Edward Arnold.

Bondurant Joan, 1958, Regionalism Versus Provincialism a Study in Problems of Indian National Unity. (mimeo) Berkeley, University of California. (Institute of International Studies) Indian Press Digests-Monograph Series No. 4

Bulsara J.F., June 1965, 'Future of India' In Marg, Vol.XVIII No. 3, Mumbai

Bulsara J.F., 1970, Patterns of Social Life in Metropolitan Areas. Mumbai, Research Programmes Committee, Planning Commission (New Delhi)

Cantril Hadley, 1965, The Pattern of Human concerns. New Brunswick, Rutgers University Press.

Caravan, Jan. 2, 1978, An Interview with Bal Thackeray ('Shiv Sena')

Cohen P.S., 1970, Modern Social Theory London, Heinemann Educational Books Limited

Dasgupta Jyotindra, 1970, Language Conflict and National Development Group Politics and National Language Policy Barkley, University of California Press.

Dasgupta H.N., 1946, Indian National Congress, vol.1, Kolkata, J.K. Dasgupta Publication.

Davies James C., 1962, 'Toward a theory of Revolution' in American Sociological Review, Vol.XXVII (Feb. 1962), 5-19.

Davies James C., 1969, 'The J-Curve of Rising and Declining Satisfactions as a Cause of some Great Revolutions and Contained Rebellion', in Graham Hugh Davis and Gurr Ted, (Eds.), 1969

Desai A.R., and Pillai S. Devadas, 1972, A Profile of an Indian Slum. Mumbai, University of Mumbai

Desai A. R., 1976, Social background of Indian Nationalism. Mumbai, Popular Prakashan (Paperback)

Deshmukh C. D., 1972, Aspects of Development. Delhi, Young Asia Publication

Deshpande S. H., (Ed.), 1973, Economy of Maharashtra. Pune, Samaj Prabodhan Sanstha.

Dhekney B. R., 1973, 'State Finances' In Deshpande S. H. (Ed.), 1973.

Dobbin Christine, 1972, Urban Leadership in Western India Politics and Communities in Mumbai City 1940-1845 London, Oxford University Press

Dollard John, Miller N. E., Doob L.W., Mowerer O. H. and Sears R.H., 1939, Frustration and Aggression. New Haven Connecticut, Yale University Press

Duchacek, Ivo D., 1970, comparative Federalism The Territorial Dimension of Politics. New York, Holt Rinehart and Winston Incorporation

Eisenstadt S. N., 1969, Modernisation Protest and Change. New Delhi, Prentice-hall of India Pvt. Ltd.

Ellefsen Richard A., 1962, 'City-Hinterland Relationships in India', in turner Roy (Ed.), 1962, India's Urban Future, Mumbai Oxford University Press

Pickett Lewis P. Jr., 1971, 'The Politics of regionalism' in Pacific Affairs, Vol.XIIV no. 2, Summer 1971.

Freedman, Robert (Ed.), 1971, Marx on Economics Middlesex, England, Penguin Books Ltd.

Friedmann John and Wulff Robert, 1976, The Urban Transition Comparative Studies of newly industrialising societies Christopher and Associates (Eds.), 1976.

Forrest George W. 1884, Selections from the Minutes and Other Official Writings of the Hon. Mountstuart Elphinstone, Governor of Mumbai. London.

Gadgil D. R., Concluding Address (Mimeo), October 1968, Metropolitan regional Planning Seminar at Pune
Metropolitan Regional Planning Boards, Mumbai, Pune and Nagpur

Gadgil D.R., 1972, Planning and Economic Policy in India, (Gokhale Institute Studies no. 59), Pune, Gokhale Institute of Politics and Economics

Gangadharan K.K., March 1970, 'Shiv-Sena Anti Social Movement', in Mainstream March 28, 1970, Vol. VIII, no. 30

Gagadharan K.K., Dec. 1970, 'The Shiv-Sena' in Sociology of Revivalism. New Delhi, Kalamkar Prakashan

Gogate Sudha, 1971, 'Mumbaiteil Bhinna-Bhashik Navagat va Tyanchi Mumbaishi Julnee' (Review Article on Neighbourhoods and migrants, 1970, TISS), Samaj Prabodhan Patrika, Vol. VIII no. 40, Pune, Samaj Prabodhan Sanstha.

Goodspeed D. J., 1962, The Conspiratiors A Study of the Coup D'Etat. New York, the Viking Press.

Gore M. S., 1970, Migrants and Neighbourhoods Two aspects of Life in a Metropolitan City Mumbai, Tata Institute of Social Sciences

Graham Hugh Davis, and Gurr Ted, 1969, The History of Violence in America Historical and Comparative Perspectives (A Report Submitted to the National Commission on Causes and Prevention of Violence) New York, Bantom Books

Gurr Ted, 1970, Why men Rebel. Princeton, New Jersey, Princeton University Press

Gurr Ted, 1972, 'Sources of Rebellion in Western Societies Some Quantitative Evidence' in short James F. Jr., and Wolfgang/Marvin E. (Eds.) Chicago, Aldine, Athanton

Gusfield Joseph R., 1968, 'The Study of Social Movements' in International Encyclopedia of Social Sciences Vol.14 The MacMillan Company and the Free Press

Gusfield Joseph R., 1970, Protest, Reform and Revolt A Reader in Social Movement New York, Wiley and Sons

Harrison Selig. 1960, India The Most Dangerous Decades. Madras, Oxford University Press, (Also Princeton Univ. Press)

Heberle Rudolf, 1968, 'Types and Functions of social movements', in International Encyclopedia of Social Sciences Vol. 14, MacMillan Company and the Free Press

Hoffer Eric, 1966, The True Believer Thoughts on the Nature of Mass Movements New York, Perennial Library Edition, Harper and Row, (First Published in 1951, New York Harper)

Honningman John, 1959, The World of Man New York, Harper and Brothers

Jackson J. A., 1969, Migration, Cambridge, Cambridge University Press.

Jayaraman R., 1964, 'Linguistic Groups in Urban Setting', in Economic Weekly, Vol. XVII no. 42, (24.10.64)

Jensen Merril, 1965, Regionalism in America. Madison and Milwaukee, The Univ. of Wisoonsin Press, Paperback, (First Published in 1951)

Joshi Heather and Joshi Vijay, 1976, Surplus Labour and the city A Study of Mumbai, Delhi and Mumbai, Oxford University Press

Joshi Ram, Nov. 1970, 'The Shiv-Sena A Movement in Search of Legitimacy', In *Asian Survey*, Nov. 1970, Vol. X no. 11, Berkley, University of California

Kapilacharya, 1967, Shiv-Sena Speaks (Official Statement), Mumbai, Thackeray Bal, *Marmik* Cartoon Weekly Office.

Karnik V. B., Strikes in India, 1967, Mumbai, Manaktalas.

Katzenstein Mary, 1973, 'Origins of Nativism: The Emergence of Shiv-Sena in Mumbai' in Asian Survey, April-1973, Vol. XIII, no.4 1975, 'Politics of Population Movements The Case of Mumbai', in Economic and Political Weekly, Vol.X, no.5, Mumbai

Khanna K.C., Feb. 1968, 'Mumbai's Pressing Problems' in The Times of India, 13.2.68, Mumbai

Khanna K.C., Sept. 1976, 'Jobs for the rural poor in Maharashtra', lead story in The Times of India. 20.9.76, Mumbai

Kulkarni A.G., 1968, A Study of Political Parties in Maharashtra with Special Reference to the Period 1947-62 Pune, University of Pune Doctoral Thesis, Dept. Politics

Kulkarni G.S., and Kulkarni A.P., 1968, Community Cost of Industrial Location at Mumbai and Nasik, Mumbai, SICOM Publication

Kulkarni K. B., 1956, Adhunik Marathi Gadyachi Utkranti, (Revolution of Modern Marathi Prose), Mumbai, K. B. Kulkarni.Kulkarni M. R., 1973, 'Transport Development', In Deshpande S.H. (Ed.), Economy of Maharashtra, Pune, Samaj Prabodhan sanstha

Kulkarni P.B., 1959, Namdar Nana Shankar Shet yanche Charitra, (Biography of Nana Shankar Shet), Mumbai, Nana Shankar Shet Charitra Prakashan Samiti.

Kunte prabhakar, 1956, Storm Over Mumbai (Pamphlet), Mumbai.

Lakdawala D.T., Sandesara J.C., Kothari V.N., and Nair P.A., 1963, Work, Wages and Well-Being in an Indian metropolis Economic Survey of Mumbai City Mumbai, University of Mumbai

Lasswell Harold and Kaplan Abraham, 1952, Power and Society A Framework for Political Inquiry. London, Boutledge and Kegan Paul (First Published in U.S.A., New Haven, Yale University Press (1950)

Lasswell Harold and Leites Nathan, 1968, Language of Politics Studies in Quantitative Semantics. The M.I.T. Press (Paperback Edition 1968)

Linton Ralph, 1943, 'Nativistic Movement' In American Anthopologist. Vol. XLV (April 1943)

Lee E.S., 1969, 'Theory of Migration' In Jackson J.A. (Ed.) 1969.

Maharashtra Economic Development Council (M.E.D.C.), 1976, Regional Imbalances in Maharashtra. (Publication no.40) Mumbai, M.E.D.C.

Malik Hirji, 1970, 'The Private Armies' in The Illustrated Weekly of India, 15.3.1970, Mumbai.

Marathi Natya Parishad, 1961, The Marathi Theatre 1843-1960. Mumbai, Popular Book Depot

Massolor J.C., 1974, Towards Nationalism Group Affiliations and the Politics of Public Associations in Nineteenth Century Western India. Mumbai, Popular Prakashan.

Mayur Rashmi (Ed.), 1975, Whither Mumbai? Planning for a Habitable City. Mumbai, Mumbai Pradesh Congress Committee.

Merton R.K., 1959, Social Theory and Social Structure. (Revised and Enlarged Edition), Glencoe, The Free Press of Glencoe.

Morris M.D., 1965, The Emergence of an Industrial Labour Force in India A Study of the Mumbai Cotton Mills. Berkley, University of California Press.

Murdoch John, 1898, Indian National Congress The Resolutions of its Thirteen Sessions, Indian Progress Since its Establishment, with Suggestions for its increased Usefulness (Pamphlet) Madras 3, Tract Depot.

Mythili K.L., 1959, A Socio-Ecological Study of an Migrant Community. Unpublished Doctoral Thesis, University of Mumbai, Department of Sociology, Mumbai

Naik J. V., 1975-76, 'An Early Appraisal of British Colonial Policy' in *The Journal Of University of Mumbai (Art)*, Vol. XLIV and XLV, Nos. 80-81, Mumbai.

Naik R.D. 1971, Profiles of Urban Youth Seeking Employment. Mumbai, Tata Institute of Social Sciences

Nair K. S., 1975, A Regional community in an Urban Setting Doctoral thesis, Dept. of Sociology and Anthropology, University of Pune, Pune

Nair P.A., 1968, Employment Market in an Industrial Metropolis. (A Survey of Educated Unemployment in Mumbai) Mumbai, Lalvani Publishing House.

Naoroji Dadabhoy, 9.3.1864, Speech at 'The Public meeting to Vote a Testimonial to the Hon. J. Sankersett' in Nilaji Balkrishna (Ed.), 1867

Natrajan S., 1962, A History of the Press in India. Mumbai, Asia Publishing House, Mumbai

Nilaji Balkrishna, (Ed.), 1867, The Late Hon'ble Jagannath Sankarsett A collection of Obituary and Other Notices Mumbai, The Mumbai City Press

Odum Howard W., 1965, 'The Promise of Regionalism' in Jensen Merril, (Ed.), 1965

Operations Research Group, 1972, Study on Economic Activity Profile for Mumbai. (Memeo) Baroda, ORG.

Overstreet Gene D. and Windmiller Marshal, 1959, Communism in India Berkley, University of California, Berkley and Los Angeles

Pendse D.R., 1973, 'Balanced Regional Development' in Deshpande S. H. (Ed.), 1973

Phadke Y.D., 1973, The Samyukta Maharashtra Movement and Congress Party, Doctoral Thesis, Dept. of Politics. University of Mumbai, Mumbai

Pinge S.M., 1960 Europeanacha Marathicha Abhyas va seva. Mumbai, Marathi Sanshodhan Mandal, Mumbai Marathi Granth Sangrahalaya

Priyolkar A. K., 1971, Dr. Bhau Daji Vyakti, Kal va kartritva (Biography of Dr. Bhau Daji) Mumbai, Mumbai Marathi Sahitya Sangh.

Priyolkar A. K., 1974, Hindustanche Don Darvaze (Two Gateways of India), Mumbai, The Goa Hindu association

Punekar Vijaya B., 1974, Assimilation A Study of North Indians in Bengaluru Mumbai, Popular prakashan

Ramachandran P., 1972, Pavement Dwellers in Mumbai City. Mumbai, Tata Institute of Social Sciences

Ramchandran P. and Pillai Devdas, 1972, The Mumbai Rent Act and Housing Production. (TISS-Series No. 24), Mumbai, Tata Institute of Social Sciences

Randive Vasant, Feb. 1956, Unhappy Mumbai A Report to Pandit Nehru (Pamphlet) Mumbai

Ray Amal, 1970, Tension Areas in India's Federal System. Kolkata, Private Ltd., Kolkata, The world Press

Riley Matilda White, 1963, Sociological Research Vol.1, A Case Approach New York, Harcourt Brace and World Incorporation

Hiley Matilda White and Stoll Clarice, 1968, 'Content Analysis' in International Encyclopedia of the Social Sciences Vol.3, the MacMillan Company and The Free Press

Riezer Kurt, 1943, 'On Psychology of the Modern Revolution', in Social Research, Vol.X, Sept. 1943.

Rudolf Heberle, 1968, 'Types and Functions of Social Movement', in International Encyclopedia of Social Sciences Vol.14, The MacMillan Company and The Free Press

Runciman W. G., 1972, Relative Deprivation and Social Justice A Study of Attitudes to Social Ineuality in Twentieth Century England Pelican Books, 1972, (Routledge and Kegan Paul, 1966)
Sadhu Arun, May 1975, 'Maharashtra Job Guarantee Plan', in *The Times of India*, 7.5.1975
Sahastrabudhe V. G., 1967, The Economy of Maharashtra, (Background of Mumbai, The Administrative Staff College of Maharashtra State, Government of Maharashtra
Sehgal, Kuldeep Chunder, 1969, 'Migration into Mumbai A factual story. in The Economic Times, Sept. 7, 1969, Mumbai
Self P. J. O., 1964 'Regionalism (Political Science)', in Gould Julius and Kolb William L. (Eds.), 1964, A Dictionary of the Social Sciences Great Britain, Tavistock Publication.
Shah A.C. and Kulkarni M.V., 1973, 'Development of Banking', in Deshpande S. H. (Ed.), 1973.
Shinde Vithal Ramji, 1958, Majzya Athavani Va Anubhav (My Memories and Experiences), Pune, Lekhan Vachan Bhandar
Short J. F., and Wolfgang, E. E., 1972, Collective Violence, Chicago, Aldine, Athaton.
Simon Walter B., 1969, Multilingualism A Comparative Study. in Anderson Nels. (Ed.), 1969, Leiden, E. J. Brill
Singh G. S., 1966, Maratha Geopolitics and the Indian Nation, Mumbai, Manaktalas
Smelser Neil, 1962, The Theory of Collective Behaviour, London, Routledge and Kegan Paul
A Special Correspondent's Report 'The Employment of the Sons of the Soil' *The Economic Times*, April 7, 1970.
Stern Robert W. 1970, Process of Opposition in India Two Cases of How Policy Shapes Politics, Chicago, London, The University of Chicago Press
Srinivasan M. N., 1964, Caste in Modern India and Other Essays, Mumbai, Asia Publishing House
Sukhatankar (Member of the Maharashtra Ekinkaran Samiti) Statement, In Shiv Sainik (Ed.), May 1969, Immortal Shiv Sena (Pamphlet), Mumbai, Rajiv Publications
Thomas W. I., and Zaniecki F., 1927, The Polish Peasant in Europe and America. 2 Vol, New York, Knopf (Originally Published in 1918, Chicago University Press)
The Times of India, Editorial, 18.8.76, 'Joining the I.A.S'
Toch Hans, 1966, The Social Psychology of Social Movements. London, Methuen and Co. Ltd

Turner Roy (Ed.), 1962, India's Urban Future, Mumbai, Oxford University Press

Vance Rupert B., 1965, 'The Regional Concept as a Tool for Social Research' In Jensen Merrill (Ed.), 1965

Visaria P. M., 1969, (Mimeo), The Pattern of Outmigration from Coastal Maharashtra in India, Mumbai University, Mumbai

Wallace A.F.C., 1968, 'Nativism and Revivalism', in International Encyclopedia of Social Sciences Vol.11, U.S.A., The MacMillan Company and The Free Press

(Rev.), Wilson John, 9.3.1864, Speech at 'The Public Meeting to Vote A Testimonial to the Hon. J. Sankarsett', in Balkrishna Nilaji (Ed.), 1967

Williams, Robin M., 1947, The Reduction of Intergroup Tensions A Survey of Research of Problems of Ethnic, Racial and Religious Group Relations New York, Social Science Research Council (Bulletin 57)

Weber Max, tr. By Henderson A.M. and Parsons Talcott, 1947, The Theory of Social and Economic Organisation London, The Free Press of Glencoe, Collier-Macmillan Ltd.

Dirth Ibuis, 1965, 'Limitations of Regionalism', in Merrill Jenson (Ed.), 1965

Zacharieh K.C., 1968, Migrants in Greater Mumbai, Mumbai, Asia Publishing House